BOONE AND CROCKETT CLUB'S

19TH BIG GAME AWARDS

Boone and Crockett Club's 19th Big Game Awards

A BOOK OF THE BOONE AND CROCKETT CLUB
CONTAINING TABULATIONS OF OUTSTANDING NORTH AMERICAN
BIG GAME TROPHIES ACCEPTED DURING THE
19TH AWARDS ENTRY PERIOD OF 1983–1985

EDITED BY WM. H. NESBITT AND
JACK RENEAU

1986
THE BOONE AND CROCKETT CLUB
DUMFRIES, VIRGINIA

Boone and Crockett Club's 19th Big Game Awards

Copyright © 1986 by the Boone and Crockett Club.
All rights reserved, including the right to
reproduce this book or portions thereof in any form
or by any means, electronic or mechanical, including
photocopying, recording, or by an information storage
and retrieval system, without permission in writing
from the Boone and Crockett Club.
Library of Congress Catalog Card Number: 86-072295
ISBN Number: 0-940864-11-8
Published November 1986

Published in the United States of America
by the
Boone and Crockett Club
241 South Fraley Boulevard
Dumfries, Virginia 22026

FOREWORD

If you are a big-game hunter, you're in for a real treat with this book. There are 87 action-packed adventures waiting for you in the section of hunting stories behind each of the trophies recognized with an award at the 19th North American Big Game Awards of the Boone and Crockett Club at Las Vegas, 1986. These stories, told in the hunter's own words, are supplemented by photographs so that you get the feeling of actually having been there. No finer collection of current hunting stories is available, and the fact that each of these trophies is at the top of its category for the period makes them even more attractive.

The trophy listings, ranked for just the three years of the entry period (1983-1985) offer the best available summary of the top trophies and top hunting areas of North America *today*. Many interesting comparisons and conclusions can be drawn in this section, with some obvious traditional areas for certain categories holding up well, while in some other cases the best areas for a certain category may surprise you.

The beautiful brown bear on the dust jacket of this book is by well-known wildlife artist Michael Coleman. This scene is from the Boone and Crockett Club's 1986 Conservation Stamp Print, one of a series commemorating our great native big-game animals, and also directly aiding the funding of the 6,000 acre Theodore Roosevelt Memorial Ranch in Montana. The TRM Ranch is a special Centennial project of the Club as it celebrates its first century of service to hunting and conservation in North America. Purchase of the Conservation Stamp Prints directly aids the ranch fund drive, with net revenues being designated for the TRM Ranch fund. Write to the Club office for further information on the series and help an important big-game habitat project.

Thanks are due to several folks for fine work on this volume. Jack Reneau has done the daily work of reviewing trophy entries, obtaining the necessary additional materials and details, and he also was responsible for the final proofing of the trophy data sections, in addition to aiding with other parts of this book. Dr. Philip L. Wright and his Records Committee members deserve thanks for their tireless work in setting standards and settling the more difficult questions of trophy measurement technique. George Tsukamoto, Chairman of the 19th Awards Judges Panel, and each of the Judges and Consultants, all spent a solid week, without pay, to carry out the judging activities. We especially thank our nearly 500 Official Measurers who love trophies so much that they volunteer their efforts to serve as measurers.

You'll find a great many photos in this book. With the exception of some of the bears and cats, there are photos for all 87 trophies receiving awards. And, there are additional photos of fine trophies that qualified for the records book, although not quite high enough in score to be invited to the Final Awards Judging. It's a great hunting achievement to make the book and I'm sure you will agree that these additional photos add greatly to this book and its ability to convey a sense of the large and growing interest in trophy hunting.

One of the great pleasures of bringing out this book is getting to read all the stories and behind-the-scenes accounts of each of the Award-winning trophy hunts. There is a unique flavor and great variety to these stories, but all of them have the common bond of "making the book." It is a book to both answer questions about big game and big-game hunting in North America today, and also to stimulate other arguments. I'll bet you enjoy reading it just as much as we have enjoyed preparing it for you.

I wish you many happy hours reading this book, and even more happy hours afield.

Wm. H. Nesbitt
Executive Director
Boone and Crockett Club

CONTENTS

Foreword v
List of Illustrations xi
The Story of This Book 1
An Overview of the 19th Big Game Awards 3
The Stories Behind the Award-Winning Trophies
    Whitetail Deer (Typical Antlers), Peter J. Swistun 9
    Whitetail Deer (Typical Antlers), Stacy Winkler & Dwight Bates 13
    Whitetail Deer (Typical Antlers), Stephen Jansen 17
    Whitetail Deer (Non-Typical Antlers), Richard A. Pauli 19
    Whitetail Deer (Non-Typical Antlers), Dean Dwernychuk 23
    Whitetail Deer (Non-Typical Antlers), Loren Tarrant 25
    Whitetail Deer (Non-Typical Antlers), Dick Idol 29
    Whitetail Deer (Non-Typical Antlers), Doug Klinger 31
    Coues' Whitetail Deer (Typical Antlers), Michael L. Valenzuela 35
    Coues' Whitetail Deer (Non-Typical Antlers), Oscar C. Truex 39
    Mule Deer (Typical Antlers), Kelly Baird 41
    Mule Deer (Typical Antlers), Erich P. Burkhard 45
    Mule Deer (Typical Antlers), Robert V. Doerr 49
    Mule Deer (Typical Antlers), James S. Harden 53
    Mule Deer (Typical Antlers), John H. Davis 57
    Columbia Blacktail Deer, Russ McLennan 61
    Columbia Blacktail Deer, James E. Brierley 63
    Columbia Blacktail Deer, Charles A. Strickland 65
    Columbia Blacktail Deer, Jim Bennett and Floyd Duell 67
    Columbia Blacktail Deer, Darrell R. Jones 73

Sitka Blacktail Deer, Donna D. Braendel 75
Sitka Blacktail Deer, William C. Dunham 79
Sitka Blacktail Deer, Timothy Tittle 81
Sitka Blacktail Deer, Timothy C. Winsenberg 85
Sitka Blacktail Deer, Edward R. Hajdys 91
Sitka Blacktail Deer, Kurt W. Kuehl 97
Sitka Blacktail Deer, Howard W. Honsey 99
American Elk (Wapiti), Gregory C. Saunders 101
American Elk (Wapiti), William E. Moss 105
Roosevelt's Elk, Sam Argo 107
Roosevelt's Elk, Ken R. Adamson 111
Roosevelt's Elk, Robert Sharp 115
Canada Moose, Mike Popoff 121
Canada Moose, Don L. Corley 127
Canada Moose, Jack E. Dunn 131
Alaska-Yukon Moose, David B. Parent 133
Wyoming Moose, Patricia A. Wood 135
Wyoming Moose, John R. Blanton 139
Wyoming Moose, Steven A. Barnard 143
Mountain Caribou, John A. Kolar 147
Mountain Caribou, Jay L. Brasher 151
Mountain Caribou, Elmer R. Kochans 155
Woodland Caribou, Gordon J. Birgbauer, Jr. 159
Woodland Caribou, John R. Blanton 163
Barren Ground Caribou, Ken Higginbotham 167
Barren Ground Caribou, Dennis Burdick 173
Central Canada Barren Ground Caribou, Raymond H. Bonar 175
Central Canada Barren Ground Caribou, George O. Poston 177
Central Canada Barren Ground Caribou, Earle H. Harder 179
Central Canada Barren Ground Caribou, Barry D. Taylor 183
Central Canada Barren Ground Caribou, Tom W. Barry 187
Quebec-Labrador Caribou, Don Tomberlin 189
Quebec-Labrador Caribou, Don L. Corley 193
Quebec-Labrador Caribou, Lynn D. McLaud 195
Pronghorn, Michael J. O'Haco Jr. 201
Pronghorn, Joseph P. Fornara 205
Pronghorn, Charles R. Sprung 207

Bison, Philip A. Sturgill	209
Rocky Mountain Goat, Timothy F. McGinn	211
Rocky Mountain Goat, Fritz Stork	217
Rocky Mountain Goat, Frank L. Stukel	221
Rocky Mountain Goat, Theodore H. Kiser	225
Rocky Mountain Goat, David J. Flemming	227
Muskox, David V. Collis	231
Muskox, Ronald L. Deis	233
Muskox, John G. Stelfox	235
Bighorn Sheep, Steven L. Gingras	237
Desert Sheep, John W. Harris	241
Desert Sheep, Jesus H. Garza-Villarreal	245
Desert Sheep, Travis K. Holder	251
Desert Sheep, Greg Koons	255
Dall's Sheep, Edmond D. Henley	257
Stone's Sheep, Greg L. Stires	261
Stone's Sheep, Paul V. Palmer, Jr.	265
Cougar, Dusty R. Cooper	269
Cougar, Jerry J. James	271
Black Bear, John F. Peters	277
Black Bear, Peter C. Knagge	280
Black Bear, Cecil W. Brown	284
Black Bear, Utah Division of Wildlife Resources	286
Grizzly Bear, Roger J. Pentecost	289
Grizzly Bear, Stanley F. Smith and Gary Fait	295
Grizzly Bear, Thomas C. Roberson	297
Grizzly Bear, DeVern Gardner	299
Alaska Brown Bear, Anthony Gioffre	303
Alaska Brown Bear, George Caswell	309
Alaska Brown Bear, Michael F. Short	313
Tabulations of Trophies Accepted for the 19th Awards Entry Period	317
Black Bear	319
Grizzly Bear	321
Alaska Brown Bear	323
Cougar	324
Jaguar	326
Pacific Walrus	327

American Elk (wapiti) 328
Roosevelt's Elk 329
Mule Deer, Typical Antlers 330
Mule Deer, Non-Typical Antlers 332
Columbia Blacktail Deer 333
Sitka Blacktail Deer 335
Whitetail Deer, Typical Antlers 336
Whitetail Deer, Non-Typical Antlers 343
Coues' Whitetail Deer, Typical Antlers 348
Coues' Whitetail Deer, Non-Typical Antlers 349
Canada Moose 350
Alaska-Yukon Moose 352
Wyoming (Shiras) Moose 353
Mountain Caribou 355
Woodland Caribou 357
Barren Ground Caribou 358
Central Canada Barren Ground Caribou 360
Quebec-Labrador Caribou 361
Pronghorn 362
Bison 367
Rocky Mountain Goat 368
Muskox 370
Bighorn Sheep 372
Desert Sheep 374
Dall's Sheep 376
Stone's Sheep 377
Charts of the Official Scoring System for North American Big Game 379

ILLUSTRATIONS

Boone and Crockett Club Big Game Awards Certificate xiv
Whitetail Deer (Typical Antlers), First Award 8
R. Parker and M. Gontarek With Their Whitetails 11
Whitetail Deer (Typical Antlers), Second Award 12
Members of the 19th Awards Judges Panel 15
Whitetail Deer (Typical Antlers), Certificate of Merit 16
Whitetail Deer (Non-Typical Antlers), First Award 18
Whitetail Deer (Non-Typical Antlers), Second Award 22
Whitetail Deer (Non-Typical Antlers), Third Award 24
J. Perry and R. Traxler With Their Whitetails 27
Whitetail Deer (Non-Typical Antlers), Certificate of Merit 28
Whitetail Deer (Non-Typical Antlers), Certificate of Merit 30
Coues' Whitetail Deer (Typical Antlers), First Award 34
D. Cabral, L. Fuller, and R. Edmonds With Their Whitetails 37
Coues' Whitetail Deer (Non-Typical Antlers), First Award 38
Mule Deer (Typical Antlers), First Award 40
R. McKelvey and J. Jarratt With Their Whitetails 43
Mule Deer (Typical Antlers), Second Award 44
W. Hart and J. Powell With Their Mule Deer 47
Mule Deer (Typical Antlers), Third Award 48
M. Selby and H. Sumpter With Their Deer 51
Mule Deer (Typical Antlers), Honorable Mention 52
E. Burkhard and J. Harden Accepting Trophy Awards 55
Mule Deer (Typical Antlers), Honorable Mention 56
S. Bulloch and M. Atwood With Their Mule Deer 59
Columbia Blacktail Deer, First Award 60
Columbia Blacktail Deer, Second Award 62
Columbia Blacktail Deer, Third Award 64
Columbia Blacktail Deer, Fourth Award 66
S. Rupp and E. Hurst With Their Columbia Blacktails 71
Columbia Blacktail Deer, Honorable Mention 72
Sitka Blacktail Deer, New World's Record 74
D. Ellis and G. Hanson With Their Columbia Blacktails 77
Sitka Blacktail Deer, Second Award 78
Sitka Blacktail Deer, Third Award 80
R. Gilliland and J. Miller With Their Sitka Blacktails 83
Sitka Blacktail Deer, Fourth Award 84
R. Pauli and M. Valenzuela Accepting Trophy Awards 89
Sitka Blacktail Deer, Honorable Mention 90
J. Brierly and E. Hajdys Accepting Trophy Awards 95
Sitka Blacktail Deer, Honorable Mention 96

Sitka Blacktail Deer, Honorable Mention 98
American Elk (Wapiti), First Award 100
D. Grimes and G. Saunders With Their American Elk 103
American Elk (Wapiti), Second Award 104
Roosevelt's Elk, First Award 106
Roosevelt's Elk, Second Award 110
Roosevelt's Elk, New World's Record 114
D. Corley, L. Hengen, and T. Tidwell With Their American Elk 119
Canada Moose, First Award 120
J. Davis and His Alaska-Yukon Moose 125
Canada Moose, Second Award 126
J. Nelson and D. Miller With Their Moose 129
Canada Moose, Certificate of Merit 130
Alaska-Yukon Moose, Certificate of Merit 132
Wyoming Moose, First Award 134
Wyoming Moose, Second Award 138
W. Conn, P. Wollenman, and R. Limbach With Their Moose 141
Wyoming Moose, Third Award 142
P. Wood and J. Blanton With Their Moose 145
Mountain Caribou, First Award 146
B. Carmichael and P. Dreeszen With Their Mountain Caribou 149
Mountain Caribou, Second Award 150
J. Kolar and E. Kochans Accepting Trophy Awards 153
Mountain Caribou, Third Award 154
Woodland Caribou, First Award 158
D. Crum and D. Skidmore With Their Caribou 161
Woodland Caribou, Second Award 162
L. Corley and M. Kelleyhouse With Their Barren Ground Caribou 165
Barren Ground Caribou, First Award 166
R. Jacobsen and C. Nadler With Their Barren Ground Caribou 171
Barren Ground Caribou, Second Award 172
Central Canada Barren Ground Caribou, First Award 174
Central Canada Barren Ground Caribou, Second Award 176
Central Canada Barren Ground Caribou, Third Award 178
K. Poston, W. St. Germaine, and D. Senter With Their Caribou 181
Central Canada Barren Ground Caribou, Fourth Award 182
E. Foster and D. Tomberlin With Their Quebec-Labrador Caribou 185
Central Canada Barren Ground Caribou, New World's Record 186
Quebec-Labrador Caribou, First Award 188
Quebec-Labrador Caribou, Second Award 192
Quebec-Labrador Caribou, Certificate of Merit 194
E. Davis, R. Petitt, and M. Dominy With Their Pronghorn 199
Pronghorn, New World's Record 200
C. Holland, J. Taylor, and J. Hlavacek With Their Pronghorn 203
Pronghorn, Second Award 204

Pronghorn, Third Award 206
Bison, Certificate of Merit 208
Rocky Mountain Goat, First Award 210
Portion of 19th North American Big Game Awards Trophy Display 215
Rocky Mountain Goat, Second Award 216
D. Fediuk and S. Sullivan With Their Rocky Mountain Goats 219
Rocky Mountain Goat, Third Award 220
S. Gingras and T. Holder Accepting Trophy Awards 223
Rocky Mountain Goat, Fourth Award 224
Rocky Mountain Goat, Honorable Mention 226
J. Munsinger and R. Mondike With Their Muskox 229
Muskox, First Award 230
Muskox, Second Award 232
Muskox, Certificate of Merit 234
Bighorn Sheep, First Award 236
Desert Sheep, First Award 240
Desert Sheep, Second Award 244
S. Polich, R. Hartford, and R. Jackson With Their Sheep 249
Desert Sheep, Third Award 250
J. Turcke, H. Grounds, and R. Card With Their Sheep 253
Desert Sheep, Certificate of Merit 254
Dall's Sheep, First Award 256
Stone's Sheep, First Award 260
D. Collis, C. Leerberg, and D. Campbell With Their Sheep 263
Stone's Sheep, Second Award 264
L. Finger and E. Henley With Their Dall's Sheep 267
D. Cooper and M. Hubbard With Their First-Award Cougar 268
B. Dear and C. Mockensturm With Their Black Bears 275
J. Peters With His First-Award Black Bear 276
W. Hellebrand and J. Whyne With Their Black Bears 287
R. Pentecost With his World's Record (Tie) Grizzly Bear 288
R. Pock and G. Engebretsen With Their Grizzly Bears 294
T. Roberson With His Third-Award Grizzly Bear 296
D. Gardner With His Fourth-Award Grizzly Bear 298
J. Malady and V. Holleman With Their Grizzly Bears 301
A. Gioffre With His First-Award Alaska Brown Bear 302
J. Revelle, W. Kemp, and L. McCurry With Their Ak. Brown Bears 307
G. Caswell With His Second-Award Alaska Brown Bear 308
G. Caswell and M. Short Accepting Trophy Awards 311
M. Short With His Third-Award Alaska Brown Bear 312

BOONE AND CROCKETT CLUB'S
19TH BIG GAME AWARDS

BOONE AND CROCKETT CLUB
NORTH AMERICAN BIG GAME AWARDS

This is to certify that the

grizzly bear 26-9/16

entered by

S. F. Smith & G. Fait

in the 19th. North American Big Game Awards was awarded

Second Award

this 28th day of June 1986

Jack Reneau
Director, Big Game Records

Philip L. Wright
Chairman, Records of North American Big Game Committee

The Boone and Crockett Club Big Game Award Certificate. The Certificate and the Boone and Crockett Club Medal (pictured at the top of the Certificate) are both given to those trophies certified by the Final Awards Judges Panel for a place award. The Certificate only is given to trophies qualifying for other awards such as the Certificate of Merit and Honorable Mention.

THE STORY OF THIS BOOK

Wm. H. Nesbitt
Executive Director
Boone and Crockett Club

Mention the name Boone and Crockett Club to a big-game hunter, and he will nearly always associate the Club's name with the big-game records keeping for North America. Of course, the records keeping is but one of many projects over the years for the Club, and the story of the numerous and significant conservation achievements of the Club is well-told in the Club's book, *An American Crusade for Wildlife*.

The all-time records book, *Records of North American Big Game*, is the universally accepted reference for data on the native big game of North America. But, the all-time records book is published once each six years, quite a long time to wait for the average hunter. And, while the all-time records are the definitive bench-mark by which to measure a trophy, many hunters are even more interested in what size animals are being taken *now*. For this and other reasons, we brought out the first Awards records book in 1984. Titled *Boone and Crockett Club's 18th Big Game Awards*, it was a records book of just the entries accepted during the 18th Awards entry period of 1980-1982. In addition to the listing and ranking of trophies in their categories, the hunting stories and photos for each of the 68 trophies that received an award at the 18th Awards (Dallas, Texas, 1983) were included. This format proved very popular with readers, especially since it allowed easy determination of the largest specimens for the past few years. More than a few folks have indicated that they liked the hunting story presentations, told in the hunter's own words, fine "armchair hunts."

This book that you are reading is thus the second in the series of Awards records books. The schedule of publication of the all-time records will be maintained, with publication after two full entry periods of trophy entry (six years), and an Awards records book will be published after each entry period. The all-time records will continue to be the final standard against which to measure a trophy, while the Awards records will document *current* conditions and the better areas for trophy hunting. The Awards records minimum entry scores are slightly lower than those for the all-time records, resulting in additional trophies receiving recognition in the Awards records, and also adding weight to conclusions that may be drawn by the reader in regard to current big-game populations and hunting conditions.

The final scores and data shown in this book supplement those of the latest edition of the records book, *Records of North American Big Game* (1981). In the case of asterisked trophy scores, the asterisk indicates that the score shown is tentative, subject to final confirmation by either a Judges Panel or additional verifying measurements. For the first time, the trophy listings of this book have the asterisked trophies separated from the other trophies and unranked. This is the only fair way to treat such trophies until the asterisk can be removed by a proper final score determination, either by rescoring by an Awards Judges Panel (the *only* solution for any potential World's Record) or by submission (and only with permission of the Records Committee) of two additional, independent Official Scorings of the trophy by qualified Official Measurers. This same procedure for listing asterisked trophies will be followed in the next edition (9th) of *Records of North American Big Game*, expected publication date 1988.

As you enjoy this book, you will notice considerable variation in length and details provided in each of the hunting stories printed. All contributors were asked to prepare their material to the same standards of length and details. But some of them just naturally have less to say, although they may well have taken one of the larger trophies, than another. And, I think you will be struck, just as I was, by the great variation in difficulties encountered and time spent in taking these outstanding trophies. For some, it was just a hunt that resulted in a larger-than-expected animal. Others, after careful planning and preparation, worked long and hard, and often had some help from Lady Luck to find their trophy. The mix makes for enjoyable reading indeed.

Several of the hunting stories are about bow kills. A good number of trophies are taken each hunting season with bow and arrow, even though use of the bow places obvious restrictions on the effective killing range. It certainly appears that the limitations of bowhunting spur its users to develop their skills of woodcraft better to compensate for the limited range of the arrow. It also underscores that the choice of the hunting tool is not nearly as important as the skills of the person using it. The finest rifle in the world can only shoot as straight as the person using it. Also noticeable in this volume is the increasing number of women and younger hunters making the "book" with their trophies. This seems to reflect some expansion of interest in trophy hunting, with its emphasis on quality rather than quantity in hunting.

Trophy hunting is indeed alive and well today. The 50 percent increase in trophies accepted for the 19th Awards entry period over that of the 18th Awards shows the overall good health of our big game populations. The growing interest in trophy hunting, passing up ordinary specimens in search of a real "keeper" can only be good in an age of shrinking wildlife habitat. The trophy hunter does not have to "make meat" in order to count his hunting trip a success; rather, he usually rates his trophies (at least in part) on the difficulties involved, with those demanding the most exertion being his favorites.

AN OVERVIEW OF THE 19TH AWARDS

Philip L. Wright, Chairman
Boone and Crockett Club Records Committee

The 18th Awards records book was published in 1984. It was based upon the single Awards entry period of 1980, 1981, and 1982. It included data on 951 trophies accepted during this period. More trophies were entered for the 19th Awards than for any comparable period since the Club started in earnest on a trophy ranking program in 1950. With some 1,447 entries accepted, we are up about 50 percent over the 18th Awards entry period results. Trophy hunting is obviously flourishing for most of the species being hunted. Much of this increase in entries comes from more entries in the whitetail and pronghorn classes. A number of new World's Records were set in the 19th Awards, as explained later in this chapter.

In the black bear category, 60 trophies are listed, from 19 different states and provinces. This includes bears from Newfoundland to Alaska, and south to Arizona and North Carolina. British Columbia leads the list of 51 grizzly bears with 30. The largest grizzlies occur along the coast of B.C., where they feed on spawning salmon. The standing World's Record grizzly was tied by a monstrous bear taken by Roger Pentecost, and his hunting story is in this book. Big grizzlies also occur over much of interior Alaska, and a few are taken in Alberta.

In the Alaska brown bear category, the 29 entries are about equally from Kodiak Island and from the Alaska Peninsula. Kodiak Island bears tend to have the skulls shorter and wider than those from the peninsula, but they are not necessarily higher scoring.

Although polar bear are being legally hunted in the Canadian arctic, specimens cannot now be legally imported into the U.S. At present, Pacific walrus is in a similar situation. All of the walrus specimens listed were picked up, as no legal sport hunting is currently allowed for this species.

The single jaguar listed in this book was taken legally by a Canadian citizen, hunting in Mexico. Since jaguars cannot be imported into the U.S., there was no legal way that this skull could have been sent to the Final Awards Judging in Las Vegas. Fortunately, it was not large enough to be called in.

Cougar hunting remains popular. There were increased numbers of cougars entered from 11 states and provinces. Colorado and Montana each had 10 entries.

The number of whitetails entered continued to climb, with over 400 entered in the 19th Awards program alone. This is more than double the number entered in the 18th Awards program. Only 28 of these were scored below the all-time minimums of 170 (typical) and 195 (non-typical), and thus qualified *only* for publication in the Awards records book. About 80 percent as many whitetails have been entered from the last six years as were known from all of the previous recording periods. Minnesota, with 67 trophies in this period, leads the list, with Wisconsin, Maine, Alberta, Georgia, and Kansas each with 20 or more entries. This indicates that large-antlered whitetails are occurring in increased numbers over a wide portion of the continent. But, it also shows that some 140 whitetail trophies that were taken earlier than the start of this entry period have now been entered. There must be many more older trophies still in existence that have not been scored by an Official Measurer. We urge the owners of older trophies to get them scored and properly entered.

In the American elk category, we see that Arizona and New Mexico are emerging as top states for trophies, whereas Montana, Wyoming, Colorado, and Idaho, the traditional American elk states, are now yielding only a few big trophies. Various Indian tribes in Arizona and New Mexico have developed management programs for the production of large trophies, and they have become very successful. Bull elk have to live six years or more before producing really large antlers. The game departments of the Rocky Mountain states to the north have concentrated on producing large numbers of elk, rather than large trophies. Thus, bull elk that are allowed to live long enough to produce fully-matured antlers are now quite scarce in these states, although total elk populations may be near or at all-time highs.

Roosevelt's elk trophies continue to be entered in good numbers from Oregon, Washington, and Vancouver Island, B.C. The Milo Raichl trophy, the previous World's Record, was beaten by two monstrous trophies entered by Harold Stepp and Sam Argo. These two trophies were favored by a ruling reached at the December 1985 meeting of the Records Committee. That ruling decided that *any* points on a Roosevelt's elk rack beyond the G-4 point would be regarded as normal, and that such points need not be symmetrical in order to count fully into the score. Thus, both the Stepp and the Argo trophies would not score as well if they were American elk, where symmetry has always been an important part of the scoring system.

At the Final Awards Judging, there were several exceptional caribou trophies, with near-record trophies in the mountain, barren ground, and Quebec-Labrador categories. The new category for Central Canada barren ground caribou brought a number of entries from northeast of Yellowknife, where animals from the Bathurst herd have been hunted by sport hunters only since 1981. Surprisingly, the top two entries scored over 400 points each. The new World's Record, taken by a native hunter, came from Rendezvous Lake, several hundred miles farther northwest where the Bluenose herd occurs. This latter herd had not been sport-hunted by non-residents until 1986. It will be interesting to see what quality of trophies may be forthcoming. All but two of the 17 entered trophies had double shovels. The largest of these racks weighed about 12 pounds, whereas the antlers and skull cap of a very large Alaskan barren ground caribou may weigh 30 pounds or more, and would be much more massive. Hunting for the Central Canada barren ground caribou is also available on the Melville Peninsula, on the northwest side of Hudson's Bay, but no entries have come from this area.

The top barren ground caribou, taken on the Alaska Peninsula by Ken Higginbotham, shows a most unusual quality. The left antler has a long, but narrow, brow that is $5 2/8$ inches wide and it extends down almost to the left nostril. It also has a well-developed bez formation, with seven points in the usual position. But, lying between the brow and bez is a single, additional long point which comes off the main beam separately. It was regarded by the Judges Panel as simply a random point, and thus it added only slightly to the total score. There are *no* abnormal points on a caribou antler according to the scoring system.

It has been gratifying to see some 11 entries of woodland caribou in this entry period, and 10 from the 18th Awards period, all from the rather small population of Newfoundland. The numbers of trophy caribou from this province have increased since 1960, indicating that this population is being properly managed by game authorities there.

Most of the entries in the Canada moose class are from British Columbia, as is usual, but increasing numbers have come from Maine where sport hunting was reinstituted in 1980. There are eight entries from Maine in the 19th Awards period to go with the three in the 18th Awards. Two entries came from Manitoba, a province that had not been represented in recent years.

In the Shiras (Wyoming) moose class, two of the top three trophies on display at Las Vegas were taken in Idaho, and 10 of the total 35 entries came from Idaho. Moose hunting in Idaho is a once-in-a-lifetime affair, and non-residents cannot apply for permits. Wyoming continues to be the top state for Shiras moose trophies, with 16 in this entry period.

It has been known for many years that the Sitka blacktail deer grows antlers much smaller than those of its cousin, the Columbia blacktail deer of farther south. The Sitka blacktail category was established in 1985 as a result of careful review of the situation. It was well-known that Alaska hunters felt that the Sitka blacktail was a fine trophy animal, despite its smaller antlers. Frank Cook, Records Committee member from Anchorage, Alaska, had been maintaining records of antlers of these deer from Kodiak Island for several years. It was he who suggested the 108 minimum entry score for this class, and he urged its establishment. We were happy that 17 entries were received for the 19th Awards entry period. Our newly established world's record, scoring 123 4/8, came from Kodiak Island, as did most of the top entries. However, at least three of the trophies were taken on Prince of Wales Island in extreme southeastern Alaska. Trophies are also eligible from the Queen Charlotte Islands of British Columbia, but no entries were received from that region. All 17 deer accepted were taken from 1980 and forward. Whether any number of earlier-taken trophies are still in existence, only time will tell.

Columbia blacktails continue to be entered in good numbers. Oregon and California are contributing many more trophies than Washington and British Columbia, at present.

The number of entered mule deer, in both the typical and non-typical categories, continues to be far below that of the whitetail and Columbia blacktail classes. Mule deer populations in general have not been thriving as well in recent years, continent-wide, as have the whitetail populations.

The number of entries in the pronghorn category remains very high, which suggests that the species is thriving in those portions of its range where it is hunted. The new World's Record pronghorn was taken by Michael O'Haco. In score it exceeds the previous record, taken by Edwin Wetzler, by four-eighths of a point. The O'Haco trophy was so impressive that the judges voted to recommend the awarding of the Sagamore Hill Award to it. Both the O'Haco and Wetzler trophies came from Arizona, where only limited numbers of permits are available. It seems clear, with 16 other pronghorns in this period also from Arizona, that horns of pronghorns may grow to larger size there than farther north where the winters are more severe. Wyoming still leads, by a comfortable margin, in the total number of entries with 55.

British Columbia is still the region where most of the trophy Rocky Mountain goats come from, with 24, while 11 came from coastal Alaska. Washington, surprisingly, has seven goats entered in this period, from either Snohomish or Okanogan counties in the North Cascades.

Review of the muskox entries shows that there is an increasing number of sites in the Northwest Territories where these animals can be hunted. Snowmobiles or three-wheeled vehicles are legally used by the native Inuit guides, but NWT regulations require that the hunted animals be approached on foot for 3.25 kilometers (2 miles), helping retain good sporting character to this hunting.

The number of bighorn sheep trophies increased over the 18th Awards period. Most are from Alberta (24), while Montana produced 22. In Montana, some very large trophies are coming from areas into which sheep have been transplanted where they had formerly occurred. Although traditionally the largest horns are from animals near the end of their life span (12 or 13 years), some of these trophies from Montana are from animals as young as six years. These transplanted sheep may grow their horns at a very rapid rate as compared with those living in continuously occupied habitats.

With more intensive management of desert sheep, the number of trophy specimens is holding up well. Baja Calif., Mexico, Nevada, and Arizona contribute about equally to the list of trophies. An exceptionally large set of picked-up horns from Pima County, Arizona, was scored by the Judges at $201 3/8$ points. This is only the second desert sheep ever to be scored by a Judges Panel at over 200 points. It is exceptional also in that it is a very tightly curled head, with much beyond a full-curl, even though a lot of horn material has been broomed away.

The Stone's and Dall's sheep categories are again represented by a relatively small number of entries. In Alaska, this is in part due to the fact that much sheep range has recently been set aside as National Parks, National Monuments, or other kinds of preserves in which hunting is prohibited. The Stone's sheep range is primarily in northern B.C., where it is intensively hunted but carefully managed to prevent over-harvest.

In using this book you will no doubt enjoy seeing trophies ranked for just the awards period. Where trophy scores are shown with an asterisk, they are *not* considered as final due to the unanswered questions represented by the asterisk. The asterisk is applied to those trophies that fall in the top 10 of the category in the latest edition of the all-time records book (or they fall in the top few of the category for the Awards entry period), or they present scoring interpretation questions unresolved in the normal manner by the entry measurement. In this book, for the first time, such asterisked trophies appear at the *end* of the category list and they are *unranked*. In the case of a potential World's Record, the trophy *must* come before the Judges Panel; only they can declare a new world's record. In the case of other asterisked trophies, the Records Committee *may* allow submission of two additional, official scorings (total of three original score charts, filled-out and signed by three separate Official Measurers) from which the Records Committee *may* decide to accept one score chart as final for the trophy and thus remove the asterisk for future listing(s) in the all-time records book, *Records of North American Big Game*. Once the asterisk is removed, the trophy will be shown in the usual manner in the trophy listings, with rank determined by its final score.

Trophy owners should note that this separation of asterisked trophies from the regular, ranked listing will also be followed in the next edition of the all-time records book, *Records of North*

American Big Game, to be published in 1988. Owners of asterisked trophies, either from the recent Awards entry periods, or from earlier editions of the records book, may well want to contact the Record Committee through the Club's office address to determine if the alternate route of additional scorings can be followed for their trophy so that it can have the asterisk removed before the 1988 records book is printed.

Photograph by Wm. H. Nesbitt

WHITETAIL DEER (TYPICAL ANTLERS)
FIRST AWARD
SCORE: 200 2/8

Locality: Whitkow, Sask.   Date: November 1983
Hunter: Peter J. Swistun

WHITETAIL DEER, TYPICAL ANTLERS 200 2/8

Peter J. Swistun

On the third day of the 1983 hunting season, November 17th, I tagged my prize, a Canadian record whitetail. I could not have guessed as the day began that it would be my prize hunting day.

I live on a farm four miles from a small farm hamlet called Whitkow, 30 miles from the city of North Battleford on Highway 16, which links Winnipeg and Edmonton. I am 41 years old, and I have been farming in the area all my life. As usual, the day began early on our farm. On the two previous days, we had been out hunting at dawn.

The weather had been nice for some time. This morning, as Dale (my hunting partner) and I were preparing, it was cloudy and there was a little sprinkle of snow that ended by the time we were finished with breakfast. The temperature was about 40 degrees. We decided to check a certain area we knew, driving around looking for signs of deer. My gun was a .30-06 Remington, while Dale used a .308 Savage. As we drove, not saying a word, I thought about the big one I had seen a month before, grazing in my oat field. I wondered whether it would still be in the area and if I would see it again. That big buck was really the one I was looking for. That was the one I wanted to find.

Our morning of hunting ended in vain, for we did not see any bucks at all. We decided to quit hunting and go back home for dinner.

After dinner, we went to feed the cattle. We drove into the field to pick up a load of hay bales. As I proceeded to load the truck with the bales, I looked around for any sign of deer. I saw a dark object moving slowly and cautiously in the distance, approximately three-quarters of a mile to the east of our position.

"Look at that big buck trying to sneak by," I said to Dale after taking a closer look. "Let's go and get him."

We jumped into the truck and drove over the thin layer of snow to where we had seen the buck go into the bush. After making a complete circle around the bush without seeing any sign of the animal, I marveled at how successfully it had disappeared and camouflaged itself in the leafless trees.

Dale got out of the truck at the bottom of the hill, and I drove up top to flush the bush. My heart pounded in my chest as I walked through the bush with my gun in hand. I was sure the big buck would have to reveal himself now, and one of us would have a good shot at it soon. It wasn't long before I had gone through the entire bush and was forced to realize that I was skunked!

I went back to the truck disappointed, but still very determined. Dale wasn't there yet, so I decided to walk along the hillside to another bush. Walking there and back, I didn't see anything. As Dale came closer, I walked around a second time, this time closer to the bush. It was then that I heard a loud snap and saw the buck bolt out of hiding straight for Dale.

"He's coming for you," I shouted as Dale began firing. "Too much buck for you," I teased, laughing at him after the buck had leaped away and was out of sight once again. We were very excited now, as we began following the tracks. We concluded that the buck would probably stop in the next ravine. The truck wasn't far away, and I drove it up on a hill to wait for Dale to come and join me. As I waited, I watched for the buck to come out of the ravine. I was so sure that we would see it again that my heart began to pound.

Dale and I talked, planning our strategy. It wasn't long before we saw a small buck appear in front of us. As it started to cross the open field, I shouted to Dale, "The big one should be coming soon!" Sure enough, he came moving slowly and proud, with his huge antlers held high.

"Shoot!," I yelled and Dale began firing. He fired a few shots, and then yelled that he was out of bullets. The buck ran about 400 to 450 yards away from us, and stopped in a field. I got out of the truck, raised my rifle and took careful aim, and fired once. The deer buckled but didn't fall. It then turned into the brome grass along the edge of the field.

"I got him," I said with assurance. "Let's go and pick him up." We got into the truck and drove up to where we thought it had dropped. There, at the edge of the hill, we saw the little buck running along the bottom of the hill with the older one following behind it.

Dale and I jumped out of the truck as the deer started to turn up into the next ravine. Once again, I took careful aim and fired. It was a neck shot and the buck went down. We raced toward the animal, with Dale getting there first.

We worked quickly and it wasn't long before we had loaded the animal carefully onto the truck. We admired its antlers at close range: they were large and magnificent. I was very pleased but I had no idea that it would be rated so highly. I was sure of one thing though, and that was that I wanted to have the head mounted.

The next day, I phoned the taxidermist in North Battleford and asked him if he would mount it for me. He said he would, so I took it in. It was there that excitement filled me when I learned that this could be a World's Record set of antlers. I found out later it wasn't quite that large, and I have to admit that I was quite disappointed.

The antlers were scored at $204 6/8$ for entry into Boone and Crockett. That is about $1 3/8$ below the current standing world's record of $206 1/8$ that was shot by Jim Jordan in Wisconsin back in the year 1914. I was told that my buck may have indeed been a World's Record had it not been for one non-typical point and that the fifth point on the right side was missing, apparently broken off in some battle.

Photo Courtesy of Robert L. Parker, Jr.

Robert L. Parker, Jr. took this fine typical whitetail 165 4/8 on the Glass Ranch in Maverick County, Texas, in December, 1982. With seven normal points on each antler, it weighed 125 pounds field-dressed.

Photo Courtesy of Mark Gontarek

Maplewood State Park, Otter Tail County, Minnesota, was the site of Mark Gontarek's 1983 whitetail deer hunt that netted him this fine buck that scores 162 6/8 points.

Photograph by Wm. H. Nesbitt

WHITETAIL DEER (TYPICAL ANTLERS)
SECOND AWARD
SCORE: 194 2/8

Locality: Vigo Co., Ind.   Date: November 1983
Hunter: Stacy Winkler and Dwight Bates

WHITETAIL DEER, TYPICAL ANTLERS 194 2/8

Stacy Winkler and Dwight Bates

Our names are Dwight Bates and Stacy Winkler. We live in the midwestern town of Terre Haute, Indiana. We have been very good friends for over five years. We are both 18, and we both graduated from Terre Haute South Vigo High School in 1986. We are both avid hunters, and we hunt anything and everything in season. But never in all our dreams did we think we would ever take a trophy deer that would end up as one of the largest in the U.S.

We had begun several weeks before hunting season to scout the woods of Southern Vigo County, building deer stands and looking for signs of deer. The first day of hunting season, we were up for breakfast and out early. We both hunt with 12 gauge shotguns. We spent the day hunting, but we had no luck. We did find an arrow shaft, and we decided to bring it home.

November 13, 1983, was the second day of hunting season. We left in the early morning, but again had no luck. In early afternoon, we returned to the woods. It was a rather nice day: not too cold, with a light breeze. We each climbed into our tree stands and began our quiet wait. Around 5:00 p.m., Dwight saw deer off at a distance, but out too far to shoot at. Dwight climbed out of his tree stand, and walked over to Stacy's stand, where he held Stacy's gun while he climbed down. After standing there for a few minutes, they saw a small herd of approximately 10 deer, but they were still too far away. We couldn't get a shot at them. We went quietly through a bean field to some artillery bunkers that were in the area. Here we split-up, hoping to fill our tags with deer in sight.

We both saw the deer, and we knew he was close enough to get a shot at. We went in opposite directions, hoping to get this one. Dwight could hear the deer snorting close by. He proceeded to turn slowly, catching the first glimpse of what was to be our trophy. At this time, Dwight got over buck fever and took his first shot, which Dwight knew had hit the buck. The deer went down, then jumped up and ran in Stacy's direction. Stacy heard Dwight's shots and lifted his gun, ready for action.

The deer ran in front of Stacy, about 35 yards away. Stacy took his first shot, and then shot once more. The deer kept going, and we met back where we had split-off to look for a blood trail, feeling sure that we had gotten him. We found some blood, but it was starting to get dark so we went to the house for lights to continue our search. Three of our buddies were at the house, and they came with us to help in our search. We went back to the blood and started to search.

About 50 yards from there, we found our deer. The first thing we noticed was the rack above the beans. We cautiously proceeded, not knowing what to expect. When we walked up to him we could tell that he was dead. Knowing that his rack was big, we started to count the points and thought it to be about 15 points. We sent one of the boys back to the house to get the truck, knowing the deer would not fit into the trunk of the car.

While the truck was being brought around, Dwight and Stacy tagged the deer and field dressed him. When the truck returned, we each grabbed a part and put him into the truck. Then, we returned to Dwight's house, honking and shouting all the way home in joy. We took the deer to the barn and hung him, with all the family as excited as we were.

After hanging him, we checked where we had shot him, discovering we had each placed a vital shot a rib apart on the same side. After checking the deer over, we found a broadhead in the deer's spine and removed it. We found that it matched the shaft that we had found the day before.

We each felt that we could not have killed this deer alone and we have shared in everything 50-50. We butchered the deer and had the head and feet mounted. At that time, we did not realize that this deer hunt would make our friendship stronger with a bond of happiness to share forever. Knowing we had to take the deer to a checking station, we were allowed the next day off from school. At the station we found that our buck weighed 203 pounds and was 16 points, not the 15 we had thought the night before. We took lots of pictures.

We knew we had a large deer, but not a possible record, until we took it to a State deer measuring show in Bicknell, Indiana. At that time, we found out that our deer ranked second in the state of Indiana, scoring $193\frac{7}{8}$ typical. Then the publicity and excitement really began.

Since then, we have been invited to and attended several showings of our trophy across the state of Indiana. We never dreamed our deer would get all the recognition it has. We just knew it was big and we were proud. We never expected to be published in the Indiana records book, let alone to make it into Boone and Crockett as one of the largest trophies ever taken in North America. All this publicity has not changed us in any way. But, we do find ourselves now waiting for another big one, passing up several chances that went by.

Dwight got a 10-point buck in 1985, and again we shared the thrill of bringing another big deer home. We still hunt together and see each other every day. We plan to continue this for years to come, with a long-lasting friendship wherever we may be as we grow older.

The 19th Awards Judges Panel. Standing, (l-r): Frank Cook, Alaska; Charles E. Wilson, Jr., Michigan; Walter H. White, Minnesota; John G. Stelfox, Alberta; Mike Wickersham, Nevada; Murff F. Bledsoe, III, Texas; Dave Boland, Minnesota; Philip L. Wright, Montana. Kneeling (l-r): C. Randall Byers, Idaho; Glenn St. Charles, Washington; George K. Tsukamoto, Chairman of Judges Panel, Nevada; Frank E. Bertoia, Alberta; Horace G. Gore, Texas; Thomas A. Cavin, Nevada. Also shown are the new World's Record pronghorn, Ohio's "hole-in-the-horn" non-typical whitetail, and the new No. 2 desert sheep.

Photograph by Wm. H. Nesbitt

WHITETAIL DEER (TYPICAL ANTLERS)
CERTIFICATE OF MERIT
SCORE: 204 2/8

Locality: Beaverdam Creek, Alta.   Date: October 1967
Hunter: Stephen Jansen

WHITETAIL DEER, TYPICAL ANTLERS 204 2/8

Stephen Jansen

Back in the 1960's, most of us small ranchers northwest of Calgary, Alberta, took off a few mornings to add some venison to our winter's supply of meat when the deer season opened. We did not have far to go. This is wonderful deer country, with several areas of uncleared, bushy land within a mile of my home.

The hunt itself is largely forgotten. But, my son-in-law and two neighbors who were with me have reminded me of a few details.

The day was mild, with only a few patches of snow on the ground, not good for tracking. We had hunted unsuccessfully for some hours. Carson Schultz (my son-in-law) and I were waiting for the others to join us in an open area below a big hill. Suddenly, over the top of the hill, a large whitetail buck sauntered into my line of vision. He was only about 150 yards away. The wind was in our favor and he didn't even notice us. I loaded my Husqvarna .270 and fired from where I stood. It was the easiest whitetail I've ever shot.

None of us had ever seen this big buck before. And since we were out for meat, we didn't particularly appreciate the large antlers because they weren't perfectly balanced. I did, however, hang them in an old shop where the head dried and provided a home for mice and the horns made a handy rack for V-belts.

About a year-and-a-half ago my nephew, Daryl Harrison, decided to measure them. He was very excited over the apparent score, and he then contacted Russell Thornberry, a trophy guide, who sent me to an official Boone and Crockett scorer, Fred Walker of Red Deer, Alberta. Mr. Walker's entry scoring won me the non-current Whitetail Deer trophy for 1984 presented by the Eckville Fish and Game Association, a branch of the Alberta Fish and Game Association.

This story is not really about a "trophy hunt;" perhaps "trophy resurrection" would be a more correct title.

Photograph by Wm. H. Nesbitt

WHITETAIL DEER (NON-TYPICAL ANTLERS)
FIRST AWARD
SCORE: 267 3/8

Locality: Peoria Co., Ill.   Date: November 1983
Hunter: Richard A. Pauli

WHITETAIL DEER, NON-TYPICAL ANTLERS 267 3/8

Richard A. Pauli

I've been hunting deer in Illinois since 1957 and have always said that bagging a buck of such proportions as my trophy is about 99 percent luck. Good fortune was in the tree with me on that morning of opening day of the 1983 firearms season.

I farm about 105 acres in Peoria Country in rural Dunlap. The property is located near the Illinois River, and I spend many hours glassing the area with binoculars to look for deer and other wildlife activity.

I was aware that a big buck had been passing through my property for several years because of its large tracks. But, I never was able to get a real good look at his antlers until that morning in the tree stand when he suddenly was standing directly under me. I had seen him twice from a distance while bow hunting, and I got a closer look one night when I went out with the cattle.

In 1981, I was bow hunting in a deep washout when I heard something about 15 feet behind me. I was in a position where I couldn't turn around, and there was no way I could shoot left-handed. All I could see was his tail. He just walked to the top of the hill and then came out in plain sight.

Another time, in the same creek bed, I noticed a maple tree had fallen, and I planned to cross over on it. The buck bolted from the brush and was gone. It scared me more than it scared him, and it was the only time I caught him bedded down. But, the best glimpse of this deer came about a month before the shotgun season in 1983.

My wife Donna and I had been to a relative's house for supper that night. It was dark when we arrived home. Since we had planned to drive the cattle to another field, we drove to the pasture, which includes a pond. Donna drove the car so we could use the headlights to see the cows. It was then that the beams hit the big buck, drinking at the pond. He turned around and looked at us, then turned his head around over this shoulder and just walked off. He never did break stride or change his pace. He acted like he was king of the hill, and he probably was.

It was a once-in-a-lifetime thrill just to see a deer like that. In the headlights, he looked like that big stag Hartford Insurance uses in its advertising.

The bow season had already started, and I went after him but never saw him again until that lucky morning of shotgun season. It was dark that morning when I left for hunting with my Browning Sweet 16. I had planned to hunt a spot on the north side of the farm, but my plans changed soon after I stepped through the gate and into the field about 30 yards behind my home.

I was about half asleep, but I sensed there was something else in the field with me. I looked up and the big buck was in the same field. He had been crossing my path 20 to 25 yards ahead of me. We saw each other about the same time and just looked at each other for awhile. I just stood there and relaxed, and he walked off. I really thought that was the end of him and that he would go bed down somewhere for the day.

After he left, I stood for 10 to 15 minutes before moving. Then, as I began to walk toward the spot, I recalled that this buck always had a habit of going crossways with the wind. He had gone southeast, so I figured he would eventually go straight west. I was playing a hunch that changed my plans. I thought if I saw him again, he would be in a most unlikely spot, because I had always seen him when I didn't expect it.

I wanted to find the biggest tree in the direction I thought he might go. The only one I could think of was on a high hill in the middle of nowhere, in an old pasture surrounded by timber. That's just where I went. I recall having difficulty climbing the tree, but I finally found a comfortable limb and settled down.

About five after seven, I heard a shot to the west of me. I thought deer must be moving. I had been facing the southeast where he might come from, so I turned around to see if anything was coming from the direction where the shot was heard. Nothing. I just sat there, relaxed, with my gun up over two limbs. I never keep the gun in my hands. I figure if the shot is not good enough for me to take my time, I don't want it anyway.

Another shot came from the west, but there was no movement. Then, about 10 or 12 minutes later, I heard a sound behind me. A deer's got a peculiar walk and sounds kind of like a person. I knew something was back there, but I didn't know what. I didn't want to turn around, so I just sat quietly.

About 15 minutes later, I looked down and there he was, standing right underneath me and about 15 feet away. All I could see were his ears and his antlers. I tried to figure out how I could get to my gun without making any noise, because the deer was awfully close. I moved a little bit, and when I did, my feet knocked a piece of bark off the tree, and it hit him. I thought all I'd see next was his tail up and he'd be gone, but he didn't move. He soon disappeared under a big limb. As I lost sight of him, it gave me time to pick up the shotgun.

Soon he appeared again, about 20 yards away. He was moving crossways with the wind, like he always did, and he was moving away from me. He turned just a little to his left to look. Then, he turned to right. When he did this, he exposed his neck to me. That's my favorite shot.

I fired one shot, and as soon as he went down he got the second one. Then I relaxed and had my usual cup of coffee. I don't get out of a tree after dropping a deer for at least 10 to 15 minutes. I was still sitting in the tree when my cousin came walking up. He had heard the shot, and he asked, "What'd you do, miss?" I said, "Yeah—he's lying right there on the ground." He couldn't believe the size of the buck when he saw it.

At the time I didn't realize how big he was. Even after I had checked it in, I really wasn't as excited as everyone else. It took a couple of days before it hit me. The field-dressed weight was 197 pounds. In 1968 I killed a big buck that weighed 263 field dressed, but naturally it didn't carry the rack of this one. We have three old does here that are as big as cows. I'd bet they weight more than the big buck did. I'm almost sure he was related to one of these three does. I know one doe is probably 17 years old and another 15 years or so. They're protected here. And, ironically, I took my buck about five miles from where Mel Johnson took his Sagamore Hill Award-winning 204 4/8 points typical buck in 1965.

I don't go deer hunting to get a deer. I go because I enjoy it. I can sit in a tree all day long. I've spent a lot of hours sitting with a shotgun but never with more satisfying results than this hunt.

Photograph by Wm. H. Nesbitt

WHITETAIL DEER (NON-TYPICAL ANTLERS)
SECOND AWARD
SCORE: 241 1/8

Locality: Bighill Creek, Alta.   Date: September 1984
Hunter: Dean Dwernychuk

WHITETAIL DEER, NON-TYPICAL ANTLERS 241 1/8

Dean Dwernychuk

Whitetails are easily the most popular big-game animal in North America, both in the U.S. and also in Canada. A number of the provinces of Canada have fine whitetail hunting, and Alberta is usually one of the best.

Dean Dwernychuk had his equipment ready. He was familiar with his hunting bow, a Martin Warthog pulling 70 pounds. His arrows were the reliable Easton XX75's, topped with Wasp three-blade broadheads. He was going to a good spot, with good chances for seeing bucks. Should the hunting gods smile on him today, he just might get a real trophy.

Dean arrived at the hunting area at 6 a.m. The area was in the Municipal District of Rocky View, about four miles east and four miles west of Cochrane, Alberya. As a resident of Calgary, Dean knew this would be a good area for whitetails.

The date was September 25, 1984. There was clear sky to the west, but the heavy cloud overhead promised snow or other happenings soon. The heavy overcast and light wind made nearly ideal conditions for hunting. Dean had a good feeling as he moved into the woods.

It was just 7:15 when the big buck moved to scarcely 30 paces away. It was close enough, well within range for Dean's powerful bow. Full-draw, followed by a steady release, resulted in a well-placed shot that soon brought the big buck down. Dean now had time to study his trophy.

What a rack! There had to be nearly 40 points on the two antlers. It would certainly have to be scored as a non-typical, and it sure would require scoring. With an inside spread of 18 inches, and all those points, it was going to easily qualify for the records books, both Pope and Young Club and Boone and Crockett.

Photograph by Wm. H. Nesbitt

WHITETAIL DEER (NON-TYPICAL ANTLERS)
THIRD AWARD
SCORE: 234 2/8

Locality: Alfalfa Co., Okla.   Date: November 1984
Hunter: Loren Tarrant

WHITETAIL DEER, NON-TYPICAL ANTLERS 234 2/8

Loren Tarrant

Oklahoma is known for many things: Indians, oil, the Dust Bowl, and beautiful women, but outsized whitetail bucks are definitely not on the list. In the last edition of *Records of North American Big Game*, only five deer from Oklahoma were listed, three non-typicals and two typicals. However, in 1982, after hunting deer for 27 years, I finally connected on a pretty fair buck. He field dressed 218 lbs. and scored 144 5/8 Boone and Crockett points. At the time I thought he was the biggest buck I would ever take, but then the 1984 season came along. But first I'd better introduce myself.

My name is Loren Tarrant and I'm a 42-year-old masonry contractor. I've been interested in hunting since my eighth birthday, when my father bought me my first .22 rifle.

In 1981, my partner, Mark Blackledge, came to work with a very impressive broken antler. His brother had punctured a back tractor tire with it while plowing in a new field along the Salt Fork River. Mark invited me to go hunting with him, but Alfalfa County is about 75 miles from Crescent, where I live; and besides, I always had a "big" one going, either along Skeleton Creek or over in the Blackjacks by the Cimarron.

Finally, in 1984, after Mark had hunted the "Monster" for three years without success, I put everything else aside just to concentrate on this one deer.

Bow season began in early October, and Mark and I pitched a tent on the sandhills above the Salt Fork. The open grassland with just a sprinkling of trees along the river was far different than any of the country I was used to hunting, but from the amount of sign present, I knew it was deer heaven!

Due to our work, we only bowhunted that one weekend, but we resolved to spend the whole nine-day muzzleloader season going after that one special deer. Donnie Elmore and John Cunningham (my nephew and my good friend), were asked to come along as gun bearers. Our communication must have been flawed somehow, because the only guns they carried were their own. We all ended the hunt by taking a smaller buck, but John came in one evening ranting about the biggest buck he'd ever seen. So we pinned our hopes of taking him on the upcoming rifle season.

Just Mark and I pitched our tent the night before the gun season opened. From all the sign around camp it looked like the rut was in full swing. Our plan was to drive Mark's Bronco across the river and park, then ease along the back boundary for about 1/2 to 3/4 mile, depending on the wind, until we came to our vantage points. His was a cottonwood tree that was almost impossible to climb, and mine was an old, unused tank battery.

Our hopes were still high on Tuesday, November 21, because Mark had turned-down shots at five bucks and I had passed-up two. His run seemed more active than mine, so on the walk in that morning I asked if he wanted to switch places. Naturally he turned me down, so I left him at his tree and walked another quarter-mile to my stand.

The wind was blowing about 20 miles per hour out of the south, and at first light a doe came easing around me to the north. She got my wind and quickly evaporated. I turned to the east and saw what appeared to be two moving ink spots along the river. At that time of the morning everything seems to move, so I wasn't in any hurry to raise my Zeiss binoculars to look at them. They were much too far away to shoot anyway. When I looked at my ink spots at 8 power, one turned out to be a doe. But, the other was the biggest buck I had ever laid eyes on!

All I could do was watch as they went through their mating ritual for about 30 minutes. When he finally tired of her, instead of dropping back into the trees, he came toward me at a quartering angle. When he got to the point where I thought he might get my wind, I squeezed the trigger on my old .25-06 Remington. He went down hard at the shot, but came pulling back up on his front legs. I settled down as best I could and put the next one right behind his front leg. He was mine!

Mark came over at the shots, and really took it pretty graciously that I had killed the buck that he'd been hunting for years. We measured the distance from my stand at 264 yards, which is one of my better shots!

My buck measured 232$\frac{5}{8}$ points after 60 days' drying time, and his field dressed weight of 235 lbs. puts him right up with the best ever taken in Oklahoma.

I don't know how I'll ever top him, but the way I figure it he has to have a father, or maybe a big brother. Even if I don't beat him, they'll probably be singing about me around the campfires for years.

Photo Courtesy of Joseph A. Perry, III

Niobrara County, Wyoming, yielded this symmetrical 6-pointer to Joseph A. Perry, III. Shot late in the afternoon of opening day in 1985, it scored 170 3/8 points.

Photo Courtesy of Roger J. Traxler

Roger J. Traxler bowhunted Winona County, Minnesota, in 1980 to take this whitetail 170 1/8, that also qualified for the Pope and Young Club's records book.

Photograph by Wm. H. Nesbitt

WHITETAIL DEER (NON-TYPICAL ANTLERS)
CERTIFICATE OF MERIT
SCORE: 328 2/8

Locality: Portage Co., Ohio   Date: Picked Up 1940
Owner: Dick Idol

WHITETAIL DEER, NON-TYPICAL ANTLERS 328 2/8

Dick Idol, owner

Seldom has a trophy had more fanfare, more publicity, and even more misinformation written about it than this particular trophy. It began several years ago, when Dick Idol, well-known outdoor writer and avid antler collector, acquired these antlers from a hunting club in Ohio. The antlers had been in the hunting club's lodge for several decades, ever since the deer was killed by a train in the 1940's.

Dick is very knowledgable of the measuring system, although not qualified to measure officially for the records book. Even before he acquired the antlers, he knew there was an outside chance, depending upon the interpretation of certain points on the antlers, that this trophy could be a new World's Record for the category. Once he had acquired the antlers and had them officially measured for entry, his suspicion was sustained. The entry measurement totaled more than the current World's Record trophy from Missouri. But Dick was cautioned by the Official Measurer that this was an entry measurement only, and that the Final Awards Judges' measurement might indeed be quite different. Only their measurement would be final, the score that this trophy would carry into the next edition of the all-time records book, *Records of North American Big Game*.

Dick decided to take a chance, and he started calling this trophy a new World's Record. Several stories calling it a new World's Record appeared in magazines that Dick writes for, and mass confusion occurred among the readers. Those who contacted the Boone and Crockett Club were reassured that the Missouri whitetail was still the World's Record, and would remain so until at least the Final Awards Judging and Awards of the 19th Awards (the period in which Idol's trophy was entered).

After the Final Awards Judging had been conducted, this fine trophy was indeed the all-time second place trophy for the category, with the Missouri trophy still reigning supreme. The slightly lower score found by the Judges Panel, as compared with that performed for entry of this trophy, is explained by the necessary interpretation of several points on the beam as being either typical or non-typical. This makes a considerable difference in the final score, as it affects both the point scoring and the location of circumference measurements.

Photograph by Wm. H. Nesbitt

WHITETAIL DEER (NON-TYPICAL ANTLERS)
CERTIFICATE OF MERIT
SCORE: 277 5/8

Locality: Hardisty, Alta.   Date: November 1976
Hunter: Doug Klinger

WHITETAIL DEER, NON-TYPICAL ANTLERS 277⅝

Doug Klinger

It was the last day of the 1976 season. Ron Jackson and I had decided that we would get an early start so that we could come home around 10 a.m. to do the chores. As it turned-out, we covered the dependable areas where we usually had good luck dropping nice bucks in other years. But it was not the case this morning, so we returned empty-handed. We stopped for coffee and toast at Ron's before leaving to feed the range cattle, which were about three miles away. We loaded the truck with the grain that we needed and headed-out.

It had just snowed lightly that night. What tracks there were that morning, we knew had to be fresh enough to warrant a second look. When we got to the gate, I jumped out of the truck to open it, allowing Ron to drive through. I made sure to close it again behind us.

The rangeland that we were now on was solid bush, extending for miles in every direction. To the east, this bushland leads into the Battle River Valley. We had only driven about a quarter-mile down the trail when Ron spotted a fresh set of tracks.

We got out of the truck to take a closer look, discovering that there were two sets instead of one. One was larger and more distinctive than the other. Ron suggested that they were probably a couple of bucks, travelling together, just the way they usually react when they heard us coming down the trail. He also speculated that the larger set of tracks could possibly belong to a particular buck that we had been chasing for the past three years. He was almost sure that this was the buck that carried an odd-looking set of antlers, a real non-typical.

Both sides of the rack of this buck were shaped differently, consisting of some additional drop tines, points that grew downward because of damage to them in the velvet stage. One hunter from the neighborhood remarked, after seeing this big buck, "It looked as if he was carrying a willow tree on his head!" Many hunters in the area claimed to have seen this buck. Some even admitted having shot at him, but they always missed.

As soon as we realized that this might be the buck that we were after, Ron suggested that I should stay out along the fence, to the east side of the bush. He thought the deer would run downwind when they spooked. He would track them, hopefully pushing them out for me. I knew that if he was right, they wouldn't be wasting any time crossing the clearing to get to the next bush. I would have to be alert if I was to get one of them.

Ron and I separated to carry out our plan. As soon as I reached the fence, I slowed down enough to give Ron the time he needed to get on the tracks and start pushing the deer. I walked a few yards, then I stopped, listening for even the slightest sound to indicate that the deer were on the move.

After 15 minutes, I found myself almost back to the road where we had come through the gate. I had not heard a sound. I realized that they might have come through already, or they might decide to cross on the south side of the bush, like the old buck had done so many times before. He was smart, but nearly everytime we chased him, he had crossed at the same place— beside an old corral, along the south side of the bush. This seemed to be what he might do this time as well, so I headed over to the next hill in order to see the corral and yet still have a view to the east.

Reaching the crest of the hill, still some 50 yards or so from the corral, I stopped to listen. After a couple of minutes, I heard branches breaking. I readied myself, as I knew from experence that he would be coming out of the bush at full speed, crossing the clearing as quickly as he could. I expected that I would only get one good shot at him before he reached the silver willows across the clearing.

I was ready when he came out of the brush, but I didn't think that he would be as large as he was. And his antlers, unbelievable! What a majestic buck he was! One could only wonder at how he managed to get through the tight bushes of his hiding places.

I was wrong about one thing. I had expected him to come out of the bush on the dead run; instead, he came out at a slow trot, which never changed, even as he got further out into the clearing.

I stood there, stunned. I realized as I watched him, that he hadn't even seen me. He didn't know that I was there. I shook off whatever had control of me (known as "buckfever" to most hunters), and raised my gun. Just as the big buck jumped the fence, I squeezed the trigger. I heard the bullet hit with a thud. I knew that I had not missed. A feeling of regret came over me as I watched the great buck hit the ground. I stood there for a moment, asking myself what I had done. I knew that it was irreversible.

The buck had a broken back and had to be finished off. I ran as hard as I could, over to where he was. When I got there, he was trying to get up. He would gather his feet under him and jump straight-up into the air. I was amazed at his will to live, but then, it was his life he was fighting for. No matter what direction I moved to try to get closer to him, he would keep me back by swinging those huge antlers. He was fully aware of what was happening around him. The only thing that I could think about at the time, was that I didn't want him to suffer too long.

I knew that I couldn't get close enough to stick him with a knife, so I reloaded my .270, placed it near his masive neck, and fired. The 130 grain slug seemed to have no effect, so I fired again. By this time, Ron had made his way over to the buck and me. The buck was still alive and trying to get up to run as Ron fired two more rounds into his neck, finishing him off.

After tagging the buck, we covered him with willow branches, leaving him on the hill where he fell while we went to feed the cattle. Later, we loaded him on the truck and went home.

My father was quite excited when he saw this buck. At this time of my life, my family almost lived on wild game. We made use of everything we got. We thought that the meat of this buck would be particularly tough, so we canned it, making it quite tender and rather tasty. Grain-fed venison is always very good.

At the time, other hunters tried to prompt me to have the head scored according to the Boone and Crockett system, but I didn't feel right about doing so. A deer with non-typical antlers was regarded as being a freak of nature, not worthy of trophy consideration. Besides, I was looking for venison for the table. I was certainly not trophy hunting when I shot this buck.

One day, out on the rigs during a rare quiet moment of relaxation, I was leafing through one of the many magazines left in the rec room. It was a copy of North American Whitetail and the story that caught my eye was "World Record Shattered! Ohio's Hole in the Horn Buck Breaks Missouri Record To Claim Title of World's Biggest Whitetail". Hey, I have a rack that looks a lot like that, I thought out loud. Both of those monstrous deer were "pick-ups" (found dead). Mine was taken in Fair Chase.

When I was back at home, the first thing I did was to go out to the old shed and see if the antlers were still there. After all it had been six long years since I left them there. I had almost forgotten about them. They were there, still intact. They were none the worse for wear; mice hadn't touched them in all that time. Only the ultra-violent rays of the sun had lightened the antler color somewhat. Since they had been been kept inside, high and dry under the roof, rainwater and moisture had not damaged them either. Unfortunately, the cape of the original buck was never saved for a mount.

So, I retrieved the old skull and antlers of my whitetail and took them home with me. Now I was really curious and I wanted to find out just how they would measure up to the big ones. I simply couldn't wait any longer. I think it was this point in time that I became a trophy deer hunter.

Taking the antlers to Edmonton to be officially measured for the non-current entry in the annual provincial Alberta Fish and Game Association's trophy competitions, I eagerly awaited the final tally on the bottom line of the scoresheet. They had to strip some velvet that still clung to a couple of the drop tines in order to get an accurate measurement. My score, $270\frac{1}{8}$ Boone and Crockett points, is now officially Alberta's best non-typical whitetail ever taken. Little did I dream any of this on the day that I bagged the buck.

The head now accents our family room, bringing back memories of this hunt every time I look at it. They say that the chances to get such a buck happen only once-in-a-million. I believed that until two seasons ago, when I got another chance at such a monster but missed. Could this have been my buck's grandson? I think it is possible. They also say that records are made to be broken. In Alberta, that has been happening a lot lately. The big deer have always been there, but it's only been the last few years that Alberta's hunters have started becoming trophy-conscious. More and more vintage trophies are beginning to appear out of the "woodwork" each year.

I don't hunt as much as I used to, but I try to get out at least twice each season. If for nothing else, the fresh air is healthy and exhilarating at that time of the year, and the idea of another Battle River giant prowling the willow-bottoms somewhere stirs the hunter's imagination as long as there will be hunting seasons.

Photograph by Wm. H. Nesbitt

COUES' WHITETAIL DEER (TYPICAL ANTLERS)
FIRST AWARD
SCORE: 118

Locality: Santa Cruz Co., Ariz.   Date: November 1982
Hunter: Michael L. Valenzuela

COUES' WHITETAIL DEER, TYPICAL ANTLERS 118

Michael L. Valenzuela

In southern Arizona lies the beautiful mountain range of Patagonia. I have hunted these mountains for nine years, enjoying the beauty of its desert landscape and habitat.

In the winter of 1980, a hunting party consisting of my youngest son (Mark), my brother (Jerry) and his son (Jay), Joe Meza, and I were into the second day of hunting for javelina to no avail. It always seems that during deer season the javelina are so thick that we constantly run into their packs, but that day they seemed to have vanished into thin air. The cool, sunny day was coming to an end, and it was time to head back to camp. My son and I remained a few minutes behind, enjoying the sunset and hoping that the game would sense the withdrawal of the hunters.

I saw the buck for the first time as he crossed over a mountain ridge. He made such a majestic image against the setting sun. In all my hunting years I had never seen such a splendid animal. I motioned to my son, so that he could witness this beautiful creature in the wild. I could hardly wait for deer season; this was going to be my trophy deer.

In 1981, after hunting for him with no success, my brother saw him and shot, but missed. It was at this time that I become determined to get him. I prepared myself, both physically and mentally. My body was totally out of shape. I started on an exercise program, gave up drinking (hardest of all), and changed my diet. I had to be fit.

I compiled everything I knew about this buck. All the little details. Like how he used every little bit of cover in the area he was always in, and no matter what was chasing him, he would stop, look, and listen before going over the mountain ridge.

I started going to the shooting range every weekend, firing an average of 200 rounds each time. I had hunted many years with a Remington 700 BDL in 7mm, which had served me well; but, this was going to be a special hunt for a special animal with a special rifle. I chose a new Ruger Model 77 in .243 caliber, fitted with a Weaver K4 scope. November seemed years away, instead of just months.

On November 10, 1981, we left Phoenix for Patagonia. We arrived in Temporal Canyon about 8:30 a.m. As the longest day of my life wore on, we prepared camp for the 15 hunters who would be arriving. That night, we sat around the camp fire telling tall tales and having a relaxing, good time before the day of the hunt.

When the alarm went off on November 11, I had no problems getting up. We dressed around the campfire and drank hot coffee, anticipating the hunt. Then, we loaded up, Jerry, Jay, Joe and me.

The time was 5:30 a.m. We were almost to Mount Bitch, when I realized, that in all the excitement, I had forgotten my permit. So, back to camp we went. Everyone took it well except me; how could I do something so dumb?

The sun was coming up, and the wind was blowing hard, when we left the jeep to start the climb up Mount Bitch. The mountain gets higher and the air thinner each year, or am I just getting older? It was over 35 minutes since we started climbing, and before me lay the canyon. The shadow of the morning still lay on the canyon floor, and the wind was still blowing. How I wished I had worn heavier clothing.

I spotted a little knoll, with some sun shinning on it; maybe it would be warmer there. As I worked my way to it, I looked and listened for game. It was a good spot, I could see quite a distance around. I must have sat for over an hour before I saw Jerry and Jay. A little later, I spotted Joe. I lost track of all of them for about 30 minutes. Then, I saw Joe sitting down and looking hard at something. Jerry and Jay joined him. I wondered what they were looking so hard at for such a long time. Joe stood up and started throwing rocks, as if to flush something out. Finally, they all started down the draw. Isn't there a bottom to this canyon?

As my sight returned to the ridge, there he was. This was the moment I had dreamed of (this was what the other hunters had been looking at). I knew that as he had made good his escape, he was laughing and thinking how smart he was; after all, he didn't get to be the boss of the canyon for nothing.

My heart was pounding out of my shirt as the safety went off and the cross hairs came down on his shoulder. I shot. Damn, I missed. He had been moving along at a good clip, but now he was in high gear. I fired and missed again. I had only one more shot. If I missed again, it would all be over. He had to be farther away than I thought! The trophy I had waited for all my life was about to vanish. I had to lead him a little farther. I threw the cross hairs past his nose and slowly I squeezed the trigger. As the shot rang out, the deer stumbled. How hard was he hit? Was he down for good? I couldn't see him! I threw two more rounds into the rifle and waited. Nothing moved.

I stood up and started toward him. My eyes never left the spot where he went down. Then, I saw him. He was bigger than I thought. My hunting companions were at the top of the ridge. When they came down, nothing had to be said. They knew it was the boss of the canyon, a name that I had given him when I first set eyes on him. Even in death, he was a splended sight.

Hand shaking and back slapping were in order. Picture taking and other chores had to be done, before we could start back out of the canyon. It took four men over three hours to carry him back to camp. My hunting dream had come true. The Boss of the canyon was mine.

Photos Courtesy of David Cabral and Luther E. Fuller

(Left) David Cabral was hunting in Annapolis Valley, Nova Scotia, in 1984 when he connected with this non-typical whitetail that scores 196 points. (Right) Luther E. Fuller shot this big non-typical whitetail that scores 223 4/8 points in Hawkins County, Tennessee, during the 1984 deer season.

Photo Courtesy of Randy Edmonds

Randy Edmonds shot this fine typical whitetail that scores 175 2/8 points in Union County, Illinois in 1984.

Photograph by Wm. H. Nesbitt

COUES' WHITETAIL DEER (NON-TYPICAL ANTLERS)
FIRST AWARD
SCORE: 143 5/8

Locality: Pima Co., Ariz.   Date: December 1983
Hunter: Oscar C. Truex

COUES' WHITETAIL DEER, NON-TYPICAL ANTLERS 143 6/8

Oscar C. Truex

When you decide to go whitetail deer hunting in southern Arizona, you will find there are between 14,000 and 16,000 die-hards applying for permits.

We hunt the southwest end of the Santa Rita Mountains, about 60 miles south of Tucson. We go into the foothills through the widespot at Amado on the Nogales Highway, (I-19).

Robert Koch and I have hunted together since we were carpenter's apprentices during 1948-1951. Our group in camp includes Robert's sons (David and Kelvin), my son (Richard) and always a friend or two. We always seem to do o.k. We have camped the first weekend of the season at the same place for 12 to 15 years.

About five years ago, I went down to set up camp early, two days early, in fact. After the camp and fire wood were prepared, I decided to take a short hike, just before sunset. I was moving slowy, in and out of the low hills and ravines, when I spotted three bucks about 50 yards away. Any one of the three would have made it a great deer hunt, but the season did not open until Friday. Same old story, "no see", when the season starts. Of course, we knew already that there were "great" antlers in this area. That year, we took out five bucks, not bad for seven hunters. Two years later, in the same camp, David Koch and Kelvin Koch got nice three-point bucks (Arizona Count). I missed one on Friday. My son came in on Saturday morning, and we did not get a shot that day.

On Sunday, November 11, 1983, we broke camp. On the way out, we hunted a large flat of mesquite and grass between two canyons. I took the easy side, up high. After about ½ to ¾ mile of walking, watching the flat and canyon bottom, there by the stream was the "one". One shot and a lot of hollering later, Bob and my son came over to see what happened. They could see that I had one fine deer, looking from the rim down. They stayed on top, hunting while I found a way into the canyon, after about twenty minutes.

About noon, the work was done and the truck moved. Richard came back with me to help out. The deer weighed 112 pounds, field dressed. The canyon sides were steep, and it took us an hour to get to the truck. I was on "Cloud Nine" all the way to Tucson, where I have lived since 1948.

Photograph by Wm. H. Nesbitt

MULE DEER (TYPICAL ANTLERS)
FIRST AWARD
SCORE: 208 5/8

Locality: Rio Arriba Co., N. M.   Date: November 1984
Hunter: Kelly Baird

MULE DEER, TYPICAL ANTLERS 208⅝

Kelly Baird

Hunting the Carson National Forest for the big mule deer of northern New Mexico had become tradition among our close knit group. We were camped on the same site my father, Lavall Baird, and his hunting companions had first found some 20 years earlier.

A light rain had fallen the night before opening day of the 1984 New Mexico deer season. We were cooking breakfast and making plans for the impending hunt before the first light of dawn appeared. Mike and Danny Sullivan (sons of Bruce Sullivan, one of the original hunting party), Eric Smith (nephew of the Sullivans), and I headed out of camp ready for a full day of hunting. Mike and I were going to hunt down the canyon about three miles, then circle back to a large drainage where Danny and Eric were to be waiting for us on stands. We had made this same drive with success in previous years. With the early snow pushing deer out of the high country to the north, I knew our chances of spotting and bagging a trophy were as good as I had seen in years.

The sun was starting to peek through the overcast as it climbed over the eastern horizon. Fog hung on the higher ridges as Mike and I split up. I took the top rim, while he was going to work around a lower bench. Almost immediately, I could see deer moving-out ahead of Mike but I was unable to see antlers on any of them. We had hunted almost a mile when I saw some deer drop off a point ahead of me. I worked around the head of a small canyon and was approaching the point where a game trail dropped off the rim. Indian pottery shards were scattered on the ground around me, just as they were on almost every point up and down the canyon.

I was watching for Mike as I neared the edge of the rim. It was just before 7:00 a.m. when I stepped out on a sandstone rim overlooking Cabresto Canyon. About 250 yards below me I spotted a deer standing in the dark shawdows of a large juniper tree. We saw each other at the same instant. As I stood motionless, I could see his massive antlers towering above his head as he looked up the ridge at me. Deer were moving out of the trees behind him and starting across the sagebrush. My attention was fixed on this deer in the shadow as he started to move around the base of the hill, leaving the other deer behind.

I moved to another rock to improve my field of view and lay down as the big buck stopped to look my way again. My heart was pounding as I cautiously brought my rifle up and found my target in the crosshairs. He was standing broadside as I pushed the safety forward and squeezed the trigger of my .22-250 Remington Model 700. The 55 grain bullet found its mark, slamming the big buck to the ground. As I ejected the spent brass, I could see him throwing his head from side to side, trying to stand. I jacked-in another cartridge as he staggered to his feet. He started trotting through the sagebrush, heading across the canyon as I fired another shot. There wasn't any evidence of a hit or miss, so I again loaded and fired. He stopped in the chest-high sagebrush as I quickly reloaded.

I momentarily lost sight of the buck as I brought my binoculars up from my chest. I spotted him as he started to trot again, widening the already huge gap between us. As he crossed the arroyo, he looked even bigger than before with his antlers outlined against the light sand. I fired again. As he scrambled up the far side of the arroyo, I fired a last shot as he disappeared into a stand of trees 500 yards across the canyon from me. Through my binoculars I could see several does standing on the hillside above the trees but there was no sign of my buck.

Mike was coming around the hill below me as I picked up my brass and started down the hill to meet him. I told him of the activities of the previous 15 minutes as we followed the buck's tracks in the sagebrush. Occasionally spotting a few flecks of blood in the brush, we traced the tracks to the arroyo. Mike crossed the canyon and circled the trees, and I sat down on the bank of the arroyo with a good view of the hillside. If he jumped the buck out of this cover, I would be sure to spot him.

Mike neither jumped or found sign of the buck, so I hit Mike's trail and stalked into the trees. I hadn't gone more than 50 yards when I saw a set of antlers protruding over a small tree. My heart leaped into my throat as I crept around the tree to see my trophy lying there, not 10 yards ahead of me, dead.

Mike and I congratulated each other as we worked to cape and dress out my buck. We could see that my first shot had hit him in the top of the back between his shoulders. It hadn't broken any bones, but he had absorbed quite an impact. Two more bullets had entered his chest cavity and never exited. A fourth had hit him low in the chest. Yet, except for the first shot, he had never shown any signs of being hit. We moved him under some trees where he would be nice and cool, then headed out to make our rendezvous with Danny and Eric.

We had crossed the canyon and started up the ridge when we jumped a small herd of deer. Mike got a shot off and dropped a nice three-point buck on the run. We made short work of him and started out again. At our rendezvous, we found that Danny had scored on a nice four-point buck early that morning. We swapped stories as we headed to camp.

Getting my trophy back to camp that afternoon was anti-climatic to the morning's activities. We moved him back to camp without too much trouble. That night, after dinner, as my mind wandered back to the adventures of the morning, my father and Bruce told stories of years gone by when the deer hunting used to really be good. I just smiled.

Photo Courtesy of Rod McKelvey

Rod McKelvey was hunting in Wapello County, Iowa, in 1983 when he shot this non-typical whitetail that scores 200⁶/₈ points. McKelvey was shooting a 20 gauge shotgun.

Photo Courtesy of J. D. Jarratt

It was 1930 in Zavala County, Texas, when J. D. Jarratt shot this fine non-typical whitetail with his .30-30 rifle. This big buck scores 220²/₈ points.

Photograph by Wm. H. Nesbitt

MULE DEER (TYPICAL ANTLERS)
SECOND AWARD
SCORE: 205 5/8

Locality: Lincoln Co., Nev.   Date: October 1983
Hunter: Erich P. Burkhard

MULE DEER, TYPICAL ANTLERS
205 4/8

Erich P. Burkhard

My hunting buddy, Sandy McHenry, and I waited expectantly for the morning light of October 22, 1983, to grow bright enough to see reasonably well. The air was crisp and clear as we waited at the outlet of the wash. This particular wash had a lot of promise. Yesterday, Sandy had taken a nice buck, only a stone's throw from where we now waited. The amount of sign that both of us saw yesterday while scouting this wash made it almost certain that I would try to fill my tag here this morning.

We had only waited a few minutes when we started working our way up the dry, sandy wash. It wasn't too difficult keeping quiet; we only had to avoid the dead branches littering the draw while looking for the deer that had to be nearby.

After about a half-mile of slowly working our way up the wash, Sandy motioned for me to stop. There, behind a dead juniper 100 yards away, was the movement of antlers. It was difficult for us to differentiate between what might have been antlers and the branches of the dead tree, since we were looking directly into the area of the eastern sky where the sun would rise in a few minutes. After a few seconds (which seemed like ages), the buck decided he didn't want to stick around.

As soon as he took off uphill, both of us could see that he was a very large buck. "You'd better shoot, it's the largest deer I've ever seen," shouted Sandy. I was aiming through the scope of my .270 rifle, and the crosshairs were jumping all over the place. I thought to myself that I'd never hit the running deer like this, and Sandy was beside himself with excitement. I frantically looked around for a place to use as a rest for a good shot. With all the commotion going on down below, the deer wasn't wasting any time getting out of there.

The only place I could find to take a steady shot at the buck was a dead tree located about 30 yards in the opposite direction from the escaping deer. By the time I ran to the tree and found a branch to use as a rest, the deer was most of the way up the hill. I knew that the buck would disappear over the ridge in a matter of seconds, but I didn't want to miss the only shot I might have at him.

Placing my rifle in the palm of my left hand, which rested on a branch of the dead tree, I took aim. My buddy was looking at the buck and shouting, "Shoot, shoot!" The buck continued to move and I knew that shooting at a moving target at 300 yards is risky, at best. Rather than take the chance on a running shot, I guessed that the buck would stop for a last look at us before disappearing over the ridge. My gamble paid off when the buck stopped just below the horizon.

I knew that this was my chance and I squeezed the trigger. With the recoil, I lost sight of the deer.

After recovering from the recoil, I could see only the body of the buck. Because of the distance and the glare from the sunlight, neither Sandy nor I could tell whether the deer was up or down, hit or missed. I told Sandy that I was going to shoot one more time and I aimed at the spine and squeezed the trigger. I heard the bullet hit and knew that the buck was mine!

I left Sandy in the wash and took off up the hill as fast as I could go. It was a good thing that Sandy stayed in the wash, since I had a hard time finding exactly where the deer had fallen. With a little direction from Sandy below, I found the buck.

When I saw him up close, I sat down in astonishment! Everything about the deer was enormous, and I couldn't take my eyes off those magnificent antlers. As it turned out, my first shot struck the animal just as intended, killing the buck immediately. The second shot missed the spine by a fraction of an inch, only clipping the hide and some fat. I don't know what I would have done without Sandy's help in dressing the deer out and hauling him out of there. We were both glad when the buck was in the back of the pickup and we had the chance to rest.

Even if this buck had not made the records book, I still would treasure the thrill, the excitement and the companionship of my most memorable big game hunt.

Photo Courtesy of William B. Hart

Sanders County, Montana, was the site of William B. Hart's 1984 mule deer hunt that resulted in this "keeper" that scores 195 4/8 points as a typical rack.

Photo Courtesy of James E. Powell, Jr.

Garfield County, Colorado, yielded this big non-typical mule deer that scores 240 1/8. James E. Powell, Jr. killed it on a hunt in 1983.

Photograph by Wm. H. Nesbitt

MULE DEER (TYPICAL ANTLERS)
THIRD AWARD
SCORE: 204 5/8

Locality: Eagle Co., Colo.   Date: November 1982
Hunter: Robert V. Doerr

MULE DEER, TYPICAL ANTLERS
204 5/8

Robert V. Doerr

On November 13, 1982, we rose early for the first morning of a five-day hunt. Everyone in camp was eager to begin the trek, high into the serene mountain tops to stalk the elusive mule deer.

My guide, Rick Martin, was also the outfitter for this trip. Rick and I loaded our gear into a four-wheel drive vehicle with chains on all four. At first I was curious about the tire chains, but as we made our way up the mountain, I realized they were a necessity. The narrow roads were extremely rough and we soon encountered snow, some 18 inches of it!

Once we reached our destination, we immediately began glassing. After about 15 minutes, we spotted our first buck walking toward a poplar thicket. He was in the brush before we coud tell just how big he was, so we quietly moved in the direction of the thicket. As we neared the area, we spotted him again. Rick wanted to be sure he was large enough, so we hesitated. After what seemed like hours, Rick finally said, "Take him". But, by this time the deer was running about 300 yards from us. I let go two quick shots and raised my head in time to watch as he ran into the distance.

After failing on our first attempt, we decided to walk toward an area on the other side of the canyon. We walked continuously for two hours. When we reached a height where our viewpoint improved, we began glassing again. Thirty minutes passed and we hadn't seen anything. Finally, we noticed a nice mulie resting in the underbrush below.

Once again we started down to stalk the buck. As we neared our destination, I suddenly noticed several deer to our left. One was a nice heavy buck. I shouted to Rick, "There's one". His immediate response was, "Take him". I quickly dropped to a resting position and drew a bead. The buck, now about 350 yards out, stopped and turned broadside to me. With the cross hairs at the top of his shoulders, I slowly squeezed the trigger and saw the deer fall back. I knew the bullet had connected.

The buck was stunned, but he quickly regained his sense of direction and headed out. I again took aim and fired four rapid shots. And once again, I watched as the buck raced off.

Pat Bollman, another member of our hunting party, heard my shots and found the buck running his way. He fired also, but did not make a connection.

Rick and I went to the point where the buck staggered. There, we located a small blood trail which we followed. The trail lead us in the direction of another poplar thicket. Pat and his guide had started around the other side of the brushy area. Suddenly, out of the thicket, came three bucks. Rick said, "He's the first one—take him!" I swung the rifle up to my shoulder and located the buck in my sights, about 250 yards out. I let off five shots as he kept running. My heart was pounding in my ears as I squeezed the trigger one final time. I knew I had connected with this final bullet, but the thicket was so close he managed to get inside.

Rick and I raced towards the thicket where we were able to locate only two small drops of blood. Rick concluded that I had not hit him very well. I was feeling very frustrated—I mean *very* frustrated, and Rick even worse. After all, I had discharged my rifle 13 times and had nothing to show for it, except a slightly bruised shoulder.

We decided to head back to camp. After lunch we rested for two hours and planned our afternoon strategy. The rest was truly appreciated by me; my feet ached, my body ached, and most of all my pride ached!

We went back to the same area where we had located the two spots of blood. I found a plateau overlooking the thicket and waited there while Rick proceeded to enter the underbrush in hopes of kicking something out to me. Thirty minutes passed as I waited impatiently at my perch, my eyes trained on the brush below. Finally Rick yelled, "Come on down, I've found him."

Excitement raced through by body as I ran down the steep slope, stumbling and falling at least a half-dozen times. As I neared Rick, all I could see was the rack, thick, massive antlers. The bullet had hit a main artery and my buck had bled to death internally.

After all the picture taking and celebration was completed, the work of dragging him out began. My emotions were running so high, it actually seemed a pleasure.

The impact of the deer's size didn't really hit home until I received the measurements. He measured $180 \frac{7}{8}$ points for Safari Club, which will be a new number one all-time.

This hunt was an experience of a lifetime, and I have Rick Martin to thank for everything.

I have hunted 16 different North American species over the last 15 years and I have a Boone & Crockett non-typical whitetail in my collection.

Photo Courtesy of Manuela Selby

Wayne Selby guided his wife Manuela to this fine typical mule deer that scores 196 7/8. That's "Ela" with the big smile. The hunt took place in 1984 in East Kootenay, B. C.

Photo Courtesy of H. C. Sumpter

Pulaski County, Kentucky, was home to this fine non-typical whitetail that scores 226 5/8. H. C. Sumpter killed it on a hunt in 1983.

Photograph by Wm. H. Nesbitt

MULE DEER (TYPICAL ANTLERS)
HONORABLE MENTION
SCORE: 202 4/8

Locality: Garfield Co., Colo.   Date: November 1982
Hunter: James S. Harden

MULE DEER, TYPICAL ANTLERS 202 4/8

James S. Harden

When I learned of my job transfer to Glenwood Springs, Colorado, I was quite excited about hunting and fishing there. But, I had to wait almost a year for the next hunting season.

November finally arrived and my hunting partner, Rudy Lawler, and I were quite ready to go. We received permission to hunt some private land (approximately 2,000 acres) that had been hunted relatively little except by the owners and a few others. The area is approximately 10 miles southeast of Glenwood Springs, near Colorado Mountain College. This area of Colorado (Garfield County) gets quite a bit of hunting pressure each year, not only from locals, but also from out-of-state hunters, with literally hundreds of hunters from Texas, Utah, California and many other states. So, it was quite pleasing to be able to hunt this area.

I picked-up Rudy on November 8, 1982, at the Mexican restaurant where he is the Manager. It was evening, and I had my truck and camper to make the 10-mile trip to our spot. The weather forecast called for a new snowfall that evening of up to four to six more inches of snow, so we chained up, even though I had a four-wheel drive.

Our hunting area is quite hilly, and we wanted to be more safe than sorry. Glenwood's elevation is 5,700 feet. When we reached camp, we figured we were at around 7,000 feet. We fixed our supper and eagerly awaited the morning.

Waiting for light the next day, we took off up the nearest hill. It was full of scrub oak and oak brush, with a nice fresh blanket of snow and tracks galore. We spotted many does and finally we saw a buck, a small three-pointer about 200 yards away. But, in the twinkle of an eye, he was gone, too high up the hill for a chance at all in this terrain. We spent the rest of the day still hunting and driving, deperately wanting to spot another buck, but to no avail.

That night we planned the next day. We decided we would try the next hill south and take some food with us. Next morning we walked and climbed together for quite awhile, then split up. Rudy stayed on a stand halfway up the hill, and I went about 200 yards above him and took a stand. We had quite a view and could see many areas for possible deer.

I was looking through my binoculars very closely and very slowly, searching for any sign of movement; parts of a deer, maybe an ear flicker, or part of a rack, or even legs—something, anything; but nothing could be spotted over a 180 degree view. I could see Rudy's bright hat below me and he never moved, so I felt he was content to stay where he was. Suddenly and without warning, a loud snap sounded to my left, an area I had just painstakingly gone over with my binoculars.

There he was, in full body sight, something that just never happens, but did. I thought for a split second he was a bull elk by the size of his rack. My heart started beating rapidly as I shouldered my .30-06, lining up the crosshairs of my variable scope quickly at the top of his shoulders, since I estimated the distance at better than 300 yards. The first round, as I found out later, broke his right front leg. He went down in the snow, then jumped right back up and went behind some oak brush and then down again.

Rudy yelled back that he would try to locate him if I guided him with my binoculars, which I did. While Rudy was on his way, the buck took off again, over a ridge and out of sight. I yelled to Rudy that the buck had taken off, and then I did the same. I must have caught up to Rudy in record time. Huffing and puffing, we started tracking the buck.

We could tell his leg was broken by the drag marks in the snow. With the blood and fresh snow, we thought this would be a piece of cake. Surely the animal couldn't keep going. To our total amazement, we found where he jumped (on three legs) a four-wire barbed fence . After at least two miles, we came to an opening and saw no more blood or tracks. We waited and looked around frantically. Then Rudy grabbed my arm and shouted "There he is!" My heart was in my throat as I took final aim. The big buck looked me in the face as I squeezed off the shot at only 50 yards. He went another 15 feet and dropped. We approached him and gasped at the size of his rack.

Many unbelievable things happened on this hunt. For one, we were able to drive my truck to within 20 yards of the kill site. Secondly, the buck qualified for Boone and Crockett. Finally, this was my first muley ever and only my second deer (the first was a three-point whitetail in northeast Washington state).

Photograph by Charlie Crunden

At the 19th Awards (Las Vegas, 1986), Erich P. Burkhard accepts the Second Award for his typical mule deer from Dr. Philip L. Wright, Chairman of the Records Committee.

Photograph by Charlie Crunden

At the 19th Awards (Las Vegas, 1986), James S. Harden accepts the Honorable Mention Award for his typical mule deer from Dr. Philip L. Wright, Chairman of the Records Committee.

Photograph by Wm. H. Nesbitt

MULE DEER (TYPICAL ANTLERS)
HONORABLE MENTION
SCORE: 202

Locality: Idaho Co., Idaho   Date: November 1981
Hunter: John H. Davis

MULE DEER, TYPICAL ANTLERS 202

John H. Davis

In 1981, I was invited by long-time friend and hunting partner Leland Schneider to again join the successful and respected Ures-Schneider Group near the Chamberlain Basin in the Idaho Primitive Area. We meet in Salmon, Idaho in early November to board planes for the 40-minute flight to base camp. There, we pack up and ride out of base camp the same day for the three hour ride to our spike camp.

Spike camp consists of a cooking and dining tent and two sleeping tents. There are saddle horses for the hunters and four pack animals. A normal day consists of riding out of camp at about dawn to our hunting area. We then hunt on foot all day, meeting at the horses around dusk, to ride back to camp.

The horses are usually trailed around by one of the wranglers to where we are meeting that evening. Whoever gets there first starts a fire and gathers wood for the wait until all the hunters are accounted for.

On this trip, we hunted for 10 days and had been fairly successful with four or five good bulls and a like number of nice mule deer bucks. Since there were nine of us on this hunt, we decided to stay an extra day and hunt in a little different area. The terrain was typical Idaho: very steep, timbered drainages that ranged from relatively open sugar pines to very thick lodge pole and jack pines.

On this last day, our group rode about two hours and then split up to cover a very large mountain. Perry O'Laughlin and I dismounted and left our horses with the wrangler to be tied farther around the mountain. When we looked up, we could see we had our work cut out for us. We would have to climb to the top of a 2,000 foot mountain in a light rain. We shouldered our packs and started up.

We were about half-way up when we stopped in a small saddle to rest and eat our lunch. That's when we heard Pete Dittmer on the far side of the drainage to our left fire several rounds. Since the slope to our left was covered with very thick jack pines, Perry and I decided, in a quickly whispered conversation, to climb up the ridge until we could see.

We had just started up the crest of the ridge, when a very nice six-point bull elk stepped from the thick pines and stopped in front of me at about 60 yards. I quickly motioned for Perry to stop, then raised my .270 caliber Model 70 and shot. The bull whirled around and immediately disappeared. I ran around the hill and Perry ran up to where the bull had gone into the pines. He found the bull dead, about 50 yards from where he was shot. The 160 grain Nosler bullet had passed through both lungs and out the other side. I was, needless to say, a very excited elk hunter with my first elk. We later found that Pete had also connected on a six point bull.

It was about two in the afternoon when Leland, Frank Ures, Perry, and I finished taking pictures and cleaning the bull. I was still very excited and looking forward to the story-telling over drinks that evening. We again split-up and headed around a huge bowl, with Frank and Leland above me, and Perry below. We were more or less making a loop, ending up back at the bottom of the mountain, where the horses should be tied.

I was about half-way around, moving very slow in sugar pines interspersed with patches of "Christmas trees", when I stopped and sat on a rock to relace my boots. I had just removed my pack, when I heard a shot coming from the direction of where we separated. I figured that could only be Pete, again coming-up from behind after finishing with his bull. I left my pack and walked back about 30 yards and listened. I did not hear anything for about five minutes, so I returned to my seat. I no sooner started to finish with my boots, than I heard something moving fast through some "Christmas Trees" just below me. I picked up my rifle and waited.

I could not believe my eyes when a very big buck mule deer stepped-out, stopped, and looked directly at me. I automatically raised-up and shot in one motion. The buck dropped in his tracks.

As soon as I walked up to the deer, I could not believe it. He had the biggest rack I had ever seen taken. I just walked around him muttering to myself. The other guys seemed to take forever getting over to where I was. I just could not believe my luck, to take my first elk, a six-point bull, and a trophy mule deer in the same day, muchless a lifetime, was too much to believe.

Pete told me later that he had finished cleaning his bull, and he had then climbed up to about where my bull was lying. He was basically following our group around the bowl, when he saw this buck running through the pines. He took a quick shot (the shot I heard), but missed.

It is indeed a good friend that runs a six-point bull elk and a Boone and Crockett trophy mule deer buck to you in the same day. Thanks, Pete.

Riding up with the wrangler and the pack animals the next day proved to be more of a chore than I expected. After we loaded both bulls, we headed for the buck. It had snowed about a foot the previous night and I could not find any of my flags pointing to the location of the deer. We rode around that big bowl for about two hours, and I was getting very nervous, when I finally spotted a red marker.

We flew back to Salmon the next morning, ending the most exciting hunting trip I have ever had before or since. I would like to again thank my friends who made it possible; Leland Schneider for the invitation and for showing me how to sneak up on elk and deer, Pete Dittmer for pushing both these animals by me (I hope I can return the favor), Perry O'Laughlin for his slow trigger, and the rest of the hunting gang (especially Lady Luck) for one hell of an experience.

Photo Courtesy of Scott M. Bulloch

Hunting season of 1985 gave Scott M. Bulloch the opportunity to kill this big typical mule deer in Washington County, Utah. It scores 195 5/8 points.

Photo Courtesy of Michael Atwood

It was Michael Atwood's first mule deer hunt, back in 1967, in Utah County, Utah. It turned out really well, with this big non-typical that scores 262 falling to Mike's .30-30.

Photograph by Wm. H. Nesbitt

COLUMBIA BLACKTAIL DEER
FIRST AWARD
SCORE: 159 4/8

Locality: Mendocino Co., Calif.   Date: September 1984
Hunter: Russ McLennan

COLUMBIA BLACKTAIL DEER
159 4/8

Russ McLennan

The hunt for my record blacktail began on September 9, 1984, when my son, Don, and I left our home in the Sierra Nevada and headed for the rolling hills of Mencocino County. There, we met my friend, John, and spent a pleasant northern California evening in the town of Hopland. Since I was beginning my hunt late in the season, I felt crowded for time and wondered if I would even see a decent buck before the season ended. John had bragged about the hunting in Mendocino County for years, and now I told him we'd see how much of his talk was just that.

Early the next morning, we drove out of Hopland and headed west. John and my son dropped me off in a brushy canyon where I took a stand on the hillside and waited, the several deer trails that wove back and forth across the gully below. It was still the rut, so I knew there was a chance I'd see some large bucks. As I waited, a couple of small forked-horns browsed through.

At about 9 a.m., seven does, followed by the best buck I'd ever seen, crossed the gully and I knew my wait was over. When he was 150 yards away, I raised my Winchester .270 and lined him up in the cross-hairs.

When John and Don came back, I had nearly finished field dressing him. They drove the truck right to me. We loaded my buck and started back.

We knew he was good. But, it wasn't until later, much later, that we found out how good. Well, okay, John, the deer are pretty big in California.

Photograph by Wm. H. Nesbitt

COLUMBIA BLACKTAIL DEER
SECOND AWARD
SCORE: 158 2/8

Locality: Josephine Co., Oreg.   Date: October 1983
Hunter: James E. Brierley

COLUMBIA BLACKTAIL DEER
158 2/8

James E. Brierley

There was no wind, and the overcast sky was just what a serious deer hunter would have ordered. Deer were likely to be moving some, but there wouldn't be any reflected sunlight from a gun or binoculars to spook them.

Jim Brierley was enjoying himself. It was a good day just to be out in the woods. It was November 30, 1983. Thanksgiving was over, and it was still several weeks till Christmas, but Jim had a feeling that this was going to be a memorable hunt.

Jim had been hunting for several hours. It was now after 8 a.m., but still a good time, with the overcast conditions, to find a good buck. Jim was hunting in the Applegate River area of Josephine County, Oregon. Some good Columbia blacktails come out of there each year, and Jim knew the area well.

The clock had moved to 8:15 a.m., when Jim found his big buck. He worked to within 30 yards, before he shouldered his .300 Winchester Magnum. A careful squeeze of the trigger, and the beautiful buck was down for keeps. Amazingly, even the overcast sky seemed brighter as Jim began field-dressing his prize.

Photograph by Wm. H. Nesbitt

COLUMBIA BLACKTAIL DEER
THIRD AWARD
SCORE: 158

Locality: Trinity Co., Calif.   Date: September 1984
Hunter: Charles A. Strickland

COLUMBIA BLACKTAIL DEER 158

Charles A. Strickland

Charles A. Strickland is a resident of Pittsburg, California. As such, he is well aware of the excellent hunting available in Trinity County. Therefore, it was no surprise that he picked Trinity County as the site for his blacktail deer hunt in 1984.

To get to the hunting area was a five-mile hike from where the car was left. But, this helped eliminate the hunting pressure, and it gave him a much better chance for success. Chuck reached his camp on September 20. He settled in for the night, hoping for good luck during the next several days of hunting.

The first couple of days of hunting proved fruitless. Chuck did not find the good buck that he was seeking. But on September 22, Chuck's luck changed. It was late in the day, just about 6:15 p.m. He had worked his way to within 75 yards of the very fine blacktail buck. It was time to make the shot. His .300 Winchester Magnum did its work well, and the trophy was his.

Photograph by Wm. H. Nesbitt

COLUMBIA BLACKTAIL DEER
FOURTH AWARD
SCORE: 155 7/8

Locality: Pierce Co., Wash.   Date: October 1983
Hunter: Jim Bennett and Floyd Duell

COLUMBIA BLACKTAIL DEER
155⅞

Jim Bennett and Floyd Duell

It was the opening day of the October 1983 deer hunting season. We had stayed up late the night before preparing for a trip into an area we had explored the previous summer that we hoped would produce some big bucks. It was our third year of hunting together, and we had been very successful at taking both deer and elk with bows and rifles. This was a rifle hunt, and we were both looking forward to hunting and learning a new area.

It was an area about two hours drive from where we live in Olympia, Washington. More precisely, it is southeast of the small town of Buckley, Washington, located in Pierce County. It is an area of steep terrain, mostly covered with second growth fir and alder, with some brushy draws we felt would be productive.

Legal time to shoot wasn't until 7 a.m., but as is our custom, we like to arrive and be in place at least 45 minutes before daybreak. So, Jim picked me up that morning at 4 a.m., after only a few hours of shut-eye for each of us. With a few cups of coffee in us, and a lot of good-natured razzing, we were raring to go when we arrived right on schedule about a half-hour before sunup. We had driven to a high ridge with the intention to hunt down it into some good-looking patches of timber. When we arrived, the wind was blowing straight across the ridge at better than 20 miles per hour and raining about as hard as it can rain here in Washington (which is one helluva lot). Both of us dislike wearing all that noisy raingear, but this certainly was going to be an exception. We compromised and decided to wear only rain jackets, leaving the noisy rainpants in the truck.

As we set in the truck sipping coffee, we listened to the rain beat sideways against the truck and we could feel the truck move as it was buffeted by strong gusts of wind. We both looked at each other. Someone made the comment that the only other person crazy enough to leave a warm bed, with little sleep, drive for two hours to the top of a ridge to go walking around in a driving rain is a duck hunter, and as everyone knows, they are totally crazy!

We had driven to the end of a road. As we anxiously waited for daybreak, we both hoped other hunters wouldn't show up at the last minute and cause us to get started before we could see in the timber. We were also somewhat concerned that the timber may not be the best place to be with the high winds. However, it was second growth and a pretty thick stand, so we figured it would be all right. Our luck held good; no other hunters showed up. I guess the sensible hunters were down low, out of the storm.

As soon as it was light enough to see antlers, we flipped a coin, with Jim winning the toss. He elected to go down the ridge and hunt parallel with me, while I stayed nearer the top of the ridge. We hunted this way for several hours, meeting up with each other at pre-determined places to compare notes. We hunt well together and pretty well know each others pace and habits. With the use of hand signals, we can do a lot of "communicating" several hundred yards apart.

We had both jumped several does, and another hunter had downed a small buck, but we had yet to see a deer with antlers. We weren't discouraged though; the storm had broken and the sun was out, and neither one of us was "back at the office" doing paperwork.

It was close to 11 a.m. when I spotted Jim and made my way over to the edge of the timber to plan our next move. Since the weather had been so poor the night before, we figured a nearby draw might still be holding a few late-feeding deer and we walked over together to have a look.

When we got to the draw, I sat down to get out my binoculars while Jim gave the draw the once over. I had just bent over, when Jim exclaimed, "There's a buck!" Even though he had said it in hushed tones, I knew Jim had seen a "keeper". I looked where Jim pointed, about 175 yards away, and I could see a very nice buck looking straight at us at the top of a hill. You didn't need binoulars to see those antlers. They were silhouetted against a blue sky and were quite large.

I raised my .30-06 and turned the variable scope up to eight power to get a good look at the buck. I watched the buck as Jim quickly looked for a rest. The walk had been up hill, we were both a little winded, and the front of a deer isn't the largest target if you want a clean kill. As I watched the buck through my scope, I could tell he was getting very nervous and I hoped Jim would shoot quickly. I didn't shoot, as Jim had seen the buck first and by rights should have first crack at it. I told Jim the buck was going to go and he had better shoot or get off the pot! He raised his .270 Ruger, which was enough for the buck. As he started to go, I fired, at the same time as Jim. The buck went down hard and I knew we had us a fine animal. But, before we could catch our breath, that buck was up and running. I could tell he wouldn't go far, but sometimes they can fool you, so we each fired one more round, putting the buck down for good.

The shots had startled a couple of deer below us, so Jim took a stand while I made my way over to the buck. We jumped two more does but no bucks. Our buck had gone over the crest of the hill and died very quickly. It was the biggest buck either of us had ever seen on this side of the mountains.

The easy part was over. We were at least a three-mile walk, uphill, to the truck, with about four hours of daylight left. While we didn't weigh the buck, we extimated the weight to be in the neighborhood of 250 pounds. The pack boards were back at the truck, and we figured it would be past dark by the time we got them and came back to the buck. So, we caped and quartered the buck and left it hanging in a tree, not sure when we would make it back. After a tough three hour-climb, we were back at the truck. We decided to return home to pick up our Honda Trail 90's which would allow us to use a ridge trail to cut our packing distance in half.

By the time we got to Olympia, loaded the bikes and grabbed a sandwich, and made the return trip, it was close to 9 p.m. I had talked my wife Pam into coming with us to see the big buck. I assured her this wouldn't be one of our "wild-hair" trips, it would only take a couple of hours and she wouldn't get cold, as she could wait at the truck. Jim's wife, Laura, couldn't go as she had to take the car and their daughter Anya. (Or, maybe she just knew us too well.)

We unloaded the Hondas and headed down a ridge trail into a fog shrouded patch of old-growth timber. Several times we missed the trail in the fog, ending up down the side of the ridge. We would then have to "muscle" the bikes back up to the trail. About the fifth time this happened, we weren't so sure how much of an energy saving device these bikes really were.

After a couple of hours of this fun-and-games, we decided we were a little lost and had missed the ridge we wanted. We decided to turn around and very carefully look for the other ridge. We had only gone about 50 yards when my trailbike quit. Being a patient man (and having left my rifle at home), I couldn't shoot the damn thing, so I began checking the spark, etc. Well, as it turned out, I had to take the entire carburetor apart and clean the jets with only the aid of one of those "disposable" flashlights. Our other light had been lost when we went on one of our off-trail excursions earlier.

I was rewarded though, as it fired right up when I got it back together. It ran fine for a whole hundred yards before it quit again! I had just bought the bike from a guy who had stored it in his garage for five years without draining the gas tank. I unscrewed the gas cap and looked inside; I've seen frog ponds that were cleaner!

We shoved and pulled my bike until we found the ridge we were looking for. We left my trail bike there and headed out on Jim's, when Jim remarked that we had forgotten to put gas in his bike. Upon checking his tank, we found it was almost empty and would never get us back to the truck. We also found the key to Jim's truck and realized there would be no way for Pam (remember Pam, my long-suffering wife) to keep warm in the truck.

We went back to my bike with the intention of straining the gas from it into a container to then put into Jim's bike. That was a fine idea until we discovered that we had no container. Jim did manage to find a used plastic sandwich bag, with holes in both corners. (Have you ever tried to pour gas out of a baggie with holes in it, into a little round hole in a gas tank? In the dark?) Well, we managed to soak our pants and the ground, and we even got about a quart of gas into Jim's bike.

Off we went, down the ridge riding double on Jim's bike. After our third spill, we decided to walk. We finally found our marker, don't ask me how, and by another stroke of luck walked right down to the deer. By this time it was almost 4 a.m. and we had been up some 24 hours on very little sleep. In our shape, there was too much deer to pack in one trip, and not enough to pack in two trips. Know what I mean? So we each made one trip back to Jim's bike, then he made trips back to my disabled bike while I made the last trip.

Finally, a little past daybreak, we had the deer mostly loaded on the disabled bike, with part of it on the back of Jim's. With a lot of pulling, shoving, cursing, and muscle, we got back to the truck at approximately 9:30 a.m. We found Pam huddled on the floor of the truck, covered only by our unused rain pants, and very cold. My, "Hello honey, look at the nice buck", wasn't met with the greatest of interest. All in all, she was a pretty good sport; it was several months later that she divorced me.

Thirty-six hours after our little adventure began, we had the deer hanging in Jim's garage, clean as a whistle, and we were headed for the sack and some much needed rest.

We were both so sore the next few days that we could hardly walk, but we were laughing and looking forward to our next adventure together. Neither of us knew we had a buck that would make the records books, and I was surprised when Jim told me how high it had scored.

We split the cost of having the cape mount done, and now we each take turns displaying the rack in our living rooms.

While neither of us will ever know which bullet did the old buck in, I don't think either of us really cares. We shared the work, we shared the costs, we shared the fun, and we'll share the credit. After all, that's what having a hunting partner is all about.

Photo Courtesy of Steve Rupp

This huge Columbia blacktail deer was killed by Steve Rupp in 1983 near Cultus Lake, B. C. Scoring 153 7/8 points, it was only 45 yards from Rupp when he pulled the trigger.

Photo Courtesy of Edmund L. Hurst

A happy Ed Hurst with his fine Columbia blacktail deer killed in 1984 near Port Blakely, Washington. It scores 135 7/8 points.

Photograph by Wm. H. Nesbitt

COLUMBIA BLACKTAIL DEER
HONORABLE MENTION
SCORE: 154 5/8

Locality: Siskiyou Co., Calif.   Date: September 1984
Hunter: Darrell R. Jones

COLUMBIA BLACKTAIL DEER
154 5/8

Darrell R. Jones

Darrell Jones was looking for a good blacktail buck. He was hunting in the Klamath River, east of Happy Camp. This is in Siskiyou County, California, a good area for blacktail deer. His chances of taking a buck were good, but he had already been hunting several hours without seeing the desired trophy.

Darrell found his big buck at 8:30 a.m. He was only 75 yards away, when he carefully aimed his .270 Browning and brought his prize down.

It was a fine buck, just what Darrell had been looking for. Now the hard work of dressing and taking care of the meat began.

Photograph by Wm. H. Nesbitt

NEW WORLD'S RECORD SITKA BLACKTAIL DEER
FIRST AWARD
SCORE: 123 4/8

Locality: Uganik Bay, Alaska   Date: November 1983
Hunter: Donna D. Braendel

SITKA BLACKTAIL DEER
123 4/8

Donna D. Braendel

We go to Kodiak Island to hunt blacktail deer every year. Since Karl (my husband) is a guide and I work in a guiding camp every fall, this is the only time we can do any hunting ourselves. We have hunted there every year for nine years.

I wanted very much to get a buck good enough to mount. Karl has taken a few really nice ones, including a buck that scored well enough to make the "book".

In November of 1983, we went down for a week with Dennis Johnson and his wife Andy, and my brother-in-law, Eric. We spent our first two days tent-bound due to the usual weather conditions of high winds and heavy rain.

On the third morning, the aqua-colored bay had turned mud brown from the flooding creeks and river, but the rain had diminished to a drizzle. Such days are very wet, but quiet, and you can see many deer, though seldom do you see the big ones, who are too clever to show themselves. This is why, on the last day, we had all taken meat deer except for Eric, who had gotten a beauty up the valley; the rest of us had not had a chance at really big bucks.

This last day was cold and clear, and the wind was not blowing. We had only a half-day to hunt. The plane would be in to get us in the morning and we still had to break camp. Karl and I decided to go out early, up the valley.

We made our way very slowly, since on such mornings it is noisy traveling. We stopped periodically to glass for deer. We had reached the last glassing knob, and we had spotted a number of deer, though none were large. We were thinking of heading back when Karl spotted several deer farther up the valley. He was fairly sure that one of them was a good buck, but it was too far away to be certain. We debated going after him, but we were short on time and chances were good that the deer would be long gone by the time we got there. We had, in fact, started back when Karl stopped to glass the knob one more time.

Well heck, I wanted to go after that deer, and I knew he did too, so I said, "Let's just go look at him closer if we can. We won't be that late." "Okay, let's go." And off we went, going as quietly as possible, hoping that the buck would remain on the knob with his lady friend in the sunshine.

When we were about 250-300 yards away, Karl spotted the big buck in a dense brush patch, looking right at us. He had not actually seen us, but he could hear our crunchy progress. We could go no further without spooking him. We stacked our packboards on top of each other, which made a good shooting rest. From there we watched him. We could see very little of his antlers, but when he turned his head several times to look in the direction of the other deer, I thought I could see a fairly good length. I could see his head and neck, but it was far too brushy to shoot. For at least 10 minutes the buck stood staring at us without moving. Then he turned in his tracks and started to walk away.

Karl said, "Well, that is that." Right then, the buck stopped and looked again toward the other deer, making a bad decision. Let me say here that it was jealousy that did in that buck. He turned and walked toward the other deer.

In his path was a very small clearing. I followed him with my scope, and when he was totally clear, I aimed high on the shoulder and fired.

I use a 6mm with a thumbhold stock, and I am very comfortable with it. Loaded with 95 grain Nosler partition handloads, it has taken several deer for me with one shot. I was pretty sure that I had done all right and that the deer was down.

At this point, we had no idea how big that deer was. I had not looked at his antlers when I shot, and we had never seen them clearly before that.

We climbed up the hill and Karl found the buck lying about four jumps from where I shot him. He was unbelievably big, a beautiful deer. When we butchered him, we found that my shot had gone through the heart. The range had been about 275-300 yards.

We got back to camp, late of course. When Eric saw those antlers, he realized that our huge dollar bet had slipped from his grasp. It was a blow, but he took it well.

Photo Courtesy of Douglas G. Ellis

Doug Ellis hunted in Marion County, Oregon, in 1984 to find this Columbia blacktail deer that qualified under the lower entry score required for the Awards records. Doug's buck scores 125 5/8 points.

Photo Courtesy of Guy Hanson

This Columbia blacktail deer easily qualified for the 19th Awards records book with a score of 122 3/8 points. It was taken by Guy A. Hanson in 1984 in Pierce County, Washington.

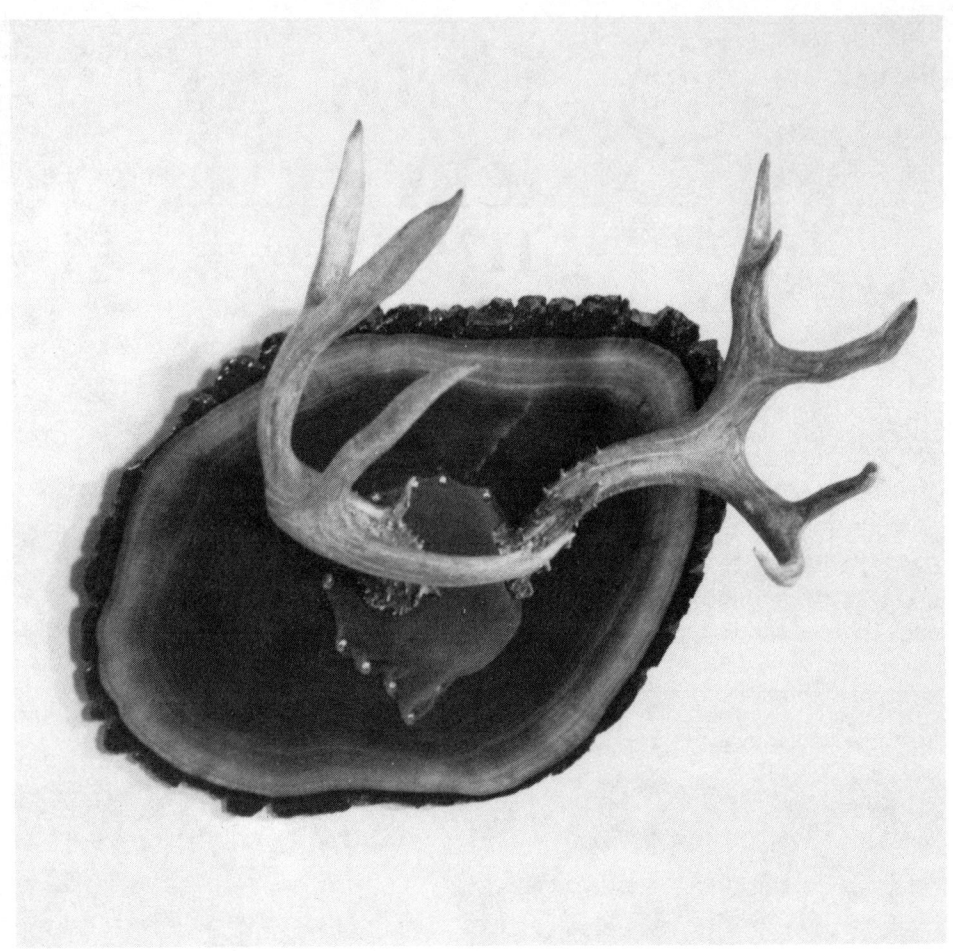

Photograph by Wm. H. Nesbitt

SITKA BLACKTAIL DEER
SECOND AWARD
SCORE: 117 1/8

Locality: Baird Peak   Date: August 1984
Hunter: William C. Dunham

SITKA BLACKTAIL DEER
117 1/8

William C. Dunham

William C. Dunham was on his annual blacktail deer hunt on Prince of Wales Island, Alaska. It was August 3 of 1984. The light rain was not at all unusual weather for the island.

It was barely good shooting light, just 5 a.m. But there the buck was. Dunham wasted no time, carefully aiming his 25-06 Remington and bringing his prize down. It was a very good buck, but little did Dunham realize at the time that it would qualify for the newly-established category of Sitka blacktail deer. When he heard of the category, Bill had his trophy measured, and indeed it qualified, ending up as one of the best taken in the category during the 19th Awards entry period.

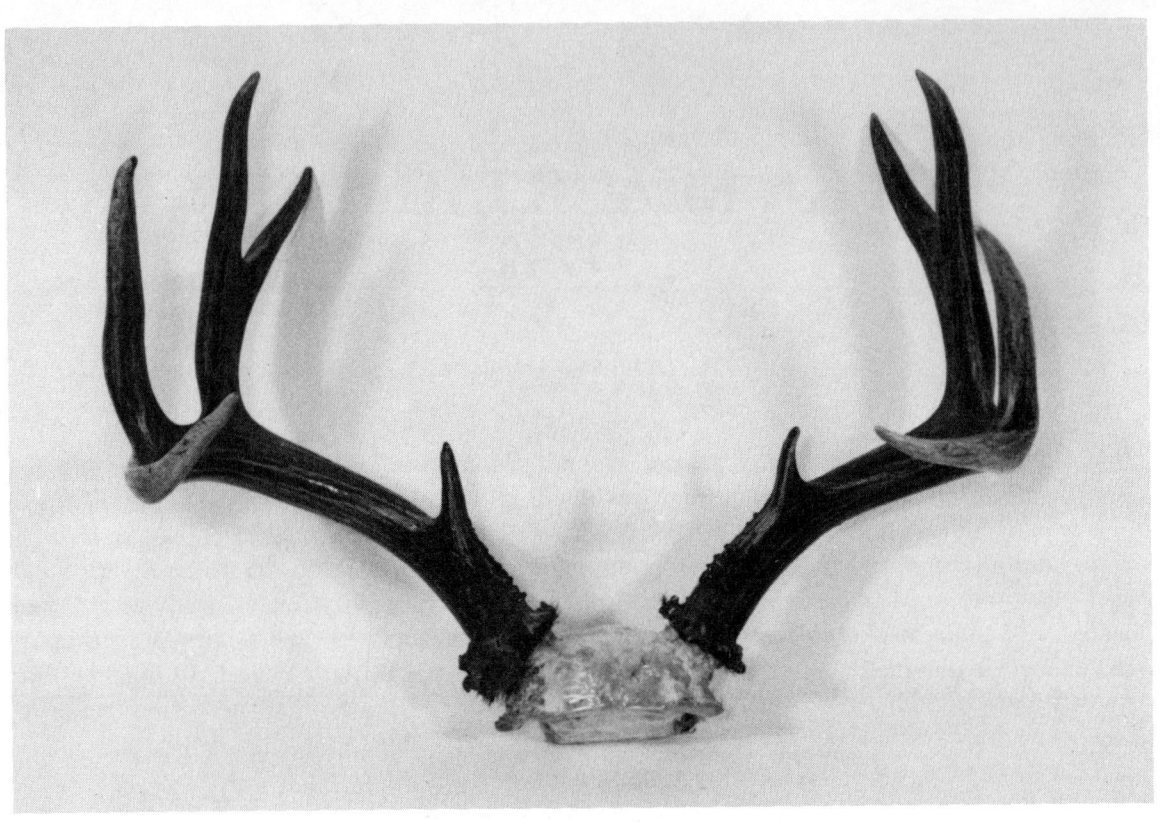

Photograph by Wm. H. Nesbitt

SITKA BLACKTAIL DEER
THIRD AWARD
SCORE: 116

Locality: Kiliuda Bay, Alaska   Date: October 1984
Hunter: Timothy Tittle

SITKA BLACKTAIL DEER 116

Timothy Tittle

The hunt started off just like all the rest. Get up at 6:00 a.m., eat a good breakfast, and head out. We knew we could get all the meat we wanted, and maybe a nice buck to go with the bunch. My hunting partner, Tom, and I had no greater expectations than normal.

Just being there on south Kodiak Island, away from the crowds, was enough. Beautiful scenery, along with fishing, duck and fox hunting, and lots of big brown bears to watch was almost perfect in itself. But we were here on our annual hunt looking for deer meat.

We headed out in my Zodiak to our hot spot, a deep ravine that is thick with alders running from the beach to the top of the mountain 1,200 feet above. Only one thing was wrong, my knees. As usual, they had locked up on me after our first deer chase the day before, and I was destined to hobble around for the rest of the week.

Tom took pity on my sore knees and volunteered to flush the ravine. I agreed to walk the high lip of the ravine, ready to pop anything extra that he might kick out. He was out of sight for only about five minutes when his .223 rang out. The first thought, of course, in this country was, "I hope it's not a mean old bear." Nonetheless, I ran as best I could up the hill to the top of the lip. I had a good view about half way down the crevice and stopped and waited. More shots indicated that Tom was into something.

Suddenly, there was a doe running out of the deep ravine towards the lip. She stopped and looked back over her shoulder towards Tom, and I dropped her from about 50 yards. I said, "All right, deer meat," and started walking toward her. Suddenly, out came this big rack with a deer under it. He stood there, with the sun sparkling off his antlers, looking back at Tom. He didn't even see me. A quick shot from my 7mm Remington Magnum dropped him, and he rolled about 40 yards down the hill.

Tom had bagged a doe and a spike below, and he didn't see my big buck until I dragged the buck farther downhill toward him. By this time, my knees were just about shot, so Tom dragged the other three deer to the beach before I got halfway there with my buck. Then, he came back to help me.

In this country, it is wise to get your deer out of the woods as soon as possible. Otherwise, the bears will smell them and possibly take them right away from you. Many times this happens within the hour after the kill.

It was 10:00 in the morning and we were headed for camp three miles up the bay with four deer. Not a bad morning's work. After hanging our deer up in the cottonwoods, we had a large lunch, followed by an ice cold beer or two for celebration purposes.

The crisp 25 degree, clear and windy weather was perfect for curing our meat. Before the week was out, we almost ran out of trees to hang our meat in. My big buck proved to be the biggest rack taken in four years of hunting on Kodiak, but he was not the biggest deer in body size. The 29 deer (19 bucks) taken by the seven of us in six days of hunting was quite a hunting accomplishment. But, just being able to enjoy the hunting, companionship, and the great outdoors was the real prize.

Photo Courtesy of Robert D. Gilliland

This fine Sita blacktail deer scores 118 3/8 points and was invited to the 19th Awards Final Judging. It was killed in 1983 on Kodiak Island, Alaska, by Robert D. Gilliland.

Photo Courtesy of John A. Miller

Kodiak Island, Alaska, grew this big-bodied Sitka blacktail deer that fell to John A. Miller's gun in 1984. It scores 104 2/8 points.

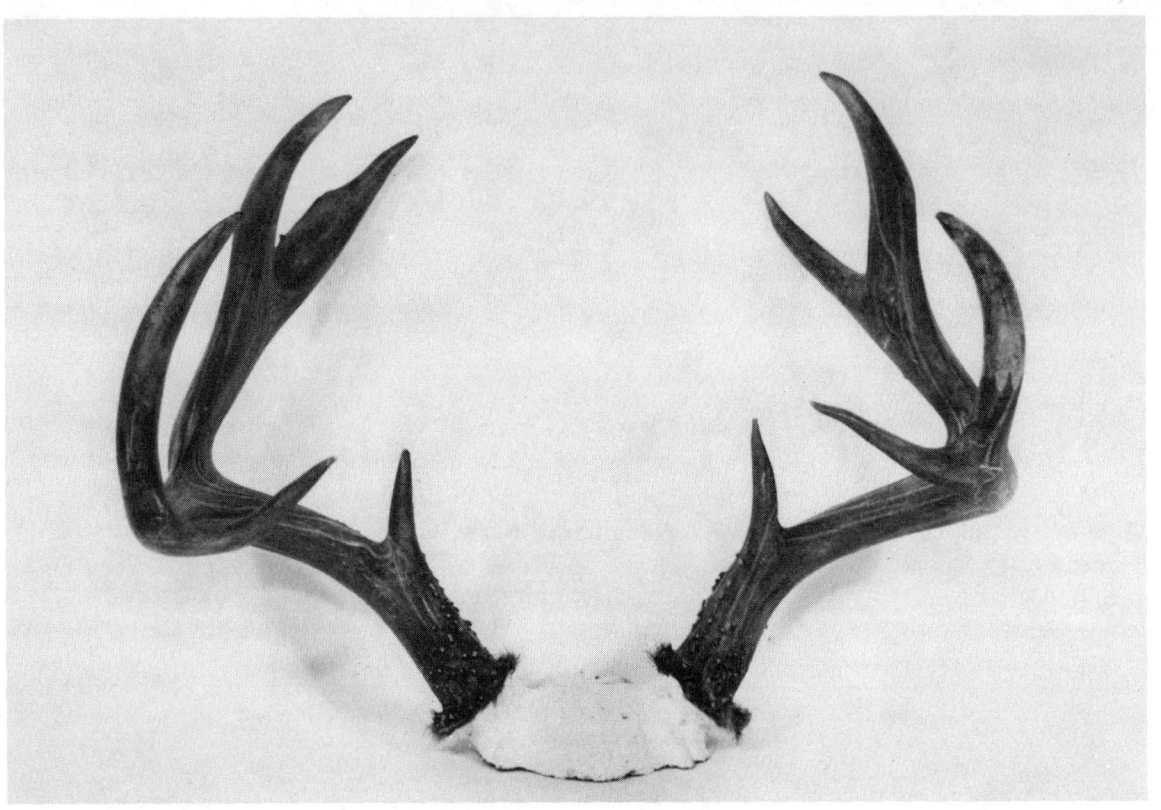

Photograph by Wm. H. Nesbitt

SITKA BLACKTAIL DEER
FOURTH AWARD
SCORE: 114 7/8

Locality: Control Lake, Alaska   Date: August 1985
Hunter: Timothy C. Winsenberg

SITKA BLACKTAIL DEER
114 7/8

Timothy C. Winsenberg

I glanced at my watch as I approached the rock quarry. Only 2:10 p.m., time to make one more trip before quitting time and the beginning of my four-day weekend. I was working on a road construction project at 12 Mile Arm, on Prince of Wales Island, Alaska, driving an off-highway rock truck. I was working a 10 day on and four day off schedule, so I had plenty of hunting time during deer season.

Deer season in this area of southeastern Alaska begins on August 1st and runs until November 30th, with a bag limit of three bucks. I prefer alpine hunting to the clearcuts and low muskegs, so I like to hunt in August and September.

Opening weekend I hunted with a friend from Ketchikan. We had intended to hunt as I had hunted, with good results, in the early 1970's. It was a long hike, but the mountain has very little hunting pressure due to rough climbing conditions. My hunting partner of the 70's called it "22 Mile Mountain". The mountain has no name on the map and it is located 22 miles from the town of Thorne Bay, thus the nickname "22 Mile".

Opening weekend was typical southeastern Alaska weather, with rain and heavy clouds. Our chosen mountain was covered in a thick layer of clouds, so we were forced to hunt a lower mountain. That weekend ended with my partner bagging a fork-horn and a small three-point. I also killed a small three-point.

On August 15, 1985, the weather was very warm and sunny, without a cloud in the sky. It was time to climb 22 Mile! I'd planned to drive to the town of Klawock after work, spend the night there, and drive the remaining 25 miles to my chosen mountain in the wee hours of the morning, then day hunt the mountain.

While driving my truck to the shop for weekend maintenance, I suddenly decided to take advantage of the beautiful weather and climb as much of the mountain that evening as daylight would permit. I'd then spend the night, contining to the top the next morning. Hopefully, that would give me more hunting time in the early morning while the deer were feeding.

I parked my truck at the shop, then rushed to my travel trailer to throw a pack together. My gear included a mountain pack, matches, sleeping bag, plastic tarp, rope, knife, camera with two lenses and tripod, extra socks, trail mix, sausage, cheese, rifle and ammunition. If it turned to rain, I was going to be in real trouble as my gear was set up for a dry camp and nothing more.

I drove to Klawock, fueled my pickup, and continued on to the junction at Control Lake. Only six more miles before my hike would begin. I arrived at my destination around 5:30 p.m., which left me 3 to 3½ hours of good daylight before I would have to make camp.

I had planned to follow the same route my friend and I had used 13 years earlier, following a wash up a steep canyon to a saddle below the southeast side of the peak. I hoped to reach the saddle by dark, as I knew there was a good camping spot there. No time could be wasted if I was to make it by nightfall.

I realized when I reached the bottom of the wash that 13 years had made a big difference in climbing conditions. The salmon berry brush and devils club had almost concealed the wash and every step was a fight. I was tempted to turn back for fear of having to sleep in a salmon berry thicket on a pile of rocks. But, my stubborn nature wouldn't allow it so I pushed on.

I reached the saddle about 8:15 p.m., with daylight growing dimmer by the minute. I climbed a little farther until I found a suitable place to camp. I used a small amount of rope from my pack to hang the tarp from nearby trees to provide shelter from possible rain and early morning dew. I had a meager dinner of sausage, cheese, and trail mix, then settled down for the night.

I awoke at about 4:30 a.m. It was growing light, but it was still too dark to finish my climb, so I had a snack, dressed and waited. A cup of coffee would have been pure heaven!

At earliest light, I left my makeshift camp, aiming to reach the peak as early as possible. The mountain top was a series of bluffs and rock outcrops, with grassy areas and mountain hemlock clumps. The climbing was slow, but the distance wasn't far. I reached the summit after a 45 minute climb.

I sat for a moment to catch my breath and take a brief look at the morning. All was quiet— total silence except for a faint stirring of the brush in the breeze. The dew on the grass and mountain hemlocks shimmered in the early morning light. The valleys were covered with a thick blanket of fog. All that could be seen in any direction were mountain tops, dressed in a pastel orange haze and the sun was a bright orange fireball in the east. It all added up to the promise of a fantastic day.

The fog drifted away from a ridge directly below me and I spotted a spike buck standing in a mountain pool about 100 yards below me. Suddenly, my mind snapped back into the hunting mode and the scenic beauty and solitude of my mountain was forgotten. As the fog continued to drift from the ridge, exposing more terrain, I spotted five more deer, all does or young bucks. Three were still bedded down. They were just coming out of their beds to feed. Perfect timing! I knew from past experience that the deer would feed in the early morning, then bed down again by 11:00 a.m. to noon, and then stay bedded down for the early afternoon. This would give me about four hours to try to find a buck worth packing off this knob.

I watched the six deer for a few minutes, then shouldered my pack and moved to the north side of the peak. This area was a series of bluffs, ravines and very steep talus slopes. I gave a sigh of relief when I glassed the area with my rifle scope and found no deer. I really didn't relish the thought of packing a deer out of that area.

I walked across the top of the peak, sat on the edge of a bluff, and checked out a bench area below me. Nothing. Suddenly, as the fog began to burn off a large alpine bowl beyond the rocky bench below, I spotted two reddish spots about 800 yards away in a large meadow. Deer! I rested my rifle over a rock and checked it out. Even at that distance, I could see the antlers of two big bucks feeding in the meadow. As the fog continued to clear, I spotted 11 more deer feeding approximately 200 yards to the right of the two bucks. I swung the rifle to the right and looked them over. I couldn't see antlers on any of the other deer, so I assumed that they were all does or young bucks.

I moved the scope back to the two bucks and looked them over again. They had stopped feeding and now were lying down in the meadow. One appeared to have a real tight, high rack and the other had a very wide rack. At that range, with only a seven power rifle scope, it was impossible to tell if they were trophy class or just big deer. A real big, even trophy class rack on a Sitka Blacktail is hard to come by. It is not at all uncommon to get a buck that is a perfect four point (western count) on one side and only a fork or three points on the other.

It was time to begin my stalk. I shouldered the pack and began to carefully pick my way down a steep, rocky gorge to the bench below. During this time, I was in plain sight of the herd, so very slow, quiet moves were necessary to avoid alarming them. After about 10 minutes of careful descent, I reached the bench which consisted of alpine vegetation, bordered by rocky outcrops. Again, I looked over the deer below. The didn't seem to be disturbed, so I continued trying to stay low and behind any available cover.

I worked my way to the edge of the bench and started down a steep talus slope toward a fringe of high mountain timber that lay between me and the meadow.

I was quietly making my way through the fringe of scattered timber when a deer snorted below and to the left of me. I whirled around to see two does bounding off through the timber. My heart sank like a rock. I was sure that would spook the bucks. My heart was pounding as I slowly worked my way through the timber until I found a small opening that offered a vantage point. I wasn't able to see the rest of the herd, but the two bucks were still bedded down in the meadow. I propped my rifle against a tree and tried to get a better view of the racks on the two. The range was still too great (I estimated that I was still 500 yards from them). I was maybe 100 yards above the edge of the meadow, which had a couple of tree covered knolls in the middle of it. I figured that if I was careful, I should be able to get to one of the patches of trees undetected and get a better look at the bucks and also be in better range for my 7x57.

When I had descended to the edge of the meadow, the deer were hidden behind one of the tree covered knolls. I was in luck, or so I thought at the time. I left my pack at the edge of the trees and started across the opening toward my chosen ambush spot. As I rounded a clump of mountain hemlock, I froze in my tracks. There stood two does, not 25 feet away, calmly looking at me. Suddenly, they bolted and trotted behind the clump of trees in the direction of the big meadow. Damn! I hurried to the clump of trees and peeked around the edge of the brush. There was a shallow ravine in front of me, so I slid down into it, crossed the mountain stream at the bottom, and clawed my way up the other side.

When I reached the top and looked across the meadow, there were deer everywhere, but they were on the move. They were all going in the same general direction, away from me! I walked a little farther and spotted the two culprit does standing approximately where my two bucks had been bedded down, nonchalantly looking at me. My eyes caught movement above them. There, at a distance of 300 to 400 yards, was the buck with the wide rack and a smaller buck trotting toward the ridge top.

I threw the rifle to my shoulder. I could make out four points on one side of the biggest one, but I couldn't make out the other side before the bucks had topped the ridge and were gone from sight. Where was the other big buck? None of the other deer I had seen were big bucks. Where did he go? I had promised myself at the start of this hunt that I wasn't going to pack anything off this mountain smaller than a nice four point. I had venison in the freezer from opening weekend, there were over three months left in the season, and I wanted a big buck.

Feeling dejected, I started tromping across the meadow in the direction the herd had gone, thinking that with a little luck I might get a nice one yet. I glanced across the meadow, and to my surprise, the buck with the high rack was standing in the shadow of a couple of mountain hemlocks at the upper edge of the meadow watching me. I was shocked! He'd only moved a couple of hundred feet from his bed and had calmly stood watching the whole show.

There I stood, smack in the middle of an 80 acre alpine meadow with no cover whatsoever, with a very large buck looking right at me from approximately 200 yards away. I slowly raised my rifle. He had a heavy high rack, though not an extremely wide one, and was still in velvet. I suddenly got excited! How long was he going to stand there?

I spotted a large round boulder peeking out of the deer cabbage just ahead of me. I took a chance, slowly moving toward it, keeping the rifle at my shoulder and not taking my eyes off the buck. He still didn't move a muscle. When I reached the rock, I gently laid down and rested the rifle over the rock and peered through the scope. He was a dandy, but I still couldn't distinguish how many points he had with him looking straight at me and standing in a shadow. I could see that he had nice long eye guards, and it appeared to be a heavy rack, but being in the velvet makes the antlers appear heavier than they actually are.

Suddenly, he lifted and turned his head and I could plainly see four points to a side—nice long points. He was getting nervous and starting to move up the slope. It was now or never! He'd taken about three steps when my pre-1964 Model 70 barked. He collapsed and slid down the slope, coming to rest behind a big boulder. I couldn't remember squeezing the trigger! It was like a dream.

I lit a cigarette and waited, watching for movement. I finally started toward the hemlocks to admire my prize. There, in a heap, lay the nicest buck I had ever killed. I grabbed an antler and lifted his head to get a better look. The fall down the slope had torn the velvet and it was hanging like old, dirty socks from his antlers. Counting the eye guards, he had six points on the left side and five on the right.

I dragged my deer down the slope to a level spot, then walked back to get my pack. When I returned I took a few pictures using the timer on my camera, and then I began the chore of butchering and boning-out the meat for the pack off the mountain.

I arrived at my camp at 11:30 a.m. I added my sleeping bag and other belongings to my already too-heavy pack and started down the wash toward my pickup. The trek seemed like it would never end. I was ready to drop when I finally reached the road at 2:30 p.m. Five-and-a-half hours with a heavy pack was almost too much for an out-of-shape truckdriver. I loaded the pack into the pickup, drank a cold soda from my cooler, and started for home, very tired but also very happy.

It wasn't until four days later, when a friend and I took some measurements, that I realized that I had a records class buck. That made the sweat, scratches, sore back and legs, all well worth while. You know, I may just go back next year and look for the other one.

Photograph by Charlie Crunden

At the 19th Awards (Las Vegas, 1986), Richard A. Pauli accepts First Award for his non-typical whitetail deer from Dr. Philip L. Wright, Chairman of the Records Committee.

Photograph by Charlie Crunden

At the 19th Awards (Las Vegas, 1986), Michael L. Valenzuela accepts First Award for his Coues' typical whitetail deer from Dr. Philip L. Wright, Chairman of the Records Committee.

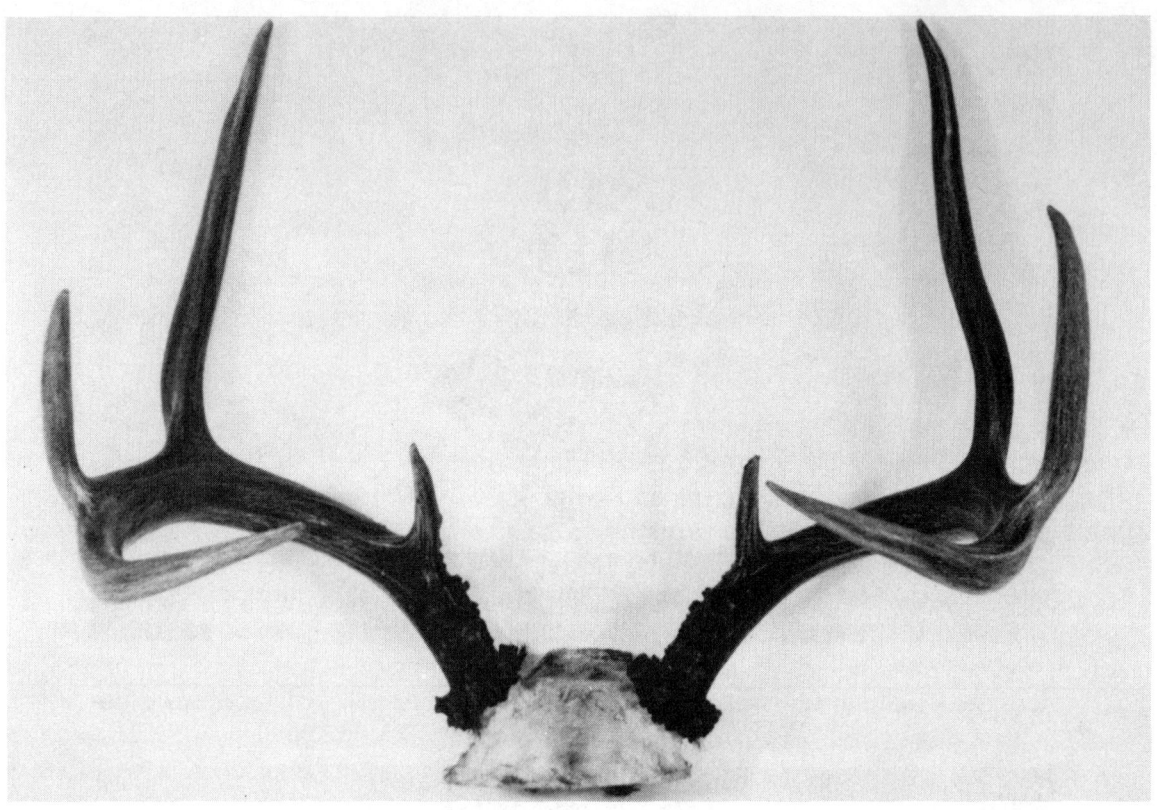

Photograph by Wm. H. Nesbitt

SITKA BLACKTAIL DEER
HONORABLE MENTION
SCORE: 113 4/8

Locality: Viekoda Bay, Alaska   Date: November 1980
Hunter: Edward R. Hajdys

SITKA BLACKTAIL DEER
1134/8

Edward R. Hajdys

It was the first week of November on Kodiak Island. Dale Sade, my hunting partner, and I were preparing for a week of deer hunting on a remote part of the island. We had chartered a Cessna 206 to fly our gear to a cabin in Viekoda Bay, about a 25-minute flight from the town of Kodiak.

We had hunted the same area the previous season (1979) but during mid-December. The weather was exceedingly cold for Kodiak that month, with temperatures in the lower teens, and there was two feet of snow. We spent a week fighting the heavy alder brush, with a reward of a very small button buck. The only time we were warm was while hunting, since the small oil stove did little to warm the drafty little cabin in those temperatures. We did, however, learn the country, or at least where not to hunt. The area looked promising, so we had decided to give it another try this season.

We were prepared for anything this year. Lots of fuel for the stove, extra food in case we got weathered in, lots of warm clothes, and insulated boots. Dale even brought a sleeping bag that was rated to minus 40 degrees. We also deided to take our shotguns and Bumper, my black labrador retriever. We had seen several mallards and goldeneyes in a cove near the cabin the first year. If we couldn't find deer, we at least could shoot some ducks. So, here we were, spending a lot of money to fly into an area not noted for many deer on an island that had other areas of much higher deer population that were much easier to hunt. But, we had spent a miserable week learning the area the year before, and by God we were going back!

The area was steep, with miles of 8 to 10 feet tall alder brush, but it was fantastically beautiful when a vantage point was reached. When the clouds weren't down, we could see into Shelikof Strait, and on a clear day, one could actually see the mountains on the Alaska Peninsula. The bottom area around the cabin was made up of large patches of brush, interspersed with large, rolling hills of bluejoint grass, thick and up to five feet tall. This abruptly stopped at the ocean edge, with 20-foot cliffs that dropped down to rocky beaches. From the rolling hills, the terrain rose sharply to over 2,000 feet. Thick alder brush covered the mountainside up to 1,100 feet, where the brushline abruptly halted, giving way to large open areas covered with grass and forbs, small patches of head-high willow and several stunted Sitka spruce. This was the reason we returned to the area: if this wasn't good deer habitat, then I would eat my hat (or at least a can of beans and wienies)!

It was the morning to leave on our hunt. The weather was clear and the drone of aircraft could be heard in the distance. On Kodiak, this is a signal that travel is possible. It is not uncommon to spend half of the hunt drinking coffee in town (until your bladder almost bursts) while wondering if the fog, rain, snow, and/or wind will ever stop.

Before long, we were landing at our cabin. As we taxied up to the beach, a flock of mallards took off. Dale smiled at me and patted Bumper. We unloaded the plane in record time. Ralph Wright (our pilot) confirmed our pick-up time and wished us good luck. In a matter of minutes, his plane was a speck in the sky, on its way to pick up another group of hunters. After packing our gear to the cabin and making a light lunch, we decided to check the nearby area for deer sign.

In light of our previous experience, our plan was to find a route to higher country and hunt the pass above the thick brush. We spent the afternoon finding a route to the top, but we were disappointed in not finding much deer sign. On returning to the cabin, Dale spotted the mallards on the beach. We grabbed our shotguns and Bumper, and tried not to alarm the mallards. There was a berm of sand and driftwood, covered with tall beach rye, so we got to the beach edge easily. The mallards had moved into the surf and had started to swim away from the beach. We decided a charge down the beach was our only chance for a shot. So off we went and up they went. To our surprise, each of us knocked a duck down and Bumper retrieved them both. We spent another hour waiting for the mallards to return. They never did, but we managed to bag a couple of goldeneyes. Well, at least the duck hunting looked promising. However, the lack of much deer sign had me concerned.

The next morning we were up early, had a good breakfast, and were ready to head up the mountain. The weather was warm, so we decided not to wear our wool pants. Leaving at first light, we walked a game trail to the mountain base. Along the way, we noticed something else—snow flakes! We didn't want to lose our early start, so decided not to go back for the wool pants. Dale split off to the right as we worked our way up through the brush. I found a pretty good route through some 10-foot tall brush, and then I stood in an opening waiting for Dale to catch up. Suddenly, in a draw to my left, I could hear deer moving. I quickly moved to where I could see into the draw and got a glimpse of a doe, just as she dissolved into the brush. I could hear another deer moving in front of the doe, but the brush was too thick to see it. It was then that I noticed a deer feeding on the hillside on the other side of the draw.

The snow was still coming down, but the visibility was still fairly good. When the deer lifted his head, I could see his antlers. I guessed him to be at 400+ yards. I did not feel comfortable shooting my .30-06 at that distance without a solid rest. I could hear Dale coming up the hill, so I motioned him over my way. I told him about the other deer, and I pointed out the buck. Dale had a 7mm Remington Magnum and he felt he could hit the buck. But, when he looked through his scope, he discovered both ends were packed with snow; he had neglected to bring scope covers. In the meantime, a snow squall moved through, reducing visibility to 20 feet or less. By the time Dale cleared his scope, and the squall moved on, the buck was gone.

The squall had dropped several inches of wet snow. As we moved up the hill, our blue jeans became soaked. It was like walkin in a pool of ice water. Squalls were now moving through every few minutes and visibility was lessening. As we topped the hill, we spotted several deer in the distance and started toward them. They had spotted us and were moving as fast as we were. We split-up, hoping one of us would get a shot. The squalls had turned to a blizzard and visibility was minimal. I had a glimpse or two of deer, but my cold legs were not moving well. When I met up with Dale, he said he ran into a nice buck but could not get a clear shot before it disappeared into the storm. His legs were also giving him problems, so we decided to head down before we got ourselves into trouble. (That was the last time either of us hunted on Kodiak without wool pants.)

The third morning, we left before light, wearing our wool pants. The weather had cleared-up the previous evening and much of the snow had disappeared. After an hour and a half, we were at the place where we had first seen the buck. In clear weather, the from where the buck had stood was no more than 250 yards. The snow storm had made distances look a lot further. So far, we had not seen a deer.

A short distance above us was a knob with a solitary Sitka spruce on it. We moved up to the tree, where we had a clear view of the mountain pass. After looking around for a few minutes I spotted a buck. It was definitely out of range and moving away from us. Between us and the buck was a shallow draw. We split-up, with Dale going below the buck while I went above. We had lost sight of the buck as we crossed the draw. Emerging from the willow brush, we moved cautiously, but the buck had vanished. The open area where the buck disappeared sloped into brush-filled draws on either side. We figured that the buck had to be in one of those draws. Dale moved left, while I moved right.

I stood on the edge of the slope, peering into the brush below me—nothing moved. There were still enough leaves left on the brush to into the tall grass, along with my camera. The buck stood broadside looking directly at me. I put the crosshairs on his neck, fired and he was down for good. He had not given up easiy. My first shot had hit him in the backbone above the shoulders. To me, it looked as if his backbone was shattered. it was amazing that he had gotten up again.

Dale and I had shot many Oregon blacktails and mule deer, so we were not greatly impressed with the antlers of this buck. He was a three-point, with extemely long tines. We were more impressed with the body size of this buck. Our guess was that he went at least 175 pounds, maybe more. The doe was probably 100 pounds. These Sitka deer weren't the little guys we had heard about. The rest of the day was spent dragging the deer over to our route down to the cabin. It was still two miles to the cabin. Dale's knee was bothering him, and my legs were still sore from the previous day's snow-soaking. We would never make it back before dark with both deer, so I made a pack out of the doe and Dale carried the guns. We dragged the buck to the solitary tree where we would pick him up at first light. It was dark by the time we reached the cabin. We used the lantern to hang and skin the doe. There was no trouble sleeping that night!

It was dark when we left the following morning. We had decided to take our pack boards and meat bags with us, since the buck was too big for one of us to drag or carry. As we approached the tree, an immature golden eagle took off from beside the carcass. It was quite a sight. Bald eagles are quite common on Kodiak, but goldens are not. After skinning out the buck, cutting it in half, and putting it on the pack boards covered by the meat bags, we hunted for a couple of hours. The wind was bitterly cold, and we saw no deer, so we decided to pack out the meat and duck hunt. We almost left the antlers for the mice, but, because it was my first Sitka deer, I tied them on to Dale's pack. He still reminds me that they poked him in the legs all the way back to the cabin.

We got one more deer, a small three point, before Ralph flew in. The limit was four deer each and we would have tried for more if our knees had held out. But, we had plenty of meat with those three, plus our ducks. We would find out later that leaving a deer overnight or even for a few hours is inviting brown bear trouble. I lost a nice buck the following year to a bear after leaving it for only an hour. This year we were lucky.

The first indication that I had an exceptional deer was when Ralph commented on his size, both body and antler-wise. After landing back in town, my neighbor said the antlers were trophy size. I showed them to Roger Smith, the Kodiak game biologist for the Alaska Department of Fish and Game. Soon several biologists had gathered around while a rough measurement was made of 113 points. I entered it in the Big Buck Contest at Kodiak and, to my surprise, I won. It was a conversation piece that I showed to everyone who came to Kodiak to hunt with me in later years. We took several larger bucks out of the same area after that year, but none ever scored as high as that first buck.

When Boone and Crockett made a category for Sitka blacktail deer, I had the antlers remeasured in Anchorage. They scored $112\tfrac{1}{8}$ points and were accepted by Boone and Crockett. Dale and I still shake our heads when we think that we almost left those antlers on the mountain.

Photograph by Charlie Crunden

At the 19th Awards (Las Vegas, 1986), James E. Brierley accepts the Second Award for his Columbia blacktail deer from Dr. Philip L. Wright, Chairman of the Records Committee.

Photograph by Charlie Crunden

At the 19th Awards (Las Vegas, 1986), Edward R. Hajdys accepts the Honorable Mention Award for his Sitka blacktail deer from Dr. Philip L. Wright, Chairman of the Records Committee.

Photograph by Wm. H. Nesbitt

SITKA BLACKTAIL DEER
HONORABLE MENTION
SCORE: 113 1/8

Locality: Wadding Cove, Alaska   Date: October 1984
Hunter: Kurt W. Kuehl

SITKA BLACKTAIL DEER
113 1/8

Kurt W. Kuehl

It was a sunny, clear day, with an inch of snow on the ground. It was October 20, 1984, and the blacktail deer season was open in Alaska. Kurt Kuehl had left his home in Ketchikan early in order to get to his favorite hunting area.

After hunting for several hours, Kuehl finally found his buck. He worked to within 45 yards and made his decision to shoot. His .308 performed well, as it always did. The fine buck was down, and Kuehl was able to admire his trophy.

Later, Kuehl had the antlers measured officially for the newly-created category of Sitka blacktail deer, and found that they were among the top few entries, based upon the entry score. An invitation to the Final Awards Judging added the icing to this hunting cake.

Photograph by Wm. H. Nesbitt

SITKA BLACKTAIL DEER
HONORABLE MENTION
SCORE: 108 2/8

Locality: Whale Passage, Alaska   Date: November 1985
Hunter: Howard W. Honsey

SITKA BLACKTAIL DEER
108 2/8

Howard W. Honsey

While working on a bridge-building project in the Whale Pass area of Prince of Wales Island, I spent most of my spare time deer hunting in the numerous logged-off valleys and hillsides. These clear-cut areas provide a haven for deer because of the new growth of shrubs and berries. And because of the good long-range visibility, they are a favorite area for hunters too.

Up until October 28th of 1985, I had seen several does, but unfortunately, not one buck. However, with the weather conditions worsening and the heavy snowfall driving the deer out of the higher elevations, I anticipated better luck. It was with this thought in mind that I decided to try out a new area early the next morning.

About an hour before daybreak, I drove to a small drainage named Snoose Creek. I had barely entered the area when, to my surprise, a buck with the biggest rack I had ever seen ran across the road right in front of me and vanished into the pre-dawn darkness. I parked my truck right there and impatiently waited for sun-up to begin my hunt.

For the next four hours I scanned the clear-cuts and tried my best to track him. But, I only caught a quick glimpse of him as he topped a distant ridge. This time, he seemed to be gone for good, into the heavy timber where I couldn't pick up his trail.

I concentrated my hunting on that area for the next five days. Taking advantage of the increasing snowfall, I could tell the deer were still moving towards low ground. So in the late afternoon of November 2nd, I followed a hunch and walked down an old washed-out logging road. I hadn't gone 100 yards when I rounded a corner and there stood four does, and the big buck. Maybe I shouldn't have raised my rifle so fast; the movement spooked him and he jumped off the road and down into the clear-cut before I could aim. I flipped the safety back on and hurried to where he had left the road.

I saw him below me as he tried to sneak away between the small trees. At 75 yards, it was an easy shot with my .30-06. The bullet struck him low in the back of the neck, and dropped him in a heap. I field dressed him and managed to drag him back up to the road just before darkness set in and it began to snow.

Needless to say, I was delighted with my trophy. Although my persistence played a big role in bagging this buck, I feel luck played a larger role, as it always seems to.

Photograph by Wm. H. Nesbitt

AMERICAN ELK
FIRST AWARD
SCORE: 385 3/8

Locality: Otero Co., N. M.   Date: September 1985
Hunter: Gregory C. Saunders

AMERICAN ELK 385 3/8

Gregory C. Saunders

It was 3 a.m. on September 21st. I lay awake, waiting for the alarm to signal the start of my first bull elk hunt. I wondered apprehensively whether the previous three months of physical conditioning and the hours spent on the rifle range would pay off with the big bull that I wanted.

My thoughts wandered back to my arrival on the previous afternoon at the Mescalero Apache Reservation in southwest New Mexico. As our truck had climbed from the flat, barren desert floor into the forested mountains and canyons of the reservation, I was awestruck by the magnificent, undisturbed wilderness that surrounded me. The pre-hunt dinner that evening had been equally exciting. There I first met my guide, Jimmy Runningwater. Jimmy was a big, powerfully-built native Mescalero with a no-nonsense approach to hunting. "I'm picky," he told me. "We will take only a big one. I hope you're in shape, I'm going to walk you." The conversation left me with mixed feelings of apprehension and excitement.

The 4 a.m. alarm finally sounded. And, after a big breakfast for the guides and hunters, we were off. Following a kidney-bruising ride in Jimmy's pickup, we arrived at our primary hunting area. As we left the truck, dawn was breaking. It was cool and clear, with no wind, a perfect day for our hunt.

We stepped into the brush to bugle for our bull. Having never heard an elk bugle in the wild, I couldn't see how what looked like a turkey call on the end of a car radiator hose would get us any closer to a big bull. As Jimmy blew through the call, a high pitched "EEEEeeeeugh, Ugh! Ugh!"resounded through the canyons. We waited in silence—no answer. Jimmy repeated the call, again no answer. "No bulls here," he said as he trotted off towards the truck. "Let's move it to another spot."

Twenty minutes and one kidney later, we arrived at Whitetail Springs, Jimmy's second choice for our hunting area. "I heard some bulls bugling here last week," he said. "Let's try it". Again we walked into the brush and repeated our bugling. This time, from a considerable distance, came our awaited reply of "EEEEeeeeugh, Ugh! Ugh! Ugh!". "There's a bull on the other side of that mountain," Jimmy said, as he pointed to our left. "Let's check him out".

Our stalk began. Moving silently, I followed in Jimmy's footsteps up the mountainside. Elk sign was everywhere: large, rounded-off hoofprints, scattered droppings, and bushes battered by the antlers of the rutting bulls. Stopping halfway to catch our breath, Jimmy bugled and again received an immediate reply. On we went. As we reached the top, Jimmy suddenly dropped to his knees and motioned for me to do the same. Pointing left, he whispered, "There's a cow over there watching us. If we spook her, she'll warn the bulls." Sure enough, as I peered around the bush in front of me, there she was, staring directly at us.

After crawling for 30 yards to get past her view, we slowly stood to survey the surrounding canyonwalls. "Mule deer," said Jimmy, as he pointed up the canyon to our right. Sure enough, there stood a high, basket-horned, eight-point buck in the midst of several cow elk. "There's the bull," he whispered as he looked through his binoculars directly across the canyon. After watching this bull for a moment, he shook his head and said, "Only a five by five, not what we want."

As we stood up to move on, I caught a glimpse of movement near the first bull. "What about that one?" I asked. Peering through his binoculars, Jimmy replied, "He's a six by six, but at this distance, it's hard to tell how good he is. Let's bring him closer." At that, Jimmy raised his bugling tube and issued our challenge.

The big bull immediately stopped and looked across to our side of the canyon. One more bugle from Jimmy brought him moving down the canyon, heading in our direction. For the next few minutes, we tensely waited for our quarry to reappear. "There," I whispered, pointing directly below us to the bottom of the canyon. For the last time, Jimmy raised and sounded his bugling tube. This time, with his massive head reared back, the big bull answered our challenge with his piercing reply and began walking toward us. At 60 yards to our right, he stepped into an open clearing, giving us an unobstructed look at him. As I watched him through my binouculars, he continued coming toward us. Looking him over at such close range, I recalled Jimmy's words of the previous evening. "We want a six by six, no less," he had said. "He must have long, heavy royal points and at least 12 to 14-inch fifth and sixth points". As I watched this bull, I thought that surely he had to be our bull. I raised my .300 Magnum Weatherby in anticipation. To my complete amazement, Jimmy lowered his binoculars and said, "We'll pass this one". Not knowing what else to say, I replied, "O.K., you're the guide".

As the bull continued his approach, Jimmy again raised his binoculars, silently staring. When the bull reached his closest approach, he stopped, broadside to us at only 35 yards. He turned his massive head in our direction, seeming to stare right at us. Jimmy slowly lowered his binoculars, looked at me and said with an excited, hoarse whisper, "Shoot him!". Quickly I raised my rifle, sighted on the bull's front shoulder, and pulled the trigger. A resounding boom and telltale "thud" broke the silence, telling us that my shot had found its mark. The old bull tensed, quivered, and then straightened up. Lowering his head, he began slowly walking back down the canyon. "Shoot him again!" Jimmy whispered excitedly. I raised my rifle, sighting between the bull's shoulder blades and fired again. The impact of the second shot stopped him, and after a moment, brought him crashing to the ground.

"He's magnificent," was all that I could say as I surveyed my downed trophy. He was big, heavy, ivory-tipped, and as his entry score of $387 \tfrac{3}{8}$ later revealed, the trophy bull of a lifetime. After congratulations and pictures, I worked up the courage to ask Jimmy why we almost passed this bull up. "Don't like to shoot on the first day of the hunt," was his reply.

Sometimes you have to make exceptions.

Photo Courtesy of Don H. Grimes

Don H. Grimes and his guide, Stan Reiser, with Don's fine American elk that scores 377 points. It was shot near the Clearwater River in Alberta in 1985.

Photo Courtesy of Gregory C. Saunders

A happy Gregory C. Saunders with his American elk that scores 385 3/8 points and received First Award at the 19th Awards. It was shot in 1985 in Otero County, New Mexico.

Photograph by Wm. H. Nesbitt

AMERICAN ELK
SECOND AWARD
SCORE: 382 6/8

Locality: Apache Co., Ariz.   Date: October 1985
Hunter: William E. Moss

AMERICAN ELK 382 6/8

William E. Moss

Bill Moss is a builder in McLean, Virginia, and business is very good in this suburb of Washington, DC. In fact, business is so good, it's hard for Bill to get away on hunts. But, Bill had wanted a big elk for a long time. So when the word finally came that he had been accepted to hunt on the White Mountain Apache Indian Reservation in Arizona, Bill pushed aside the things on his schedule in order to make the hunt. It was too good an opportunity to pass up; the White Mountain Reservation produces some very fine wapiti trophies each year and Bill was ready to go.

Bill arrived in Arizona and was met by his host on the 29th of September, 1985. The hunt would continue until October 3, when Bill had to return to the city.

It was October 2. The sky was sunny, and the air was clear. The light wind was an aid in staying downwind from the big bull. It was just 9:30 a.m., and Bill and his guide had worked to within 175 yards of their quarry. It was a big bull, a fine 6 by 6, with massive beams and long points. It was just the sort of trophy that Bill had been seeking.

Taking careful aim with his .300 Winchester Magnum, Bill sent his 200 grain Nosler handload on its way. The job was quickly done, and the big bull was down. Now the celebration could begin. Bill had his big bull elk.

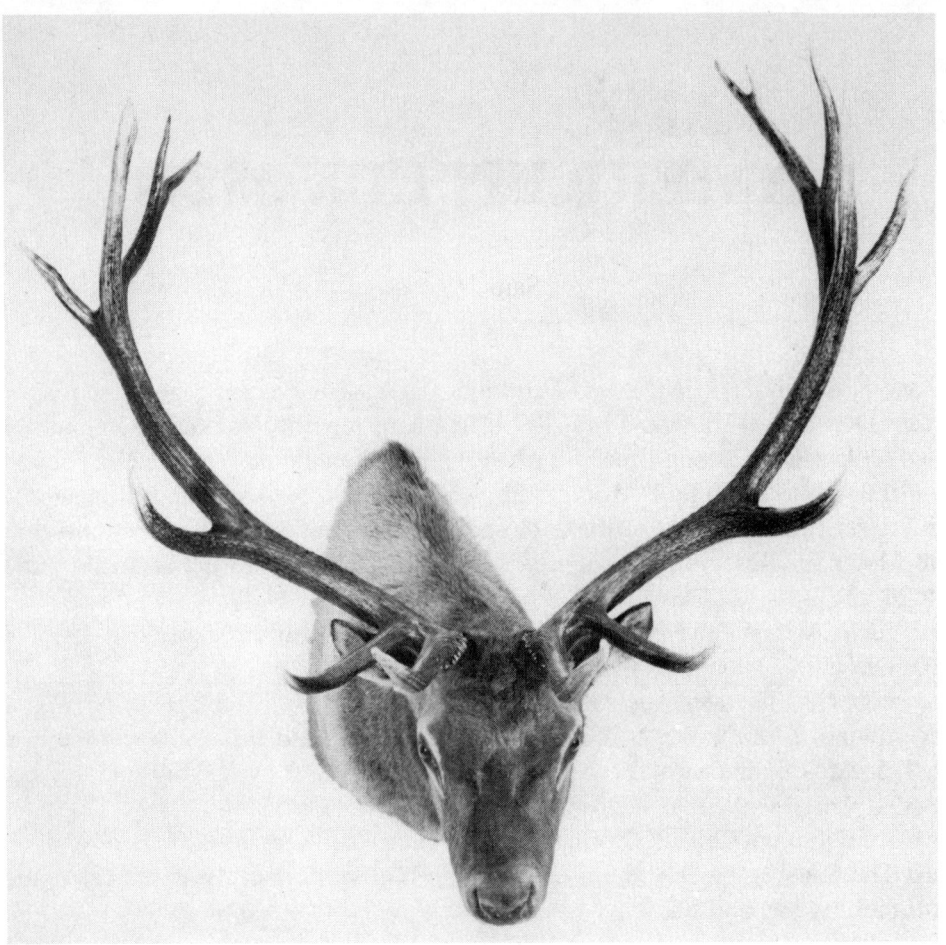

Photograph by Wm. H. Nesbitt

ROOSEVELT'S ELK
FIRST AWARD
SCORE: 380 6/8

Locality: Jefferson Co., Wash.   Date: November 1983
Hunter: Sam Argo

ROOSEVELT'S ELK 380⅝

Sam Argo

The outcome of this hunt culminated a decade of serious trophy hunting. But, somehow it fails to possess the excitement and challenge associated with an era recently ended in the quest of Suzzie and Clyde, a pair of records class bull elk that successfully outwitted the Wolfpack Hunters. Despite tenacious pursuit, involving the use of virtually everything in the book and several other unpublished tactics, these bulls beat the odds to die of natural, elemental causes. Well over the hill, Clyde was found half-submerged in a beaver pond, the result of being stuck in the mud and dying of exposure. Old Suzzie merely vanished into history, in much the same way he had appeared. Shed antlers from Suzzie, plus off-season views, had revealed him to be probably the largest elk in North America since the turn of the century. Given a 40-inch spread and 10 points in deductions, he would have scored 430 Boone and Crockett points.

To find a replacement, continual year-round scouting plus relentless investigation of rumors, tips and sightings, coupled with a spot in one's brain jam-packed with elk hunting and elk habit information, paid off in an almost instant and unbelievable spur-of-the-moment hunt.

On November 23, 1983, I received a telephone call from Russ Meade, an Ohio native now living in the Northwest. Russ had just returned from an unsuccessful elk hunt on the Olympic Penninsula of Washington State, and he had a hot tip for me on a mammoth bull elk they had seen crossing the road at dusk on the way home. This bull, Russ claimed, was probably bigger than any in the Wolfpack Hall collection in Carbonado.

This description was no small matter, since there are several bulls that score over 400 points in that collection. But of special interest to me was his description of the rack which indicated several bifurcated points on the top side of the fourth points. The bull had stumbled on the road in front of their car at very close range, and, although vision was impaired by fog, Russ said the lights reflecting off the antlers gave them a story-book view. (This probably added to the size of the antlers also.) Keep in mind that Russ is a regional salesman for Timex watches and has a gift of gab for getting the point across.

Of even more interest to me was the location Russ gave for the sighting, as it was almost exactly the same spot as a previous tip for an "exceptional bull," a "Keeper," as we call them. This information was given by another friend, Jeff McCart, a non-hunting camera buff who has logged in the Fork's area for years. Other tips by Jeff had always been accurate, and this now compelled me to act.

A few quick calls to family members produced negative results, as I was reminded that of over 40 bulls they had taken near the sighting locations in previous years, only a few scored over 300 points. They chose instead to stick with previous plans to hunt close to home where some good bulls had been seen. A call to Doug Nearhood, my number-one hunting partner and as dependable as rain on the Olympic Peninsula, was more fruitful. I knew the answer before the call was made. Always ready for a challenge, and willing to change plans on the spur of the moment, Doug's response was, as always, "Let's go for it."

As the location is about a five-hour drive from home, we decided to hit the road as soon as possible. Our packboards and gear are always ready. Most of our group have two or three sets of packboards and duffle bags filled with old military sleeping bags, extra clothes, and some dry goods. In coastal western Washington, it rains daily, and extra dry clothes and sleeping bags are a must in November.

Within two hours, we were headed down the highway with high hopes and illusions of grandeur. We arrived at what we believed to have been the correct location of the monster bull and got a couple of hours of sleep before daybreak.

Anyone who has hunted on the Olympic Peninsula in an area of second-growth trees, trees 10 to 20 years old, will understand what a frustrating experience this can be. Visibility in the brush is poor until about two hours after sunup. We scouted the highway for tracks, but we found nothing of interest. We finally started to do some serious probing. We circled and came up with nothing. We were testing our wits against the odds. Our plan was a simple one. Locate fresh tracks and stay close. Finally, we decided to line out on the course of least resistance, through the undercover. Keep in mind that in this cover good visibility is 20 yards, and normal visibility is point blank. We did happen upon a set of tracks that looked real promising, both in size and freshness.

We always hunt in pairs, since it is so brushy in western Washington. One person moves slowly and keeps his eyes on the ground, following tracks and signs. If you're watching tracks, you cannot be watching for animals. That is the other guy's job, to move closely behind you, watching both the sides and straight ahead for any movement or color that may resemble an elk. Split-second timing is critical in thick-cover elk hunting, and our refined method of stalking elk, using two brains thinking as a single unit, has brought success many times under adverse conditions. On this specific hunt, I was tracking and Doug was looking, when he gave me a tap and pointed ahead at a 45-degree angle. There was a very large elk rear visible, but no antlers in sight, and the animal was moving. Then, the familiar sound of horns hitting brush and a better view gave me a shot.

This whole time frame was two to three seconds. The animal was not down but moving, and the chase was on. A fast-moving elk can sound like a bulldozer in the brush, crushing and running over most items in its path. Then in the next step, it moves with the grace and quietness of a big gray ghost. You often wonder, was that an elk, did I really see something?

When hunting elk, we have concluded that you must act in a split second. When an animal may only move a foot or two and be completely gone from sight, you have to have your senses fine-tuned and be willing to make a decision as to what you have just seen and fire at the same time. Too often, the hunter waits. Waiting in the brush is very costly and is an advantage only to the elk.

We were moving very fast on sight, sound, and the strong scent of elk, firing repeatedly. Remember, this is heavy brush country. We were able to catch the bull and finish the job. Six shots were fired. Five shots hit home. This seemed like a lifetime with the adrenalin flowing; but in reality, it was only about two minutes.

We took our time and made quite a day out of packing and talking. We cannot say this is the exact bull the reports were on, but we did have a most successful hunt on tip information we had received about the area. Our only regret is that the bull was only 6½ years old. Given two or three more years, it might have been a real monster. It has eight points on each side and is quite even in score for a Roosevelt's elk.

After we had packed out our animal and were headed home, we stopped to gas up at Hoquim and showed the head to the service station attendant. He looked it over and said he'd seen two that day, at least that big. I truly doubt they were of that caliber, but big elk are where you find them and not necessarily where you expect them. Their ability to survive against tremendous odds is a tribute to these magnificent animals. This animal was living in an area adjacent to Highway 101 where no one would normally hunt. As one hunter said, while stopping at our van as we packed-out some meat, "Must be a small bull to go through that brush patch." Small bull? No, just smart to have found an area with no pressure. As Doug would say, "Just nested up in the brush, the brush the Roosevelt's call home."

Photograph by Wm. H. Nesbitt

ROOSEVELT'S ELK
SECOND AWARD
SCORE: 353 4/8

Locality: Washington Co., Oreg.   Date: September 1985
Hunter: Ken R. Adamson

ROOSEVELT'S ELK 353 4/8

Ken R. Adamson

There were a thousand thoughts zipping through my mind as I crouched in my makeshift blind, straining to hear a hint of sound that would let me know that I was not all alone here in the woods. Thoughts such as, did I blow it? Did the wind spook the bull? Should I just pack up and leave quietly to return tomorrow? Should I have tried stalking the noises that I had heard? Will I hit a branch if I get a shot? Is this hunt going to be one of those that end up as a good story, but no meat?

I felt the bull was still in the vicinity, and I wanted to be ready if I got a shot. So, I checked the pulley wheels of my compound bow for obstructions, checked the sight pins, drew a couple of times, and checked to make sure my broadheads were tight and aligned. By this time, I was as ready as I was going to get. I figured the elk, if it was an elk, should be settled down now after a half hour to forget the sound and/or scent that had spooked it.

My previous bowhunting for elk hadn't produced anything in the way of meat or antlers. The Oregon bow season had opened the last weekend in August, and I had hunted for a full week with family and friends. We saw elk, but didn't manage to bring home any antlers. Since then, I had managed to hunt four evenings, with the same results.

Most of my hunting is done on private land, owned by the timber company that employs me as a Forest Engineer. So, I do have the advantage of being in good elk hunting areas several times throughout the year. My best friend and hunting partner, David Showerman and I have been hunting together for about 15 years. We have taken several elk and deer, but we were still waiting for the "Big One". Unfortunately, he was not along on this hunt.

I had spent many hours practicing with my Golden Eagle Hunter on a bale of cardboard in the barn, and I felt competent to put the 2219 Gamegetter arrows where they would do the most good. The day before this hunt, I had set my Hunter up from the 75 pound pull I had been shooting to 85 pounds, for a little extra "oomph".

Saturday morning, September 7, 1985, I left home before daylight and spent a couple of hours bowhunting with no success. I had promised my wife and her brother that I would attend the grand opening of the building where her brother works. That took up most of the midday, but if I hurried, I could still get in a couple of hours of late afternoon bowhunting. I wasn't about to pass up that opportunity.

I had seen several herds of elk on a 300 acre tract of land owned by our timber company earlier in the season, so I figured this would be a good place for the evening hunt. My wife, Theresa, and two kids, Jeramy and Leslie, hopped in our four-wheel drive pickup and we all headed for the hunting area 50 miles west of Portland.

We arrived at 5:00 p.m., which would still give me three hours of good bowhunting daylight during the best part of the day. The sky was cloudy and completely overcast, with the feeling of rain in the air. For this country, rain is a pretty common occurance, and I knew my wool hunting clothes would take care of keeping me warm even in a downpour. Theresa agreed to pick me up along a logging road (about a mile away) in three hours, so I headed for the woods.

My favorite elk bowhunting method is still hunting and stalking, as the cover is too dense for good glassing. There is plenty of feed for the elk in the logged-over areas, so they seldon venture into the more open meadows and parks. I spent lots of time practicing my bugling, using a Jones diaphragm call and grunt tube. But with all the bowhunting competition in the area, the bulls are getting cagey and will seldom answer a bugle any more. Over the past couple of years, I have had several bulls sneak silently into my calling and catch me completely by surprise. To date, I had not bugled-up a good bull to get a shot, but that didn't stop me from being ready.

I hadn't gone far down the old logging skid trail, when I began to see lots of fresh elk tracks in the trail. It had rained the day before, so I knew the sign was fresh and that there were elk in the area. I try to stay on good trails when hunting, because it is much quieter and easier to move through the dense vegetation. I had traveled about a half-mile during the first hour, and I was seeing more and more fresh signs, when I heard brush breaking in front of me. About the time I heard the racket in the brush, I spotted a huge track in the muddy trail that I was sure had been made by a large bull. The huge track and breaking brush combined to get my adrenaline pumping, and I had to force myself to slow down.

I eased forward and could definitely hear what I took to be elk, moving through the heavy brush ahead of me. The wind had been in my face since I left the truck; but, as luck would have it, it was now swirling around in several directions. I tried to move off the trail and circle to see what was making the noise, but I couldn't because the underbrush was just too thick to get through. The only route open was a direct approach, which I didn't particularly care for. The decision was taken from me when a stray breeze blew down the back of my neck and I heard branches and limbs breaking, as whatever was ahead of me moved off.

In my experience with Roosevelt's elk, I have found that if they get a whiff of human scent, they will move off but usually not leave the area. They do stay on the alert, and movement or more scent will put them in high gear. However, if the hunter backs off and lets things calm down, the elk can usually be approached again, with caution. I moved back 100 yards up the trail, where I decided to build a blind to hide from what I was hoping was a bull elk. I draped bracken ferns from alder limbs until I had an almost solid blind facing the direction where I had heard the brush breaking.

After half-an-hour of planning and checking equipment, the time had come to do something. I bugled and grunted to the best of my ability. Almost immediately a bull came running into the small clearing on the trail that I had just vacated. My blind was too good, as I couldn't see much of his antlers through the hanging ferns. But, I could tell by his body size that he was not a small bull. He looked around for a minute, and then crossed the trail and went back into the heavy brush and timber, where he proceeded to tear up the brush with his antlers. I waited through another 10-15 agonizing minutes of silence, trying to figure what he was up to. I bugled again, and glimpsed the bull as he moved cautiously through the trees and up a small ridge, where he again started tearing up the brush.

I was beginning to wonder if I shouldn't just pack it up and go home. I didn't seem to be gaining anything, and I was sure that I had spooked the bull to the point where he would never come close enough for a shot. My blind was no longer in the right position, so I slowly moved up the trail until I could get around a small bend and out of sight. I bugled once more, and once more the bull started tearing up the brush quite a distance above where I crouched. A few minutes later, I heard a sound in the opposite direction and more brush breaking. The bull had circled around and seemed to be stalking me from the opposite direction.

I figured I had only about 20 minutes of good shooting light left, and I knew I had to do something to get things off dead-center. I found a limb and started thrashing it through the brush, at the same time squealing for all I was worth with the diaphragm and tube. The bull went berserk as he headed my way, tearing and thrashing the brush and limbs. He was about 75 yards away and coming steadily, so I eased out onto the trail and came to full draw. He was moving through the brush, looking around, while I was concentrating on all the things a bowhunter should do at this point of the game. I argued with myself as to whether I would try a shot through the brush. I figured if I couldn't get a good shot, then I wouldn't take any.

The bull took a couple more steps, stopped, and then moved into a small clearing at about 40 feet and stopped again. He turned his head slightly, and as he did, he took one more step forward with the front leg on my side, giving a perfect "behind the shoulder" angle. I put the 20-yard pin half-way up his chest, and about 10 inches behind the shoulder, then lowered it about four inches to allow for the short distance, and released. The bull jerked, and then trotted about 30 yards, where he stopped and stood looking at me. I remember wondering, as he stood there 40 yards away with the arrow embedded up to the orange vanes, why I hadn't shot completely through him as I had supposed I would at that range.

I don't know how long we stared at one another before I thought to myself, "Man, get another arrow into him if he's just going to stand there." I got another arrow on the string just as he turned and started off. I let go with a bugle, hoping to stop him for the shot; but all that did was scare him into an all-out run for the heavy timber. He disappeared in a second, leaving me standing there with a sinking feeling, wondering if I had really gotten him as good as I thought, or if I would have to track him all night or maybe lose him in the rain that was just starting to come down.

The light was fading fast when I got to the spot where I last saw him, but there was still enough light to see the quantities of blood that seemed to be everywhere. Another 20 yards and I could make out his huge form lying on the forest floor. What an elk! His body was so big that I really didn't take a full look at the antlers before heading back to the truck to tell my wife and kids, and get all the help I could to get him home.

We were able to get the truck to within 150 yards of the bull and bring him out in one piece. He measured 12 feet and four inches from hind feet to nose and would have stood 5½ feet tall at the shoulders. The meat weighed 580 pounds, which would have put his live weight at somewhere in the neighborhood of 1,200 pounds. His massive rack was six by six, with a couple of little extra points, and a score of 353⅝ points.

Photograph by Wm. H. Nesbitt

NEW WORLD'S RECORD ROOSEVELT'S ELK
CERTIFICATE OF MERIT
SCORE: 384 3/8

Locality: Clatsop Co., Oreg.   Date: 1949
Hunter: Robert Sharp
Owner: Harold E. Stepp

ROOSEVELT'S ELK 384 3/8

Robert Sharp

The season was October 25 to November 3, 1949. I had chosen an area south and west of Saddle Mountain, south of Seaside and Cannon beach, and north of Highway 53, in Clatsop County, Oregon. It turned out that my timber-falling partner could not hunt at this time. So, as I had been in this area once and had seen the possibility of a fair hunt, I decided to give it a go alone.

With my Enfield rifle, a cleaver, a small knife, a coffee can of food, and my Alaskan pack board, I left the Gods Valley Camp Area before daylight, and then felt my way across an old railroad trestle. Daylight was long in coming, as a real dark and stormy night had preceded this day. I liked this blustery weather, as it clears the leaves from the trees and also makes for a quiet approach.

Once on the north side of the North Fork Nehalem River, with daylight coming on, I thought about my approach into this vast area. Believing I would be the only fool to do this bit, I felt at ease to hunt my way. That is, to just get lost and keep the wind in my face as much as possible. Also to watch every movement, regardless. There were lots of deer. I saw two nice bucks, and a coyote packing a large piece of meat that looked like a deer fawn or ham. He paid me no mind, as I did him. The weather cleared a bit and the fog coming in was snow; this happens on the coast, one has to tolerate some real changes, all in the same day.

I have argued this with many, but my thought is: if you have never picked up the smell of deer, elk, or a bear, then you've been staying too close to your horse or vehicle. The elk scent was strong and I was in a low area where I couldn't see much. I crossed a small creek and crested a ridge. There they were, about 20 or more cows and two spikes. I worked back so as not to spook them, then I made tracks getting away from them.

The area I was going into now was more tall fern and berry vine. I usually choose to go under an area of brush, vine maple and hemlock with lots of cedar windfalls, but as it is so often with me, I felt, "No, go above them"—Gosh knows why. So I went above, only to come to a cedar windfall that I had to climb like a ladder to get over. On the other side, the packboard didn't feel right, so I set my rifle down, took off the board, and redid the straps. Once set to go again, I checked my scope. I hadn't moved yet, and didn't, but I had the strangest feeling, even though I never knew what it was.

All at once, 50 feet in front of me, this huge elk bull stood. I had never seen anything like it, seasoned though I am. There before my eyes was this big, big animal, and in a position so that I could not shoot. Rump and horns were all I had, and I had no place to move, so it was up to the bull to make a move. I took the safety off, then stood and waited as I glanced around to guess what was next. I could not believe it, there was another bull, standing facing me! I guess he had not seen a man before. His head lowered and his ears cocked, he was like a statue there and looking straight at me.

I placed the crosshairs on his left ear and moved a little to the right, which put the impact at the base of his neck and fairly high. I didn't really feel or hear the rifle go off. The bull laid his head back, mouth open, and just stood. I placed the second shot a foot lower and laid him down like a ton of bricks. I didn't see the first bull leave, or whatever he did. To this day, I can't imagine his big rack, since I never really got a good look at any part except his rump. But the horns matched his hindquarters, and they were big! But, I did have his buddy on the ground.

I approached this big boy carefully, then stuck the barrel into his eye to make sure he was dead. He had fallen forward onto his head somewhat, and I was unable to move him. I got my cleaver and whacked the head off. It took some time to free the head, but, "Careful is the thing, and this fella is big," was my thought. When I was cutting off the head, I accidentally missed and hit the base of the right antler. This knocked a small chunk out of the base and left a meat cleaver mark in the antler. I gutted him on his side, skinning and butchered him there on his hide. I boned the meat as I cut him up, placing the meat on a log near me.

I had to make a move quickly, as time was going fast. I loaded the heart, liver, neck, and some small parts on the packboard, with the head upside down on the pack. I never went far like this, as the horns were hung up all the time. So, I packed them on one shoulder, loose so I could control and see where they were. I went east as fast as possible. I needed to reach the ridge I had been on previously. A good elk trail was on this ridge.

Before I realized it, I was there and on the trail I wanted. I also found where I had been before when scouting this area. Then, I had only gone as far as a fork in the trail north and uphill from me. I wanted to get to that point. I left the pack and ran up the trail quite a way. Luck was with me, I came out on a flat at the end of a railroad grade. Someone had built a fire there earlier that day, and it was was still warm. I ran down the hill, gathered my stuff, and returned to the fire site, where I left my things and hid the head. I took the cleaver and the can of food and headed out the grade east. I marked the spurs as I came to them, finally giving in to hunger to eat the food I had.

It was now dark, and I figured I just might be in trouble. I was wet with blood all over, tired, and with no way to light my way, I would have to feel my way or hole up and be miserable all night. I had no matches, so I felt I had let myself down. But it wasn't anything to be worried about, except my main concern was that my family didn't know where I had gone. I felt good that I had a big bull. I was working my way on the grade when I heard a vehicle in the distance. It sure sounded good and encouraged me a lot.

After some time, I fell off the railroad grade right onto Highway 53. What a relief! I found some big rocks and marked the side of the road, then headed west not knowing how far away my car was. It took forever to get to my car. There was no traffic, and no one would have loaded me in anyhow! I almost missed my car, the sky's light in the headlamps is what I saw.

My family was worried, and it was near midnight. My friend Gib Raymond had not returned.

So next morning, with food, gas lantern, rope, shovel, ax, and my trusty food can, we were back at the grade. It took some effort to get the Ford on the grade, but with ax and shovel work, I managed to get the car clear to the fire. The work was now to begin with the pack, hopefully. A bear, cats, or coyote didn't get into my meat pile. I did take a look at the head before I headed down the trail.

Now this was a day to remember! One can't believe all the meat in one animal. I packed all day and into the night. By the map it was a mile to my car uphill, from the kill. I had put my Ford back on the railroad grade, some four miles from the highway, and the hunt covered some three miles before I killed the bull. Yes, I was one tired and worn-out dude. The maps show I was still 1/4 mile from Grassy Lake, but still in Grassy Lake Creek drainage. I have hunted south of this area, for deer, and once for elk. That time I got a five by five, a big one also.

To finish with my bull, it took the gas lantern. I did stop to cook a piece of the meat, with no salt, and it was filling. The meat was all cared for in Nehalem. My wife said it was the toughest I ever brought home!

After packing the meat out and getting it all home, the word spread about the large bull I had killed. Several friends came to see the antlers, and if any of them were alive today, they might recognize them.

Then in 1952 or 1953, some fellows in St. Helens asked to borrow the antlers. There was a parade being held, and they wanted to put them in it. After the parade was over, I expected the antlers would be returned. This wasn't to be, and thirty years would pass before I saw them again.

On January 12, 1984, I was reading the local newspaper. A photo of a set of elk antlers was featured, and the owner, Harold Stepp of St. Helens, was asking if anyone had any information about them. I couldn't believe it. I was certain it was my set of antlers. I called my son and told him to look in the paper also. There was a phone number listed, so I called Mr. Stepp right away.

When I reached Mr. Stepp, he asked if there was any way I could be sure these were my antlers. I remembered the cleaver mark in the antler base and told him to look there. He placed the phone down for a moment and then returned, stating that this set of antlers had the missing chunk and the mark where I said it should be.

Later on, I went to look at the antlers, and I'm positive they're my missing antlers. These were so big and unusual that it would be difficult not to recognize them even after that many years. Harold was trying to find the hunter so that the antlers would be recognized by the Boone and Crockett Club as having been hunter-taken, and therefore truly identified as Roosevelt's elk and also shown as hunter-taken, and not as a pickup trophy, in the records books. I'm sure glad he was so persistent.

Now, all my family are successful hunters. Both my sons have killed lots of big bulls. I dedicate all this to Helen, my wife of 50 years, and my sons Bob and Ben. They deserve it for being great outdoorsmen and hunters, and she for her hard work and many hours cutting, wrapping, and cleaning up after us. Thank you all, and thanks to Boone and Crockett, the members of the Museum, and all those that worked so hard to make this possible for me.

(Editor's Note: Both Robert Sharp and Harold E. Stepp were present at the 19th Awards, and they both participated fully in all activities, including the presentation of the award to this outstanding trophy. It was heartening to all present to observe the friendship and sportsmanship of these two gentlemen, linked by their common love of this trophy.)

Photos Courtesy of Don L. Corley and Leonard L. Hengen

(l) Don L. Corley's fine American elk scores 380 5/8 points. It was killed on the White Mtn. Apache Indian Resv., Arizona, in 1984. (r) Leonard L. Hengen found his big bull elk on the Panther River, Alberta in 1977. It scores 386 5/8 points.

Photo Courtesy of T. R. Tidwell

T. R. Tidwell hunted on the White Mtn. Apache Indian Resv. in Arizona in 1983 to find this big American elk that scores 399 4/8 points.

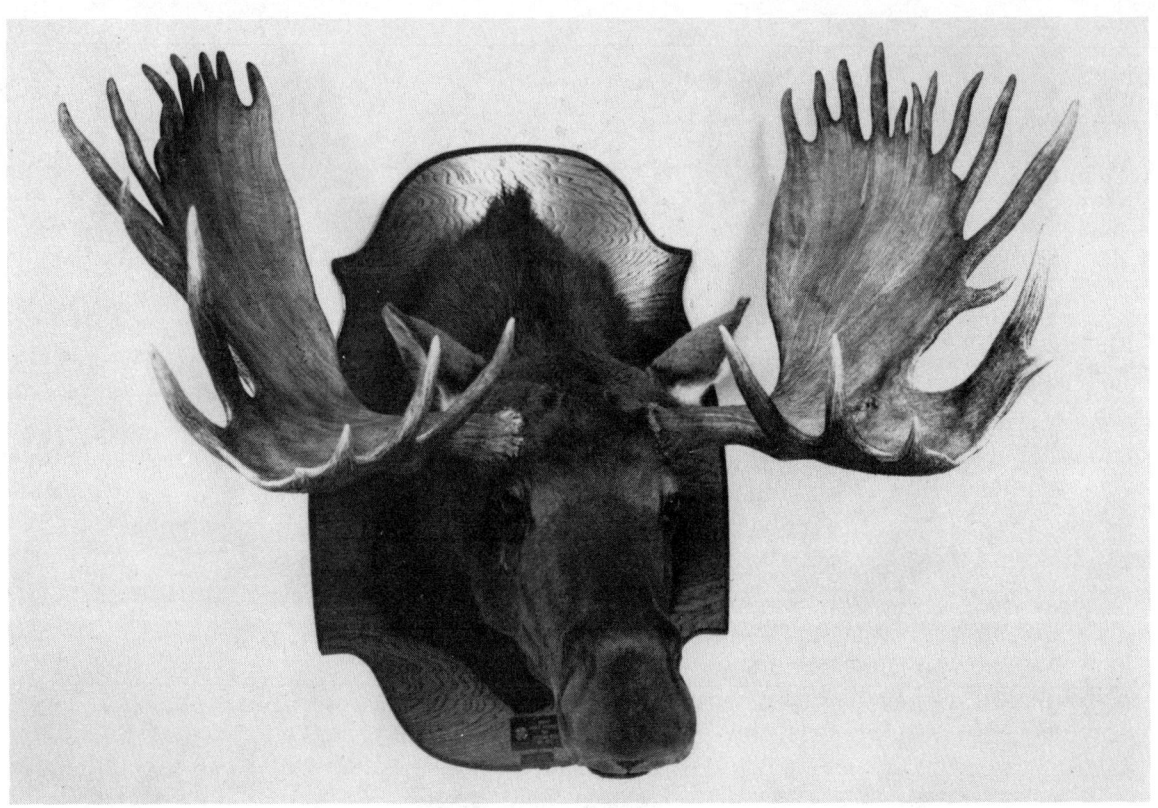

Photograph by Wm. H. Nesbitt

CANADA MOOSE
FIRST AWARD
SCORE: 218 6/8

Locality: Kennicott Lake, B. C.   Date: September 1984
Hunter: Mike Popoff

CANADA MOOSE 218⅝

Mike Popoff

During the summer of 1984, Eb Kerbach, my regular hunting partner, and I had our hunting trip all planned out, as we'd done for many years. It was going to be another fly-in and hike-in trip. But, no matter how carefully or how well planned, things do come up to disrupt the best of plans. In this case, Eb's elderly father got sick and things didn't look good for him. So naturally Eb went to Europe to visit him and thus used up his holidays. I was left with the decision of going it alone, or changing my plans completely and taking someone else. None of my other partners were too keen on my plans for the hike-in trip. I planned to hike-in and backpack for 16 miles with our crossbows for goat and sheep. We had been in a few years before without any success, although we had seen animals.

I knew the area and knew what to expect, so I decided to go it alone. After some thought, I decided to take my Honda 90 trail bike as far as I could, to make my pack in easier and also to help me bring out my trophy goat and sheep that I was sure I was going to get this year.

On August 31, I left my home in Richmond, B.C., and in the next few days, I drove approximately 1,100 miles. Upon getting to my destination, I parked in my usual spot, packed everything for my trip, and then relaxed in order to be ready to leave early the next day. Next morning, did fairly well on the trail bike except for two times, when the mountain was so steep that I went over backwards and was lucky enough to steer the bike clear of me when it came down. Several other times, I was able to catch the bike before it went over. Upon reaching the plateau, I found that the snow level was down the mountain to the plateau, and as I was making my way across, there were patches of snow to show that the plateau had already had a good fall of snow. It was quite warm and sunny, so I wasn't too concerned about the weather. I made my way across to a deep ravine that would have been very difficult to cross with the bike. From here I would go on foot.

The odometer on the bike read 12 miles, so I only had four more miles to go. It took several hours to cover this last stretch to get to the fork in the two little streams where Eb and I had camped before. After setting up my pup tent, gathering a pile of firewood and having my supper, I set out for my lookout spot. Sure enough, there were the goats on the same slope as last time.

Next morning, I circled the slope. Throughout the day, I could have shot four goats, but none was trophy size. Also, there was a good chance I would have lost two of them over the cliff if I had shot them. I did take some pictures, and seeing as I was going to be here a whole week, I would have a lot more chances.

Late in the afternoon, it started to drizzle and blow. I could feel the temperature dropping.

Next morning, when I poked my head out of the tent, I was dismayed to find two inches of fresh snow, and more coming down as well as a heavy fog. I knew that I could cut straight down the mountain and get back to my truck, but my main concern and thoughts were that I didn't want to leave the bike there over winter. I wasn't sure if the snow would stop. So after a quick breakfast, I packed up and headed back to the bike.

It was quite an experience, slipping and sliding my way back across the plateau. When I reached the crest of the mountain, I was out of the snow. But, the steepness of the mountain made me feel like I was tobogganing down on my bike.

So much for my hike-in trip. I carried on to Dease Lake in preparation for my fly-in trip. Not knowing my schedule, I had not reserved a plane. The B.C.-Yukon airline was down to two planes at Dease Lake, a Beaver and a Cessna 180. The Beaver was booked days ahead, but the Cessna 180 was free for part of the day. Since I was alone, the Cessna was able to handle me and my camping gear quite easily. It was quite foggy that morning, so we had to wait a few hours.

Near noon, Ray Sande, the owner of the airline, thought we would give it a try. We had to detour and take a roundabout way, but we finally landed at our little lake, approximately 80 miles west of Dease Lake. I made arrangements to be picked up in two weeks, on September 20. It was drizzling as we unloaded my gear, and we had to cover it.

I went up the bank to a clump of trees where Eb and I had camped five years earlier. There was our table, cupboards and bench, that we had made out of poplar poles, still standing. I did have to spend an hour reinforcing it and propping it up. It was about a 50-yard pack, and it was showering intermittently. So, between showers, I managed to get all my gear packed up and my tent set up without getting anything too wet. The rest of the day I finished setting-up my camp, bringing in firewood, water, etc.

When Eb and I had been there five years earlier, we had each taken a nice caribou out. Mine had scored 354 and Eb's was a bit smaller. We had seen several cow moose and calves on that trip, as well as some real big tracks, but we had not seen a bull moose. On one of my long excursions I had come across a whole skeleton of a bull moose and had cut the antlers off and packed it several miles back to camp. It had a 50-inch spread and scored just over 180. On that trip, we had concentrated mostly on caribou; but, we both felt there were some nice bull moose in the area, and that was my reason for being here. I was going to spend one week trying to find a trophy bull moose and one week trying for a big bull caribou with a double brow.

That night, it poured real heavy, with quite a strong wind. When I woke up, I saw my tent hadn't been shut properly and the wind had blown in rain, soaking part of my sleeping bag and foam mattress. Fortunately, I had some nice big sunny breaks and got everything dried off.

The first two days, I didn't do too much hiking. I had three lookout spots picked out, and I spent most of my time in these, glassing the surrounding area for signs of wildlife, but saw nothing. The following day, I covered a valley that wasn't too far away. I was very discouraged at the lack of signs; most of the tracks were a month or so old.

I decided that the following day I was going to go up to where I had found the skeleton, then over to another little lake four or five miles away, and then circle my lake back to camp. Next day was wet and drizzly, and my rain gear made it a lot more tiring. I had covered all of the area, and I was about to circle my lake. I had seen no fresh sign at all. At the end of the lake, I climbed up on a bit of a knoll where I thought I would sit for 10 minutes or so.

I had sat there only a few minutes when, out of the corner of my eye, I thought I caught a white flash near the top of a little mountain I had just circled. I concentrated on that area. Sure enough, I caught another white flash. I brought up my binoculars, and after a few minutes, I was able to make out the antlers of a moose feeding, way back in the poplars. They weren't too clear, but they looked huge; maybe not trophy size, but certainly bigger than any of my other ones. The white flash had been the sun's reflection when the moose turned a certain way. How lucky I was to have sat at that particular spot and caught that bit of white flash!

I sat for 10 minutes or so while I planned my stalk. The drizzle had stopped, so I was able to take off my rain gear. I would have to backtrack a half-mile or so, because of the swampy open area between him and me. Then, I would cut over at the base of the mountain to the gully that had a few scattered evergreens on it. Then up to that big patch of evergreens and that should put me around 100 yards from the moose. The wind was in my favor, so I set out with my plan well entrenched in my mind.

Everything was going fine. I was only about 20 yards from my clump of evergreens, when I suddenly realized the wind had shifted and was blowing my scent directly toward the moose. Panic almost set in. It was too late to circle back. He probably had gotten my scent already. I took a few more steps, and sure enough, there he was about 100 yards away looking in my direction. He hadn't seen me, but he had my scent. All I could see was his head and antlers, looking around this huge clump of willows. I dropped down to my knees and crept as quickly as I could to try to see his body for a shot. I stood up and could see his chest. I was still puffing from my climb up the mountain, but I had no time for a rest. As I was raising my rifle, he wheeled around and took off directly away from me. I put my cross hair on his hump and squeezed off a shot. I heard a thud. Got 'em! But he didn't drop. He disappeared over the knoll.

I ran as quickly as I could in his direction. When I got to the knoll, there he was, coming out of a gully at full speed. Just as he got to the top of the crest, he turned broadside. I got my cross hairs on his hump, just as he was going down the other side. This time, when I squeezed off my shot, there was no doubt that I had hit him good. His legs just went out from under him, and I'm sure his hitting the ground would have registered on the Richter scale. I couldn't see where he had dropped, but there was no doubt in my mind that I had him as I made my way through the heavily willowed gully up to where he was.

When I got to him, I saw that he was huge. My rifle laid across his antlers was a foot-and-a-half shy of his spread. There was a bullet hole through his right antler that I think was my first shot. As I stood admiring him, I found it hard to believe that just one 180 grain slug from my .30-06 could drop such a big, majestic animal. Looking back across the gully, I could see that it was at least 150 yards.

It was just about 7:00 p.m., getting a bit dark for picture taking. I had a two or three mile hike back to camp, so I concentrated on just cleaning him that night and then getting back to camp.

Next morning, I made my way back to my moose with packboard, saw, etc. I could use the meat, so I was going to bring it out. I had dropped my two-man rubber raft at the lake shore.

After inspecting the immediate area, I found that he had been there for quite a while, just fattening up for the rutting season. My God, he looked even bigger than the day before.

I halved him and skinned one side of his neck for the cape. I had to take off one front shoulder before I could turn him over to skin out the rest of his neck. The head and antlers were so heavy and big that I had to skin out the head right there and cut off part of the skull in order to pack out the antlers. I could barely move the hind quarters, so I had to skin, debone and halve them. It was another drizzly day, but I was so happy, I hardly noticed it.

I cut away the damaged part of the hump and left the ribs. I put all the meat sections into cheesecloth sacks to protect them from the blow flies. I had about a half-mile pack down to the lake. I made it in 10 trips, and they were all heavy trips. Once at the lake, I was able to haul all the meat and antlers down the lake to my camp in only two trips. That rubber raft once again paid for itself many times over. Back at camp, I made a rack with poplar poles set a few feet off the ground right at the water's edge, and put all my meat on it, shading it with a tarp. This all took me two full long days. It's not an easy job when you're by yourself, but it's not the first one I have packed out alone.

After all the meat was taken care of, and the antlers were deposited by my tent, I sat by the fire and started to finish the cape. I turned the ears inside out, and began skinning the nose. I remember thinking that there was no end to the nose, and that this was definitely going to be the last moose I would ever cape. But, I had said this twice before when I was caping out the other two moose I have mounted. The nights were fairly cool, so I had no problem keeping the meat, and my cape was well salted.

The rest of the trip went fairly quickly. I went up to the plateau and camped there for four days, looking for caribou. I did spot four; but, when I crept up to them, I saw they were a cow and a calf, a small bull, and a large bull, not big enough to make a decent trophy. I did find a beautiful red fox, which I shot and skinned out to make a rug for my trophy room. I also saw a silver fox, but he didn't wait long enough for me to add him to my fur rugs. I spent a few leisurely days just loafing and exploring. The lake was loaded with fish, so I spent a bit of time fishing. Most of them were 8 to 12 inches long.

On September 20, I was all packed and waiting for the plane. I had caught my limit of rainbows in the morning. Ray's son Ernie came in with the Beaver to pick me up, only an hour late. Ernie was quite pleased to see my nice set of antlers. By the time we loaded the meat, gear and antlers, we had quite a load for the Beaver.

On my way home, I detoured through Vernon to drop the meat off at Simon Dengal's place. Simon, an old friend and semi-retired meat cutter, was to cut up the meat for me. We weighed all the meat and were surprised that even with all I had cut away and deboned, I still had close to 800 pounds of meat. I sent a tooth from my moose to the Fish and Game Department, and they informed me that he was eight years old. The meat was very tender, so I not only got a real nice trophy, he was also terrific eating.

When I arrived home, I purposely underscored my antlers so that I wouldn't be too disappointed if he shrank a lot. Imagine how pleased I was, when after the drying out period went by and I took him to Gordon Smith (our Boone and Crockett Official Measurer), he scored my moose as 221! Not only did my moose make the records book, he placed quite high in it. My taxidermist, Jack Gibson of Trophy Taxidermy, did a real fine job of mounting him. So, I am very pleased and happy with the final outcome of this hunt.

John C. Davis of Soldotna, Alaska, hunted near Pilot Point, Alaska, in 1984 to take this excellent Alaska-Yukon moose that was scored for entry at 227⅞ points.

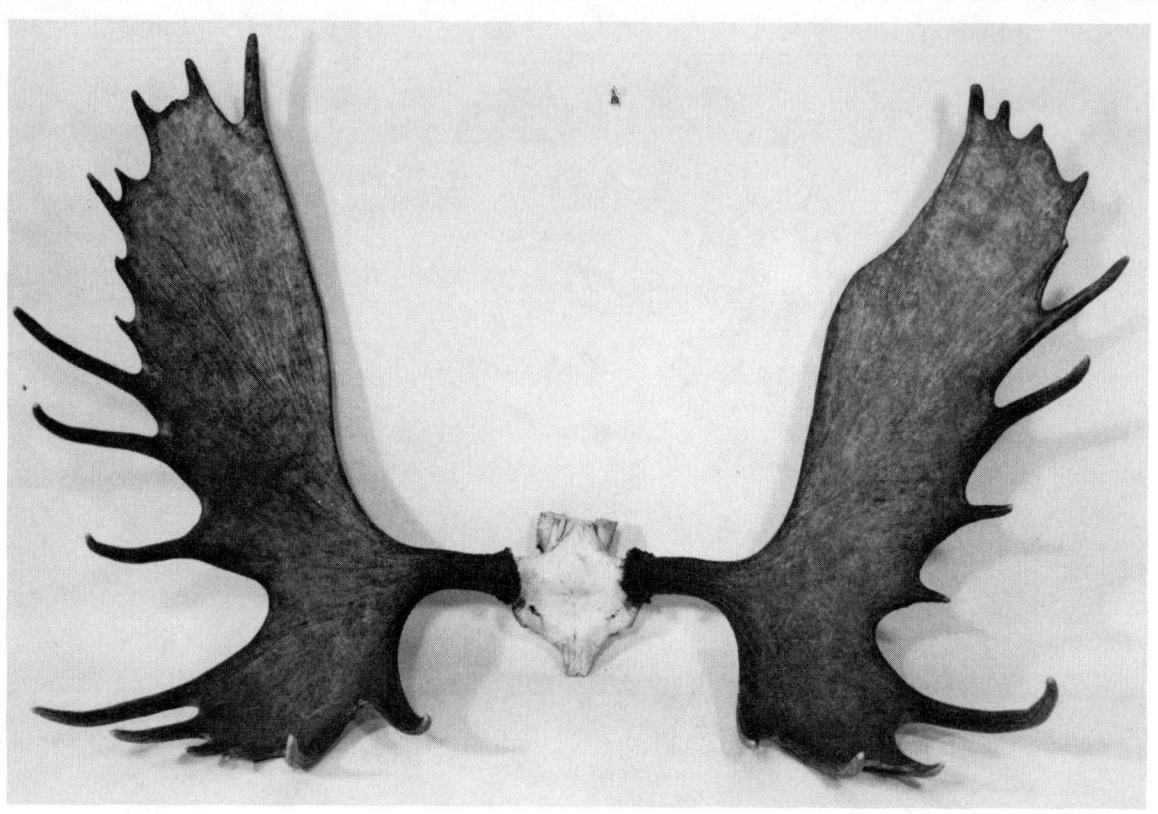

CANADA MOOSE
SECOND AWARD
SCORE: 216 2/8

Locality: Cassiar Mts., B. C.   Date: November 1984
Hunter: Don L. Corley

CANADA MOOSE 216 2/8

Don L. Corley

Our destination was Watson Lake, Yukon. As I was leaving Dallas/Fort Worth, Phil Stago left Phoenix in order for us to meet in Edmonton. Phil arrived before me, and when I first saw him, he seemed to be in shock at the 20 below weather he found in Edmonton. We left the next morning at 11:00 a.m. for Watson Lake, Yukon.

We finally arrived at 5:30 p.m., and we were met by Myles Bradford and 40 below weather. I was expecting Myles, but not quite such cold weather. He told us that an unexpected Artic front had moved in and it was unusually cold. It was Phil's first trip to Watson, and my 33rd since 1969. Bradford operates the late George Dalziel's hunting area with the help of his wife Sherry and her brother Byron "Butch" Dalziel. We spent the night in Watson with Butch. When the temperature had warmed up to 20 below the next morning, we headed for the Horse Ranch camp.

The Horse Ranch camp is 40 miles south of Watson. This is where all the horses are wintered, and this would be our home for the next 15 days. It is not only a wintering area for the horses, but also a perfect place for moose. The rut was over, and the bulls were all back together. We had moose north, east, south, and west of us, lots of them. Our problem was the weather. Occasionally it would warm up to minus 10, but the majority of the time it was between 20 and 50 below. Also, we were confronted with up to two feet of snow and no wind, which made for a bad hunting situation.

For the next two weeks, we chased many bulls around and almost connected several times, but not quite. A bull moose can hear you and a horse coming a long way off in snow, especially with no wind. During the entire hunt, we experienced extremely cold temperatures, and never once a good wind.

Myles, his wife Sherry, Phil, and I shared a cabin. We had lots of time and many big bulls close by in a 10-mile radius. Myles and Phil started hunting, and Sherry and I set out 30 or more marten and lynx traps. With a little help from Myles, we became full-fledged trappers. For the next 11 days, Myles, Sherry, Phil, and I trapped, hunted, cut wood, cooked and washed dishes. Who would ever believe that 11 days had passed and we had still not taken a big bull? We saw trophy bulls daily, but 500 yards was as close as you could get, and then the ears would go up and the moose was off and running.

Finally, on the 12th day, Phil and Myles got a bull moose. Phil's bull scored 195.

In the meantime, I was becoming quite a successful trapper. I was seeing moose daily, but not "Mr. Big." Myles and I got serious on the 13th day of the hunt; however, no big bull. The next day, we saw a glimpse of something that looked good. Several hours later we got a better look, and it was truly a big moose. We tied the horses up and started following six bulls on foot. They were feeding and we were downwind, so fortunately they were not spooky. Still, there was very little wind. All of this started about 1:00 p.m.

Approximately three hours later, our bull lay down on a small hill. We started our stalk. We were within 500 yards, 400 yards, 300 yards and look out! Trouble. We ran into two of the six bulls. They jumped up and started running. Myles and I climbed a small ridge and started glassing for "Mr. Big." Two bulls went to the left, two ran fast to the right, and the other two went straight down below us into a creek bottom. After a quick look at all six moose, we spotted "Mr. Big" in the bottom of the creek, 250-300 yards away. Three or four fast, off-handed shots with my .300, and down he went. As we approached the big bull, I told Myles that he looked more like an Alaskan moose than a Canadian moose.

He measured 64 inches, a truly outstanding trophy. After pictures were taken, and the bull was caped out, we quartered him and packed what we could take back to camp with us. It was after 5:00 p.m. by then, but luckily, with the snow and the moon for light, we arrived back at the Horse Ranch cabin around 11:00 p.m. The temperature gauge registered 25 below zero on the tree in front of the cabin. Sherry and Phil had the cabin warm, and moose stew was waiting for us.

The next day, Myles took an extra horse and returned for the remainder of the meat, while Phil and I checked the trap lines. We had now been at Horse Ranch for 15 days. Yes, 15 days and two moose, but what moose they were! One scored 195 and the other 220.

For Phil's first trip north, the experience was nothing short of a true adventure. Sharing Phil's excitement, learning to trap, and spending time in the bush with friends, was indeed another highlight in my hunting career.

Photo Courtesy of James E. Nelson

This huge Alaska-Yukon moose was killed by James E. Nelson in 1985 near Worm Lake, Yukon. It scores 233 3/8 points.

Photo Courtesy of Don Miller

Don Miller was hunting near Pink Mountain, B. C., in 1985 when he killed this fine Canada moose that scores 198 6/8 points.

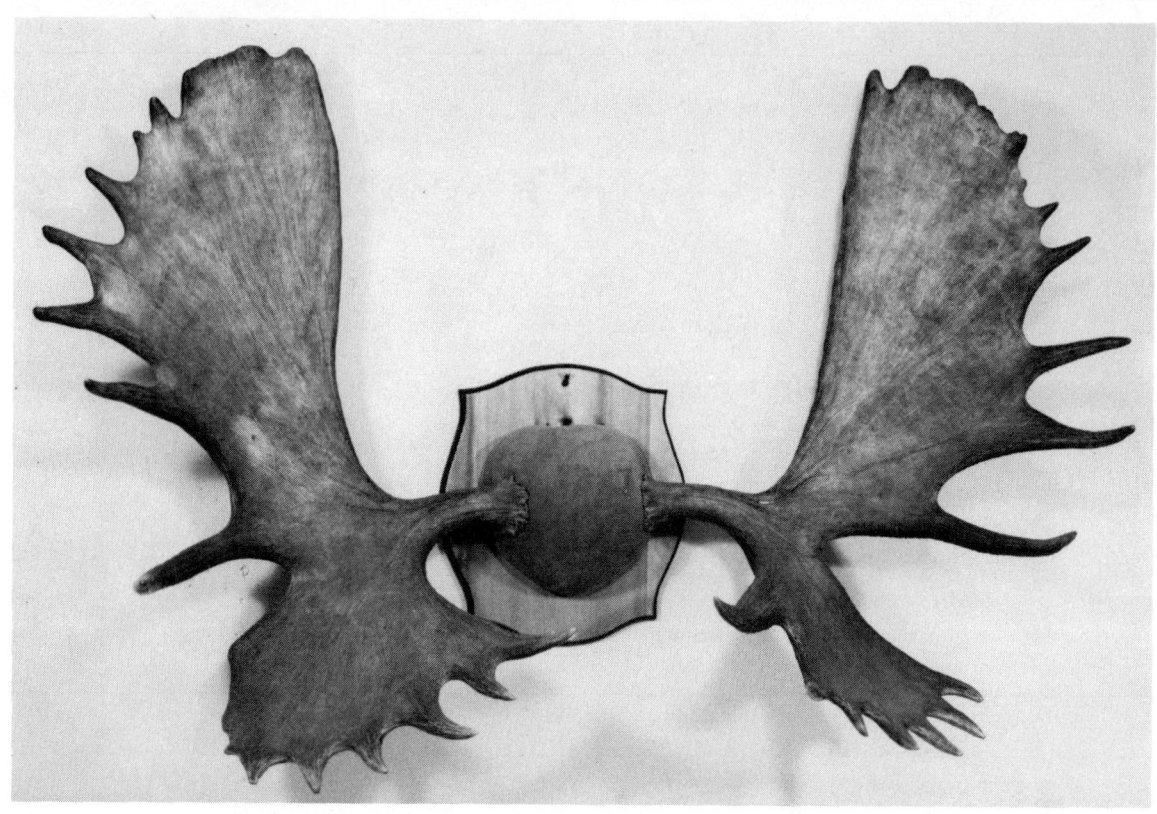

Photograph by Wm. H. Nesbitt

CANADA MOOSE
CERTIFICATE OF MERIT
SCORE: 223 5/8

Locality: Island Lake, Man.   Date: 1980
Hunter: Indian
Owner: Jack E. Dunn

CANADA MOOSE 223 5/8

Jack E. Dunn, owner

This huge Canada moose was taken by an Indian hunting under tribal treaty rights in September of 1980. Very little is known of the hunt other than the hunting season date.

The trophy was acquired from the Indian hunter by a second individual, who in turn, transferred ownership to Jack E. Dunn. Mr. Dunn is in the jewelry business in Winnipeg, and is also an avid sportsman. He recognized the trophy value of these fine antlers and acquired them to enjoy with others in his collection.

This huge bull moose certainly proves that there are some really big moose in Manitoba.

Photograph by Wm. H. Nesbitt

ALASKA-YUKON MOOSE
CERTIFICATE OF MERIT
SCORE: 249 1/8

Locality: Granite Mt., Alaska   Date: September 1982
Hunter: David B. Parent
Owner: Earl D. Hahn

ALASKA-YUKON MOOSE 249⅛

David B. Parent

I have a small placer gold mine on the Seward Peninsula in Western Alaska, approximately 140 miles east northeast of Nome, Alaska. This is open country, with tundra covered hills and some patches of willows in the drainages that sometimes extend quite far up the hillsides along these drainages. The valleys have willow and cottonwood, and farther downstream, fairly good size spruce. The big game animals found in this area are grizzly, caribou, moose, and reindeer (the latter are actually privately owned). Moose are a recent arrival, having only become abundant over the past 30 years. They seem to have been on the increase during the past 15 years that I have been coming here.

On September 1, 1982, my partners and I were operating our mine, when we noticed a bull moose on the hillside about a mile away. He was browsing at the edge of a willow-covered drainage. We were out of meat, and this presented an excellent opportunity to replenish our supply. Two of us decided to go get some meat. We walked up opposite sides of the brush patch, staying out in open tundra. As chance would have it, I was on the downwind side. We were both carrying Model 70 Remingtons in .300 Winchester Magnum, with Leupold scopes. Meanwhile, the moose had disappeared into the tall brush in the course of his browsing. I couldn't see my partner because of the brush.

About two-thirds of the way up the hill, I heard a crashing in the brush, so I stopped. In a matter of seconds, the moose came out of the brush and into the open at a full run, about 40 feet from me. He was too close and moving too fast for my scope to be of any use. I just aimed down the barrel and fired at his neck. I was lucky. He dropped like a rock, a clean kill.

We field dressed the moose and hauled him to camp whole. There we hung him up to skin and quarter him. We then hung the quarters up to age. At this time, the rack didn't seem that unusually large, as all the moose we had taken over the years had been over 60 inches. I measured the rack the next day at just under 72 inches and decided I had better save them. When an airplane big enough to fly them out arrived, I took them to Fairbanks and gave them to Mr. Earl Hahn, who now owns them.

Photograph by Wm. H. Nesbitt

WYOMING MOOSE
FIRST AWARD
SCORE: 182 6/8

Locality: Caribou Co., Idaho   Date: October 1983
Hunter: Patricia A. Wood

WYOMING MOOSE 1826/8

Patricia A. Wood

My husband Rod has never been patient when it comes to waiting for the results on a big game drawing. So, I wasn't surprised when I came home one day to find him waiting for me with a big grin, "You've been drawn on the moose hunt!" After telling me this, he lost his smile. Mainly, because I wasn't smiling.

All I could think of was the hunting season the fall before. I had been drawn on an elk permit. The hunt was only 12 days, but it was an extremely hard hunt for me. Our children were quite young that year. I would spend my precious time at home doing a day's worth of work in two or three hours. Then, I would hunt with Rod and his friends almost every daylight hour. I didn't even get an elk. I had a chance for cows and calves. But, I wanted a large bull that would make a nice mount. Of course I took a lot of ribbing from people about how picky I was.

I wasn't always picky. I was raised in Grace, Idaho, about 12 miles away from my present home in Soda Springs. My dad, James Parkhouse, started my hunting career when I was 14 years old. Being raised with three brothers, and no sisters, brought on the responsibility of hunting for game meat as a family. Opening day of my first hunt, I got the only buck shot that morning. I shot him in the lower spine. Dad always bragged about what a good shot I was.

Rod brought me back to the present by saying, "I thought you would be happy." Well, I was happy. I just couldn't imagine keeping up the pace which I had on my last hunt for the 30 days allowed on the moose permit.

The afternoon before the opening of the hunt, Rod took me to practice with the Remington .270 I was going to use. For over a month, all Rod could tell me was that a .270 just would not put down a moose with one shot. I was only able to take three practice shots. I had hurt my right shoulder previously, and I didn't want it to get too sore to shoot during the hunt.

I was still concerned about our children. Our son, Larry, was only 10 and our daughter, Suzie, was eight. At the time, though, we had a 17 year old exchange student from Sweden, so I left them in her care.

Opening morning was October 5, 1983. My area was 376-1, which runs next to the east side of Soda Springs. We decided not to camp out, it would be just as easy to load our horses and drive to the hunting spot each day. Opening day, our friends, Jerry and Candy Young, were going to hunt with us. Another friend, Terry Sanderson, had an elk permit in the same area.

Terry started from a different canyon, saying that he would meet us later in the day. The Youngs, Rod, and I, saddled our horses and headed over the mountains. Later that morning,

Rod and Jerry were in front of us a little way. I told Candy that moose hunting was a little more fun than elk hunting, because Rod didn't think that I needed to be as quiet as we had to be when elk hunting. As I turned to talk to Candy, I saw a moose. It was a long way off. As I got off the horse, Rod was looking with binoculars to see if it was a good-sized bull.

Just as I got the moose in my sights, it ran. I hurried back on the horse, and we took off after the moose. Jerry and Candy rode along the bottom of the hill to push it back if it came into the open. Rod and I rode as far as we could on the horses, then started walking through the trees, hoping the moose would stop. He was much better at running through the dense forest than we were. After earnestly searching for him to no avail, we decided he had given us the slip.

After a long hunt that day, we rode back to the horse trailers. We unsaddled our horses, then sat in the grass for a while to rest. Terry Sanderson drove up. He didn't have any luck finding an elk, either.

He did say, however, that he had seen a moose in the trees on the mountain next to our horse trailers! After a long, hard day this was very ironic. Pretty soon, as we sat talking, the moose came out of the trees and started to wander across a clearing. We looked through scopes and determined that he had a small rack. Rod asked me if I wanted to try to shoot him. I said that I hated to shoot such a small moose on opening day. Candy then told me that she had heard how picky I was, but hadn't believed it until now. So, we calmly sat and watched the moose cross back and forth in the open.

The next day, Rod, Terry, and I took our horses onto a friend's land. It was a quiet hunt, and we didn't even see any game that day.

The third day of the hunt was Friday, October 7. I was so saddle sore that I begged to walk. Rod, Terry, and I drove into Angus Creek area, about 15 miles northeast of Soda Springs. We saw a nice moose early, but the silly thing had a beautiful antler on one side, and only a spike on the other. Rod asked me if I would want to shoot him. I said that I only wanted a nice mount. Then, I joked that maybe our taxidermist, the local Fish and Game officer, could add a plaster antler on the other side so that we could hang the moose in our family room.

As we went on, we spotted another bull moose walking across a clearing. It was the same size as the one we saw opening day by our horse trailer. Then, Rod and Terry spotted something moving in the quaking aspen below the small moose. They saw two moose, one with what seemed to be a nice rack. The moose were laying down at the edge of a large triangle, thinning to a small patch at the right of the moose. Other than that, it was open mountain side. Rod and I left to find a position where we could better see the moose.

Terry went to the place where the quakies thinned. If I only wounded the moose, he would try to drive it into the open. If it went any other direction, I would have a second shot. Rod and I had to cross a very large beaver pond, with narrow footing. I'm not at all fond of water, so this was not exactly a thrilling experience for me. All I could think was that if I fell into the water and couldn't shoot my .270, I would have to use Rod's 7mm. I didn't want to shoot his rifle. Well, I thought, once we cross, it will be easy from there on. Hah! Have you ever walked on a steep slope covered by deer brush? It was impossible to be quiet.

I knew when we finally got into position that the moose must have heard us and would be miles away. We went around the hill, and I took a look through my scope. The early morning sun was glaring in the scope. We decided to walk back behind the hill and then go lower. It wasn't the best idea. When we got into position, the glare was worse. I wanted a clear shot. The other moose lying by the bull was a cow, so I really needed a better vantage point. Rod suggested that we climb the north face of the hill and look down on the moose. We climbed another 200 yards through deer brush. Finally, we came out in the open.

Bad news. From the bottom of the hill, the hill looked flat; it wasn't! Now we could not see the moose because of a slight ridge between our position and that of the moose. Rod said, "Let's crawl on our hands and knees to the juniper tree in the middle of the sagebrush on the rise." We crawled out to the tree, holding our rifles up with one arm. It must have been another 100 yards. You should have seen the juniper tree. It might have been six inches taller than the sagebrush!

Rod told me to steady myself and raise up and shoot. I told him that I hadn't really had a clear look at the pair of moose yet. I didn't want to shoot before I was sure that the cow was out of my line of fire. He told me to raise up a little, take a look, then stand and shoot. I raised up and whispered, "He's got his back to me." At that point, I forgot my sore shoulder. I stood up, took steady aim at the middle of his back, and fired. What happened next, I never expected. He started to raise up on his front legs, then toppled over. We found out later that the bullet severed his spine right behind his hump.

I'm not a very mature hunter, based upon what I did at that point. I glanced at Rod who was standing, staring at the moose, completely stunned that he was down. I don't remember traveling the 150 yards to the moose, but I do remember crying and yelling, "I got him," the whole way. The moose was thrashing around, so a final bullet through the neck killed him almost instantly.

The action was all over by 9:30 a.m. I was so excited. All I could think of was what a nice, even mount he would make. Terry had brought a camera, by chance, and he took our only pictures in the field. The first clue that this moose was very large was when I tried to place my rifle across the rack. It fell through!

Rod and Terry then told me that it was time for me to clean my kill. The hide was so thick, I couldn't get the knife through. After laughing at my predicament, they pitched in and did all the work. It took them until midnight to finish, and also deliver the meat to the store to be butchered.

I have to admit that my husband is the best hunter I know. If it wasn't for his skill in locating the game we hunt, I surely would never have gotten my beautiful trophy. It was one of the most exciting days of my life.

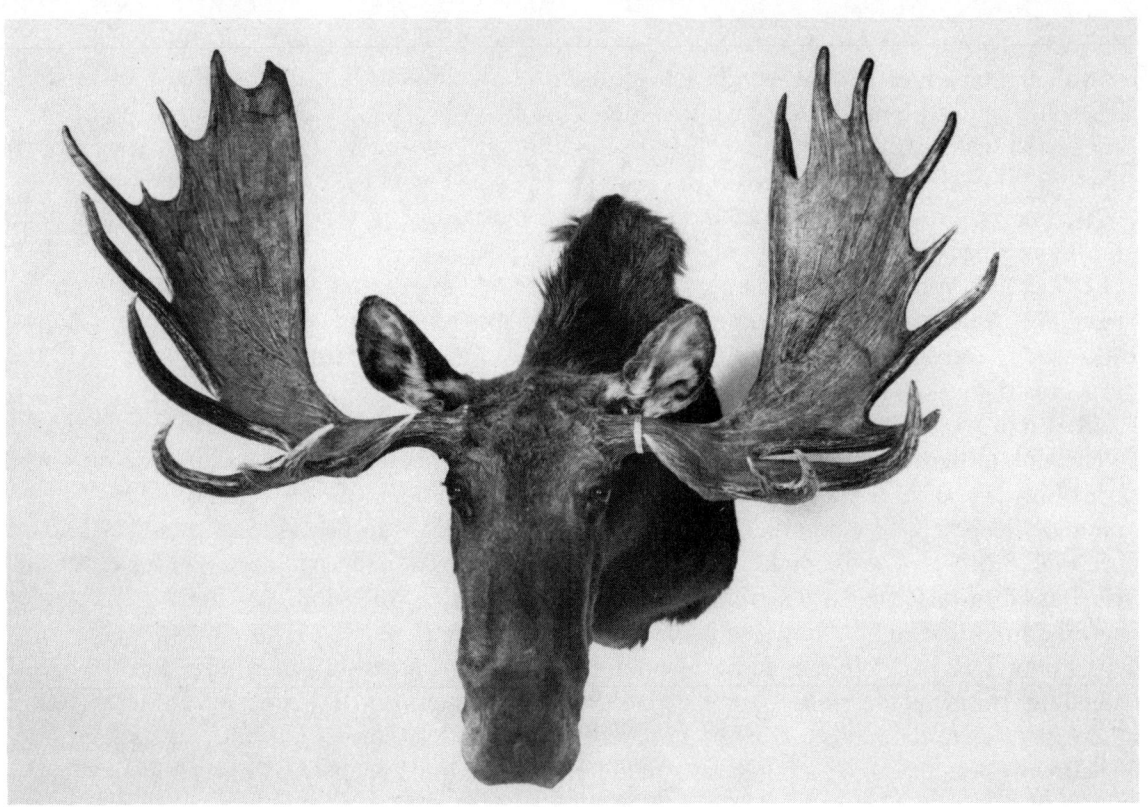

Photograph by Wm. H. Nesbitt

WYOMING MOOSE
SECOND AWARD
SCORE: 177 5/8

Locality: Teton Co., Wyo. Date: September 1985
Hunter: John R. Blanton

WYOMING MOOSE 177⅝

John R. Blanton

What a week! I always try to live life to the fullest, but the third week of September, 1985, proved to be especially action packed.

Friday the 13th (proving to be lucky) was the date of my 50th birthday (September 14, 1985) party. After a wonderful celebration party and dinner, with 80 friends in my home, I slept a few hours and left for Kerrville for the Y. O. Ranch Gala. Upon returning to Dallas on Sunday, I packed the gear for my long anticipated hunt in the Tetons. I had been trying for a moose permit for three years, and finally I received it through the Jackson Hole Outfitter's Guide Association.

Ridge Taylor, the outfitter, welcomed me to Jackson. Bed came early, due to a 4:00 a.m. departure for our camp area. The drive next day through the Tetons was breathtaking.

We didn't waste any time. After several hours of glassing and spotting, we saw a magnificent bull through the 60 power scope. We watched the bull bed down about mid-morning. Ridge knew that this was the trophy we should be after.

Riding through the heavy timber, I knew I was in for a strenuous day. I hadn't been on horseback for a year. But, it was about 40 degrees and the day was sunny.

After hours of riding, we reached a high meadow in mid-afternoon. There, we began to spot and glass again. Suddenly, the earth shook and I heard charges of dynamite being set off. This went on for half an hour, and I feared my bull would be badly spooked.

Ridge and I worked our way on foot upward through the boulders, looking carefully in the timber as we went. When we came upon a clearing, there he was with a couple of cows, about 50 yards away! We took cover; the underbrush was too heavy for taking a shot. We worked in closer to beat the darkness. The moose awoke on full alert! I took an off-balance shot with my Winchester .300 Magnum, but it was directly in the heart. Ridge had probably never seen a man so excited.

It wasn't until after we field scored him that I realized what we had! After elation and shooting photos, we had to cape and quarter him by flashlight. All this on a 45 degree angle of slick wet tundra! We wrestled with the horses and moose, finally getting loaded-up at 11:00 p.m.

Covered by blood and mud, we had been stomped, kicked, and run over. Not only that, but a storm was supposed to blow in by morning. But, maybe we didn't have all the poor luck. A friend, Don Corley, had hunted here 10 days prior and had slipped on the ice, breaking his shoulder blade.)

We began our hazardous descent in pitch darkness, walking and leading our horses packed with the meat, cape, and horns. (Wyoming requires that you bring back all edible meat.) The rack continued to hang up in the heavy brush and trees. We were busy with constant re-tightening of the packs. By 2:00 a.m., we gratefully found a horse trail. My light had burned out, and Ridge's was dim. Physically, I was in total exhaustion. Ridge kept encouraging me by saying, "It's only another mile." He lied well.

As dawn was breaking, I saw a wonderful sight, our truck and trailer! Ridge left me at the hotel about 8:00 a.m., then picked up two hours later to drive me to the airport. I slept all the way home.

This had to be the toughest 30 hours of my life; but, the rewards were great. My moose is No. one in SCI, and it should also rank well-up in Boone and Crockett.

Photos Courtesy of William V. Conn, Jr., and Paul Wollenman

(l) William Conn hunted near Atlin, B. C., in 1983 to find his Canada moose that scores 189 3/8 points and qualifies for the Awards records book. (r) Paul Wollenman was hunting near Mayo, Yukon, in 1984 when he shot this Alaska-Yukon moose that scores 227 4/8 points.

Photo Courtesy of Richard B. Limbach

Richard B. Limbach was near the Hess River in the Yukon in 1985 when he killed his Alaska-Yukon moose that scores 224 4/8 points.

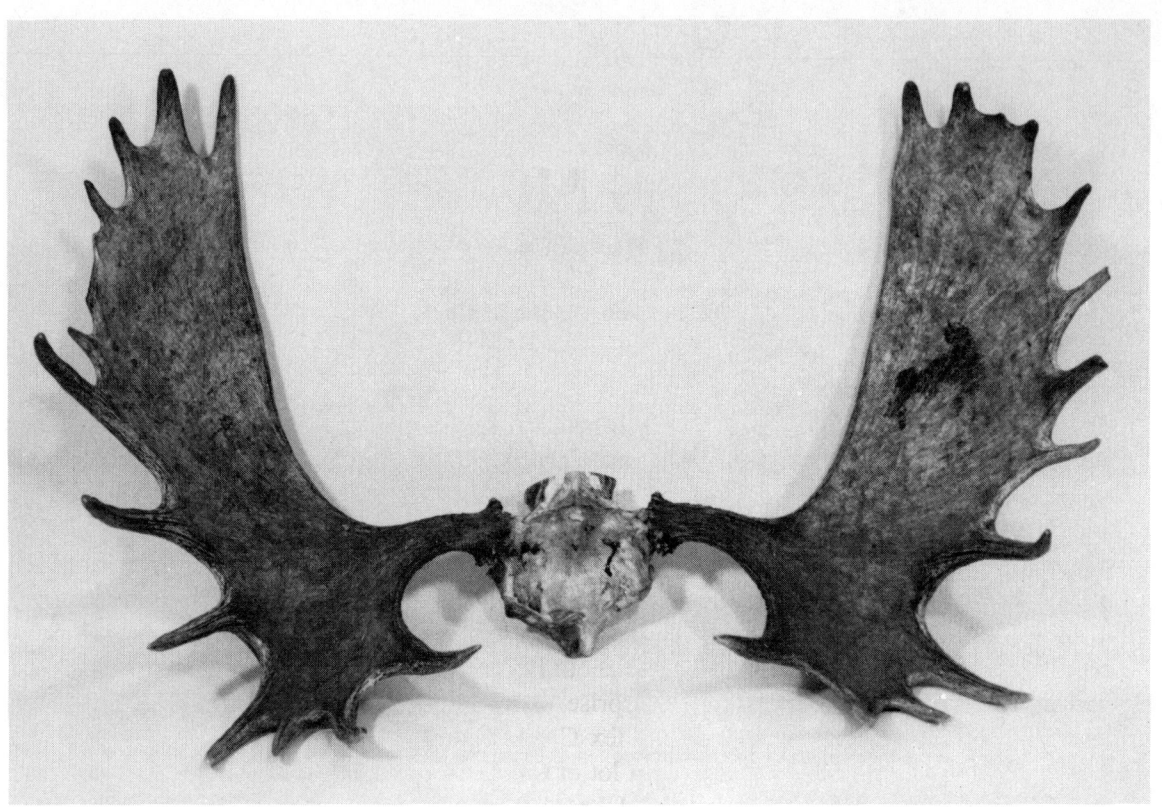

Photograph by Wm. H. Nesbitt

WYOMING MOOSE
THIRD AWARD
SCORE: 176 2/8

Locality: Bonneville Co., Idaho   Date: October 1985
Hunter: Steven A. Barnard

WYOMING MOOSE 176 2/8

Steven A. Barnard

It was early in June 1985, and the time had arrived to mail the application forms for the state's special hunting permits. It has become a practice at the Barnard home to put in for moose each year, knowing full well that no one would ever draw one of the six permits given in our choice area. However, by putting in year after year, I reasoned it would at least lower the odds for that once-in-a-lifetime experience. My wife, Linda, even looked forward to this part of the hunt. I had to send in $75 with each application for my two sons and myself. Linda reasoned that if we had this kind of money to spend, then each year when the refund came back with the news that we had not been drawn, she should take the checks and go shopping.

In August, we were both in for the surprise of a lifetime. My son, Doug, and I had both drawn moose permits! Our hunt was the Tex Creek area east of Idaho Falls. Since I practice dentistry in Idaho Falls, and I also spend a lot of time either four-wheeling or horseback riding, I was somewhat familiar with this area. I knew there were quite a few moose in this area. However, I was not aware that this area was the home of a records class moose, which I would later take.

Since the hunt opened at the end of August, we did not have a lot of scouting time. A friend, Kim Ryan, had taken a large bull the year before in this same area. He was a great help in deciding where to go and when to hunt. Kim also knew what a records class moose looked like, and he cautioned me not to shoot the first "little moose" I saw. Kim accompanied us on several trips, both scouting and during the hunt. Again, his help was vital in taking my prize trophy.

We started hunting on opening day, which was in the last part of August. The leaves were still on the trees, and the bulls were not very visible. We did find one fair-sized bull, but we held-out, hoping for a larger one.

We hunted at every opportunity. But, we were limited mostly to weekends when my son was home from working construction in another state. We usually saw at least one bull and a number of cows on each trip. So far, we had followed Kim's advice and let the "little ones" go. We had seen several in the 35 to 40-inch class.

In late September, it was time for Doug to return to his studies at the university. So, we decided it was time to take the next 40-inch, or better, bull that we saw. Doug took a nice young bull with a 43-inch spread. We were really excited! I could see that we had our winter's supply of meat, and we also had enjoyed the greatest hunt a father and son could ever hope to have. I made the decision that I would not take a moose now unless he was of records class. I continued to hunt when I could, and I glassed many fine animals, none of records class.

One Friday evening in early October, Kim and I were checking out a wallow area. The rut was in full swing now, and the bulls were a lot more interested in the cows than they were cautious. It was just about dark when, way across the beaver ponds and in the edge of the timber, this large, black figure appeared. We glassed him for nearly an hour, until it was dark. We had found him too late and too far away for a good stalk, and much too far for a sure kill.

That evening, I called Doug and very excitedly told him to come home and hunt with me on Saturday. We took my dental assistant, Debra Rudd (soon to be my daughter-in-law), my 13-year-old daughter Lori, and my nephew Paul, and went back to the area on Saturday morning. It was a beautiful October day with a good "Idaho" wind. The leaves were colored, but only about half-gone from the trees. We spent most of the morning working slowly through the trees, hoping that someone might push the bull into an opening. Several times, we got close enough to smell his "courting time" perfume, but we did not see him. I guess he didn't get that big by being dumb!

Along about mid-morning, I was glassing an area when I noticed a tree moving down where the wind wasn't blowing. I watched for what seemed like forever until finally I could see the dark figure of a cow moose. Now I knew we were on track. As I continued to watch, I finally caught sight of one big antler. My heart made a giant leap and began to beat like a bass drum. I was shaking like a leaf on a tree and my mouth was spitting cotton. I have hunted since I was 11 years old, and I have killed deer, elk and other game, but I still get very excited on every hunt as though it was the first one.

We decided that our little hunting party should move down into the grove of trees and try to push the bull into an opening for a clear shot. I would stay high and in the open, so I would have the advantage of unrestricted shooting if he did move into an opening. As the boys moved into the trees, they hadn't gone far when the bull decided it was time for him to get out of there. The noise he made sounded like someone driving a tank through the grove. It was an awesome sound!

I readied my shaking self and my custom-made .280 Remington Express for what was about to take place. My first sighting of this fantastic bull's full figure was at about 200 yards, and he was running full-out. Again, this was an awesome sight! I brought the .280 into position and fired. Down he went! I put another shell into the chamber and watched. In an instant, he was on his feet and running full speed again. The .280 barked once more and it was over! Both 150-grain bullets had smashed into the lung area about eight inches apart. The result was very final.

After much celebrating, measuring, and picture-taking, we began the chore of field dressing and just plain hauling moose!

This was the hunt of a lifetime, with a moose of a lifetime. What a blessing to live in a great land where a person can hunt and be free with nature. There is a solemn beauty to a trophy like this that few will understand and none can explain.

Photo Courtesy of Patricia A. Wood

Patricia A. Wood is obviously happy with her fine Wyoming moose that scored 182-6/8 points and received First Award at the 19th Awards. It was killed in Caribou County, Idaho, in 1983.

Photo Courtesy of John R. Blanton

Teton County, Wyoming, was the site of John R. Blanton's Wyoming moose hunt in 1985 that resulted in this trophy that received the Second Award at the 19th Awards and scores 177-5/8 points.

Photograph by Wm. H. Nesbitt

MOUNTAIN CARIBOU
FIRST AWARD
SCORE: 444

Locality: Mountain River, N. W. T.   Date: September 1984
Hunter: John A. Kolar

MOUNTAIN CARIBOU 444

John A. Kolar

My plans for a Dall's sheep and mountain caribou hunt began in the Spring of 1984. With advice from three hunting friends who had previously been there, I made a phone call to Stan Stevens of Mackenzie Mountain Outfitters, Northwest Territories, Canada. Fortunately, there was one opening. Stan told me his area, approximately 8,000 square miles, is located southwest of Norman Wells, between the Mackenzie River and the Yukon border. The mountains are approximately 3,500 to 9,000 feet. He recommended backpacking to get into the more remote areas. The hunt would be for 12 days, and I could expect to see several nice rams, plus a good selection of mountain caribou.

I loaded my backpack with 40 pounds and started my training the next day. Alternate days were spent running and packing. I also worked with weights twice a week. During the summer, I spent many hours on my rifle range. A load of 162 grains of IMR 4831 powder with a solid base 140 grain Nosler bullet was finally perfected. My Browning 7mm Magnum bolt action will group five shots in 9/16 of an inch at 100 yards. A 22-inch chest-size target was used out to 600 yards, though shots of 100 to 200 yards could be expected.

Finally, on August 30th, the long-awaited trip from Wisconsin to the Minneapolis airport arrived. My wife, Judy, wished me good luck as I started my journey to Edmonton, Alberta. Yellowknife, the capital of the Northwest Territories, was the next stop and then finally Norman Wells. Stan's wife, Helen, greeted me and another hunter, and arranged for hunting licenses and last-minute packing. Five inches of snow were on the ground.

Later that day, we flew from Norman Wells to base camp where we were greeted by our guides and camp cooks. Stan flew me and my guide, Paul Weisser, into our hunting area the next day, September 1st. We made a spike camp along the mountain river, and we watched a band of ewes and lambs feeding on a distant mountain.

The temperature was 30 degrees early the next morning as Paul and I started our climb from camp. Within an hour, we spotted a small ram and six ewes. About noon, we found four rams bedded on a gradual slope, with 11 younger rams and ewes 500 yards higher. Two of the rams were legal; one was about 36 inches. We decided to move higher and for four hours, we followed a fresh caribou track to a pass between the mountains.

Suddenly, we discovered fresh tracks everywhere. The early snow must have started the caribou movement. Immediately, I spotted 12 caribou on a far ridge. They were a half-mile away and moving in our direction. We watched a huge caribou cross the top of the same ridge. Paul was very excited about getting close to the big bull. The wind was right as the caribou herd moved down into a valley and out of sight. We jumped from our position and ran to a spot where we hoped they would cross.

Almost magically, the bull appeared 120 yards away. Dried velvet clung to his huge antlers like moss on a cypress tree. I waited for more of his body to appear over the knoll. When I could make out his shoulder, I shot. Down he went!

What a beautiful animal! Not only were his antlers massive; the hair color pattern was very pretty with its mixture of grey, brown, black, and white, a perfect blend to match the surrounding tundra. As a taxidermist, I thought how beautiful a full body mount would be, but eventually elected for a more practical shoulder mount.

Over 30 caribou, including two exceptional bulls, passed by within 300 yards as we prepared my trophy for the long pack out. One of the bulls had a longer shovel than mine.

Struggling with our heavy packs, we left the kill site. After climbing over a hill, Paul spotted a silver-tipped grizzly. We watched him feed along a distant hillside and knew the remains of my caribou would not be wasted.

We arrived in camp at 10:00 p.m. It had been one of the most exciting and exhausting days I have ever spent hunting. If only a man could afford to do this more often; what an experience in this vast wilderness.

The next day was spent fleshing and salting the cape. I wanted to make sure this trophy had proper care and would end up on my wall.

Stan flew Chris (another guide) and Peter (his hunter) in for sheep and moose. He dropped off the river raft and flew out the caribou meat and antlers. When the rack didn't want to fit into the plane easily, Stan smiled and said that this one would go into the records book!

Chris and Peter took a nice 3/4-curl ram that day, so we readied the raft and headed downstream with them. Paul and I went after sheep and they continued looking for moose. Foggy, rainy weather forced us to hole-up in our tent for a day-and-a-half. Finally, on the sixth day of my hunt, I killed a beautiful wide-flaring, full curl Dall's sheep. He was the largest of eight rams in the group. We also saw a wolverine, a nice finish for the perfect hunt.

Photo Courtesy of Brooks Carmichael

Brooks Carmichael was hunting in the Mackenzie Mountains of the N. W. T. in 1984 when he killed his fine mountain caribou. It scores 399⅝ points.

Photo Courtesy of Patricia M. Dreeszen

A happy Pat Dreeszen with her big mountain caribou that scores 416⅝ points. It was killed in 1984 at Little Dal Lake, N. W. T.

Photograph by Wm. H. Nesbitt

MOUNTAIN CARIBOU
SECOND AWARD
SCORE: 442 7/8

Locality: Spatsizi Plateau, B. C.   Date: October 1984
Hunter: Jay L. Brasher

MOUNTAIN CARIBOU 442 7/8

Jay L. Brasher

In 1979, I booked a hunt with Collingswood Brothers to hunt on the Spatsizi Plateau for Stone's sheep. I had a very successful hunt. Because of the wonderful area they have, and the vast amount of trophy game, I decided that I would very much like to return someday and hunt with them again.

It wasn't until the fall of 1984 that I was able to book with Collingswood Brothers again. This time it would be for moose, mountain caribou, and grizzly bear.

On October 4, 1984, we (Dr. Lou Elorza and I) landed at Hyland Post. Unstable weather kept us close to base camp, where we hunted moose along the Spatsizi River. After a few days, there was a break in the weather, so we (Dr. Elorza, Reg Collingswood, Tim Mervyn, the wrangler, and I) headed out to Upper Ross camp to hunt on the Blueberry Plateau. We arrived about six hours later, and set up camp, with Lou making supper while Reg and I scanned the mountains and spotted several caribou herds. That night, we heard and observed many wolves on the outskirts of our camp. The next morning, we headed out in crisp air and fresh snow from the night before. As we were hunting, we could see the wolf tracks following us along our trail.

We arrived at the top of the mountain just before noon. We encountered a lone bull caribou along the way that Reg said was both shootable and over 350 points. A closer evaluation showed the caribou was following tracks up to the high plateau where the deeper snow was. Figuring the caribou had a better sense of where he was going and would probably be joining the rest of the herd, we kept pace with him. He lead us up to a large basin. Here we spotted a herd of 20 caribou, with one trophy bull in the middle and three respectable bulls on the outside. The lead bull constantly took runs at the three anxious companions, but they were unwilling to take him on. With all this courting going on, the caribou didn't seem alarmed with either the horses or hunter, who was about 40 yards off.

Reg's assessment of this bull was that it was heavy in the bezes and double shoveled. Reg continued to glass the area, and he spotted another herd of 40 in which he found one truly massive bull caribou. He told me this was the one to go after. We planned our approach. We were able to get to within 20 yards of the herd, as this magnificent bull seemed more occupied with keeping his harem in line than watching us. I was having trouble getting an opportunity to shoot, as the large bull always kept 5 to 10 caribou around him. But, soon enough the opportunity arose when the herd broke into a run and the bull came out into the open. I took a single shot and the caribou was down. Reg commented that I had probably taken the new World's Record.

Back at Hyland, rough measurements were taken. But because of the uniqueness and peculiar points, it was difficult to arrive at a final score. The rack has beams of 47 inches, with a total of 51 points, double shovels, and an inside spread of 41 4/8 inches. The most unique factors of the rack are the width and the heavy main beams. There were two offshoot points with lengths of 18 and 30 4/8 inches. Rough scoring of the rack varied from 442 to 465 5/8 points.

After arriving back at Hyland Post and measuring the caribou, we found that the same grizzly that had been in the camp the previous year was pulling the same tricks. He had torn up the meat house, making off with a goat hide, moose quarter, etc. He also tore up a brand new tent that had been put up down river. I was anxious to get the grizzly, so I stayed up for two straight nights, but he didn't show. The third night, I stayed up again. Just at the break of morning, the bear started tearing boards off the meat house. I watched the bear from about 10 yards away in the wrangler cabin. When the bear moved around the corner of the meat house, I shot him. The bear dropped. I watched him lay for a minute, all of a sudden he stood up. I let off another shot and had him. This put an end to a most eventful trip for me and a fine ending for the hunt at Hyland Post.

Photograph by Charlie Crunden

At the 19th Awards (Las Vegas, 1986), John A. Kolar accepts the First Award for his mountain caribou from Dr. Philip L. Wright, Chairman of the Records Committee.

Photograph by Charlie Crunden

At the 19th Awards (Las Vegas, 1986), Elmer R. Kochans accepts the Third Award for his mountain caribou from Dr. Philip L. Wright, Chairman of the Records Committee.

Photograph by Wm. H. Nesbitt

MOUNTAIN CARIBOU
THIRD AWARD
SCORE: 411 1/8

Locality: Keele River, N. W. T.   Date: August 1981
Hunter: Elmer R. Kochans

MOUNTAIN CARIBOU 411⅛

Elmer R. Kochans

In February of 1980, I began to plan a hunt in the Northwest Territories, in the Mackenzie Mountain Range for sheep, barren ground caribou, and grizzly. I guess I could call this hunt both agony and ecstasy. I've been hunting big game in North America for some 15 years now. I know with most hunts there is some agony, but with this hunt it started before we got afield. My partner, Don Hoemke, and I had done the usual homework, selecting Skyline Outfitters for a Dall's sheep hunt. Skyline is owned and operated by Bill Moynihan, whose camps are located about 100 miles northeast of Norman Wells. Deposits were mailed in February of 1980 for a hunt in the fall of 1981.

Before I go into any detail of great length, let me give you some background information into the agonies of this hunt. First, my partner (Don) became seriously ill. After several months of tests, it was determined major surgery would be required. He would have to cancel on our hunt.

In July, six weeks before the hunt, I spent an eventful weekend at my lakeside cottage in northern Michigan. After spending a day on the boat, I jumped from the boat to the dock. Suddenly I found myself on my left shoulder instead of my feet. The final diagnosis was a broken elbow.

A couple of days before it would be time to leave, I went to the doctor for x-rays and a decision. I had about 60 percent usage of the arm. I could straighten it enough to reach the forearm of my Sako 7mm. The fracture was about 70 percent healed. My doctor advised me to be careful, and to tuck it in if I fell.

Forty-eight hours before flight time, the air traffic controllers walked out on strike. The Canadians supported the Americans and would not allow American planes in Canada. I switched to Air Canada, but I had to go on stand-by for the first leg to Winnipeg. I made the flight, and from there on it became sheer ecstasy.

We stayed overnight in Edmonton. I say we, because I met my hunting partner at the airport. C.W. Conn was able to replace Don on short notice from his home in Beaumont, Texas. This was his first big game hunt outside Texas.

We left for Norman Wells at 7:00 a.m. It took four hours to reach Yellowknife, and then about two hours more to Norman Wells. By noon, we were in a four-place Piper Cub, headed for camp about 100 miles southwest. The main camp was located on Godlin Lake, in a beautiful valley. Moynihan has two other camps, Ram Head (a backpack camp) and Mackenzie (a river camp). Boats are used to hunt game along the river. Hunting from the main camp was with horses, using spike camps. That was the method we selected.

The next morning, we packed up and headed for Caribou Pass, about a 25 mile trip. About 10 miles out, we spotted a grizzly. C.W. attempted a stalk; he was unsuccessful. We set up temporary camp for the night; we would continue hunting the next morning.

About noon, we spotted another grizzly about a half-mile away on a hillside. With C.W. spotting for us, we took off. The stalk took us across the Ekway River, which is about 100 feet wide and two feet deep. We took off our boots to make the crossing. The horses were left with C.W. Keeping an eye on C.W., we started to climb. After two ours of searching, there was still no sign of the bear.

That night, we made camp at Caribou Pass, along the Ekway River. This would be home for the next 10 days. The mountains weren't too high, 6,000 to 8,000 feet. There was no timber, just some scrub brush. We really had to scrounge for firewood. Ernie Muvhill, my guide, proved to be a great outdoorsman and a super guide. He didn't talk much, but that was O.K. too.

On the first full day of hunting, the weather was poor, with light rain and some fog. We could not see the mountaintops. Ernie suggested we go look for caribou. After about two hours in the saddle, we turned up a valley with high, rolling hills on both sides and the greenest grass I've ever seen. It looked like a never-ending golf fairway. It was magnificent. As I rode along, crossing little streams here and there, I was so at peace with the world that I think I forgot why I was there.

About an hour into the valley, Ernie dismounted and pointed to a knoll about a mile away where there were eight caribou. Looking through the spotting scope, they all looked like bulls, and two or three were big. It looked like it would be an easy stalk. Wrong. every time we got close enough to look, they would move away from us. Finally, we came around the side of the hill. When we peeked, they were looking right at us, and they were on the move. But, they were in range. Ernie suggested that I hit the fourth one from the lead. I shot. I hit him low and too far back. He made a right turn, going straight up the hill. My second shot was high over his front shoulder, but it spun him around. My third shot was high in the left shoulder. He was dead when he hit the ground at 250 paces.

This was my first mountain caribou. He would score $452\tfrac{5}{8}$ points for Safari Club, and $417\tfrac{3}{8}$ points for entry into Boone and Crockett. The National Rifle Association awarded me the N.R.A. Silver Bullet Award for him.

The weather cleared, with temperatures ranging from a low of 20 degrees at night to a high of 60 in the day, perfect for sheep hunting. Two days of hunting produced only lambs and ewes. On the third day, late in the afternoon, we spotted three rams. One, we thought, would go over 40 inches. It was too late for a stalk that night.

We started out the next morning, after the rams of the previous day. We got to where they had been, but we couldn't spot them. Then, Ernie saw the big one about three miles away and up high. We started out not knowing if we could even get close to them. About an hour later, and a half-mile up a shale slide, I saw what appeared to be two sheep. But, I had spotted so many "stone rams", I didn't say anything to Ernie until I put the glasses on them. We were indeed looking at two rams. A look through the spotting scope showed that one was a young ram, not quite full-curl. The other one was a full-curl, but might not go 40 inches. It looked like an easy climb, so we took off for a closer look.

After about an hour's climbing, we came out above them. The bigger of the two rams was smaller than we thought, maybe 36 inches. We were about to leave, when Ernie noticed something about the ram's rear leg. We took a closer look. Something was wrong. At about 100 yards, we stood up to see what he would do. He got up and started to move away. He seemed all right until he started up the hill. The leg seemed useless. Our consensus opinion was that he wouldn't make it through the winter. His cape just came back from the tanner, and the mount should be ready in a couple of weeks. I doubt that too many people will know he only measures 36 inches.

By the way, Don Hoemke's surgery was successful and he is well on the road to recovery.

Photograph by Wm. H. Nesbitt

WOODLAND CARIBOU
FIRST AWARD
SCORE: 347

Locality: Rocky Pond, Nfld.   Date: October 1984
Hunter: Gordon J. Birgbauer, Jr.

WOODLAND CARIBOU 347

Gordon J. Birgbauer, Jr.

It was the middle of October, and I was hunting with Fred Webb and Gerry Phumphrey in the Long Range Mountains of southwestern Newfoundland. Fred is a professional hunter, developing and operating hunts in several areas of northern Canada. I had enjoyed successful trips with him that ranged from bear hunting in New Brunswick to caribou hunting with the Eskimos up on Ungava Bay. So, when he told me that although I had hunted Newfoundland for several years with other outfitters, he thought I would be happy giving him and Gerry a try, I went along with the idea. He pointed out that Gerry had several camps, strategically located in one of the finest areas of the Island, and would provide an all-out effort.

The first couple of hunts were for moose only, but I could see that with Gerry's flying skills and ambition to satisfy the clients, the chances for a successful moose-woodland caribou hunt were excellent. The 1984 hunt was set up with that in mind.

Fred advised me that when planning a mixed bag hunt, it's best to keep in mind that although several species may be in season at the same time, usually any particular week is not best for all of them and the best hunting for all may not be in the same immediate area. On this hunt we had picked a top week for moose and a fairly good one for caribou. We also planned that if the need arose, we would move from one part of the area to another.

Three days' hunting, camping out with a guide named Harvey, produced a moose. Not a records book animal, but decent for an eastern Canada moose, and one that would provide mighty fine fare for my game dinner which we put on annually for a good number of sportsman friends in our home area. As caribou sign had been observed in other areas, Gerry decided to bring us into Hungry Grove (one of the main camps), for a comfortable night and a couple of good meals put on by the ladies there. Here, I parted with Harvey and was introduced to Tom, a younger guide, who would accompany me on the caribou portion of the hunt.

That evening, plans were made for another camp-out, starting the next day. Apparently this was going to be a late fall; the caribou just were not herding up in the usual manner and they were not passing through the normal range near the permanent camps. It was planned, therefore, to make spike camps in an area lying between two of the camps, in hopes of intercepting some of the small bunches gradually working through the country.

At midnight, the sky was clear, and the lake dead calm. The wind started to rise a few hours before dawn. At first light, Gerry and Fred arrived in the float plane, in a rising gusty wind, which they reported was much worse up on top of the plateau. Regretfully, it was decided that the only safe course was to tie the aircraft down, go back to planning and telling tall tales, and wait until conditions improved.

Finally, late in the afternoon, the wind swung around and lessened a bit. Gerry was not long in depositing Tom and me, with a minimum of gear, in another chain of lakes east of Fox Hole Brook, where our chances of seeing caribou should be excellent.

Camping in the lee of a knoll where we were out of the wind, we spent a reasonably comfortable night. Glassing from the top shortly after sunup revealed several groups of caribou filtering down in our direction. One group in particular seemed to contain at least a couple of really good stags, so we started moving in a direction to intercept them if they held to their present course. Further glassing convinced me that one stag in particular looked pretty impressive, even though not as immense as the Quebec-Labrador caribou I had seen on other hunts.

By now, the herd was moving along at a fairly good rate so that it became necessary to close in more quickly before they got out of range. At last, we got into the position we wanted. I rested my .300 Winchester Magnum on my back pack and prepared for the shot. With a bit of luck at having the stag stop for a second, without being hidden by the other animals, he was mine.

While the congratulations and the picture-taking were going on, it began to dawn on me that this was really quite a caribou. Tom kept telling me, while he was caping it out, that while he didn't know what it took to enter the records books, this was as good a stag as he had ever seen on the ground.

Sometimes everything seems to go right. Back at camp, Gerry and Fred had talked things over, deciding that since Gerry had to fly out for supplies, it would be a good idea to take a pass over us to see how we were making out. Spotting my stag on the ground, Gerry landed nearby. In short order, we had carried gear, meat, cape and antlers to the plane and we were quickly moved over to Hungry Grove camp again.

Within a few minutes, Fred had the measuring tape out and was writing down figures on the back of a beer box. As he became more impressed, he dug out some Boone and Crockett and SCI forms and did a more careful job. When he finished, his advice was, "Gordon, we better not split that rack for transportation. I know it will go fairly high in both books, so you had better take it to official scorers as soon as you are able."

As it turned out, it did exceed the then number one SCI animal, and eventually it ended-up number two in the new edition, edged out by another tremendous stag taken in Newfoundland the same season. Boone and Crockett officially scored it for entry as 347⁶⁄₈ points.

Not every hunt can be a "records book hunt," but all of them are enjoyable. I have hunted with Fred and Gerry since then, and I am returning again this fall, always on the quest for the bigger one.

Photo Courtesy of David H. Crum

David H. Crum and guide pose with Crum's fine mountain caribou taken in the Yukon in 1984 near the Pelly River. It scores 392 points.

Photo Courtesy of Don B. Skidmore

Saddler's Lake, Newfoundland, was the site of Don Skidmore's 1983 hunt for woodland caribou that resulted in this fine animal that scores 278⅝ points to qualify for the Awards records book.

Photograph by Wm. H. Nesbitt

WOODLAND CARIBOU
SECOND AWARD
SCORE: 334 1/8

Locality: King George Lake, Nfld.   Date: October 1984
Hunter: John R. Blanton

WOODLAND CARIBOU 334 1/8

John R. Blanton

Don Corley, Dr. Don Senter, and I departed from Dallas for Corner Brook, Newfoundland, on October 6, 1984. We were met at midnight by Joe Peddle, our outfitter, and continued on to a rustic lodge to spend the night.

Sunday morning was started with a hearty breakfast, and we enjoyed the spectacular view. Don Senter and I left by float plane for Top Lake, where we were met by brothers Garland and George, who were our guides. There, Don and I checked our rifles and gear and prepared for the following day's hunt. Newfoundland doesn't permit hunting on Sundays.

We were up and ready before daylight, and we began our search on hilly terrain. The tundra was extremely wet and the temperature was in the 20's. I immediately knew I had brought the wrong boots; leather rather than rubber.

Don Corley had hunted the area before. He had reassured me prior to the hunt that this would be fairly easy conditions to get my caribou. It didn't take long to decide that I'd been misled! My boots were soaked through. I was cold and really disappointed with the lack of game. We had walked over 20 miles and had seen only a few small caribou and two moose.

Upon returning to camp that evening, we found that Dr. Senter had taken a fine caribou that should make the next records book. During a late, candlelight supper, I discovered Don had only seen a few caribou and moose. I frankly didn't think my chances were good to take a book animal.

The next morning, October 9, 1984, Garland (my guide) and I were up for another hike. We borrowed Dr. Senter's spotting scope, which was a great help. It was foggy, with low visibility that made it almost impossible to hunt. By 10:00 a.m., the weather began to break.

While we were spotting and glassing, we noticed a nice caribou herd on the horizon. I quickly spotted a magnificent trophy. As I watched him, cold chills ran down my back. After walking three hours, we finally got within range of the herd as they grazed. As we approached, we were fortunate to find cover in some rocks, quite close to two small bulls about 200 yards away. We thought they might spook the entire herd.

We crawled and laid on our stomachs for about two hours, getting soaked and tired, but also enjoying the terrific view of the animals. When "my" bull was challenged by several other bulls, he made it clear that he was in charge.

Still about 500 yards away, we worked our way in, frightening some of the smaller bulls, which started the herd moving. I missed the first shot, but the second was a direct hit in the heart. He took a nose dive and died instantly We knew as we came nearer that he should score high in both the SCI and Boone and Crockett Club records books.

Don Senter and I continued hunting for several days for moose. Not seeing any large bulls, we decided to return to Dallas and thereby ran into difficulty. Our trip was delayed because of extremely high wind. In spite of this rough weather, the float plane took Don and me back to Corner Brook. Don, an experienced pilot, was co-piloting out of Top Lake. Some moorings had broken loose on a load of timber being shipped on the river, so that the river was almost jammed with floating logs. After several unsuccessful landing attempts, we had to land among the logs! Several of them hit the plane, but luckily caused no damage to us or the plane. Don commented that it was about the roughest flight he had ever encountered.

After a good dinner and bath, Don Senter and I returned to Dallas. We left our good friend Don Corley behind to seek his records book caribou.

Photo Courtesy of Linda Corley

Still velvet-covered, this fine barren ground caribou was shot by Linda Corley at Iliamna Lake, Alaska, in 1983. It scores 428-5/8 points.

Photo Courtesy of Madeline M. Kellyhouse

Madeline Kelleyhouse hunted along Joseph Creek in Alaska in 1984 to find her barren ground caribou that scores 405-5/8 points.

Photograph by Wm. H. Nesbitt

BARREN GROUND CARIBOU
FIRST AWARD
SCORE: 453

Locality: Alaska Pen., Alaska   Date: October 1984
Hunter: Ken Higginbotham

BARREN GROUND CARIBOU 453

Ken Higginbotham

(Editor's note: this story about Ken Higgenbotham's hunt was contributed by his guide on this hunt, Lee Todd.)

It was October 7, 1984. Mike Cowan and I had just finished packing in the meat from a caribou that our client, Jerry Tkac, from Houston had taken the day before. As always, the wind was blowing and the air was full of the fresh clean smell that the wind carries as it blows across the Alaska Peninsula. It's an odor made from salt water and salt grass mist, along with the poignant smell of the muskeg swamps that are present throughout the flats. The pack across the tundra and swamps is always tiring, but the work and wet conditions make you feel alive and part of this wild and beautiful land. The last leg of the trip had been longer than the rest. When we arrived, we plopped down on the ground, slipped the packframes off our shoulders and treated ourselves to a couple of candy bars. Mike and I were guiding from a tent camp for Keith Johnson, whose operation is based at Wildman Lake Lodge on the Alaska Peninsula.

After a few minutes rest, and another chocolate bar, we were feeling better so Mike started tidying up the camp. Since he seemed to have things well in hand, I decided to take a short break to try to shoot some movies of a band of caribou that we had spotted about a half-mile from camp. The last time we had seen them, they were bedded behind a low ridge that was out of sight of camp. I didn't take any great pains to execute a good stalk, after all they were only caribou.

As I was walking up on them, still about 300 yards off, I was spotted and the herd jumped up and started to move. Quite often a startled herd will go off only a little ways, then circle around to try and see what it was that had disturbed them. This time, I could tell by their actions that they were going to keep right on going. It was a small group with only 18 cows and two bulls in the herd; but boy did I do a double-take when I saw the second bull! I have seen hundreds of bulls in this country, and a lot of them have been Boone and Crockett trophies, but I knew without a doubt this was the biggest caribou I had ever seen.

At first, I just wanted to drop down and watch the bull through my binoculars. But, a trophy like this doesn't turn up often, and I wanted to get something on film to prove what I had seen. Excitedly, I set up the tripod, zoomed and focused the lens, and set about exposing some footage. Even as I was shooting, I knew that I was wasting flim, for by this time the herd was a long way off and moving fast. How I wished that I had taken just a little time to execute a good stalk so that I could have been close enough to get some good footage. More importantly, I was disgusted that I had run such a fine animal away from our spike camp. If we got him now, we were going to have to be real lucky, and there would be a lot of extra work. The best thing I could do now would be to watch where the herd went so that we could have a chance later on.

I returned to camp for Mike, and together we climbed the lookout hill near camp. As I was setting up my spotting scope, a snow squall moved in, obscuring visibility for some time. When the squall finally passed, we could find no trace of the herd. We were just settling down for a long wait when we heard the drone of an approaching airplane. We had been expecting Keith, so we hurried down to camp.

Keith had come in to pick up Mike and a load of meat for the return flight to the lodge. I excitedly told Keith about the big bull, while Mike lost no time jumping in the cub. Keith assured me that he would return later in the day with a hunter for me.

I still wanted to locate the herd, so I returned to the lookout hill, knowing they had probably left the country, but still hoping to see the big bull again. Finally, about four hours later, I got a glimpse of him about two miles away as he was disappearing over a range of hills with his cows. He stopped for just a moment, skylined on the ridge. I had a chance to once again admire the big rack as I watched through my spotting scope; then he disappeared.

Daylight was rapidly slipping away, and I was beginning to worry that Keith would not return with a hunter. If that happened, the bull would surely get away as any hunter coming in tomorrow would not be legal to hunt until still another night had passed. I had just about given up hope when I heard the cub in the distance. By the time I was back at camp, its big tundra tires had touched down and were bumping across the strip. As the cub pulled up to the tent, the door dropped open and I could see Ken Higginbotham sitting in the back seat. Keith swung himself out of the plane, followed by Ken, having just a little bit of trouble extracting his long frame from the awkward passenger seat of the cub.

No introduction was necessary, as Ken and I had hunted together two years earlier when he took a caribou that narrowly missed the record book. Ken is an ex-pro football player, an enthusiastic hunter, and always a pleasure to hunt with. After the usual ritual of shaking hands and good luck wishes, Keith climbed back into the cub and flew off in the last minutes of daylight.

The lantern burned late that night as Ken and I talked over what had happened in our lives since we had last hunted together. There were a lot of things to talk about, but the big caribou I had seen that day kept popping into our conversation. His rack kept growing in size, until finally I was telling Ken the bull could be a new World's Record. I didn't sleep well that night, as I was half convinced that we wouldn't be able to find the big bull in the morning. At this time of year the caribou are forming large herds and are almost constantly on the move, traveling at a ground-eating pace that leaves the hunter on foot no alternative but to wait for another herd to come by. The last I had seen of our small band, they were traveling steadily away from camp and by tomorrow morning they could be 20 miles away. There wasn't any point in mentioning that to Ken, as I could tell by the tossing and turning that he wasn't sleeping very well. Goodness knows he would need his rest.

We were up and fed long before daylight, and we were sitting on the lookout hill at the first light. Before us were several small herds, a few containing some respectable bulls, but nothing even approaching the size of the big one we were looking for. We knew the animal we were looking for and there wasn't any point in just sitting there. So, after about 15 minutes of glassing, we headed in the direction that I had last seen the big bull and his harem of cows.

We walked at a steady pace, working our way through the rolling hills, and easing over the top of each ridge in hopeful anticipation of finding our quarry behind each one of them. Three hours went by, with no sign of the big bull, but we kept moving steadily until we came into sight of a pinnacle about a quarter-mile away. I suggested to Ken that we should work our way toward it as a potential rest point. This was the best lookout in the area. If the bull was anywhere in the vicinity, we should be able to locate him from there. Ken was in full agreement, so we changed our course and made for the hill.

The tension and excitement had been rising and falling all morning. I knew that our last hope rested on the success of this lookout. Normally, when caribou hunting, we could have just walked to the top and had a look around. But, I wasn't about to make the same mistake with this herd that I had done yesterday when I tried to take a few casual pictures.

Just before we topped out on the summit, I dropped my pack and rifle and eased up to the crest. Just like a sheep hunter, I pushed back my cap and gently lifted my forehead and eyes to a point just above the crowberry tussocks, hidden by the tufts of saltgrass that grew on the summit. As I lifted myself up onto my elbows, I spotted the first of several caribou. There, about 300 yards away, was a small herd of about 20 animals. I didn't need my binoculars to know that the big bull in the middle of the herd was the bull we were after.

I dropped to my belly and slid back down a few feet to talk to Ken. I was really happy to have found our animal. As I looked at the excitement in Ken's eyes when I told him that the bull was just over the hill, I wasn't disappointed. Quickly, I grabbed my spotting scope and tripod and crawled back up to the crest. There was no doubt that it was the same fellow I had seen the day before. I set the scope up just to admire the bull, and I told Ken to have a look. This almost proved to be a mistake. Ken's eye wasn't at the scope more than a couple of seconds before he had grabbed his rifle and jacked a round into the chamber. "Ken," I whispered, "I think we can get a little closer by slipping back down the hill, and then move in under and over that small rise." "No, I think we are close enough," he responded. "You say it's about 300 yards?" I confirmed the range and helped him get in a position to shoot. I had seen Ken and his .270 perform in the past, and I had no doubts that he would do just fine.

Pulling the rifle into his shoulder, Ken took a deep breath and squeezed the trigger. The .270 cracked, with the shot hitting low in the brisket. The bull staggered, then started to run just as Ken let go with a second round. This time, the bull went down hard. He then tried to regain his feet, but a third round put him down for good. Ken muttered something about needing to go back to the shooting range, but I feel the blame could be more directly placed on my shoulders as I probably shouldn't have let him look through the spotting scope. The excitement is a major part of the hunt, and that big rack would excite anybody. In addition, I had underestimated the range. In that wide open country, it can be extremely difficult to judge distance. When we paced it off, we found it close to 400 yards.

It took longer than usual to cape and dress out the animal, since we took frequent breaks to admire the big rack and to relive the day's experiences. A snow squall hit us while we were skinning, chilling our hands but doing little to dampen our spirits.

We both returned to camp with the cape, rack, and as much meat as we could carry. I promptly left for a second load of meat, returning an hour or two later, just as Keith had arrived. When he saw the rack, Keith was just as excited as Ken and I. Once again, we relived the hunt, and only after much backslapping and congratulations, did we get around to tying the rack on the wing struts and breaking camp.

After drying, the rack scored 454 points for entry into the Boone and Crockett records, while Safari Club scored the rack as a new SCI record.

Photo Courtesy of Robert Jacobson

Robert Jacobson is all smiles with his big barren ground caribou from the South Fork of the Kuskokwim River, Alaska. Taken in 1982, Jacobson's bull scores 407 7/8 points.

Photo Courtesy of Charles F. Nadler

Charles F. Nadler is at left with his fine barren ground caribou that scores 416 points and was taken in the Alaska Range, Alaska. Mrs. Nadler and son hold other trophies from a memorable hunt for the family.

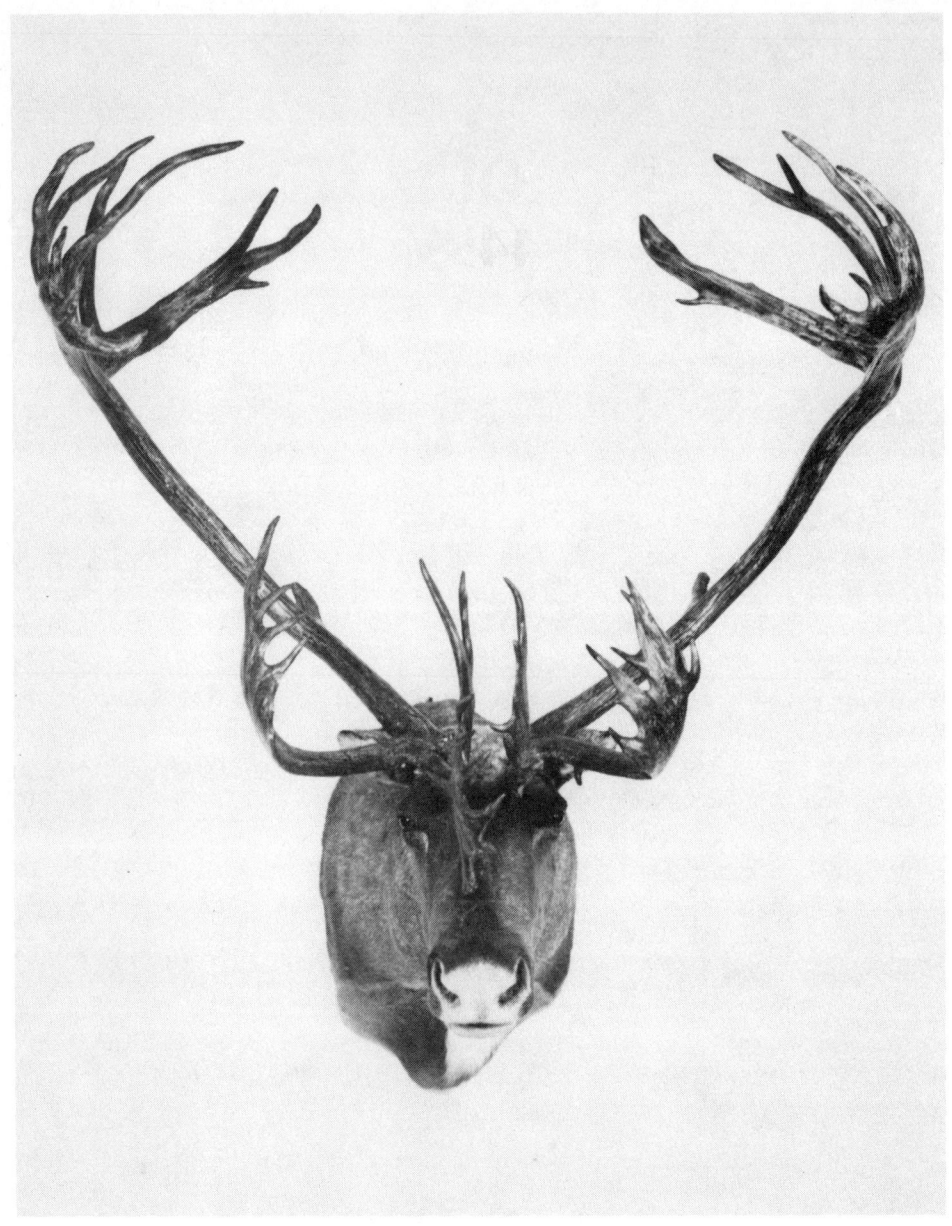

Photograph by Wm. H. Nesbitt

BARREN GROUND CARIBOU
SECOND AWARD
SCORE: 449 6/8

Locality: Lake Clark, Alaska   Date: August 1984
Hunter: Dennis Burdick

BARREN GROUND CARIBOU
449 6/8

Dennis Burdick

My first trip to Alaska (September of 1981) was a cold, snowy ordeal. I sighted only one caribou in a two-week period, and he was not close enough for a shot. Harvesting a caribou with my bow has been a life-long dream, so I returned to Alaska in August of 1984.

Since we did not have a guide, my hunting partners (Keith Hynes and his sons Neil and Troy) and I decided to drop-camp on a small lake, then hunting above timber line on a group of high rocky ridges.

It was about 10:00 a.m., when we spotted this large caribou grazing across an open area about 400 yards below us. We were amazed at the size of his antlers. Being the senior members of the hunting party, Keith and I were elected to try a stalk. We carefully descended a steep draw of slide-rock, trying very hard not to dislodge loose rocks and spook the animal.

We had to make a fast stalk to intercept him, as he was grazing at a fast walk. As we worked our way closer, there was a patch of bushes about 30 yards in diameter between us and the caribou. We paused for a moment, then deciding that Keith would circle the lower side while I took the upper. As I crept along the edge of the bushes, my heart began to pound and I began to shake, realizing that at any second I might get a shot at my first caribou. As I reached the far end, my heart began to sink as there was nothing in sight. I thought, "Oh, no, he has given us the slip." All at once, my caribou trotted to within 50 yards and stood quartered toward me.

I drew my 85 pound bow and shot. My arrow struck him in a perfect spot. He traveled about 200 yards. and went down. I have always been a do-it-yourself hunter, and I feel very fortunate to have taken such an outstanding trophy animal.

Photograph by Wm. H. Nesbitt

CENTRAL CANADA BARREN GROUND CARIBOU
FIRST AWARD
SCORE: 408 2/8

Locality: Courageous Lake, N. W. T.   Date: August 1985
Hunter: Raymond H. Bonar

CENTRAL CANADA BARREN GROUND CARIBOU 408 2/8

Raymond H. Bonar

It was not a great day. In fact, it was raining heavily; but, sometimes that's the way it goes in caribou hunting. Ray Bonar and his guide, Barry Taylor of Quivik, Ltd., studied the bull caribou. It was probably as good as they were going to find. It was time to make the decision. They decided that Bonar should take it.

It was just the first day of the hunt. Ray Bonar had arrived on August 19, 1985, from his home in Edmonton, Alberta. He wanted to hunt the beautiful Central Canada barren ground caribou, the new category being recognized by the Boone and Crockett Club. There were certainly caribou in the area, and Quivik knew its business well. The guides were able to get him close to the caribou, where they could both study them to decide whether the trophy animal that they were seeking was there.

Ray settled into a good shooting position with his .300 Weatherby Magnum, and then gently squeezed the trigger. The distance was only 150 yards, a very easy shot for this rifle.

As Ray and his guide admired his trophy, they were both awed by its huge rack. Later, after all the dust of the 19th Big Game Awards Final Judging had settled, Ray Bonar's big bull would be recognized as the largest hunter-taken trophy for the category, just a smidgen less than the world's record trophy, which turned out to be a picked up set of antlers.

Photograph by Wm. H. Nesbitt

CENTRAL CANADA BARREN GROUND CARIBOU
SECOND AWARD
SCORE: 395 3/8

Locality: Courageous Lake, N. W. T.   Date: September 1985
Hunter: George O. Poston

CENTRAL CANADA BARREN GROUND CARIBOU 395 3/8

George O. Poston

There's always a great deal of excitement in hunting for a trophy in a new category. For one thing, there isn't the background of information available on how to judge trophy quality, nor are enough specimens available to familiarize yourself with them before you go hunting. Such was the case with George Poston's hunt for the new category of Central Canada barren ground caribou. But, he had a strong advantage in hunting with several hunters who had previously hunted these caribou. Their experience and advice were welcome to him.

Poston hunted at Courageous Lake, some 150 miles north-northeast of Yellowknife, N.W.T. He arrived in the hunting area on September 14, 1985. Only one day later, they found his big bull. It was just 1:35 p.m., and the distance was 300 yards. George's guide, an employee of Quivik, Ltd., told George he'd better shoot. They wouldn't get a better chance at such a big bull. George settled in for the shot. His gun was a .25-06, certainly flat-shooting enough to do the job well. And, it did.

As George and his guide admired the big bull, George felt very satisfied. He had a mighty fine trophy, and now he could spend the next couple of days relaxing in camp and maybe doing a little fishing.

Photograph by Wm. H. Nesbitt

CENTRAL CANADA BARREN GROUND CARIBOU
THIRD AWARD
SCORE: 382 2/8

Locality: Courageous Lake, N. W. T.   Date: September 1985
Hunter: Earle H. Harder

CENTRAL CANADA BARREN GROUND CARIBOU 382 2/8

Earle H. Harder

It was September 9, 1985, and the weather was beautiful. Not at all like the blustery snow squalls my wife, Dorothy, and I experienced the first morning in Yellowknife. This was our second trip to the Northwest Territories to hunt Central Canada barren ground caribou. Last year, I had hunted hard for a week but managed only to spot a few small groups. I had made my mind up not to shoot unless it was a respectable trophy.

I knew this year it would be different. It had started well, as Dorothy and I fished Blachford Lake for two days prior to heading North to Courageous Lake with Mike Freeland of Quavvik Ltd.

As the old World War II Beaver droned north towards the Arctic Circle, and the trees gave way to endless lakes and open tundra, my thoughts drifted to the inscription written in a copy of Mark Califf's book on caribou given to me at the end of my last hunt. It read, "1984 Courageous Lake, N.W.T. NO CARIBOU EVERYWHERE." We saw no caribou on the flight to camp, and I could easily reflect on the days when the Inuits must have waited, and felt the emptiness.

Next morning, after the early mist had vanished and the hearty camp breakfast was consumed, our guide (Don Mercier), Dorothy, and I set out to hunt the northwest end of the lake. It was one of those rare picture-perfect days: still, beautiful, and cool.

An hour or so out of camp, we began to see small groups of caribou and some scattered individuals. Nothing good, but spirits were high and through the binoculars the caribou looked beautiful silhouetted against the bright colors of the autumn tundra.

We all spotted the small band of five bulls at the same time, as they picked their way up the side of the large eskar two miles away. As we approached closer, Dorothy said, "Look at the old gray one—he's the one you want".

It is amazing how fast caribou can travel over the tundra. As the small group topped the eskar, we knew it was useless to give chase. Disappointed as I was, I realized it was only the first day.

We continued traveling along the lakeshore for another two or three miles, then headed overland. As we topped a steep eskar, Don, who was leading, said, "Get down. I think it's the same group." With my heart pounding, Don and I crept forward while Dot retreated to a large rock off to our right.

The caribou were not spooked, and they were angling towards us. But, I could not see the old, gray fellow I wanted, so I inched forward. Just then, one of the large bulls topped a small ridge and walked directly toward Dorothy. He stopped 50 yards from her, staring at the rock that she was hiding behind. I strained to peek over the ridge to see the old fellow. The wind was gentle and tricky, and I wondered how long it would be before the entire group spooked.

Carefully I inched on my belly to the top of the eskar where I could make out the top of a beautiful set of antlers approximately 150 yards away. If he would just take a few steps, or if I could just raise up a little more, a shot would be possible.

Without warning, the magnificent animal stepped clear and I saw the antlers clearly through the 3 x 9 Leupold scope. I had my shot; but, I had to make sure I had enough elevation to clear the ground cover.

The silence was broken as the 140 grain 7mm Nosler from my 7x57 Ackley Improved sped to its target. The animal gave no hint of being hit as it turned and moved away with the other bulls. However, as the other animals climbed the eskar, my bull turned and went down the slope. The little Gentry custom rifle spoke again. Both bullets penetrated the lungs of the big bull and exited. He went down.

My hunt was over, but the work was just starting. The warm sunshine brought the tundra to life with swarms of blackflies that certainly made themselves felt as we packed the meat and hide.

When the antlers were scored at camp that evening, it was beyond my wildest expectations. A dream come true and well worth the extra year's wait.

Photos Courtesy of Kaye Poston and Warren St. Germaine

Two fine Central Canada barren ground caribou. (l) Kaye Poston's bull from Courageous Lake, N. W. T., in 1983 scores 357 1/8 points. (r) Warren St. Germaine hunted near Winter Lake, N. W. T., in 1985 to find his bull that scores 377 5/8 points.

Photo Courtesy of Donald F. Senter

Paulatuk, N. W. T., was the site of Don Senter's hunt in 1985. His Central Canada barren ground caribou scores 350 4/8 points.

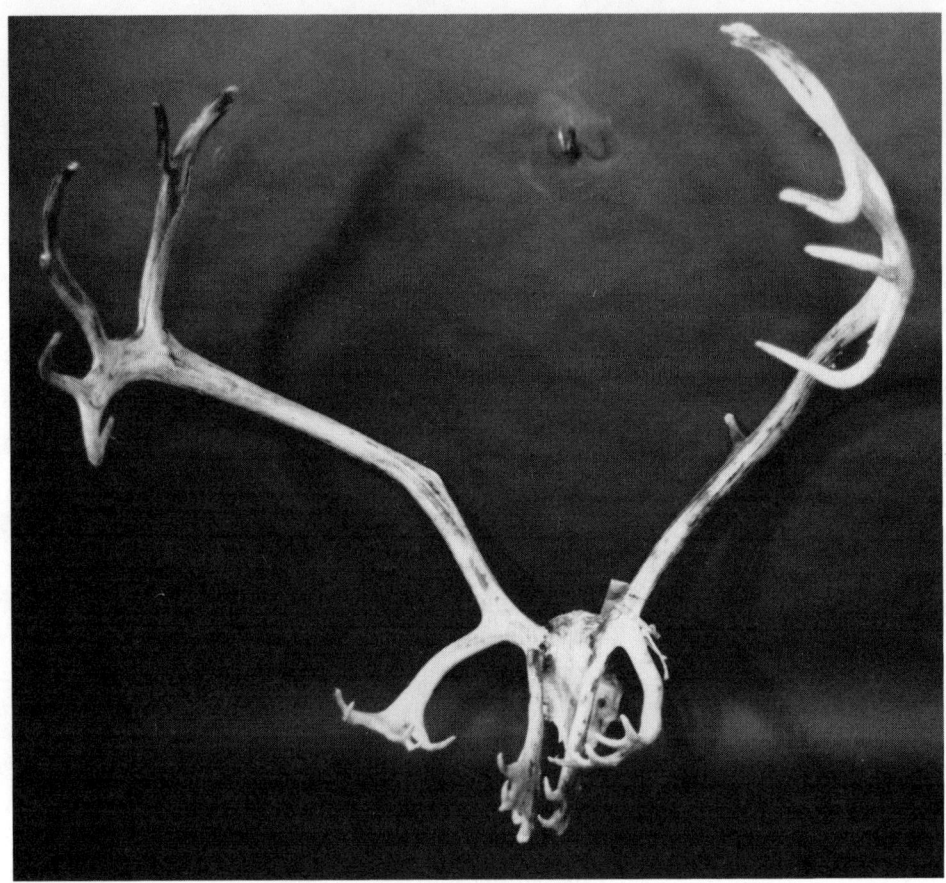

Photograph by Wm. H. Nesbitt

CENTRAL CANADA BARREN GROUND CARIBOU
FOURTH AWARD
SCORE: 369 1/8

Locality: Seahorse Lake, N. W. T.   Date: September 1985
Hunter: Barry D. Taylor

CENTRAL CANADA BARREN GROUND CARIBOU 369 1/8

Barry D. Taylor

The perfect hunting day! Sunshine, warm weather, and no wind. With me were Warren St. Germaine, Greg Robertson, and Greg's wife Ruth, all die-hard lovers of caribou hunting.

We had spent the last few days teaching big-game guiding, and this day was to be spent on practical field scoring, caping, and field care of meat. As we left camp, talk centered on the various trophies spotted the past evenings during course breaks, in particular one that bore light velvet in comparison to the normal dark, and also had the height and width to place him well up in the book. He had been spotted twice, each time at about a mile, and each time bedded down, with only the antlers showing.

About three miles back, a small group was spotted on a small rise, browsing contentedly. With no hesitation, a stalk was commenced. Our only approach would be to come in to them through some small willows with the wind at our backs. Hunkered down, away we went. Working our way through the brush, parallel to the caribou, we got to within 400 yards. Here we stripped-off our packs and began checking out the animals with binoculars and spotting scopes. "Geez, there's two good ones in there!" And there were. It must have taken 10 minutes to compare the two. One seemed a little better, but we were prejudiced. We decided to take the one with the light velvet, the same animal we had seen and admired twice before.

Well, now we had to get closer. Lining ourselves behind each other, we proceeded in a straight line to the herd, which now consisted of 14 animals. Stopping every time a head lifted, progress was slow. Eventually, we got within 150 yards; then they spooked! But that was okay, they were hemmed-in on the ridge and could only go towards camp, which would save on the packing.

Moving up to the top of the ridge, we sat down and looked over the caribou again. Our decision had been right. The light colored head was the best. Now to keep them moving towards camp. Greg and Warren would hold the rear and left side, while I took the right. But the caribou weren't in on the meeting. They abruptly headed away and to the right. A quick 200 yard dash turned them. Now they milled about, looking for a way out. This is when it gets hard. You pick out an animal, and then lose it in the crowd. Which was the good one and where did he go? There he is, going down behind the rocks. But that's not him coming out!

They took off again, this time going back toward Warren and Ruth. But where are they? I can't see them using binoculars. (Little did I know we had a ridge between us by this time.) There go the 'bou, and I don't know where the good one is! The last one has light velvet, that's him. Down quickly, it's now or never. Go for the spine, don't ruin the cape. Bang! Thwap!

He's down!

Trotting up, I see him getting up. Do it again. This time, he's down for good.

Looking him over, I did some rough scoring and guessed that the score would go in the 390's, definitely as good as any that had been taken to that date. As was remarked later, "This was definitely a course on taking big caribou."

Three days later, I guided Ray Bonar to a bull within a half-mile of the same area. His caribou green-scored 422 4/8 in velvet, a new all-time high. And, I believe there is a 450 point bull out there, somewhere. Next year will tell!

Photo Courtesy of Ernest W. Foster, Jr.

Tasituyak Lake, Labrador, was the site of Ernest W. Foster's 1985 hunt for Quebec-Labrador caribou that resulted in this fine trophy that scores 402 5/8 points.

Photo Courtesy of Don Tomberlin

Fresh out of the velvet, Don Tomberlin's huge Quebec-Labrador caribou brings a smile to his face. Shot in 1985 at Akuliak Camp, Quebec, it was scored at 439 1/8 points and received First Award at the 19th Awards.

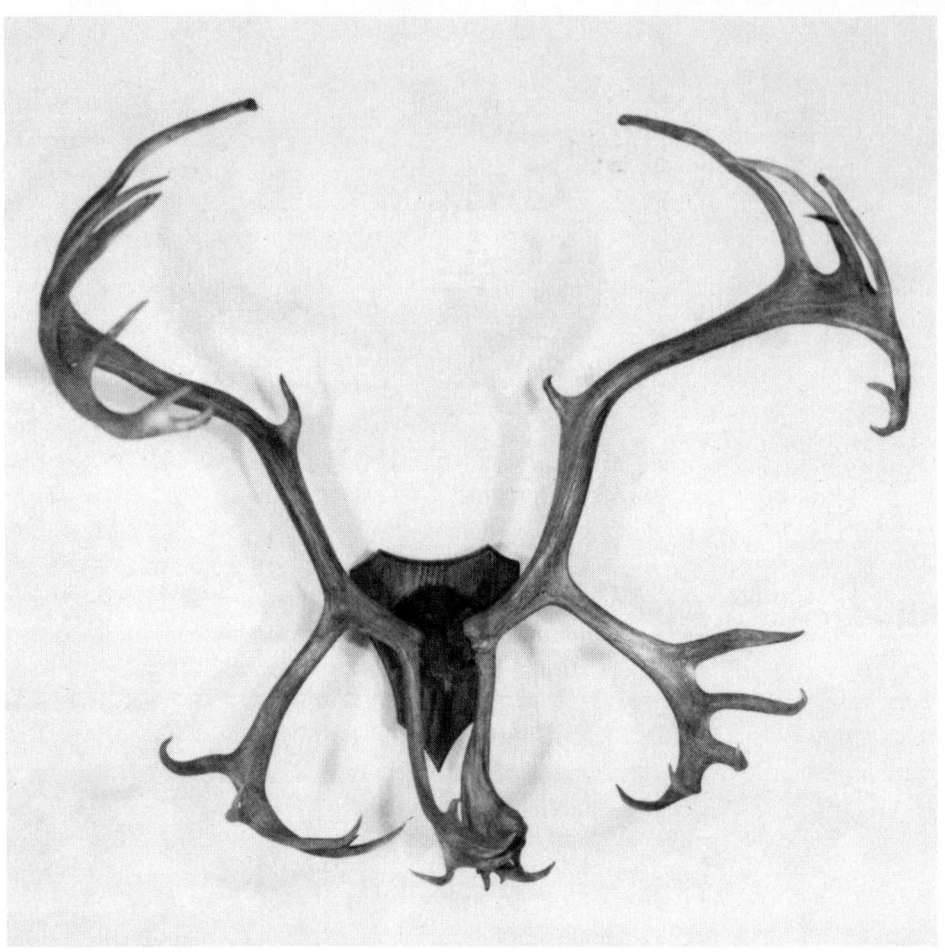

Photograph by Wm. H. Nesbitt

NEW WORLD'S RECORD CENTRAL CANADA BARREN GROUND CARIBOU
CERTIFICATE OF MERIT
SCORE: 408 6/8

Locality: Rendez-vous Lake, N. W. T.   Date: October 1982
Owner: Tom W. Barry

CENTRAL CANADA BARREN GROUND CARIBOU 408⅝

Tom W. Barry, owner

This trophy is the World's Record for the newly-established category. It is, by the Boone and Crockett Club system of trophy measurement, the largest known to be in existence for this category. It scores well over 400 points, which would make it a big caribou in any category. It's an absolutely huge trophy for the Central Canada barren ground caribou category.

This rack is from the Lac Rendez-vous area of Northwest Territories. It was found in a pine tree by Tom W. Barry. Apparently, the antlers were placed there by an Eskimo who had killed the trophy for meat. Antlers are sometimes placed this way when food animals are obtained by these native people.

Barry recognized that the huge set of antlers should be officially measured. In due course, this trophy came before the Judges Panel of the 19th Awards and they certified this trophy as the World's Record for the newly-established category.

Photograph by Wm. H. Nesbitt

QUEBEC-LABRADOR CARIBOU
FIRST AWARD
SCORE: 439 1/8

Locality: Ungava Bay, Que.   Date: September 1985
Hunter: Don Tomberlin

QUEBEC-LABRADOR CARIBOU 439 1/8

Don Tomberlin

Over coffee and doughnuts on the afternoon of our arrival at Akuliaq Camp of Arctic Adventures, Sammy Cantafio had strongly advised us that during our hunt we would be seeing a lot of caribou, and in particular a lot of big bulls.

"Take your time," he suggested, "and just look the first day. That way you will have a better idea of the size of the animals and will be better able to judge what constitutes a big trophy bull. Too many hunters shoot one of the first bulls they see and then later regret that decision. There are plenty of bulls and lots of time."

Good advice! However, we were now barely an hour-and-a-half into our first morning of hunting, watching four large bulls feeding about 200 yards below us. They all appeared big, but one was considerably larger than the others. He was carrying a large, well-proportioned rack with perfectly matched double shovels. My dilemma was this: it was very early in the hunt; I had five more days to hunt; if we could find a bull this big, this quickly, then surely we could find bigger ones; and yet, this bull was undoubtedly everything I had dreamed of and fantasized about since I had booked this hunt.

We were hunting Quebec-Labrador caribou along the southeastern shore of Ungava Bay in Northern Quebec. Hunting with me were Barry Dyar, Laurie Johnson, and Bill Gernazian from my home town of Durango, Colorado. Also with us was Gary Meine of Toronto, Canada, an old hunting companion from previous years.

After talking with a number of hunters, we had booked this hunt with Arctic Adventures of Montreal, as they had an excellent reputation for good clean camps, lots of caribou, and a very high success rate on large bulls. We had booked our hunt for September 9 through September 16, 1985.

Our guides were Inuits who lived in the area throughout the year. They proved to be very knowledgeable about the caribou in the area. Bill and I hunted together with Billy and Paul Annannak, two very fine young men who quickly became hunting partners rather than guides, which made our hunt all the more enjoyable.

We would leave the base camp early in the morning, depending upon the very high (and low) tides present in Ungava Bay, traveling in large freight canoes along the coast and up the many inlets and river mouths present in the area. From there, we would make our daily jaunt into the interior on foot. The Ungava region is composed of vast areas of large, rocky hills covered with lichens, with swampy tundra between the ridges. It made for interesting walking but was good habitat for caribou.

After mentally tossing the proverbial coin for 10 or 15 minutes, I decided to take the bull mentioned at the start of this tale. He was just too good to pass up. Besides, Quebec allows a hunter to harvest two caribou per license. Therefore, if I wanted, I could always look for a bigger bull later.

One shot later, I had my bull—and what a bull! He had 17 points on one antler and 15 on the other, with big, palmated tops and bez points. The bonus was the two, very large and symmetrical shovels. They were absolute twins. Later that evening, back at camp, we green-scored him at 401 4/8 Boone and Crockett points, well into the book.

I was totally satisfied, and also convinced that I was through hunting for this trip. I would accompany my hunting partner, Bill, while he attempted to fill his tag. I would become the "expert" trophy evaluator and assistant packer.

For the next couple of days, we scoured the lichen-covered ridges and basins, literally looking over several hundred caribou, with the majority of them good, big, mature bulls. Bill passed up several exceptional animals, always hoping that just over that next hill would be that one special trophy.

In the middle of the afternoon of our third day, Bill killed a very nice bull that narrowly missed meeting the minimum score required to make the book. As packer for the day, I was sitting on a rock catching my breath (and wishing that caribou hindquarters came equipped with wheels) when I spotted a very nice bull and a cow crossing the flats below me. The bull looked big, so I decided that my packing chores could wait while I took off to stalk these caribou.

I was carefully working my way around a large rock outcrop, when the two caribou came walking around the far end. They were about 100 yards away and feeding in my direction, so I just sat down and waited. Shortly, the bull was standing broadside, about 40 yards away and staring at the strange bump (me) staring back at him through 7 power binoculars. Every time he would start to move off, I would whistle softly and he would turn back and stare some more. We kept this up for the better part of 15 minutes, till he finally tired of the game and trotted off to catch up with the cow. All this time, I was wishing that my camera wasn't so warm and snug in the cabin back at camp.

Mentally comparing this bull with the one I had taken earlier, as well as the others that had been brought into camp, I knew that this bull was outstanding. He was definitely a once-in-a-lifetime trophy. Later that evening, I decided to spend the rest of my hunt attempting to find this big bull again. It was not a hard decision.

The next day, unfortunately, turned out to be windy, foggy, rainy and snowy. In other words, it was not a very nice day. Since our means of travel relied on canoes across the open waters of Ungava Bay, the camp manager ruled out canoe travel for the day. That left only hunting behind camp or staying in camp. We stayed in camp.

Saturday dawned little better than the day before, but there was very little wind and the horizon promised the hint of a break later on. Since it had been more than a day-and-a-half since we had last seen the big bull, our guides decided that we should take the canoe up a river inlet several miles, then hunting back toward the area where we had last seen him. Since caribou have a tendency to move around a lot, we were hoping to intercept any movements that he might have made in that time.

By noon, we had not found the big bull, but we were seriously glassing several bulls in a small basin below us. One of them was a beautiful bull with very heavily palmated tops. Bill, who had traded his rifle for a muzzleloader, decided that he would like to take this bull as it was obviously bigger than his first one. It was also in a spot where he could make the stalk close enough for a good, clean shot with his muzzleloader.

Thirty minutes later, Bill was making his final stalk and, at a distance of approximately 40 yards, took his second bull. We later scored it at 390+ Boone and Crockett points.

After lunch, we decided to hunt up a valley and across a high ridge looking for the big bull. After carefully checking out several smaller animals, we spotted two bulls bedded on the end of a long peninsula jutting out into a large lake. They were close to a mile away, and in a position where we could not tell how big they were, so we began working closer. At about a half-mile, the big one started looking better and better. We still couldn't tell if he was the one we were looking for, but the possibilities were looking good.

A short time later, we were lying on our bellies about 50 yards from the two bulls. By now, it was obvious that we had found the big bull I had so thoroughly studied two days previously. I carefully eased a shell into the chamber of my rifle and rose up on one knee. The caribou spooked, bolting toward the lake. The guides hollered not to let him get into the water, so I shot, and missed! Fortunately, the two bulls stopped at the edge of the water and turned to look back. I did not miss my second shot.

Now that we could closely examine this magnificent bull, he turned out to be bigger than any of us had imagined. He was huge! Not only was his rack big, his body was exceptionally large. Comparing his antlers with the ones already in camp, I quickly realized that I had just taken the biggest trophy of my life. Later, I would find out just how big.

We were late getting back to base camp. The following morning we green-scored my bull at $453 \frac{2}{8}$. On reaching home, I discovered that this green-score, according to the 1981 edition of *Records of North American Big Game*, would place my bull approximately number two in the all-time records. I knew that the final score made after the required 60 day drying time would be lower. However, I was confident that this would still leave my caribou high in the record listings. In late December, my bull was officially scored for entry at $440 \frac{2}{8}$, good enough to be invited to the 19th Awards Final Judging in 1986.

What a magnificent climax to a super hunt!

Photograph by Wm. H. Nesbitt

QUEBEC-LABRADOR CARIBOU
SECOND AWARD
SCORE: 434 7/8

Locality: Mistinibi Lake, Que. Date: October 1983
Hunter: Don L. Corley

QUEBEC-LABRADOR CARIBOU
434 7/8

Don L. Corley

John Blanton, his brother Butch, Don Senter, and I left the Dallas/Fort Worth Airport on October 4, 1983, for Schefferville. This was my second trip to Quebec in quest of a big bull.

On the first trip in 1980, Richard Parker, I, and several other friends, had made the same trip to the same location. I had agreed to help Richard get a big bull before I took mine. After three days of looking at hundreds of big bulls, I spotted one that looked like a book bull. I conveyed my thoughts to Richard. He said he really wanted a caribou with a double shovel. I knew this was a big bull, so I said, "Fine, I'll take him." And he said, "No, I will." Bang! As I predicted, a Boone and Crockett bull. By then it was dark so we returned to camp. The next morning, Richard and the other hunters left to return home. There I was, the only hunter left in camp. The long lines of big bulls had ended. Now there were only a few stragglers. Again, the next morning, no big bulls. The next day, as the hunt was ending, I took a bull in order to help complete my North American 30. The bull did make the Safari Club records book, but it was far from a Boone and Crockett trophy.

Now, here I was on another late trophy hunt.

The next morning, John and I hunted together but saw nothing worth taking. The following day, John, our guide Rodger Tramblay, and I hunted west of our camp. We saw a large herd of caribou passing over a small hill, going down through a pass and over to the next hill. Once we were on top of the hill, we saw caribou everywhere, with snow falling freely.

John and Rodger were glassing to our left, when I saw "Mr. Antlers" coming up out of a low spot. As soon as I could see all of his antlers, I dropped to one knee, took aim and fired. As I shot, John took another big bull 200 yards behind my bull. As we approached my bull, all our eyes opened wide. What an animal! We all knew he was large, but it was the next day before we knew how big he really was. After two years of hard hunting for a trophy Quebec caribou, Lady Luck had laid him in my lap. The George River herd had truly yielded an outstanding trophy.

Luck has a lot to do with the taking of a big trophy. However, it is important to know how to judge a book animal, especially if you are trying to put a species into the records book.

If you hunt caribou during the migration, and are fortunate enough to be at the right place at the right time, and if you also know how to recognize a book head, you have a good chance for a Boone and Crockett trophy. Good hunting!

Photograph by Wm. H. Nesbitt

QUEBEC-LABRADOR CARIBOU
CERTIFICATE OF MERIT
SCORE: 460 6/8

Locality: Ungava Bay, Que.   Date: September 1978
Hunter: Lynn D. McLaud

QUEBEC-LABRADOR CARIBOU 460%

Lynn D. McLaud

Rain splattered against the window for the second straight day, and grey, scudding clouds enveloped the water tower at the edge of town. It looked as though we'd be stuck in the Inuit settlement near Fort Chimo forever. But late that afternoon, the ceiling started to lift slightly, just enough to provide a glimmer of hope for the morning.

It had started to rain shortly before our flight from Montreal (some 900 miles to the south) touched down on the asphalt tarmac of the airport on Monday morning. By the time Bob Kilmer and I had retrieved our gear, the Canadian Maple Leaf flag outside the air terminal was already too sodden to flap. There was one consolation, at least the twin Otter aircraft which was to take us on the final leg of our journey to the land of the Ungava caribou was also held captive by the rain, poor visibility and snow squalls.

True to the evening's promise, Wednesday morning broke bright and sunny. In less than an hour we were strapped into our seats and were taxiing down the runway on our way to the George River spike camp. We'd spent more than a year planning, dreaming about, and looking forward to this Quebec-Labrador caribou hunt. It was finally coming true!

This was our first trip beyond the tree line. We'd both hunted elk and mulies in Colorado several times, and we spend the better part of every fall hunting whitetails in our home state of Pennsylvania as well as in Maine and New Brunswick. But, this treeless land of barren, wind-swept ridges that slipped away beneath the fuselage of the aircraft was totally foreign to both of us. I could feel the excitement mounting.

A little more than an hour later, the pilot banked sharply over the George River and there below us, against a back drop of stunted black spruce that managed to get a roothold in the shelter of the valley, stood a tiny collection of tent camps that we were to call home for the rest of the week. Camp manager Conlucie Annanack and his crew of Inuit guides were on hand to greet us as we disembarked. Somehow, their smiling, friendly faces immediately broke the ice.

The Snowball spike camp is one of an extensive network of fishing and hunting camps throughout Quebec's Ungava region that are owned and operated by the native people through village cooperatives. About 20 years ago, they banded together to create the Federation of Inuit Cooperatives of Nouveau Quebec and in so doing created a tourism development branch called Arctic Adventures. We'd heard from other Pennsylvania area hunters that the organization is well run and reliable, and so we wrote asking for more information.

Within days, we got a call from Sammy Cantafio, a knowledgeable hunter himself, who runs Arctic Adventures. He suggested that, considering our hunting experience and zest for adventure, we try hunting out of the George River spike camp. Though it was a bit more Spartan than the main caribou camps at Tunulik, Akuliag, and Weymouth, the hunting was excellent, with a good chance of running into some trophy animals. Best time, he told us, was during the last half of September when the big, mature bulls start migrating toward the rutting grounds. But, Sammy also warned us that bad weather frequently causes delays at this time. It was a chance we were willing to take.

Sammy hadn't exaggerated about the weather. By the time we'd stowed away our gear, changed into our hunting duds, and checked over our rifles, the ceiling had dropped once more and the thermometer had plummeted. We hunted in the ridges behind camp, but it was a half-hearted effort in the damp, bone-chilling cold. Up on the ridges, racing snow squalls had left patches of snow here and there. Even Charlie Koateak, our wizened guide, was skeptical about seeing caribou, but he also understood that we needed to stretch out cramped muscles after being cooped-up for several days.

By Thursday morning, we were back into the sunshine and we could sense an electrifying excitement in the camp. We quickly forgot about the previous day's disappointment as guide Charlie pointed the prow of the 22-foot freight canoe downriver. Somehow, he knew that this would be an eventful day.

About three quarters of an hour from camp, Charlie spotted a big black bear lumbering along the steep flank of the barren ridges beside the river. After a hurried consultation, we decided to try for him. Black bear are relative newcomers to the Ungava region, as Sammy Cantafio had explained to us prior to our trip. Apparently, they've followed the encroachment of civilization into the barrens over the past decade or so and are now quite numerous in the George River Valley. What's more, they grow to an enormous size in the barren land. Blackies weighing upwards of 400 pounds are quite common now. This one looked as though he'd go that much, and probably better.

Leaving the canoe on shore, we picked our way up the steep slope, using grey, weathered boulders for cover until we were within 300 yards of the unsuspecting bear. Through my 3 to 9 power variable scope, I watched the lustrous black pelt shine in the morning sun. As I prepared to squeeze the trigger, I felt Charlie's hand tighten on my arm in warning.

Turning around, I found him pointing to a distant ridge on the other side of the river. "Tuk-tuk," he said urgently. Caribou. There would be other black bear, but we were here to hunt caribou. And, with time running out, we wanted a closer look at them. For all his years, Charlie trotted easily down to the canoe, crossed the river and headed up the next ridge with Bob and I in tow. The climb left us both gasping for air and determined to get into better shape next time around.

From the distance, we hadn't been able to tell how big they were. But, as we got closer, we could see only small bulls and some cows in the band of about half-dozen animals. It had hardly been worth the trek over, yet it was nevertheless exciting just to see game.

By this time, it was noon. We were just gathering up some twigs to build a fire for tea, when Charlie's sharp eyes picked out a band of some 50 caribou on a distant ridge. Even at a distance of some two or three miles, we could make out the high racks of a dozen or more big bulls. After tracking their direction for a few minutes, Charlie judged that they were headed toward the George River which we had crossed less than an hour earlier.

It took us the better part of an hour to reach the top of that last ridge, a half-mile from the river, where we figured we could intercept the herd. To my dismay, there were no caribou in sight; could Charlie have misjudged the animals? Or, had we somehow spooked them? I caught the dark eyes of our Inuit guide in a silent question and the answer that came back was reassuring.

Within minutes, we sensed the presence of game. Perhaps we subconsciously picked up the sound of their breathing, or the hunter's instinct captured the warm, musky scent of game in a vagrant breeze. Over the lichen-stained, grey boulders scattered across the crown of the ridge, we could now see the crowns of their nut-brown antlers moving along, swaying from side to side as they walked parallel to the ridge line. Instead of coming over the top, the herd had decided to angle up and then cross at the point of the ridge some 250 yards away. We watched the forest of antlers for what seemed to be an eternity before the first of the caribou came into sight.

Bob lined his cross hairs on a big bull that came through. He knew it wouldn't quite make the records book, but it was nevertheless enormous. At the report, the herd wheeled, and in their confusion, came directly up the ridge toward us. My heart was pounding like a big bass drum as I anxiously searched for the white-maned bull I'd seen when we first spotted the herd. I didn't know if he was coming or not; but, I knew that if I shot a caribou, that was the one I wanted.

At that stage, the first few animals in the herd had reached us and were passing us on both sides. One of them almost stepped on Bob, who was still in the prone position after taking his shot. At the tail end of the herd, the last of the stragglers had rounded the point of the ridge. My big bull was still nowhere to be seen. Frantically, I searched through the disappearing herd once more, thinking that maybe I'd missed him somehow, but he wasn't there.

Then, I heard Charlie mutter a warning. I snapped around just in time to see an enormous bull caribou come up onto the ridge. His white mane reached almost back to his haunches and the sun's rays played across incredibly long tines and massive beams. This was my bull. I quickly lowered my cheek to the polished comfort of the rifle stock. The 150 grain bullet from my 7mm Remington Magnum did its work quickly.

Looking at the other caribou, I quickly realized that this was an above average trophy, but I didn't think it would make the records books. I just knew it had awfully long points and it looked really good to me.

Back at the spike camp, the rack created quite a stir when the camp coordinator excitedly hauled out his measuring tape and went about the task of green-scoring. The double shovels went 22 inches wide, one of the bez points reached 16 inches, and the back points were 10 inches long as well. All told, we came up with an informal score of 465 points, some 90 points over the minimum score for Quebec-Labrador caribou and just a few points less than the existing Number One Boone & Crockett bull taken in 1929!

Now that Quebec game authorities have increased the limit to two caribou per person (a regulation passed in 1983, four years after my eventful trip to the George River spike camp), hunters are no longer under pressure to take the first animal they see, and the chances are good that some of the longstanding records will tumble one by one. Whatever happens, nobody will ever be able to erase from my mind the sight of that big, white-maned Ungava caribou bull as he crested the ridge and stood momentarily silhouetted against a backdrop of rolling tundra ridges and the sun-washed afternoon sky!

Photos Courtesy of Ernie Davis and Ronald Pettit

(l) Ernie Davis killed his fine pronghorn in Hartley County, Texas, in 1984. It scores 82 2/8 points. (r) Ron Pettit was south of Wamsutter, Wyoming, in 1983 when he killed his pronghorn that scores 83 4/8 points.

Photo Courtesy of Matthew Dominy

Matthew Dominy hunted in Coconino County, Arizona, in 1984 to take this fine pronghorn that scores 83 2/8 points.

Photograph by Wm. H. Nesbitt

NEW WORLD'S RECORD PRONGHORN
SAGAMORE HILL AWARD
FIRST AWARD
SCORE: 93 4/8

Locality: Coconino Co., Ariz.   Date: September 1985
Hunter: Michael J. O'Haco, Jr.

PRONGHORN 93 4/8

Michael J. O'Haco, Jr.

It was the first weekend in August, 1985, and I was out of town. I called home because I knew the Arizona hunting permits should be in the mail. My wife Linda said there was good news and bad news: I said I wanted the bad news first. She said that I had not received an elk permit. However, the good news was that I had received a deer and pronghorn permit. Already having a mule deer in the Arizona state records book, I was pleased at having drawn a deer permit, but not half as pleased as I was with the pronghorn permit. This was the 20th time I had applied for an pronghorn permit; the 19 previous times I had been rejected. The computer finally came through.

After getting home, I called my hunting partner Phil Donnelly. We got together to plan how we were going to scout the unit we had been drawn for. Being a rancher in that same area, I would scout the top half of the unit, while Phil would scout the lower half. The top half was closer to where I was working cattle, and the lower half was closer to Winslow, where Phil lives. We got together after a couple of weeks and discussed what we had seen. He seemed to think that he had two records-book bucks in the lower half of the unit, and I thought I had three records-book bucks in the top half, but one buck was exceptional.

I tried to get a look at the bucks Phil had spotted, but I was unable to find them. I kept track of two of the bucks I had spotted, but I couldn't find the big buck. I almost panicked! After a little research on pronghorn, I found that during early September in Arizona, a buck will be looking for his harem, but will return to his own territory after putting them together. The big buck did, and I found him again the week before the hunt. I explained to Phil where I had seen the buck the day before, and asked him to take a look. Phil came by the ranch that night and told me this definitely was the biggest buck he had ever seen. We agreed the buck would go high in the Boone and Crockett records book, but we didn't realize how high.

The afternoon and evening before the hunt, we decided to watch the big buck until he bedded down for the night. Phil watched until he couldn't see him in the spotting scope anymore, then he returned to the ranch. After supper, he explained to me exactly where the buck had bedded down. My family has ranched in this area for years, so I knew exactly where the buck was. We talked about using horses, or going in on foot, and if we should come in from the north or from the northeast. We decided that foot would be better, and that the northeast route would be the best. This way, we would have everything working for us, with the wind and the most cover, and also the sun at our backs.

Since this was my first pronghorn permit, I would get the first shot. If I missed, it was anybody's ball game. I had worked up a super accurate load of a Sierra 85-grain, hollow-point bullet, a Remington case and primer, and 41.5 grains of IMR 4350 powder. This load would be used in a Sako .243 rifle, with a two to seven variable power Leopold scope. I didn't intend to miss!

That night was one of the longest of my life, as my mind was filled with thoughts of the next day's hunt on my mind. Would the buck be there in the morning? Would we spook them before I could get a shot? Would I miss? Finally, about 3:00 a.m., I couldn't take it any longer. I got up and put the coffee on. Phil got up and asked how I felt. I said that as many times as I had shot that pronghorn in my dreams, we should be able to drive out there and load him up.

We drove to within a mile of where the buck and his does had bedded down for the night. It was still an hour before daylight. We discussed how we would make our stalk, and tried to visualize all aspects of the stalk so there would be no mistakes.

Finally, it was light enough to make a move. We had to crawl over a fence and then use the scattered cedar trees for cover. We moved slowly. When we were about 300 yards from where we had seen them the night before, I spotted the does but couldn't see the buck. Now we were crawling slowly and easily. When we were about 200 yards from the pronghorn, something caught my eye to the left. It was a buck. Phil was about 20 yards to my left. The buck was looking straight at me, with a slight right turn, and I could see just part of a shoulder. Not being able to tell if it was the big one, I whispered to Phil, "Is that him?" I knew the buck was big, but I couldn't see the prong from my angle. Phil said, "That's him." I shot. The buck broke and ran. I thought I had missed.

I jammed another shell into my rifle. I hollered at Phil to shoot. He said, "No, he's hit hard." The buck slowed down, then stopped and looked back. I shot again, nothing. The adrenalin was really pumping through my body and I couldn't hold the cross hairs steady. Phil said to use his shoulder for a rest, but he was shaking worse than I was. I took a deep breath, got my composure, and squeezed. The buck finally went down and didn't get up.

When we got to the buck, we took a quick measurement and were awed by what we totaled. Two days later, I had Jerry Walters, an official Arizona state measurer, measure the buck and he came up with a $95\frac{2}{8}$ green score. After the 60-day drying period, the buck was officially scored by Mike Cuppell, a Boone and Crockett measurer, at 94% for entry into the records program. It was beginning to look like we just might have a new World's Record on our hands.

Editor's Note: This trophy, and the fine, Fair Chase hunt for it, received special recognition at the 19th Awards with the Sagamore Hill Award, the highest trophy award made by the Club. This was the first time ever that the Sagamore Hill Award was given to a pronghorn trophy. It was only the 13th time this award has been made, and it was the first time the award had been made since 1976.

Photos Courtesy of Charles L. Holland and Judy Taylor

(l) Charles Holland found his pronghorn that scores 82 points in Coconino County, Arizona, in 1984. (r) Washoe County, Nevada, was the site of Judy Taylor's hunt in 1983 that resulted in this fine pronghorn that scores 84 2/8.

Photo Courtesy of John W. Hlavacek

John Hlavacek was north of Harrison, Nebraska, when he shot this big pronghorn in 1983. It scores 85 4/8 points.

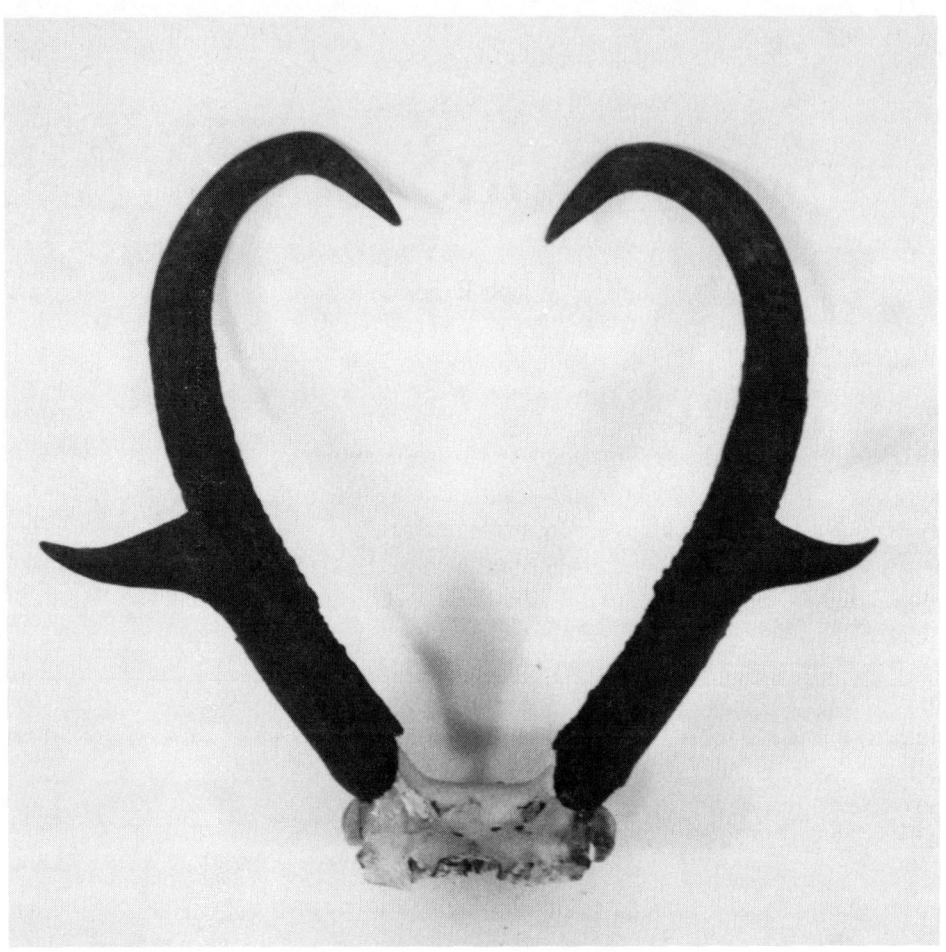

Photograph by Wm. H. Nesbitt

PRONGHORN
SECOND AWARD
SCORE: 90 4/8

Locality: Yavapai Co., Ariz.   Date: September 1984
Hunter: Joe P. Fornara

PRONGHORN 90 4/8

Joseph P. Fornara

As a native Arizonian, Joe Fornara knew where he wanted to hunt. Big Chino Valley of Yavapai County was his choice.

He arrived there on September 27, 1984. He had several friends with him, a group that he often hunted with. They expected a good hunt, but it turned out to be much better than that. It was truly one of those red-letter hunts that all hunters dream about.

Opening day of the pronghorn season failed to produce the big buck that Joe desired. He saw a lot of bucks, does and fawns, but he wanted that one special buck.

The second day of the season was much like opening day, until 4:30 p.m. That's when Joe had worked to within 225 yards of the buck that he knew was the one he wanted. He carefully settled himself for a shot with his .270 Winchester. The shot was good, and the buck was down. As Joe looked at his trophy, he was filled with awe at the size of those horns. They were huge.

Later, a green measurement would indicate that the horns were darn near World's Record size. They ended up being one of the finest trophies entered in the Awards Program, and they earned an invitation to the Final Awards Judging and Banquet.

Photograph by Wm. H. Nesbitt

PRONGHORN
THIRD AWARD
SCORE: 86

Locality: Apache Co., Ariz.   Date: October 1984
Hunter: Charles R. Sprung

PRONGHORN 86

Charles R. Sprung

Charlie Sprung lives in Show Low, Arizona, so he knows a good pronghorn when he sees one. Arizona is becoming justifiably famous for a wide variety of big game, and it certainly produces some outstanding pronghorn each year.

Charlie had chosen to hunt in Unit 2B, which had produced some big bucks. He found his big buck on the first day of October, 1984. He had worked to within 60 yards, when he used his .243 to kill his pronghorn. He knew it was a good buck, but it wasn't until later, when the green score measurement indicated it would place well up in the book, that Charlie began to get excited. The excitement hasn't stopped yet.

Photograph by Wm. H. Nesbitt

BISON
CERTIFICATE OF MERIT
SCORE: 124

Locality: Coconino Co., Ariz.   Date: October 1984
Hunter: Philip A. Sturgill

BISON 124

Philip A. Sturgill

As we all know from reading the history books, the bison once numbered in the millions and covered the plains like flies on stale meat. Today, that is of course no longer true, and the bison is an unusual and rare trophy. Arizona is one of the few states of the lower 48 that does offer a wild and free-ranging bison hunt. For those people lucky enough to participate, it is like a step backward in time. Philip A. Sturgill was one of the lucky ones. He had been drawn to hunt bison, and now he was on his way for the hunt at House Rock Ranch, owned and operated by the state.

Sturgill arrived at the hunting area on October 18, 1984. He found his trophy bull on the next day. He managed to work to within 60 yards of the huge bull, and then made the kill with his .30-06.

The snow was lightly falling, and the sky was overcast and gloomy, but it was a beautiful day to Phil Sturgill. He had a huge bison bull trophy, and it had truly been a hunt to remember.

Photograph courtesy of Timothy F. McGinn

ROCKY MOUNTAIN GOAT
FIRST AWARD
SCORE: 52 6/8

Locality: Reflection Lake, Alaska   Date: September 1985
Hunter: Timothy F. McGinn

ROCKY MOUNTAIN GOAT 52 6/8

Timothy F. McGinn

My hunting had been directed mainly towards big mule deer bucks. Then, a couple of years ago, my brother Dan got a very good goat in British Columbia. This undoubtedly increased my desire to hunt goats.

In August of 1985, Tod, my hunting partner from Thorne Bay, Alaska, and I contacted the Alaska Fish and Game Dept. With their help, we decided on an area about a hundred miles northeast of Ketchikan that had a good population of goats and had recently produced some very large ones. This area was so rough that it could only be hunted by backpacking. It was too rough even for horses, so the hunting pressure was very light.

We contacted a float plane pilot who knew the area. He said he could land us at the "No Name" lake we had decided on, and would pick us up in 10 days.

The day of departure arrived. Although the weather was threatening, our pilot seemed certain he could get us to the lake without any problem. We understood that in August you can see until slightly after eight o'clock at night. Flying time to the lake took approximately an hour and fifteen minutes. We arrived with just enough time to set up our camp and do a little bit of glassing. In Alaska, it's illegal to hunt on the same day you fly. So, Tod and I took only our glasses and spotting scopes and climbed the nearest ridge to see if we could find some goats. I was completely inexperienced on goats and, although Tod had done a little goat hunting previously, we wanted to locate some goats to attempt to judge their horn sizes.

Right away, we could see we were in extremely rough country. There were steep ridges with rocky areas, and lots of draws and ravines running down the mountains. The mountains were not too high, about 4,000 feet, but what they lacked in height they certainly made up in steepness. Glaciers and ice fields were in abundance. After we set up our spotting scopes, we managed to locate five nannies.

Tod was hoping to get a Boone and Crockett goat. I planned to simply hold out for a 10-incher. If it made the book, so much the better. As it was getting late, we picked up our scopes and headed back to our base camp.

The next morning, we packed up all we could carry and set out to establish a spike camp farther into the back country. We planned to make daily hunts out of the spike camp. The weather kept threatening and then clearing up, always leaving us with a feeling of uncertainty.

The third day, which was really the first day of actual hunting, we left our spike camp early and headed for an area we had decided was "big goat country." We found it always took us a lot longer than we anticipated to get to a point on a ridge, due to having to cross so many ravines and hike so many ups and downs.

At one point, we stopped to carefully glass the mountains that were about a mile away. Earlier that morning we had located one billy that we guessed would go 9½ inches. Tod thought that I should take him. No way did I want to take a goat that early in the hunt. I located two bands of goats, and Tod found one. Two of these groups seemed to be nannies with kids. The third group consisted of just three goats. I told Tod that I thought they were all billies. Tod agreed. He thought they all looked like 10-inch horns, or better.

We could see their outlines and horns silhouetted against the snow and ice. One was obviously bigger than the other two, and I couldn't take my eyes off him. By this time, it was midday and we had come a long, long way from our spike camp. The goats were in a cliff area, about two-thirds of the way up the mountain. I knew I had to make a try for that biggest goat.

We talked about how far we were from our spike camp, how much time it would take to make the stalk, and whether we could get back before dark. We agreed to try. Tod wanted to get above them on the ridge, hoping we could see the goats from there. I told him I didn't think we would be able to see from the top. I wanted to circle the mountain that was between us and the goats, then make a crawl to a saddle that would put us in good shooting range.

Tod said he had been in deep trouble before trying to cross such rough, cliff country, so he would make his attempt from the ridge. We went our separate ways. I hadn't gone too far, when I had to backtrack. "Maybe Tod was right," I thought as I started again. I managed to cross a number of very difficult draws with water rushing down them, terminating in huge drop-offs. One slip would be one too many. I was plenty scared. In fact, I crossed some places that I knew I couldn't have crossed back. I had passed the point of turning-back.

I very carefully crawled around a boulder that was about as big as a car, using my left arm to steady myself. I had to squat to maneuver between the boulder and a 500-foot drop-off that was just 18 inches away. Suddenly, I heard a grinding noise. I had to sit helplessly as the boulder began rolling against me. I knew I was dead. The boulder slowly pushed my face between my legs. I pushed back as hard as I could but it was like trying to budge a house. I could hardly breathe. Suddenly, the boulder stopped. An inch more and I'd have been crushed like a bug.

I could hardly move. The water bottle in my backpack burst with the pressure, and my rifle, which was slung across one shoulder, was smashed against me. Very slowly, I worked my left arm out of the backpack strap, fearing any movement would start the boulder moving again. It took me about 15 minutes to squirm out. I realized that only incredible luck kept me alive.

My down jacket had been in the pack, with its sleeves hanging out. Now, one sleeve was pinned under the boulder. To salvage the jacket, I had to tear off the sleeve. My rifle was scratched, but otherwise seemed un-damaged. By this time I was shaking and scared, but I did notice that there was only one ravine between me and the saddle where I hoped to see the goats. I'd used up a tremendous amount of energy in that frightening ordeal. I wondered if I'd have my wits about me and be able to use good judgment when I got to the goats.

I managed to cross the last ravine, then I started my crawl to the saddle. Staying low and not raising my head, I finally reached a point where I thought I should be able to see the goats. Slowly, I raised my head for a look. I immediately spotted a goat about 50 yards away. This goat was a young billy, with horns about eight inches long. I had never seen him before. Cautiously, I looked around, there were the other two billies. But, the big one was missing. I knew I could crawl a bit farther in order to see some areas that were now out of my vision.

Carefully, I inched my way up another 15 feet. As I slowly looked up, there he was, just 30 yards away.

He was on his feet, looking right at me. The wind was in my favor and I didn't make any noise. Still, he knew I was there. His eyes were looking into my eyes. I quickly made sure that he was the biggest goat of the group. I pushed off the safety, and put the cross hairs on his shoulder. When I squeezed the trigger, down he went.

I was congratulating myself when the billy tried to get up. I ejected the spent case and ran another round into the chamber; my rifle went off, which scared the hell out of me. I ejected that shell and loaded another into the chamber. That one went off too! My goat was now walking away. I wasn't sure if I had buck fever and was pulling the trigger, or what. The third time, I carefully watched as I loaded another round. As I turned the bolt handle down, it again fired.

By now, my goat had disappeared down through the steep rocks and cliffs. It was very steep, but I worked my way in his direction. Shortly, I saw him slowly walking up the other side, about 150 yards away. I got into a good shooting position. With the cross hairs right on his shoulder again, I slowly closed the bolt handle. The rifle fired, and the bullet hit right where I wanted it to. He went down like a ton of bricks.

Then, he got up again. He headed slowly downhill towards a cliff. I knew if he reached the cliff, he would go over and that would be the end of my horns. This time, I put the cross hairs on his neck, and then slowly turned the bolt handle down. When the rifle went off, the cross hairs were right on his neck; his head jerked with the impact.

I knew he was down for good. Tod had come down the mountain and was closer to the goat than I was. He asked what all the shooting was about. I told him my rifle wasn't working right, and that I was afraid that I had hit the goat in the head. Tod hollered back that I had indeed shot the goat's horns off. Damn. I knew he was a good one and I had shot the horns off!

"Wait a minute," Tod yelled, "There's one horn left. Too bad. The one that's left is 10⅝ inches." Then he added, "Come on over!"

What a relief to find out Tod had been playing tricks on me. Both horns were okay, and what a goat he was. Each horn measured 10⅝ inches and was undamaged.

It was too late in the day to cape my goat and also get the meat back to camp, so we dressed him, and then put him over a rock in the shadiest area. The weather was threatening again, and we were hours away from our spike camp. Tod's route along the ridge was by far the easiest, so we took that course back, walking as fast as we could. On the way, we saw two goats in the fog about 30 yards from us. One goat appeared somewhat larger than the other. Tod said he was going to take the big one.

Bang! Just like that, Tod dropped him. It was a mistake, as it was a small goat with horns about eight inches long. Tod felt bad about making such a mistake. But, we dressed the goat out in a hurry and continued on our way. I think the fog deceived Tod into thinking it was a much larger goat.

Darkness closed in on us, and then to top it off, it started to rain. I noticed that Tod had been lagging behind a little. But, tired as we were, we had to keep pushing. Finally, we were reasonably sure we were on the ridge somewhere above our spike camp. The camp was at the end of a lake. We could faintly see the lake, but in the darkness and fog we could not pinpoint our location.

We were both exhausted, but Tod now showed signs of near collapse. He lay down and curled up in the fetal position, telling me he couldn't go on and he was prepared to die right there. I thought he was kidding. Then he started to retch and vomit and he vomited some blood.

"Tod," I said, "Whatever you do, don't go to sleep. I'll find the camp, but if you go to sleep, I'll never be able to find you in the dark."

I left Tod still vomiting. Within five minutes, I found the camp. I could hear Tod retching. I called to him to find out if he could see my flashlight, and he said he could.

We had set up our camp in a dry draw, but rain water was now running through our tent and our sleeping bags were completely soaked. I went back for Tod, who was still retching. Together, we made it to the tent. I fixed Tod a sandwich, but he was too sick to eat it. We crawled into our wet sleeping bags to try to get some sleep. I wasn't at all sure that Tod would make it through the night. We were completely soaked; but thank goodness, it wasn't too cold.

The next morning, to my great relief, Tod was much improved. We ate some sandwiches and candy bars, and talked over our situation. We decided it would be best for us to go down to our base camp and dry out.

After we arrived at the base camp, and got a little rest, Tod seemed to be in good shape again. So, we discussed going back to get our goats. But for two days, we were stuck in camp, unable to move due to fog and rain. We figured it was cold enough and cloudy enough to keep the sun off the cape so the hair wouldn't slip.

On the morning of the third day, we awoke to light fog, but we could see blue sky above. Tod said, "Let's go for it." We knew we had to go all the way to my goat and back in one long day. We could then easily get Tod's goat the next day, as it was only half the distance.

We started early and traveled light to make the best time possible. We ran into some bad weather again when we finally got onto the ridge somewhere above my goat. Visibility was less than 200 feet. We stopped to wait for the weather to break so we could pinpoint our position, but to no avail. Finally, we set a time limit. We agreed that if we couldn't locate the goat by that time, we would have to go back and try again on another day.

We had waited 15 minutes past our deadline. Then, like magic, a break in the clouds occurred and we knew exactly where we were. We had come about 500 yards too far. We now headed down right to the goat.

Tod started boning and I started caping. Within 45 minutes, we were headed back. It was just getting dark when we could make out the camp in the distance, still about two hours away. Again, it had been a very long, hard day.

The next day, we again had acceptable weather, so we headed back to get Tod's goat. Now all we had to do was rest, clean up the capes, and wait for our plane to pick us up.

About 7 p.m. on the tenth day in camp, we were just about to crawl into our sleeping bags when we heard the roar of our plane coming over the ridge. Boy, were we glad to see it. It taxied right up to our camp. In no time, we had everything loaded on board.

A great takeoff was followed by an uneventful flight back. We landed near Tod's home on Thorn Bay in the glow of last light.

Photograph by Wm. H. Nesbitt

The 19th North American Big Game Awards display of invited trophies offered an unparalleled opportunity to study the differences between various categories. Visible here are two typical whitetails (lower left), five unmounted Sitka blacktails (lower right), and four Columbia blacktails (upper and center). Note that whitetails have points originating from a main beam while the blacktails (subspecies of mule deer) show "Y" branching of the main beam into the major points.

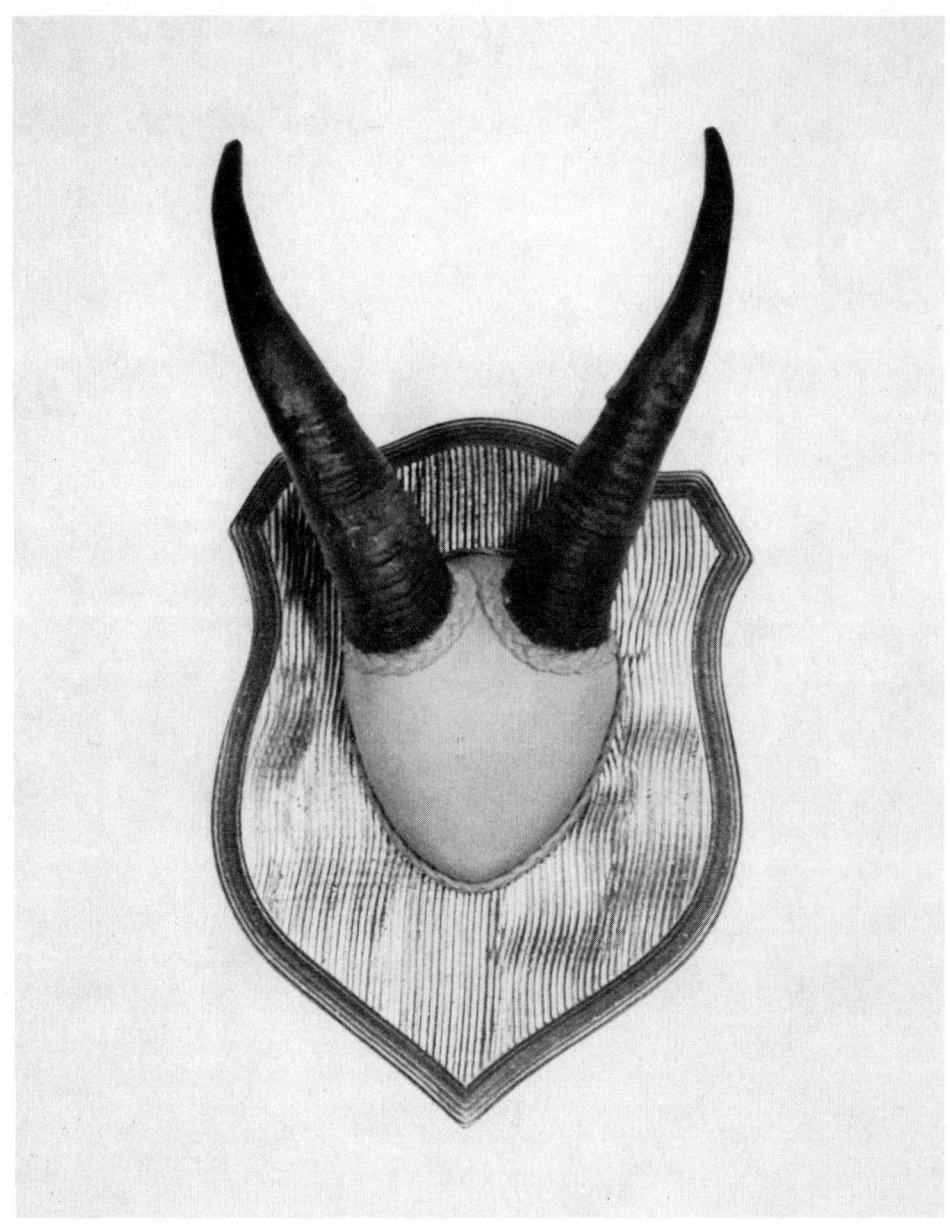

Photograph by Wm. H. Nesbitt

ROCKY MOUNTAIN GOAT
SECOND AWARD
SCORE: 52 4/8

Locality: Taku River, B. C.   Date: September 1985
Hunter: Fritz Stork

ROCKY MOUNTAIN GOAT 52 4/8

Fritz Stork

In 1983, my friend, Charles "Corky" Schmidt, and I decided to go on a hunt in British Columbia. We contacted Jack Atcheson, who booked a hunt for us with Guy Anttila of Taku Safari, Inc. We had a very successful hunt, and we both decided that we would return in a couple of years for a goat hunt, when we could take our wives along with us.

In January of 1985, I contacted Guy about a goat hunt. He booked me for a hunt beginning September 1 and continuing through September 15, 1985.

On August 30, I left my Fairview farm at 4 a.m. I was accompanied by my wife Jane, and Corky and Anna Schmidt. We motored to Toronto Airport. There, we checked our baggage and confirmed our tickets, then we enjoyed a leisurely breakfast. Excitement filled the air as we waited to hear our flight called. Corky and I knew that our wives were in for a real treat: a nice camp, good food, and good fishing. We finally boarded the Canadian Pacific Airline plane, and soon we were on our way. We arrived in Whitehorse, Yukon Territory, about 5:00 p.m. By 5:30, we were in our room at the Taku hotel.

Next morning at 8:00 a.m., we got a call from Edie, our expeditor, who picked us up and drove us to Atlin. There, we boarded a Beaver plane (Taku Air, piloted by Theresa), and headed out to camp. The scenery was beautiful, and the weather was perfect.

Waiting at the float plane dock were Elsie Anttila (Guy's wife), Rose Anne (who helped with the cooking), and Ovey Anttila, who later turned out to be my guide. We also met Jackson, a 12-year-old Pitt bull, and Trig, a year-old Norwegian elkhound.

The dogs turned out to be a lot of fun at camp. Jackson was well experienced at keeping the grizzly bears away from the camp. The camps are very comfortable. We four were in the same cabin, but it was divided by a partition so that each couple had their own privacy. There was carpeting on the floor, and a stove with plenty of wood stored nearby. The light we had to use at night was very unique, a wine bottle with a candle in the top.

Later that day, we flew out to a small lake called One Way Lake, on the Taku Plateau in the Cassiar Mountain range. There, we set up our spike camp, and then we spent some time glassing the area with our binoculars and spotting scopes. The goats were numerous on the mountains. We didn't see any moose roaming about, but it was still a little early in the season for them. It had really been a nice day, warm enough that we could walk around without jackets.

The next morning, Ovey and I started our climb up the mountain for goats. We fought our way through thick pines and devils's club. We stopped for lunch, some sandwiches, candy bars and a little rest. We continued our way up until we reached the top. After spotting several goats, we noticed a large billy on a pinnacle below us. After glassing the goat, I knew he was a real trophy. Ovey and I decided to make the stalk. Very cautiously, we crept slowly down the rocky terrain, finally coming within 200 yards of this magnificent billy. Ovey asked me if I could shoot the goat from where we were. With no waste of time, I eased a shell into the chamber of my rifle. I glanced over at Ovey, who now was taking a picture of the goat as he was standing on the peak. I took careful aim at the goat, and with one shot, he was down.

The goat fell off the pinnacle after the shot. I could hear the shale rattling down, for a long period of time, not realizing until later that it was my goat falling clear to the bottom of the mountain. We had to face a treacherous trip down. I slid on my butt down the shale slides, and we kept looking for the goat on the way down. We encountered Corky and Guy, with Corky's billy, which also qualified for the Boone and Crockett Club records. After taking some pictures, and swapping our stories, Ovey and I proceeded down the rocks and shale, looking for my goat.

We finally found my goat at the bottom of the mountain, dirty, bloody, and really banged up from the fall. The tips of both horns were broken off. Even considering the shape he was in, I knew I had bagged myself a real trophy. It later measured $54 2/8$ for entry into the Boone and Crockett Club scoring system. Guy took a piece of the goat's jaw to the branch office of the British Columbia Fish and Wildlife Dept. to determine the age of the animal. I received notification that it was $14 1/2$ years old.

Corky and Guy finally got down to the bottom. The back side of the mountain was so steep that on the way down, Corky had slipped and sprained his ankle (so we thought). We found out later that he had cracked a bone in his ankle. He still kept on hunting for the remainder of the hunt, approximately 10 days.

This goat hunt will live in my memory forever. The trip was really complete. While we were hunting, our wives were enjoying some good fishing. They caught plenty of dolly varden, and we all enjoyed eating them when we returned from the bush. They liked the warm and comfortable camps, and the food was really good. They complained when they got home about the weight they had gained from all of the good food!

Photo Courtesy of Dan Fediuk

Dan Fediuk was hunting on Bleisdal Creek, B. C., in 1984 when he found his Rocky Mountain goat. It scores 50 2/8 points.

Photo Courtesy of Steven M. Sullivan

Sheslay River Mountain, B. C., was home to this beautiful Rocky Mountain goat that scores 51 points. It was killed by Steven M. Sullivan.

Photograph by Wm. H. Nesbitt

ROCKY MOUNTAIN GOAT
THIRD AWARD
SCORE: 52 2/8

Locality: Sheslay River, B. C.   Date: August 1984
Hunter: Frank L. Stukel

ROCKY MOUNTAIN GOAT 52 2/8

Frank L. Stukel

I sat there with my brother Cal and our two guides, Doyle and Rudy Day, on a high rocky ledge overlooking the beautiful Sheslay River Valley below us. We had spotted what looked like a nice billy sunning himself on a shelf about 800 yards below. We had decided to have our midday lunch before making a final stalk. It was the 6th day of a 15-day combination hunt. My brothers Cal and Ray and I had booked this hunt 18 months previously with outfitter Fletcher Day of Telegraph Creek, B.C.

Up to that point, we had taken a Stone's sheep ram, a 56-inch, velvet-covered moose, and one Rocky Mountain goat. This was our first hunt outside the lower 48 and it was a real dream come true. Our financial situations would not normally allow such an expense. That had changed, however, when we had figured out that our South Dakota farmland and abundant pheasants could provide us with enough extra income to take a first-class guided hunt every other year. But that hot August day, pheasants were a long way from our minds as we finished our lunches and laid out a plan to get a closer look at the napping billy.

My guide (Doyle) and I were to make the downhill sneak, while Cal and Rudy stayed on the high ridge to direct us with designated arm signals. The terrain was such that we wouldn't be able to see the billy until we were right on him. We were fortunate to have Cal and Rudy sitting in ringside seats. At that point, all we knew was that the resting goat looked like a nice billy. But, because of how he lay, we weren't positive of his horn size. I had hopes of bagging a 10-inch goat, but I wasn't going to pass up any reasonable trophy. I was already so elated at just being there that record books just weren't on my mind.

Our stalk took us a long way around, in and out of sight of the guys on the cliff. But, 45 minutes later, we still couldn't find the spot where the billy lay. Finally, my guide decided to work ahead on his own to do some scouting. He didn't get more than 15 yards below me when he quickly froze and then signaled for me to stay low and quiet. After a couple of minutes of waiting, I slowly worked down the last 15 yards, searching carefully for a place to put each step. I could tell by my guide's facial expression that we were close, really close.

That last 15 yards took about 15 minutes. When I finally reached the spot, I could see we were too close for words. The billy had sensed danger and was now standing up to look around. The terrain prohibited my seeing any more than his front half, but that's all that was needed to know we had found our 10-inch goat. Shooting without a rest is risky, but at that range I was confident. I really had no choice. As I pulled the rifle up, the billy began to turn slightly, as if to walk away. One shot from the .300 Winchester Magnum was all it took. That shot was followed by the sound of rocks sliding. Before I could get my gun down, Doyle was running down toward the ledge.

My billy had fallen about 30 yards down a steep incline and was held in place by a few scrub aspen trees. Doyle was down beside the beautiful white creature long before I could make it. He welcomed me with promises of 10½ inch horns and Boone and Crockett Club records book status. Not being into record books much, I thought it was all guides' talk. I was more impressed with seeing a Rocky Mountain goat up close for the first time in my life. The single shot had made a clean kill. We later paced off the distance at 72 yards.

Our hunt continued for another nine days. Ray and Cal later took another billy and a velvet-covered moose. Each of us had bagged two animals on a British Columbia hunt in the heat of August and it was truly a dream come true. We all decided that anything this good just had to be tried again. So, the three of us booked another hunt with Fletcher for two years later.

Photograph by Charlie Crunden

At the 19th Awards (Las Vegas, 1986), Steven L. Gingras accepts the First Award for his bighorn sheep from Dr. Philip L. Wright, Chairman of the Records Committee.

Photograph by Charlie Crunden

At the 19th Awards (Las Vegas, 1986), Travis K. Holder accepts the Third Award for his desert bighorn sheep from Dr. Philip L. Wright, Chairman of the Records Committee.

Photograph by Wm. H. Nesbitt

ROCKY MOUNTAIN GOAT
FOURTH AWARD
SCORE: 51 4/8

Locality: Snohomish Co., Wash.   Date: September 1985
Hunter: Theadore H. Kiser

ROCKY MOUNTAIN GOAT 51 4/8

Theadore H. Kiser

My goat was taken in the Gunn Peak area of Snohomish County, in the Cascade Mountains of Washington. I had scouted the area for six to eight weekends prior to the opening weekend. I sincerely believe that if you are familiar with the area and the animals, your chance for success will be much better. I spotted approximately 20 goats in different areas, ranging in altitude from 2,500 feet to 6,000 feet.

On Sunday, the weekend before the season opening, we were hiking up to Eagle Lake, trying to get our legs in shape. I had spotted the goat I wanted to go for the previous day, and I figured we had a pretty good hike to get it. On our way out from Eagle Lake, we came down by Barkley Lake. Across Barkley Lake, on the side of Baring Mountain, I spotted what I felt was a trophy animal or close to it.

On Friday afternoon (the day before the season opened), my wife and I hiked into Barkley Lake. It's a short hike, only two miles from the end of the road. We set up camp, and that evening I glassed the side of the mountain for my trophy goat, but he never showed himself.

The next morning, I was up before daylight looking for my big billy. At 10:00 a.m., my two friends, Vern Lang and John Peruka, arrived in camp. They agreed to go with me. If I got a goat, they would help pack out the meat.

We decided to go up the side of Baring Mountain as far as we could go. We left the lake (elevation 2,500 feet) at 11:00 a.m. When we reached the rock face, and couldn't climb any farther, it was about 4:00 p.m. At an elevation of 3,600 feet, it was about as steep as any hunter wants to climb. We saw no goats, but there was lots of sign, and we knew that animals were in the area. We rested for about 15 to 20 minutes and then decided to come down.

We started down through a little shoot of timber that came down the side. We figured we could not go back the same way we had come up. At least in the timber we had something to grab onto. We had gone into the timber approximately 50 yards when we spotted two goats. I picked the one I could see best. He looked in great shape; the other goat was partially hidden. I shot only one shot. I was using a Remington 700 BDL in .264 caliber, with a 140 grain Remington bullet. The goat took only a couple of steps before going down.

Now our troubles would begin. It was 4:30 p.m. when I shot the goat. By the time we got the animal back to our truck, it was 9:45 p.m. I knew at the time I shot him he was big; but, I had no idea I was bringing back a real trophy.

Photograph by Wm. H. Nesbitt

ROCKY MOUNTAIN GOAT
HONORABLE MENTION
SCORE: 50 5/8

Locality: Little Oliver Creek, B. C.   Date: January 1985
Hunter: David J. Flemming

ROCKY MOUNTAIN GOAT 50%

David J. Flemming

It was a crisp Saturday morning in January, one of those fine days that British Columbia is famous for. My hunting partner, Richard Loftstrom, and I decided we would go out for a day of spotting and maybe we would be lucky. We wanted to find a good mountain goat.

We first went to a spot where we had seen a good-sized goat, but we didn't see a thing. So, instead of heading home, we decided to try the other area.

We drove about 30 miles east of Terrace, then up a logging road to the base of Little Oliver Mountain. There, we spotted what looked to be a good-sized billy. We then decided to go up the mountain after him. We left the truck, and climbed down a ravine. Then came the creek. We had to find a way to cross it without getting wet, as it wasn't totally frozen over. Once we got over that, we had to decide the best way to climb the mountain to get to the goat.

We started slowly up the mountain. For the first quarter-mile it was icy and steep, but we had trees to help us. Then, we got out in the opening, but we had to stay on the blind side so the goat couldn't see us. We wanted to get above the goat so we wouldn't spook him. We got out in the open area and the snow conditions were terrible. The snow was up to our armpits and we had to make trail all the way, so it was slow going.

Finally, about 4½ hours later, we figured we were high enough to cut across to where the goat should be. So, we started across but we couldn't see him. There were a few trees between us and the goat that we had to cut down to be able to see where the goat was bedded down. By this time, we were wet and very cold. We were really hurrying, because time was running out for us to get safely down the mountain.

All of a sudden, we looked to our right. There he was, bedded down. The goat saw us just as we saw him. He was about 400 yards across a ravine, bedded down on a rock pinnacle. We knew we couldn't get any closer. My .300 Magnum Parker Hale rifle was sighted-in to be 2 inches high at 100 yards with my 180 grain bullet. At 400 yards, I figured I could take a bead on his shoulder and let him have it. I put my rifle up and, leaning against a tree, put the cross hairs on his shoulder. I said to my partner, "Now or never!" and squeezed the trigger. Click: a dud shell. By this time the goat had jumped up, so I ejected the shell, feeling mad at the bullet. Just as I was putting another shell in my gun, my partner said the goat was starting to run. The billy had only 50 to 70 feet to go around the rock face to be out of sight. I put the cross hairs on his front shoulder, moved it ahead about a foot, and squeezed the trigger again. At that time, the goat was just rounding the rock face and my bullet hit the rock face. We thought we'd have to kiss the goat goodbye.

We stepped out into the opening and discussed what to do. We decided we would go down and come back up the next day. My partner turned to start down the mountain. I was still standing there, looking in the direction where the goat had gone. There was a ravine between us and the goat, and I looked in the ravine as I started to go down the mountain. Out of the corner of my eye, the goat re-appeared in the ravine about 300 yards below us. I couldn't believe my eyes. I didn't have time to holler to my partner. I just drew a bead on the top of the goat's shoulder blades and squeezed the trigger.

My partner yelled to ask what was going on. I told him I had shot a goat. He didn't believe me and asked where. I told him down in the ravine. By this time, he was on his way back. I figured that the goat would lie on the ledge where I had shot it, because I knew he was hit hard. But, that old billy gave one little kick, which was enough to put him over the edge, and he landed at the bottom of the ravine.

By this time, it was roughly 3:00 p.m. So, we had a choice of sliding down the steep ravine, or going around, which meant a mile to get to the goat. We knew daylight was running out fast, so we looked at each other, then jumped over the side and slid all the way down to my goat.

When we got down to him, we inspected him all over to see if he was damaged in the long fall. He was perfect. The horns looked to be over 10 inches, by our estimation. We were sure pleased with ourselves! We took quite a few pictures, and then we field dressed him and started the long drag out. By the time we had dragged the goat down the ravine, then across the creek and up the ravine to the pickup, it was totally dark.

We drove my prize to the taxidermist. He estimated my goat to be about 300 pounds and 8½ years old. I was pleased when we measured the horns and found them to be nearly 11 inches long. I knew then I had a very respectable goat.

Photo Courtesy of John G. Munsinger

Banks Island, N. W. T., was the site of John Munsinger's muskox hunt in 1985. It resulted in this trophy that scores 108 points.

Photo Courtesy of Roy L. Mondike

Roy Mondike hunted on the Parry Peninsula of N. W. T. in 1985 to find his muskox that scores 111 2/8 points.

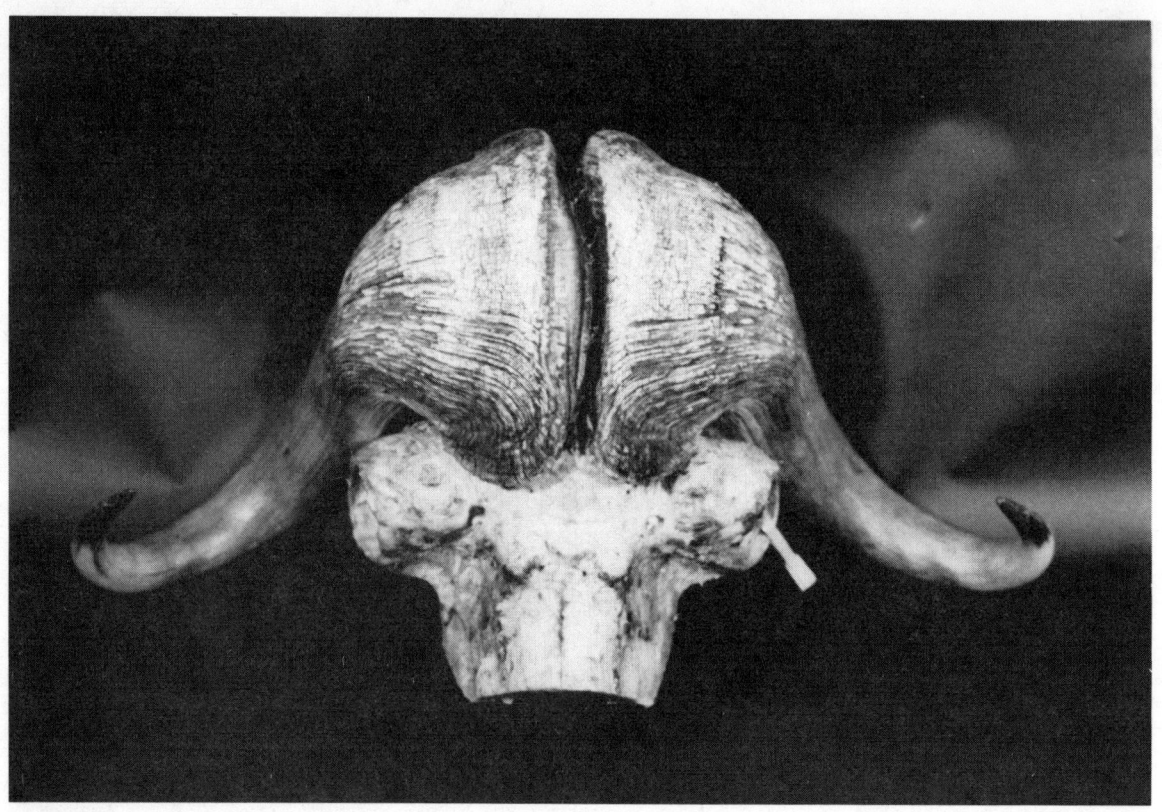

Photograph by Wm. H. Nesbitt

MUSKOX
FIRST AWARD
SCORE: 110 4/8

Locality: Banks Island, N. W. T. Date: March 1985
Hunter: David V. Collis

MUSKOX 110 4/8

David V. Collis

As I left my Florida home on March 23, 1985, heading for a muskox hunt on Banks Island, N.W.T., I didn't quite realize that I would be experiencing a 118 degree difference in the outside air temperature. The temperature at Inuvik was 35 degrees below zero when my flight was met by the hunt coordinator, Jessie Amos. From the airport, we went first to the hotel, and then on to the office to be fitted with special Arctic survival clothing. At this time, we were also issued our hunting licenses.

The next day's air service took me to Banks Island, where I was met by my guide, Mr. Roy Goose. I had the choice of staying in a lodge, or living with my guide and his family. I opted to stay with my guide. We enjoyed an evening of visiting and re-telling previous hunting adventures. Quite a few other Eskimos came over to inspect my archery equipment, as I was the only archer in our group of seven hunters.

The next morning, we packed our sleds with provisions and headed northeast, planning to stay out three or four days. The trip to the hunting area took us about 12 hours. Along the way, we were able to look at several muskox, trying to find an exceptional trophy.

We stayed in a double-walled tent, very adequately heated by a fuel oil heater, which also served as a cooking stove. On our trip out, I shot arctic hare and ptarmigan to go along with our caribou meat, which was also very delicious.

Day two was spent doing a bit of spotting and glassing for muskox. We passed up a lot of nice muskox.

On the third day, about noon, we spotted a group of three muskox, two of which were large bulls. They were feeding on a ridge that was wind blown, where the snow was not so deep. A small canyon nearby gave me enough cover to make a stalk. I picked out the largest bull, and I shot him at twenty yards. He was mine to claim in a couple of minutes, after the broadhead did its work.

We had our work cut out for us, skinning the animal for a life-size mount and cutting up the meat. A seven-hour sled ride took us back "home". We had a nice celebration in town, as this was the largest bull they had taken.

After the 60-day drying period, my muskox scored 111 6/8 for trophy entry, potentially making it a new World's Record for bow and arrow.

Photograph by Wm. H. Nesbitt

MUSKOX
SECOND AWARD
SCORE: 110

Locality: Sadlerochit River, Alaska   Date: March 1985
Hunter: Ronald L. Deis

MUSKOX 110

Ronald L. Deis

Imagine, if you will, a good-sized Shetland pony covered with 7 to 9-inch long fur. Then, add a set of horns that would look very appropriate on a Cape buffalo, and you've got a pretty good approximation of the small but spectacular muskox. Add to this its environment of the snow and ice fields of the far North, and you've got the ingredients for a very romantic hunt, one that is becoming increasingly popular with sportsmen.

Ronald L. Deis went to the Sadlerochit River of Alaska in search of a muskox trophy. Deis is a native of Alaska, so he did not need a guide. He knew this was a good locality for muskox, and he was well equipped.

He traveled into the hunting area by snowmobile on the first of March, 1985. His base was the village of Kaktovik, with the hunting area approximately 65 miles away.

On March 3, Ron found his big bull muskox. He worked to within 100 yards, then he used his Remington BDL in .300 Magnum to down his trophy. The time was 3 p.m. Ron's hunt was over, with a fine trophy to show for it.

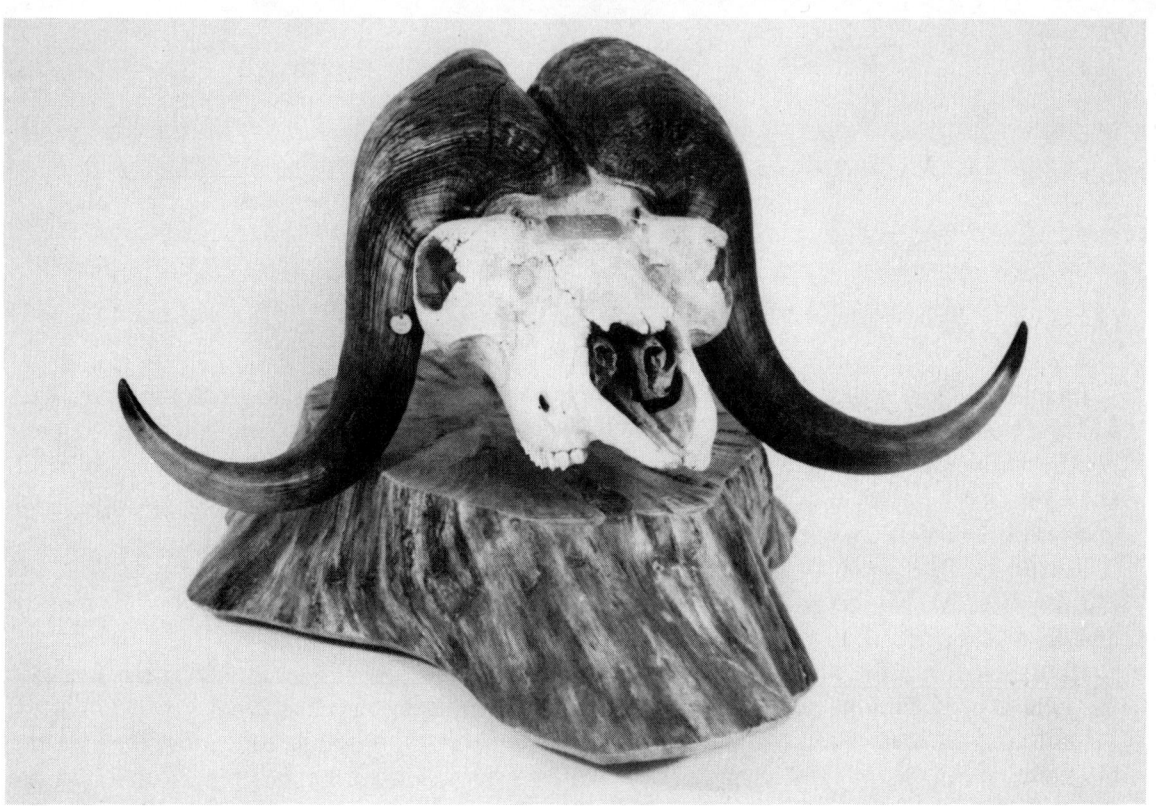

Photograph by Wm. H. Nesbitt

MUSKOX
CERTIFICATE OF MERIT
SCORE: 121

Locality: Ellice River, N. W. T.   Date: Picked Up 1983
Owner: John G. Stelfox

MUSKOX 121

John G. Stelfox, owner

Dr. John Stelfox is one of the most respected wildlife scientists of the Canadian Wildlife Service. He is well-known for his research on moose, sheep, caribou, and other big-game animals. He has also spent extensive time in Africa, working on aspects of big-game management of the wildlife of that country.

John is also an Official Measurer and has served on several Final Awards Judges Panels. He is an avid big-game hunter and a good evaluator of trophy quality afield. When he saw this huge muskox, he knew it was one that would rank very high in the records.

This muskox bull apparently died of natural causes prior to December 1983, when the skull and horns were picked up by an Eskimo, Eddie Manigyogena. The location was near the Ellice River, Northwest Territories. Later, John acquired the horns from Eddie and had them measured. That entry measurement for the records keeping totaled $119 \frac{2}{8}$, well up in the category. But, the measurement was apparently conservative, as the 19th Awards Final Judges Panel found the correct final score to be 121, just below the World's Record of 122. In fact, this fine muskox will be listed as the all-time number two for the category in the next edition of *Records of North American Big Game*.

Photograph by Wm. H. Nesbitt

BIGHORN SHEEP
FIRST AWARD
SCORE: 191 7/8

Locality: Granite Co., Mont.   Date: September 1984
Hunter: Steven L. Gingras

BIGHORN SHEEP 191 7/8

Steven L. Gingras

I was lucky enough in 1984 to draw a Montana ram permit for area 216 (Rock Creek). I spent several weekends hiking in the area, and I had previously hunted deer and elk there. I was thus moderately familiar with the area. The problem was that the rams live in another part of the range during the deer and elk season, which opens much later than the sheep season. I saw a lot of sheep sign and a few rams, but not the huge heavy rams that I knew were there.

I talked with my friend, Dr. Phil Wright, who is the Chairman of the Boone and Crockett Club Records Committee, and also has a cabin overlooking the area I was to hunt. Phil knows the area and the local people well and is an extremely knowledgeable hunter. He advised me to talk to Larry Clark, the son-in-law of the owner of most of the land that the rams live on. Larry outfits deer and elk hunters in the area, and he proved to be an excellent guide and a fine companion. Larry lives right on the area and observes the sheep year-round. After talking to Larry, I asked him if he would guide me. We agreed to hunt the opening week until I scored.

The hunting area is only about 60 miles from my home in Missoula, but 45 miles of it is over poor roads. I decided not to spend any more time scouting the area, as I just might blunder into the rams and spook them out of the area. I would rely on Larry's knowledge of the sheep for my hunt.

I stopped at the Montana Fish, Wildlife and Parks Department office in Missoula, and talked to two of my friends there. Bill Thomas, the Information Director, and Jim Ford, who is the Western Region Director, were extremely helpful. Jim, who is an avid sheep hunter, had a huge set of sheep horns lying on the floor of his office. I asked him what they scored and where they came from. He smiled at me and said that they were from Rock Creek and that they scored 193. My head filled with visions of taking a trophy such as that magnificent ram. Little did I know that I would take a ram even larger than that tremendous head.

I arrived at Larry's house on the 14th of September, the afternoon before the season opened. Larry and I talked about sheep and hunting in general, and got acquainted. He told me a lot about the sheep in the area, and I learned that they are mostly descendants of sheep that were transplanted into the area from the Sun River Herd of Montana. There was a native herd originally, but they were decimated by disease and over-hunting. The transplants have done magnificently and the horn growth has been unbelievable. Larry showed me pictures of rams that were four years old and had sixteen-inch bases and were of book class size. That night Larry showed me slides of some of the huge rams, taken in the spring, that were in there. I knew that sleep would be hard to come by that night!

We started out early the next morning on horseback, headed for the head of Capron Creek. That is the area, Larry told me, where the large rams live during the early fall and late summer. We left the horses on top of the ridge and started to hunt on foot. The rams live in the timber on the steep sides of the canyons, watering in the creek that flows in the bottom. We saw fresh sheep sign almost immediately, and was I ever excited! We saw where they had grazed, and the sheep trails had been heavily used recently. We had walked for about an hour, when we spotted two rams about 40 yards ahead of us. With my heart pounding, I got them in the binoculars, but they were not what I wanted this early in the hunt.

About 11:30 a.m., we were walking along slowly, still hunting. We noticed a small fir tree, about six feet tall and 100 yards below us, that was being violently horned by an animal. We sat down behind a large tree to glass. Rams, about 20 in one single bunch, were feeding and butting heads, milling around and jostling each other. The rams ranged from juvenile to one mature ram with about 36-inch horns, but his horns had perfect points and not much mass. The wind was in our faces and the rams were unaware of us, so we started to inch closer. We slid on our rears down the hill, from the cover of one tree to another. We kept glassing the group, and the sounds of rams crashing heads, told us that there were more rams below us, out-of-sight.

As we kept watching them, and also trying to edge closer, we suddenly noticed a different and larger ram than we had seen before. We could then count about 30 rams below us through the trees, four of which were good rams. My binoculars were shaking, and my heart was pounding. But, the steady breeze in my face, and the fact that my watch showed me that it had been almost three hours since we had first seen them (and they had still not seen us), calmed me down.

Then suddenly, I thought I saw the ram I wanted! He had just walked into the view of my eight power Zeiss rubber-armoured binoculars. I grabbed my rifle and worked a round into the chamber. It is a Ruger action in .270 Winchester caliber, with a stainless barrel from Marquart, and a Brown Precision fiberglass stock. With my pet load of 62 grains of WW 785 and a 130-grain Nosler solid-base bullet, it is a deadly mountain rifle and has accounted for more than a few trophies.

Larry saw the ram and said he was a keeper, but I should wait until he turned his head so we could size him for sure. The right side, the side I saw first, was tremendous. The horn was massive, as are those of all mature rams, but it was a bit unusual in that after sweeping down below the jaw and coming up to the eye, it flared straight out to the side to a perfect point. I was sure that it was 46 or 47 inches long. But, when he turned his head, I saw that the left horn was broken off, so I passed him up.

The sound of rams crashing heads was coming more often now. Whereas before the sound had been coming to us every three to five minutes, it was now an almost constant crashing, sounding to me almost like rifle shots. We knew that there had to be a group of large rams that were just out of sight below a steep spot in the hill, as only the large rams seemed to be butting heads. The whole time this had been going on, we were between 50 and 75 yards from them. Now, we could see the backs of some rams that were only about 30 yards from us, just over the edge of the steep spot. It was some of the smalls rams. They were between us and the big rams that we knew were just below.

We were sitting there, trying to figure out what to do, when suddenly it happened. Something spooked the whole herd. Out from under the ledge came about 10 huge rams, every one of them a trophy. In the rear was the largest ram of them all. I brought up my rifle and tried to get the cross hairs on the running ram. Then, in a stroke of luck, he stopped in an opening and stood broadside to us, looking downhill to check for whatever it was that had frightened them. (I found out later, after getting a call from Jack Atcheson of Butte, Montana, that it was Jack, coming up from the bottom that had frightened them. They had winded him.)

If I live to be 500 years old, I will never forget the sight of the ram standing there! He had stopped where the sun was streaming through the trees, and he was a sight to behold with those massive horns and dark brown, heavy body. A shot through the shoulders, and he was mine.

He had stopped about 60 yards away. As we approached him, several smaller rams, apparently confused by my ram dropping, milled around him and only moved off when we were almost to him. I looked at Larry, and the smile on his face told me that the ram was as good as I had hoped when I shot.

In the excitement of early morning, I had left my measuring tape at Larry's ranch, so we had to wait until we were back at the house to measure him. I could hardly believe my eyes when we put the tape on him. He was $41\frac{7}{8}$ inches on the one horn and 41 inches on the other. The bases were $16\frac{3}{4}$ inches in circumference.

A couple of days later, I was in the office of Jim Ford to have the horns plugged and sealed for official identification by the Fish and Game Department as a legal kill. Jim green-scored my ram at $196\frac{1}{8}$. Sixty-one days later, Dr. Philip L. Wright scored it officially for trophy entry at $195\frac{1}{8}$. What a trophy! Beginner's luck, I guess, but you can bet I am now a confirmed sheep fanatic and it won't be long before I am heading North to hunt those grand fellows again.

Photograph by Wm. H. Nesbitt

DESERT SHEEP
FIRST AWARD
SCORE: 185 2/8

Locality: Graham Co., Ariz.   Date: December 1982
Hunter: John W. Harris

DESERT SHEEP 185 2/8

John W. Harris

As far as hunting goes, sheep hunting is probably the very worst type of hunt an individual can make. The trouble lies in that sheep hunting, win, lose, or draw, is addictive. So much so that instead of being an addiction, it can actually become an obsession. At least, that is how it affected me.

My story starts 15 years ago when I made my first sheep hunt. The hunt took place in the Chugach Mountains in Alaska in 1968. A 10-day hunt turned into 17, and a missed shot saw me go home to Wheatland, Wyoming, empty-handed.

After I moved to Arizona, luck finally smiled on me. In 1982, I drew a coveted desert bighorn sheep permit for the Aravaipa Canyon unit. I say "luck", because I had applied for Arizona desert bighorn for 8 years and Wyoming Rocky Mountain bighorn for 17 years without obtaining a permit! When the permit arrived in the mail, I was probably the happiest hunter in Arizona.

After coming down from cloud nine, I realized that a lot of planning had to take place in a very short time. There had been years of waiting, and now just a couple of months of preparation would either spell success or failure. One of the first decisions to be made was whether to hire a guide or go it on my own. After weighing the alternatives, and talking with friends, I decided that I would seek assistance.

A couple of phone calls and about a week later, I had some of the best help in the state. With a permit this valuable, I figured that I needed every advantage I could muster. I spent every free moment for the next three months in Aravaipa Canyon. I talked with Arizona Game and Fish Officer Norris Dodd, who was doing research work in the canyon, and to Tom Waddell, who was the area Wildlife Manager. By the time December rolled around, I felt certain I was ready for the hunt.

Dan Artery, a friend of mine from Wyoming, came down to make the hunt with me. We met our guides, Tom Boggess and Dean Priest, at a preselected campsite on Wednesday, December 1, 1982. We got situated in camp, and then planned the hunt strategy.

Other members of the Arizona Desert Bighorn Sheep Society had come along to help. Joe Bill Pickerel and Joe Mahac had set up a spike camp across a major canyon from us to check out another area. Jim Mahac, Joe's son, had joined the rest of us in base camp. The day before season opening found us all out in the hills, scouring the area in an attempt to locate one of the two rams I was interested in. While we found over 40 sheep and 10 large rams, we could not locate either of the rams that I was after. Just before dark, we finally located one very large ram that had bedded down at the head of a feeder canyon. I had a decision to make, whether to go after this ram or continue looking for the ram I had my heart set on. It was decided that we would go after the bedded-down ram.

Opening morning found us stalking the spot where the ram had been bedded. But, he had apparently moved during the night and the only sheep we located was a nice, 3/4-curl ram. We regrouped and decided to split up. Jim Mahac and Dean Priest would go one way, and Tom Boggess, Dan Artery and I would go another. Just prior to splitting up, we heard some shooting and went to investigate. We located the other hunter, who also had a permit for this unit. He had taken the ram we had started out for that morning.

We split up. My group tried to cross a canyon, but we ended up having to backtrack over the ground we had just covered. When we got out, Dean Priest came running up to us and said that he and Jim Mahac had located a group of sheep that contained the ram that we figured was the biggest in the canyon. We had about a quarter-mile hike to the rim of the main canyon. When we arrived, Jim pointed out the big ram. The ram was browsing in a bush that blocked its horns from our view. Jim indicated that the ram was extremely big, much bigger than any of the other six rams that were with him. Since most of the other six would easily make the Boone and Crockett minimum, I took Jim's word for the sheep's size. From Jim's description, I figured this had to be the ram that we had been looking for, the one we had been watching and photographing for three months.

I sat down, resting my .280 Remington rifle over the rim of the canyon wall. The ram was quartering away to the left, about a 45-degree angle below us, and about 150 yards away. I squeezed off the shot and heard the solid smack of the bullet striking home. All the rams started to run at the shot. As the ram I was after wheeled, I shot again, striking him in the middle of the back, just behind the shoulders. He tumbled and hit another ram as he fell, almost flattening the other ram. When he came to rest, his head was stuck in another bush, so I could not see his horns. I had just killed my first sheep, and I could not even be sure what he looked like. While I am normally a patient man, this was getting to be ridiculous. I wanted to see the ram's horns, and I wanted to see them now!

Joe Bill Pickerel had come into the canyon, so we directed him to the downed ram. He pulled the sheep's head out of the bush, and I finally got a good look at my sheep through binoculars. It most definitely was the ram of my dreams!

It took us over two hours to get off the rim and down to the ram's location. We had to go down through a feeder canyon to get to the main canyon. The trail was certainly a sheep trail, as it was almost vertical and virtually non-existent in places.

When we got to the ram, the first order of business was to put a tape on the horns. With a final reading of 41½ inches in length and over 16¼ inch bases, the war whoops I made could probably be heard in Tucson, over 60 miles away.

It took us well over four hours to get out of the canyon, as we got caught in the dark. Six people trying to use one flashlight is nothing short of a three-ring circus, particularly when trying to negotiate a sheep trail. The way I felt, I thought I could fly out of the canyon. The good spirits and good friends made the four-hour trek, in less than ideal conditions, seem like a cakewalk. I have to admit, camp sure looked good when we got back.

I had finally started my grand slam, after a long period of both frustration and anticipation. Starting with a trophy of this caliber made the years of waiting, and the occasional moments of frustration, worthwhile. I have felt extremely fortunate with my success, but the real thrill, for me, is still being in the great outdoors with good friends to share the good times.

No matter where my hunting trails may lead, I know the *big* ram of Aravaipa Canyon will live on in my mind forever.

Photograph by Wm. H. Nesbitt

DESERT SHEEP
SECOND AWARD
SCORE: 182 1/8

Locality: Baja Calif., Mexico   Date: February 1984
Hunter: Jesus H. Garza-Villarreal

DESERT SHEEP 182 1/8

Jesus H. Garza-Villarreal

Before I begin the story about my hunting trip, I would like to make a brief statement about my previous experience with desert sheep. After three or four years of applying for permission to hunt for desert sheep in Baja California, it was given to me in 1980. It was for March 6 to 15, 1981, at the Arroyo Grande area, the San Matias camp, state of Baja California Norte. My hopes were set on hunting a sheep that would give a minimum score of 170. On the fourth day of our hunting trip, a little before it became dark, we located a group of seven rams, including one that had a score between 175 and 180, according to information given to us. Since we only had a little time before dark, my guides and I decided which one was the biggest, without being able to estimate its score. I shot it. It ended up having a score of 165 3/8. I was very content about this, my first sheep, and I thought that someday I would be able to kill a bigger one, one that might be included in the book of records.

I was given permission again, for the next season, to hunt at the San Pedro Martir Sierra, the El Diablo camp, during March 6 to 15, 1982. Again, my intention was to hunt for a sheep that would score a a minimum of 175, or at least one that would be better than the one I already had. In spite of this being one of the best areas for finding good sheep, I didn't manage to kill any during the 10-day hunting trip. The sierra we were on is one of the highest and most difficult ones where desert sheep live. We managed to see at least 50 sheep. These included rams, ewes, and lambs, but we could only take movies of them. We saw some rams that were legal due to their age, but their score would have been lower than the one I already had. Therefore, I did not shoot. We also saw some big rams with good scores that were not legal for hunting. They were either too young, or their horns were still short. The 10 days went by, after which I went back home, tired, and thinking that some day I would find a sheep with a good score.

I didn't get permission to hunt for desert sheep during the 1982-1983 season. I kept on applying, and during the next year, I was again chosen. This time the permission was for the La Sierrita area, the El Diablo camp, for February 1 to 10, 1984.

On January 31, 1984, I left Saltillo to board a plane in Monterrey. I was headed for Mexicali, Baja Calif. When we stopped in Chihuahua, due to a heavy snow storm, we had a mishap. This delayed my arrival at Mexicali. I got there one day later, February 1st, before noon. My friend Jorge Belloc (head of the Sheep Hunting Organization in Baja California Norte) and Ismael Castro, who would be in charge of my hunting trip, were at the airport. We went to eat Chinese food at a nice restaurant. Mario Lopez Fonseca, a biologist from the Fauna Department of the Cimarron Sheep Program, also came with us.

We were talking during dinner, with the talk about sheep and hunting. The story was told of the hunter who had been in the La Sierrita previously. His group had located a group of six rams, including one scoring 176, which had been hunted. But, there were two bigger ones. Jorge told me to tell my guide, who was waiting for me at the camp, that it would be convenient for us to go look for these sheep. We would most likely be able to find them in that area, due to the green vegetation near the camp. During that summer, it had rained more than during the previous ones.

At about 5:00 p.m., Ismael and I left Mexicali in a Bronco truck, headed towards the El Diablo camp. This camp is located 112 miles south, and is at the foot of the San Pedro Martir Sierra. It took us about 2½ hours of driving to get there. We rode on both paved and unpaved roads, arriving at about 8:00 p.m. While the cook was preparing a good dinner, Ismael introduced me to the guide, Ramon Arce, and to the three scope spotters and helpers that would accompany me throughout the hunting trip. We talked for a while. Ramon asked me what score I was looking for in my sheep. I told him I wanted a 180 score. Ramon didn't answer. After a while, he said, "O.K. We will do everything that's possible." This made me feel happy as we went off to sleep.

Very early the second day, we had breakfast and then we filled our packs with enough food, water, and drinks for three days and two nights out. Ismael, Ramon, Don Lupe, Cayo, his brother, and I, left in the Bronco, heading toward La Sierrita, a series of medium size mountains located between the San Pedro Martir Sierra and the Cortez Gulf, close to the beach. It is a one hour ride, approximately.

We got to the foot of the sierras, where we stopped the Bronco, and started spotting for sheep. We soon located two sheep about 2,500 feet away. After a while, Ramon thought that a ram might be behind that sierra, so he sent Don Lupe and Coyo to check the area on the other side. An hour later, they rushed back to tell us that they had located two sheep, of which one was a good one. We could get there by climbing up directly in front of where we were. We climbed up rapidly. Since I hadn't warmed up, I was shaking when we got to the top.

We found the sheep, and after watching them with 16-power binoculars and a 60-power telescope, the guides told me that the big sheep would score 175. I asked them if they were sure that it would not score higher. I watched it at a 450 foot range for about three minutes. I was perspiring, because I could not decide whether to kill it or pass it up. I had started hunting two hours before, and still had 10 days to go and much good land to cover. I might not find a bigger one, or even one like it. Several times, I tried to shoot, but my finger would not push the trigger hard enough. Something inside kept telling me not to do it. In a low voice I kept on telling them to check it well, to see if it would measure more. The guides kept saying that it was 175, no more. All of a sudden, the sheep jumped down the canyon. I wanted to shoot but Ramon said it was too risky; we might hurt one of its legs and then we would spend the rest of the time looking for it. I agreed with him. The sheep jumped again and we lost it. We started descending towards the Bronco, in search of a place to camp.

I was sad. Don Lupe, an old guide who was our helper, told me not to worry, we would find a bigger one. I kept on thinking about the 10 days I had spent at El Diablo without spotting a good one. That night, I couldn't sleep, thinking about what would happen if the weather changed, or if I should have problems with my physical condition, etc.

On the third day, very early, we started out for the opposite side. After walking a little, Ramon told Don Lupe to go back to the camp because he had a cold. He was supposed to wait for us there. I gave him some pills so he would get well. After walking for three hours, we located two sheep at about 3,000 feet. I could not distinguish them very well, because they were so far away. After looking through our binoculars for three hours, one of the sheep started walking towards us. When we could see it better, we were surprised that it only had one big horn. If it had both, it would have easily been a 180 score. Maybe it lost its horn in a fight or due to a fall. I thought I still had bad luck.

As we headed back to camp, we found a dead sheep whose horns were 170. Maybe it had been injured by a clandestine hunter. Before we got to the camp, Ramon told me that during the next day we would move to another area, far away, called Algodones. But, when we got to camp, Don Lupe told us that he had climbed a slope close by, in order to not get bored. There, he started spotting a sierra that was between the places where we had camped on the first and second days. He had located two rams and two ewes at about 4,500 feet. That night, we decided to look for these sheep, before moving to another place.

On the fourth day, at dawn, we started spotting the area where the sheep had been seen, but we only saw ewes. We then decided to search for the rams. We picked up the camp and walked towards the place where they could be. We sent Ismael and one of the spotters in the Bronco, so they could wait for us at a place that would be adequate for lunch. We got to a place where we could look for the sheep. Seeing that the rams were not around, Ramon told me to go to where Ismael was, so I could eat while they walked around to check the canyon that was in back to see if the sheep were there.

I was warming up the food when I saw Coyo running. He said that they had located one that was easily 180, and Ramon wanted to know if I was interested. Of course I was. I sat the food aside and grabbed my 7mm Remington Magnum. At a rapid pace, we headed to where Ramon and Don Lupe were watching the ram. When we got there, they said the ram was behind some rocks, but that the air was not blowing inside the canyon. Ramon asked if we should wait. Don Lupe said that we would have to try to to get there soon, through the canyon on the other side, in order to reach it through the top. He felt the ram was resting. It was 12:00 noon. We parted rapidly.

Ramon, Coyo, and I took only a rifle and the binoculars. As we were climbing, I started breathing faster and started getting nervous. The sheep could probably feel us getting close, and it could escape through the same canyon, without us seeing it. We got to the edge and Ramon looked down. He told us he could see the ram lying down, but it was not asleep. I peeped down. I didn't see it, because it was the same color as the rocks. Ramon told me to get on my stomach on the landslide, with my rifle pointing down, and to shoot when I saw it. He said the distance was about 390 feet, and the ram was looking up. So, I did.

When I saw the ram in my rifle scope, I noticed it was looking at me. I fired right at its shoulder blade. The horns covered up half of the body. I was surprised when it got up and trotted downwards. I asked Ramon what had happened? Where had I hit it? The sheep fell for an instant, while we were watching it with our binoculars. Ramon told me that I had hit the sheep, so I calmed down a bit, and shot again. My shot injured the ram near its knee, but it kept on running. I had to see it fall, so I fired a third bullet. It fell at about 600 feet, at last!

I was so excited that I began to remember the 13 hunting days that had gone by since I killed my other sheep; the sheep that I passed up, including the 175 point one we had seen two days ago; the climbing; the thirst; the injuries; and how tired I was.

Almost running, we made our way to my trophy. When we took a close look at it, they told me that it would measure over 180. The rest of the members of my group arrived, all of them very happy. They congratulated me, and we took pictures. Then, they took off the skin very carefully. At that moment, I thought of dissecting the whole sheep. We then climbed down to the Bronco. We went back to the El Diablo camp, where we spent the afternoon and part of the evening, talking and celebrating.

The next day, February 5, we headed to Mexicali and went directly to Jorge Belloc. When he saw the sheep's horns, he said it was the biggest one that had been killed during that season and also the one before. Later, at the Lucerna Hotel, Jorge and Mario Lopez Fonseca (the biologist) took pictures of the horns, and made a green measurement which was $185 3/8$. On July 11, 1984, 155 days after the kill, Mr. Jose Trevino, an Official Measurer for Boone and Crockett, measured my ram as $183 2/8$ for entry into the records.

Photos Courtesy of Steve Polich and Roberta A. Hartford

(l) This fine Stone's sheep scores 170 2/8 points. It was killed near the Prophet River, B. C., in 1984 by Steve Polich. (r) Petty Mountain, Montana, was home to this bighorn sheep that scores 180 6/8 points. Roberta Hartford killed it in 1982.

Photo Courtesy of Randy Jackson

This huge bighorn sheep scores 187 2/8 points. It was taken in 1984 on Plateau Mountain in Alberta by Randy Jackson.

DESERT SHEEP
THIRD AWARD
SCORE: 176 6/8

Locality: Pinal Co., Ariz.   Date: February 1984
Hunter: Travis K. Holder

DESERT SHEEP 176⅝

Travis K. Holder

I could hardly believe it. It was the first year I put in for desert bighorn and I got drawn for my first choice. I was just thirteen and very excited.

My father (Mick Holder) and I left our home in Globe, Arizona, on our way to Tucson. We met a friend, Biff McCollum, near Mammoth. From there, we drove the remainder of the way to Tucson. In Tucson, we checked in with the Game and Fish Department. The date was December sixth. After finishing up at the Game and Fish Department, we met another friend, John Harris, who was going to help guide. John had taken the number one Arizona bighorn a year ago in Aravaipa Canyon, the canyon I would soon be hunting in.

We left Tucson, heading for Aravaipa Canyon, a large canyon near Mammoth, Arizona. We reached our destination late that night, and we camped near the edge of the canyon.

We got up before daylight the next morning. It was cold and windy. We got dressed and ate a fast breakfast, then prepared for the day's hunt. I loaded my .270 Winchester, which actually belonged to my brother, Frank. I borrowed it because I was having problems with my new .25-06.

We started out by walking to the edge of the canyon and glassing it for sheep. It was barely daylight. We kept glassing for about another hour, and then we moved down the canyon. We saw no sign of sheep for quite a while, so we headed back to camp for lunch. After lunch, we walked farther down the canyon. We walked and glassed, and glassed and walked, but we still saw no sheep.

We walked a little farther down and there they were, a large band of about 20 sheep! By this time, we had three additions to the hunt. Two game wardens, Kelly Neal and Jim Jett, were there, along with Bob Masters, owner of the range we were hunting on.

We were all admiring the majestic bighorns through binoculars and spotting scopes. While we were watching, some whitetail deer ran through the middle of the sheep and split them into two groups. There were five records-book rams in the bunch, but two of these were definitely superior in size. One ram was older, with a tight curl and a chip out of his horn. The other was younger and looked a little bigger.

We all argued about which ram was bigger, but my father and I decided on the younger ram. The two of us stalked him through the rocks and brush. We went as quickly and quietly as we could, the sheep were drifting towards another large canyon. At a range of about 250 yards, we stopped and looked at the ram. He was calmly eating a bush and looking up at us every once in a while. He knew we were there.

The sheep were starting to move, so we went a little closer. The ram walked up on a small knoll. We got within 200 yards, and I got a steady rest on a rock. He was standing broadside, so it was a clear shot. My dad asked me if I could make the shot. I said yes, of course!

I held the cross hairs right on the ram's shoulder, held my breath, and slowly squeezed the trigger. The next thing I knew, I saw the bullet hit the ram. It knocked him sideways, but not down. He then went up a little higher on the knoll. By this time, some of the other sheep were calmly walking near the edge of Horse Camp Canyon, a deep canyon leading into Aravaipa Canyon. I was sure the first bullet would kill him. But, I was afraid he might run and fall into the canyon, so I just pulled up and shot him again. When the bullet hit him, my ram chipped off a piece of one of his horns. I then heard my friends yell and congratulate me.

I still could hardly believe it, but it was true. It was a perfect hunt, and I couldn't ask for a better one.

Photos Courtesy of Jim A. Turcke and Howard Grounds

(l) Jim Turcke hunted Hurricane Creek, Oregon, in 1982 to find this fine bighorn sheep that scores 179 7/8 points.
(r) The Black Mountains of Arizona were home to this desert sheep that scores 174 2/8 points. Howard Grounds shot it in 1984.

Photo Courtesy of Roger Card

Roger Card and his guides with his desert sheep that scores 168 2/8 points. It was killed at Lerto, Baja Calif., Mexico, in 1985.

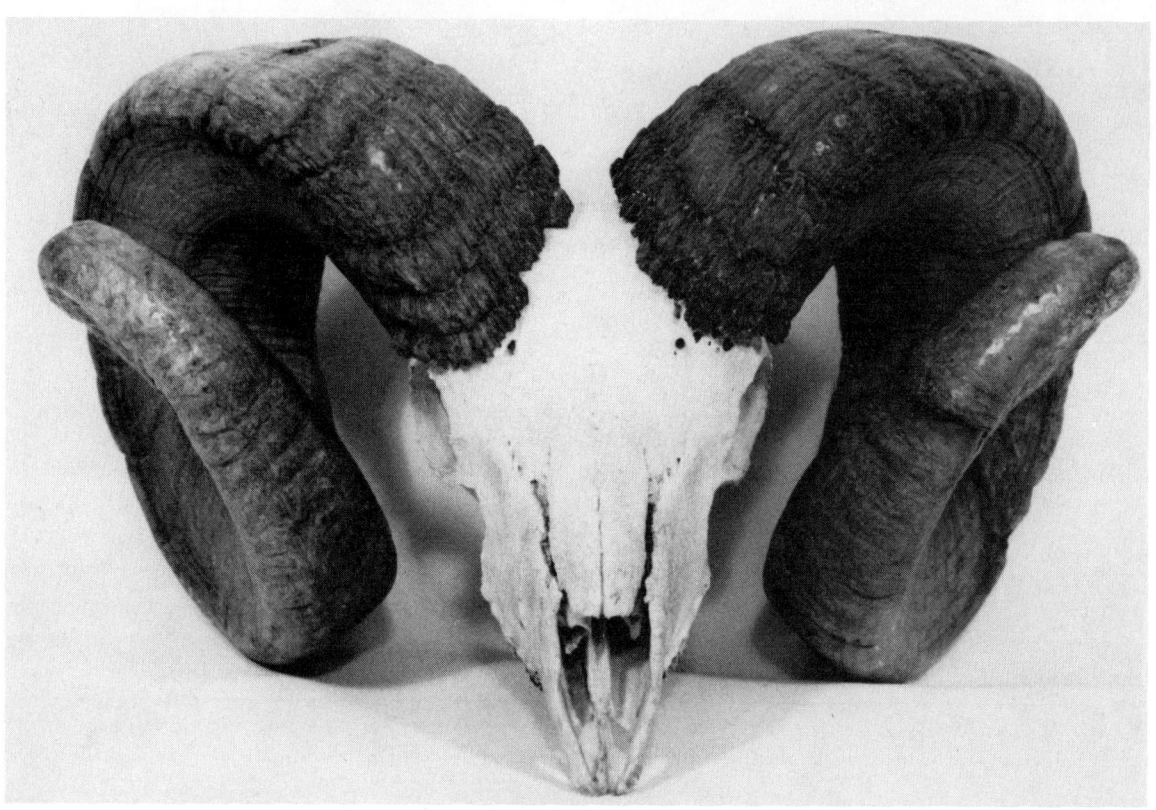

DESERT SHEEP
CERTIFICATE OF MERIT
SCORE: 201 3/8

Locality: Pima Co., Ariz. Date: Picked Up 1982
Owner: Greg Koons

DESERT SHEEP 201 3/8

Greg Koons, owner

Desert sheep are certainly one of the most prized big game animals of North America. They are beautiful animals, and hunting them involves enduring great extremes of heat and cold, as well as often scaling areas that no sane person would want to try to climb through, especially for "sport." This story is about an absolutely superb trophy animal that never fell to a sportsman's gun. Aged by the annular rings of the horns, this desert sheep was fifteen or sixteen years old when it died, apparently in the fall of 1981.

Greg Koons of Phoenix, Arizona, was out varmint hunting in Pima County, Arizona. It was February of 1982 and the weather was typically cold and brisk. It was a good day for varmint hunting, and just a good day in general to be out-of-doors.

Greg stumbled on the remains of a huge desert sheep ram. It was apparently a winter-kill, and what a set of horns. They were monstrous horns, the kind to set a sheep hunter dreaming.

Greg took the horns and skull home. They were so big he had them measured. They scored a whooping 202 6/8 for entry into the records keeping. At this score, they were awfully close to the World's Record score of 205 1/8. They easily fell into the top 10 of the category, qualifying for an invitation to the 19th Awards Final Judging.

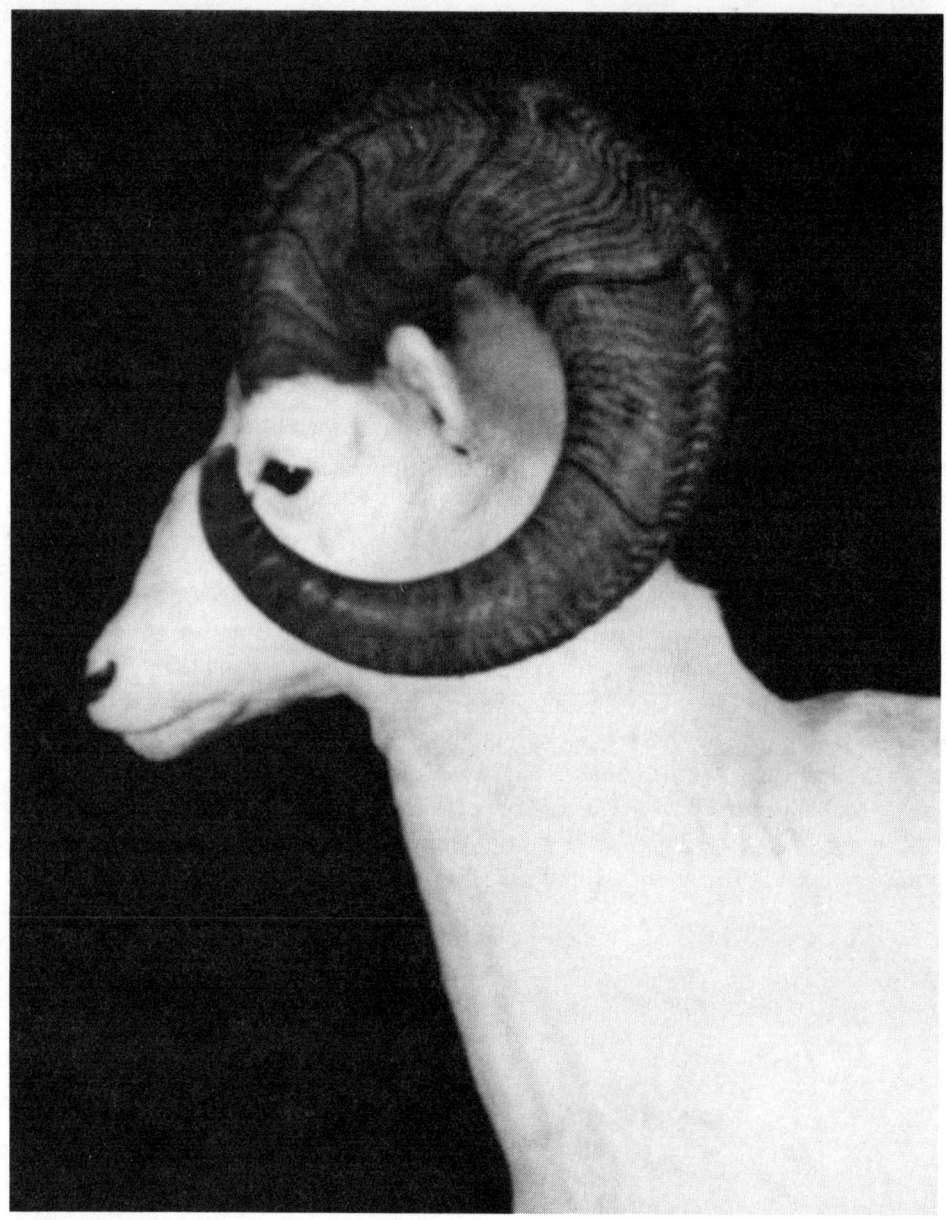

Photograph by Wm. H. Nesbitt

DALL'S SHEEP
FIRST AWARD
SCORE: 172 6/8

Locality: Mountain River, N. W. T.   Date: September 1983
Hunter: Edmond D. Henley

DALL'S SHEEP 172 6/8

Edmond D. Henley

My hunting partner, Dr. Hugh C. Nabers, and I had shared many memorable hunting experiences over a wide area of geography. Yet, our only really successful sheep hunt together had been to Mongolia in 1973. We made two trips to British Columbia in the late 1970's, but did not score. However, Hugh completed a grand slam and half of an additional one on other hunts by himself.

In early 1983, Hugh said to me that it was time to plan another mountain hunt, and he wanted me to do the planning. He suggested that I contact J & B Safaris for information about an outfitter in the Yukon Province or the Northwest Territories of Canada who could provide an opportunity to hunt better-than-average Dall's sheep and mountain caribou. That idea sounded great to me. Even though I had shot a Dall's sheep in Alaska some years before, I wanted a much better one, at least a 40-inch ram.

Beverly Wunderlich of J & B Safaris immediately recommended Stan Stevens of Norman Wells, Northwest Territories. She said Stan had a great area in the Mackenzie Mountains that was producing many 40-inch rams and also excellent moose and caribou. Stan runs a good outfit that offers horseback hunts as well as back packing. He is an experienced pilot who does much of the flying of his clients into and out of the hunting areas.

We contracted with Stan for a 10-day hunt, from September 2nd to 12th, 1983. Hugh and I arrived at Norman Wells in mid-morning of September 1st. We were met at the airport by Helen, Stan's attractive wife. She took us to their charming log home just outside of town for lunch. After lunch, we were driven to the Game Department office where we bought licenses and trophy tags. Helen then gave us a guided tour of Norman Wells, showing us, in particular, the oil development there. The petroleum in the area is mostly under the Mackenzie River, which is three miles wide there. Most of the wells are drilled from artificial islands built in the river. A few are drilled from natural islands and from shore. We watched great activity of men and machines, busy building the islands from stone quarried from the hill east of town.

Stan arrived in early evening and informed us that we would be flying to his camp at Mountain Lake the next morning, where we would meet our guides. I was to hunt with Andrew (whose last name I never learned), and Hugh was to hunt with Danny Moore.

We departed the airport about 10 a.m. the following morning, arriving at Mountain Lake at 11:30 a.m. It was a beautiful day for flying; the wilderness scenery of mountains, valleys, lakes, and rivers was outstanding. The camp had a small runway hacked out of the buckbrush, just long enough for a small airplane. Any larger aircraft would have to be equipped with floats to use the lake. This camp was ideally located for both types of aircraft.

The camp consisted of a wooden building for cooking and eating, a metal silo for storing saddles and feed, and three wooden-floored tents for the hunters and guides. Everything was neat and orderly.

Hugh and I hoped to hunt in the afternoon. But, the horses had all walked away during the night and had not returned. We found this to be the norm, because the best grass was several miles away along a tributary of Mountain River. The horses had learned this early in the season, and they went there nearly every night. We put our fishing rods together and tried to catch some grayling, but to no avail. However, it did give us the opportunity to look over our surroundings, get acclimated to the change in temperature and altitude, and observe caribou grazing on the hill south of camp. During our several days at this camp, we observed many caribou on that hill, plus several good bull moose around the lake.

There were two more days hunting from the main camp, but we found no bulls large enough to shoot. The third morning, the wranglers and guides caught all the horses early, then got them saddled and packed with our gear and food for five days. We rode to the Mountain River tributary, then turned upstream to the west. It was a six-hour ride through a light snowfall, with a stop for lunch and a cup of hot tea. Just before lunch, we watched a cow moose with calves move toward the river.

Sometime after our lunch break, a dark shape appeared in the brush to our left, about 150 yards away. This shape materialized into a fair-sized grizzly, standing to see us better. It quartered away from the direction of our trek, but stopped several times to watch us. This bear remained in the area, feeding on berries during the next few days. We saw it several times.

For three days, we hunted hard together. We saw caribou every day. We watched two huge bulls bedded on a high ridge arise and walk over the other side, then disappearing completely. One day, farther up the river valley, there were two large bull moose. Later, we surprised a wolf sleeping in the brush; he hightailed it toward the Yukon. On our return, a small grizzly appeared 30 yards away, across the creek from us. That bear acted as though it had never seen humans and horses. A quarter-mile from camp, another bear was feeding on blueberries on the hillside. (I might add that there was no open season on grizzlies in this area.) Every day, we saw several bands of ewes, lambs, and quarter-curl rams; however, the trophy rams were all somewhere else.

The fourth day, hunting from our fly camp, all of us rode down river to where we had seen the bear the first day. He was there, again. We rode up the side valley to the south to the point where it split. At this point, Andrew (my Indian guide) demonstrated how well he knew these mountains. He said we would take the valley to the left, and Hugh and Danny could go to the right. This we did.

Andrew and I rode down to and across the creek, and then up the mountainside to the left, then on toward the head of the valley. We found a level spot that was a good place to leave the horses hitched together. From there, we went on foot. After climbing about 75 yards up into the new snow, we found fresh tracks heading toward the pass. Andrew's only comment was that they were ram tracks, and fresh.

We followed these tracks around the side of the hill where they intercepted a well-worn game trail that ran straight up toward the pass. We followed this trail for approximately 300 yards to the top of the pass. At this point, Andrew moved ahead, up the mountain to the left so that he could peer over a slight rise. He crept forward, and then turned to me holding up seven fingers. My excitement could hardly be contained as I caught up with Andrew and got a look at our quarry. All the sheep but one were lying down, enjoying the afternoon sun. I could easily see that two rams were larger than the others. One quarter-curl youngster on the far left was staring straight at us.

Andrew set up his spotting scope and studied them quickly. He told me that the large ram in the center left was the best one. I used the scope and thought another ram to the right looked just as long in the horn as the other one. Andrew again told me to shoot the one on the left. By this time, they had all seen us and were standing up. So, I kneeled on the ground and then carefully shot the ram Andrew had recommended.

At the shot, the ram just stood there. Andrew told me that the ram was hit and to wait. I could envision this trophy running over the mountain, so I carefully placed another bullet behind its shoulder. This shot put him down for good. By this time, the remainder of the herd had begun to walk off. They never ran.

On approaching the dead ram, I was overjoyed to see that it was more than a full curl. Neither of us had a tape, so we used a bootlace to measure the horn, which we estimated at 40 inches. Andrew gave me his congratulations, and I gave mine to him. It was indeed a team effort, and now I had my trophy.

We skinned the sheep and quartered it, so we could transport all of it back to the horses. Hugh and Danny had heard the shots, and they came to congratulate us as we rode down the mountain valley. By Danny's tape, the horns measured roughly 41 inches on the left side and 40 inches on the right. What amazed us all were the bases, 15 inches on each side. We all decided that this ram deserved to be fully mounted, which I subsequently had done.

Upon returning to camp, we all drank a toast to my ram, which, I am sure, is a trophy of a lifetime. I may make other sheep hunts, but I certainly don't expect this kind of success again.

The following morning, our quides announced that, although Hugh had experienced no luck, we would pack up and move back to the base camp, because we were out of food. Hugh would continue to hunt for sheep in that vicinity, and I could look for a caribou.

Although I finally got a very nice bull caribou several days later, this magnificent ram was my trophy of a lifetime, and will always be the goal for me to surpass.

Photograph by Wm. H. Nesbitt

STONE'S SHEEP
FIRST AWARD
SCORE: 172 1/8

Locality: Muskwa River, B. C.   Date: August 1984
Hunter: Greg L. Stires

STONE'S SHEEP 172⅛

Greg L. Stires

I took my ram on August 3, 1984, in British Columbia, Canada. I was hunting with outfitter Garry Vince, of Muskwa Safaries.

I met Garry at the Foundation for North American Wild Sheep convention in New Orleans in 1982. I booked my Stone's sheep hunt with Garry for August 1984. Garry mentioned that he would like me there a few days early, to look the country over. I left Los Angeles for Fort St. John, B. C., with one stop-over in Vancouver.

When I landed in fort St. John, Garry was waiting for me, with another hunter, Butch White, who had arrived earlier. Garry flew us to his house, which is his main hunting camp. It was about an hour-and-a-half flight from Fort St. John. When we landed, his wife Sandra was waiting for us. We stayed at the main camp that night. At dinner that night, Garry said my guide would be an Indian named Nelson, and that I would be leaving for my hunting area the following morning.

The next morning, I had to throw my gear in a small aluminum boat to cross the river. Nelson and a horse wrangler were waiting for me. We had about a seven-hour ride to our main camp, which was a cabin located on a high lake. During our ride, we saw some elk, moose, a black bear, and some ewes and lambs along the trail. We arrived late that night at the cabin. During dinner, Nelson mentioned to me that we would be glassing the area behind the cabin for sheep the following morning, and we would start hunting the next day.

Next morning, after breakfast, we started glassing the area. We saw lots of elk, some small moose, ewes, and lambs. We came back to the cabin early that afternoon. I did some fishing, catching some rainbow trout for our dinner.

The next morning, we traveled around the lake, hunting most of the day on some lower mountains. We saw a band of rams that numbered 30 or more. There were four legal rams, but we were looking for one a little better. On the way back to camp that evening, we came upon some moose in the valley, mostly cows and calves. Nelson mentioned that night at dinner that we would be going to some higher mountains the next morning where he had spotted some good rams the year before.

When we got up the next morning, we noticed that our horses had run off. Nelson and the horse wrangler left to find them. It was about noon when they returned to camp with the horses. So, we got a late start hunting that day. That afternoon, around 3:00 p.m., we stopped to glass two high mountains. We saw a band of six rams. We didn't see any good rams at first. I set up my spotting scope and I spotted one ram lying down. Behind him, I noticed two large humps that turned out to be the curl of a very large ram.

By now, it was getting late and nightfall was coming on. We decided to go back to camp and get up early the next morning to come back to get a better look at this ram. The following morning, which was the fourth day of my hunt (August 3, 1984), we left camp real early to go back to the same spot. The sheep were nowhere to be found. We glassed for several hours. We then decided to go over to the next valley, which was Beaver Creek. There, we spotted the rams feeding. We spotted the same ram, and he looked even bigger than he had the day before. We knew that this was the one we were looking for.

The rams fed, and then bedded down on a rocky ledge that was almost impossible to get to. Nelson said we would have to go higher than the sheep to get close enough for a shot. On the way up the mountain, we ran into about 15 rams. We were afraid that we were going to spook this band of rams into the rams that were bedded down. But, luck was with us, and the spooked rams ran in the other direction.

We continued climbing to the top. When we reached the top, we had to go over another saddle to reach the rocky ledge where the rams were bedded. We could only see the smaller rams lying down. We decided to stay there until evening, when the rams would feed again.

We lay there for about four hours, until the little rams got up and started making lots of noise. Nelson got up and looked over the ledge. He could see that the big ram was still not there. At that same time, I turned around and looked below us. I saw the big ram by himself, feeding back towards the saddle we had crossed earlier that day. I whispered to Nelson that the big one was behind us. I then brought up my gun, a .270 Winchester, and took one shot at about 150 yards. The ram disappeared. Nelson said, "You got him!"

We walked over to where the ram had been, and we saw blood. We then saw that the ram had fallen off the cliff and was lying 200 yards below. We climbed down to the ram. When we lifted his head, we knew he was a good one. I had forgotten my tape measure, but Nelson had a belt on that he said was 34 inches. We put the belt along the horns. The horns were only about three inches longer than the belt, which made them approximately 37 to 38 inches long. That disappointed us.

We caped the sheep out, then packed it down the mountain and headed back to camp. We arrived two hours after dark. We had our dinner, then went to bed. The next morning, I spotted some fishing equipment in the cabin and found a fish measuring tape. We measured my ram with it. My ram's horns measured 41 inches long, with 15-inch bases. (Yes, I'm going to buy Nelson his very own tape, so some other hunter won't have a heart attack.)

The rest of the day, I did some fishing, then got to bed early. I left the next morning for the main camp. When we arrived at the main camp, Garry Vince and Butch White were already there with a nice 39-inch ram. I spent a few more days at the main camp with Garry and Sandra Vince and their family. Then, I headed for home in California.

Photos Courtesy of David V. Collis and Craig L. Leerberg

(l) David Collis hunted near the Graham River, B. C., in 1982 to kill this Stone's sheep that scores 166 2/8 points to qualify for the Awards records book. (r) Gardiner, Montana, is where Craig Leerberg found this fine bighorn sheep in 1985 that scores 178 5/8 points.

Photo Courtesy of Dennis Campbell

With a beautiful coat, this Stone's sheep scores 165 points to qualify for the Awards records book. It was shot by Dennis Campbell near West Toad River, B. C., in 1982.

Photograph by Wm. H. Nesbitt

STONE'S SHEEP
SECOND AWARD
SCORE: 171 5/8

Locality: Pink Mt., B. C. Date: August 1985
Hunter: Paul V. Palmer, Jr.

STONE'S SHEEP 171 5/8

Paul V. Palmer, Jr.

Peering over the crest of the mountain, we waited for the right moment. We were gazing upon eight rams, all with good curls, but one was more outstanding than the others. Not a drop of moisture was in my mouth as I centered the scope on the old ram, holding my breath. Hands shaking and heart throbbing, I squeezed the trigger. Damn! Eject the shell and shoot again. This time, I hit him between the shoulders, breaking the spine. Straight down, we watched the ram take one final step, dropping on his knees and then falling hundreds of feet through the air before hitting the shale slide below, where he went tumbling head-over-heels.

Our hearts panicked, as he rolled out of sight. All we could do was stand there and look. As we watched the falling ram, the other seven rams stood there, staring at us and their fallen leader. Ann (my wife) snapped as many photos as possible. My guide, Gary Dowd, stared in disappointment, as the ram's crown could be shattered from the fall. We all three moved with hesitation as we started down the bowl-like incline of shale, taking one step and then sliding three feet.

Gary approached the battered ram first, inspecting him head to toe. Gary smiled as he reached for his tape measure. We arrived moments later, not sure of our priceless kill. We were met by the congratulations of Gary. Only a few scratches on those magnificent horns. But look at the size of this ram! Horn length of 41 inches, and a base of 14 5/8. Whew! A ram of a lifetime, and not only for me. Gary's delighted face showed that years of experience and persistence had finally paid off. A king of the mountain lay majestically beside the three of us, his crown of horns curling upward toward a tearless blue sky and a wind breathing victory.

This was the seventh day of our hunt. It took us four days, riding between 7 and 10 hours a day, just to get back into the Ospeaka Mountain Range to a place no hunter had been in three years, and where two of the largest B & C rams were taken 15 years ago. This is where I wanted to go, and through hell and high water, we made it.

Gary Dowd, a guide from the R. Lynn Ross Camp, together with our wrangler (Steve) and nine horses, took us through some unbelievable country, country torn by high winds, fierce winters, and eroding weather. Animal life was abundant everywhere. The game trails were heavily used by moose, bear, caribou, sheep, goats, and other animals. Two days previous to this one, we shot one of the largest goats (9 5/8-inch horns) ever taken from this area. The shale mountains and thick forests make the hunting quite difficult. But, to be on a mountain few have touched was quite a thrill not only for my wife and me, but even for our guide. Watching, glassing, waiting, and listening for the call of the wild, is worth the effort just to be there, even if you don't make a mark. You take home an achievement beyond compare.

On our ride in, an aggressive horse had kicked and broken my scope. Unfortunately, I didn't realize this until I had the goat in sight. I shot approximately 10 times before finally bringing this massive billy down. Only then, did I want to throw the rifle away and curse every trusty steed in sight. Gary had brought an extra gun, so I took both the sheep and a fine 56-inch spread moose with his rifle.

Three weeks of good weather, beautiful country, an excellent guide, a little luck, and tremendous hunting made this a hunting trip hard to surpass.

Photo Courtesy of Leslie C. Finger

Leslie Finger hunted in the Mackenzie Mountains of N. W. T. in 1985 to find her Dall's sheep that scores 172 4/8 points.

Photo Courtesy of Edmond D. Henley

Edmond D. Henley was hunting near Mountain River, N. W. T., in 1983 when he took his Dall's sheep that scores 172 5/8 points and received the First Award at the 19th Awards.

Photo Courtesy of Dusty R. Cooper

COUGAR
FIRST AWARD
SCORE: 15 11/16

Locality: Okanagan Lake, B. C.   Date: January 1985
Hunter: Dusty R. Cooper and Marc Hubbard

COUGAR 15 11/16

Dusty R. Cooper

For years now, I've always wanted to hunt mountain lion. A few years ago, I had the chance to go on a mountain lion hunt with a couple of friends of mine, just as an observer and to take pictures. My hosts were Marc and Mike Hubbard (cousins), both of whom had cougar hounds, and have each taken cats themselves. Marc is a professional guide for cat hunters here in British Columbia. During this chase, we treed a female and kittens. We, of course, took pictures and then left them alone. This gave me the fever to go on another mountain lion hunt, and to have the possibility of shooting a cougar myself.

A few years later, I still wanted to take a cat. My chance arrived in January, right in the middle of the hunting season for mountain lion. Marc phoned me and said he had no hunters in at the present time. He wanted to know if I would like to go out and look for tracks and possibly get in on another chase. Of course my answer was yes! After discussing things on the phone, we decided that he would come up to my house to stay for a few days, since he lives and guides about 30 miles south of my home in Penticton. We would then hunt out of my home as friends, not hunter and guide.

Since neither of us knew the area we were about to hunt, we decided to call Marc's cousin, Mike, for some information. He had been hunting this area for years and knew it well. After talking to Mike, we felt there would be a good chance to come across a cat track if we looked long and hard enough in our area.

The next morning, we got up at day-break, and then left with two of Marc's cougar hounds, Rex and Gunner. After spending the entire day looking for cat tracks, and covering several miles of mountainous country with no luck, we decided to head home for the night.

Heading out the following morning, again with both hounds, we decided to try another area not far from where we were the day before. After a few hours of looking for tracks, Marc came across a set. He then came back to me, and said he had found a set of tracks, but couldn't tell how old they were. It looked to be a big cat because of its track size and stride. He said, jokingly, "It's too big for you to shoot." The snow conditions were not very good. We hadn't had any fresh snow for several days, and a crust had formed on top, which made it hard to say how old the tracks really were. So, we decided to spend the rest of the day working out the tracks. What we found were tracks going every-which-way over the whole mountainside. We could tell the cat was hunting, and we where hoping to come across a kill where the cat had been feeding, so it would give us a place to start and possibly turn the dogs lose. But, night fell, and we hadn't found any fresh kill of any kind.

That night, we were talking to Mike, when he said he wasn't working for a couple of days and would like to come along and get in on a chase with us.

The following day, the three of us went back to the tracks and began to work them out again. After a good part of the day had passed, we came across a fresh moose kill. We now knew we were closing in on the cat. It was too late in the day to turn the dogs loose, and the three of us were exhausted after walking through the snow all day long. So, we decided to be out at the moose kill first thing in the morning.

Just after day-break, we arrived back at the moose kill to find that the cat had returned during the night to finish up the last of its kill. Marc decided to turn the dogs loose. They could work out the tracks from there.

After about 5 minutes Rex (one of the dogs) took off down the road where he began following a set of tracks leading into the brush, barking with all he had. Marc said, "Let's go; he's on the cat's track!" Then, the chase was on, with the three of us trailing not far behind the two dogs.

After an hour or so, we could no longer hear the dogs as they could travel much faster then us. We started to find blood in the dog's tracks. This was not a good sign, as this meant the dogs' feet were being cut by the crust on the snow. Even if we wanted to, there would be no stopping the dogs now. Hoping the dogs were on a fresh set of tracks, we continued to follow them. Suddenly, we came across an old horse kill, which we believed the cat could have killed and fed on a few weeks ago. The horse carcass had been almost completely eaten.

Not hearing the dogs for several hours, we were concerned for their safety. Feeling that the cat might have turned on them, we tried to pick up our pace, but we all were getting tired. Then, we heard what we were all waiting for—the dogs baying. This meant the dogs had the cat treed!

Marc arrived at the tree first, with Mike and myself following. At first, we couldn't spot the cat, because the trees were real thick. Then, Mike said, "There he is," and pointed at a tree. But before much was said or done, the cat jumped from the tree and tore down a hillside. So, the chase was on again, with the dogs on his tail and us shortly behind.

After about an hour, the dogs were baying just in front of us. We rounded the corner of a large rock to find the cat cornered by the dogs on a rock bluff. Just then, much to our surprise, the cat turned and leaped off the 50 foot bluff. After a short period of time, the dogs, with us following, had made their way down the bluff, and were back on the cat's tracks.

The dogs then cornered the cat for the third time, this time against a rock wall. There was time for me to take a shot, so I took aim with my .30-06 and fired. The big cat fell down, dead.

After walking up to my trophy, we could tell that we had a big mountain lion. At that time, we felt we might have a records book cat, but we had no idea that it would be so high in the book. Our big cougar weighed approximately 210 pounds, and it measured 8 feet, 3 inches on the ground.

COUGAR 15 8/16

SECOND AWARD

Jerry J. James

My cougar hunt began in the spring of 1979 when I first decided to go on a hunt. I wrote letters to guides, and then eagerly awaited the morning mail for the replies to come. I was able to narrow my guide selection, and after calling several references, I finally decided on Bob Smith of Kooskia, Idaho. I had read about Idaho's reputation of having large cats, and the Selwy-Bitteroots mountain area has yielded numerous Pope and Young Club cats.

My enthusiasm was brightened, when upon arriving in Lewiston, Idaho, I was informed that they had a fresh snow in the high country. My enthusiasm was quickly dampened, though, when my hunt began the next day and the weather turned extremely warm. The snow quickly melted, and the possiblity of finding a fresh track was just about nil. Bob and I spent a week walking in the high country with no luck. I returned home, but I was determined to try again.

The next year was a repeat of the first, with no snow. I planned my trip for two weeks later, but little did I know that Idaho would experience a snowless winter. The hunt was spent walking, every day, but we were unable to jump any cougars. When you consider the number of miles that guides cover when there is snow to cut a fresh track, you can imagine how lucky you would have to be to jump a cougar under non-snow conditions.

My plane trip home was once again a long ride back to Minnesota. But, I was even more determined than ever to get a cat. I vowed that my third trip would only happen if snow conditions were perfect, and I planned on staying until I got a cat, or Bob sent me home, whichever came first.

Finally, in late December, 1981, I got the call that I had been waiting for. Bob said that they had 18 inches of snow in the high country, and more was expected. My first night after arriving was spent in renewing acquaintances and preparing my equipment. I shoot a 60-pound Bear Alaskan bow, with Bear Magnum arrows and Satellite broadheads. My equipment has accounted for numerous whitetails and two bears, and I knew that this would be adequate medicine for cougars. Our spirits were brightened the next morning with three inches of fresh snow.

The hunt began with Bob and I driving the back roads in his four-wheel-drive truck, along with his two best cat dogs, Chief and Ralph. Chief is an airedale and bluetick hound cross, and he has been involved in more than 100 cat kills. Ralph is a Pitbull and Walker hound cross, with a big hate for cats and bears. It was really a switch, driving back roads through more than a foot of snow, compared to our first two years. I was really amazed at Bob's ability to determine what kind of tracks there were along the road. I had never seen a cougar track, so I had Bob stop several times for tracks that I thought were those of a cat that he called elk, etc. And, he was always right.

As we drove along, Bob told me about different cougars that he had taken over the years. I told him that I wasn't fussy after two unsuccessful trips; all I wanted was a cougar, and he did not have to be a Pope and Young cat. Bob told me that if I got a cougar, more than likely it would make the book, as the cats in his area all seem to have large heads and every mature cougar would make it.

About 10:00 a.m., we cut a day-old cat track crossing a bridge and heading up the side of the mountain. We took to the trail, with Ralph on a leash while Chief was allowed to run ahead. The cat headed straight up the mountain, Bob and I following in a foot of snow. Bob told me that Chief did not have to be leashed because he would only run the trail if Bob gave the command. Once the command was given, Chief would run the trail silently until he jumped the cat. Then, the hound would take over and he would bark like crazy. Ralph was leashed so that he would not take the trail. Because of Idaho's remoteness, Bob does not want to turn his dogs loose until the trail is fresh, as his dogs could be gone for days. Four hours later, the track was not getting any fresher. My legs were suffering from cramps from climbing the mountain, so we decided to quit. I was dog-tired and soaking wet as we slid down the mountain to the Bronco.

That night, about a foot of snow fell which made it impossible to go back and follow the old track, and we found no new tracks that day. For me, it was a welcome relief, as I was still tired from the first day. That night it snowed again, and next day we cut another cougar track on the road. The cat had swum the river and headed up the mountain. Bob was really excited, as he thought the cat was a big tom with skull measurements that would easily exceed 15 inches (the Pope and Young Club World's Record scored 15^8/$_{16}$ inches). The track looked as big as a pie plate in the snow.

We started up the mountain again, with Ralph on a leash and Chief following the trail. After climbing about a mile, we came to some rock bluffs where the dogs went wild. The cat scent was strong in the rocky area, and both Chief and Ralph were barking like crazy. Bob sent Chief on the trail and turned Ralph loose, and the chase was on. The trail paralleled the river for about a mile, then headed downhill straight to the river. We tried to keep up with the dogs, but it was impossible as the snow was more than three feet deep, and we did not have snowshoes on. The terrain was too steep to wear them.

We could hear the dogs barking down by the river, so we raced down the mountain. Unfortunately, the cat swam the river, and we could not follow as we had no boat. After that, our daily equipment list included a boat, and we hunted both sides of the river. I doubt that we could have followed the cat anyway as we were both tired and it was getting late. Bob also thought that the cat had swum the river before he had even turned the dogs loose, as the cat had made a lot of tracks down by the river.

That night, it snowed again. We decided against taking a boat across the river and following the cat. The track would have been over 36 hours old, and the cat could have been 15 miles away. We drove up one back road where a tree had fallen across the road. We turned around before we got to the fallen tree, since we did not have a chainsaw to remove it. That night, it snowed again. Next day, as we headed up the road to where the tree had fallen, I joked to Bob that there probably was a cat track just beyond the fallen tree. Sure enough, there was a track only 100 yards on the other side of the tree! Needless to say, a chainsaw was added to our equipment list after that. The cat had crossed the road and walked up the fallen tree and then up the mountain. The track was already over 24 hours old, but we decided to follow it anyway, hoping the cat had made a kill on the mountainside. Unfortunately, the cat had not, because he continued to climb the mountain. Soon we were wading in four feet of snow. After about four hours of trailing, we headed back to the Bronco totally exhausted. With all of the bad luck I was having, I didn't think I was ever going to get my cat.

The sixth day, we did not cut any tracks. This was just as well, as I was still too tired from the day before. I saw more hills in Idaho in one day than I have seen in Minnesota in a lifetime. So far, my trip could best be described as plain bad luck. But, the scenery was beautiful beyond description; and during the day's hunt, we continually saw numerous deer and elk.

The seventh day was a perfect day for hunting; we had two inches of fresh snow. We stopped at a cafe to have a cup of coffee, and we were told that a truck driver had seen a cougar right next to the road two days before. We went to where the cougar had been sighted, and then spent some time in the area listening for ravens which might indicate that the cat had a kill. His track was too old to follow, so we decided to cover our daily route.

After some time, we found the track of a large cat that had crossed the road and headed up the mountain. The track was filled with snow, but we knew that it had been made during the night. We hoped that the cat was not too far away. We started our usual procession of Chief leading the way, with Ralph on a leash, and me bringing up the rear. We headed up and then paralleled the mountain, when the cat track turned and headed into a small canyon. This was into a bunch of rock bluffs. All of a sudden, Chief, who had gotten out of our sight, started barking as though he had jumped the cat and was following the trail. Bob turned Ralph loose and he headed down into the canyon in the direction that Chief was barking from. After days of walking, I was finally listening to hound music.

The chase was short; soon both dogs were barking that the cat was treed. We hurried over to the tree, and there was the most beautiful sight that I have ever seen. The lion looked golden brown against the green pine trees, and it was obviously a big tom. Finally, the moment I had worked at for the last three years was about to happen. Bob tied up the dogs as I positioned myself for a shot with my bow. I only had a small hole to shoot through as I released my arrow. The arrow deflected on a small branch and hit the cat on the side of the head. The cat started snarling, and he knocked off every branch as he started down the tree. I nocked another arrow, and took another quick shot before the cat was halfway down the tree. The arrow hit him right behind the front leg. The cat died before he could go 20 yards, as the broadhead really did the job.

I beat the dogs to the lion, but I remembered what Bob told me about not touching the cat until the dogs got there. I knew what he meant, when Ralph hit that lion wide open. I am sure he would have chewed on me too, if I had been holding that cat. Chief gave the cat the business too, but he knew he had done his job, just as he had done dozens of times before.

Later, we laid the hide on the floor. The big tom measured 8 feet, 7 inches long, and Bob thought he would score at least 14½ points, which would easily put him the the Pope and Young Club records book. Bob joked that we could stretch him a lot further, especially if we used two pickups. Needless to say, I was elated. After hunting 22 days over a three-year period, walking at least 200 miles, sliding down mountains, and crossing icy rivers in a rubber boat, I had finally got my cougar.

Fortunately, this is not the end of my story. I received a phone call from my taxidermist in the middle of July. He had sent the skull to the University of Minnesota to have it cleaned up in a bug-box. After receiving it, he had taken the skull to a Pope and Young scorer who gave it an official score of $15^{11}/_{16}$, which would make it the tentative new World's Record. My cougar was recognized as the new World's Record at the Pope and Young Club Awards Banquet on April 9, 1983, in Milwaukee, Wisconsin. It also was awarded the Pope and Young's prestigious Ishi Award, which is the highest form of recognition given by the club. The Ishi Award is presented only when a truly outstanding big game animal is taken, and the award criteria are similar to those for the Boone and Crockett Club's coveted Sagamore Hill Medal.

Never in my life did I believe this could happen to me. I called Bob Smith and thanked him for a tremendous hunt, as it had been a real experience to see Bob and his dogs work. I also reminded him about the big cat that swam the river and got away from us. There is no doubt that cat was larger than the one I shot. I am sure when someone gets him, Bob Smith and his dogs will also be there.

Photo Courtesy of Bill Dear

Bill Dear bowhunted near Big River in Saskatchewan in 1985 to find this big black bear that scores 21 13/16 points.

Photo Courtesy of Carl B. Mockensturm

Carl B. Mockensturm's black bear from Fremont County, Colorado, qualified for the Awards records book with a score of 20 4/16 points. It was killed in 1985.

Photo Courtesy of John F. Peters

BLACK BEAR
FIRST AWARD
SCORE: 22⁸/₁₆

Locality: Gila Co., Ariz.   Date: September 1985
Hunter: John F. Peters

BLACK BEAR 22⁸⁄₁₆

John F. Peters

Central Arizona may seem an unlikely place to hunt black bear, but bear do inhabit the brush and cactus covered mountains and canyons, and an inordinate number of them reach the huge proportions that hunters dream about. Maybe it's the mild winters and abundant feed, or being able to reach a ripe old age in an isolated area, but for whatever reason, there are some enormous bear in Arizona.

Ingrained in the Southwest is a long and deep tradition of hunting bear with hounds. Many of the greatest of the lion and bear hunters, men like Ben Lilly and Monteque Stevens, Uncle Jimmy Owens and Homer Pickens, the Goswicks, the Evans, the Lee brothers, and many others, did their hunting in the rugged southwestern mountains. Teddy Roosevelt made numerous trips to Arizona and Colorado to hunt bear and lion behind a pack of local hounds. And even today, there is some fine bear hunting within sight of Zane Grey's cabin, where the author wrote many of his western novels, and chased bear and lion with hounds. A man riding these hills today is following in some famous footsteps as he pursues his elusive quarry.

My own pack of seven dogs is a mixture of redticks and blueticks, out of the big game hounds of Clell and Dale Lee. I was fortunate to have hunted with Clell and Dale, and I learned by their example the meaning of persistence and long rides, of Fair Chase, and true hounds. Bear hunting from horse back, using dogs in the dry and rocky southwest, is an uncertain and sporting proposition.

I live in Show Low, Arizona, and have hunted for bear and lion with hounds for the past 16 years, mostly on the White Mountain Apache Reservation. This 1.7 million acre reservation is famous for the trophy elk taken annually from the high, aspen and pine covered ridges, and there is also good hunting for deer, bear, lion, and javelina.

One day in October, 1984, my son Joe and I decided to hunt some of the pinyon-juniper country that borders the Salt River Canyon, where I had found a particularly large bear track the previous spring. Cut a small section out of the Grand Canyon and drop it in central Arizona, you'd have a fair replica of the Salt River Canyon. It is this type of ruggedness that discourages hunters and, we hoped, had allowed some bears to grow both old and big.

The third day we hunted, the dogs trailed a giant bear track into an impossibly rough, rocky canyon where the bear whipped the dogs and escaped. Joe and I, our horses and our hounds, were physically beat as we limped back to camp by moonlight. But, we resolved to regroup and try that big, mean bear another day.

In the spring of 1985, despite numerous hunts in the Salt River area, we were unable to locate the big bear. The weather had been relatively dry, so we did most of our scouting near sources of water. At one of the cattle water catchments we found the big bear's impressive tracks. We did not find enough sign to know his exact habitat, but at least he was still alive and in the area. Not far from the water catchment was a suitable campsite with an old corral and water for our horses. The road into camp was difficult and steep, but we figured we could pull the horse trailers in by using four-wheel drive, if the weather stayed dry. We made our plans for a three-day hunt in early September. I would hunt the first day alone, and Greg and his son would haul in additional horses and camp gear for the next two days.

It was cool in the early morning darkness as I loaded my hounds and horses. Show Low is over 6,000 feet in elevation, but our campsite, 45 miles from town, was about 1,000 feet lower, and much warmer. In September it is sometimes too warm, as the hounds run out of gas quickly in hot weather, leaving only the cool, early morning hours to hunt effectively. By the time I arrived at our campsite, dawn was breaking. I hurriedly saddled my big brown horse, while the dogs whined impatiently in their boxes. The first place to check was the cattle tank where we had found the big bear's track in August.

The dogs detected no scent at the tank; so we continued down the crooked ravine that drained from the cattle tank. A mile or so down the ravine, we climbed out and headed across a series of ridges and canyons. As I rode into one particularly rugged canyon, the dogs started drifting ahead with their heads up and noses quivering, as they searched the air currents for the scent of bear. Just as they reached the bottom, my big redtick hound (Barf) announced with a bellow that he had found a bear. Immediately, the other six hounds joined in. With an excited chorus of barks, the dogs roared up the twisted canyon. These canyons are also inhabited by Coues' whitetail deer and javelina, which my young dogs will sometimes chase, so I leaped off my horse to try to find a track. In the gravel where the dogs had barked was a single large, flattened-out area. Not really much to go on, but it was a bear, and a big one, and the dogs were going in the right direction.

By the time I had remounted and urged my horse forward, the baying of the dogs had faded into the distance. My big horse, a veteran of many bear hunts, dodged between rocks and trees as he rushed after the dogs. For a long time, my goal was simply to hold on and not get wiped off by branches or brush. At the same time, I tried not to lose the distant sound of the baying hounds.

I would ride rapidly for a quarter-mile or so, then stop and listen for the dogs. This stop-and-go procedure continued for quite a while, until one of the times I paused to listen I thought the dogs sounded louder. Then, within minutes, I could hear clearly the excited barking, mixed with angry growls. The dogs had jumped the bear, and he was headed back down the canyon in my direction. I quickly dismounted, and withdrew my Model 99 Savage in .250 caliber from its scabbard.

As the furious sound of the hounds came closer, I searched for movement. Finally, I saw him, a huge black bear running easily ahead of the dogs. But, before I could get the rifle up, he was hidden by juniper trees and then was gone on down the canyon, the dogs thundering behind him. From my brief glimpse, I could tell that he was indeed a big bear. But, he was more of a lean, raw-boned fighter, not a fat, roly-poly butterball. He was remarkably tall, and he ran effortlessly. This could be a long chase.

Again my horse carried me at a fearful rate between boulder and branch as we plunged down the canyon after the bear and hounds. For a time, we held our own; but, it gradually became apparent that we were falling farther behind. Despite our best efforts, the bear was getting away and the dogs would soon be out of hearing. From a high vantage point, I could barely discern some faint echoes as the dogs and bear were swallowed-up by the immense Salt River Canyon. And then, when all appeared lost, there was a strange silence. For a long minute, I strained to hear above the breeze, until finally a solitary bark emanated from the distant chasm. Then, there was another bark, and another, until there was a thunderous roar from the depths of the canyon; the bear had treed!

I couldn't believe my good fortune! I rode rapidly to get closer. From a promontory, I could see a solitary ponderosa pine in the canyon bottom. The excited chorus was coming from it.

About 400 yards from the tree, I dismounted and, leaving my horse, approached the tree from downwind with a cartridge chambered in my rifle. When approaching a treed bear, it is best to keep out of sight and smell until you can dash under the tree; this helps keep the bear up in the tree. There can be real havoc if a bear comes down into a pack of dogs who are trying to impress their owner. It's the bear who usually makes the biggest impression.

Luck was with me that day, as I was able to approach within 40 yards undetected, then rushing under the tree before the huge bear could decide what to do. He was standing on his hind legs on a limb about 15 feet off the ground, and he would occasionally emit a low rumbling growl and snap his cavernous jaws. Immediately, I knew that this bear was one of the big boys. Even though he was not fat, there was no doubt that he was a tremendous bear with an awesome head and neck, and formidable, pile-driver front feet. He appeared to be an old bear, well past his prime, but still in good shape and the obvious kingpin of this area. I had a momentary impulse to tie the dogs and let this old warrior go. But, this was the bear of a lifetime, so I raised my rifle.

After he was dead, I sat for a while and admired him, alone with my dogs and my thoughts. I was feeling proud that I was able to catch this old monarch. But, I was also melancholy that my sons weren't here to share this moment, and that by killing this old bear, there would be a void in these hills and canyons. Perhaps we, as hunters, need to dwell more upon these things. Happily, there were to be many more hunts with my sons, and bears to take the place of Old Big Boy.

BLACK BEAR 22²⁄₁₆

SECOND AWARD

Peter C. Knagge

I hunted bear in the Galiuro Mountains for several years, but September 9, 1982 was to be a day that I will never forget. It began very much like all my previous hunts. After two days of calling without spotting any bears, and two unfruitful stands on the third day of this season, I set my Circe call on the ground and began to light my pipe.

A hunter needs to be alert after calling, but the lack of success had my guard down. When I heard the faint sound of an animal walking through the small pebbles on the ridge, I was surprised. My first thought was "fox," since the sound was so soft. A few seconds later, more stones crunched under foot of the animal. Looking around for the sound, I saw a black object moving toward me. From behind the large rock I was using for cover, the critter moving through the thick brush looked like a black Angus cow that was nearly starved to death. The animal appeared to be nothing but a bag of bones.

When I finally recognized the animal as a bear, I was not very excited. I was sure this bear was not the bear that left the huge track I had been following for so long. This bear was in such bad shape, and so skinny, he could not possibly last through another winter.

Watching the bear come in, I tried to decide whether to shoot. I caught a glimpse of the bear as he passed through the brush. I could see the hair hanging from his belly, which indicates, just as with cattle, a male. I knew that a boar was necessary to make the 22-inch official score that I wanted. I had called in at least 30 bears, most of them sows and cubs and a few small boars. After five frustrating years of calling so many bears, and not getting a single shot at a big boar, the temptation to shoot grew.

When the bear cleared the brush at 35 yards, I drew my 82-pound pull Laser Magnum bow. I held the 30-yard pin on the top of his scrawny back as he presented an excellent front-quarter shot. At this time I decided to take this bear.

In my entire life, I never imagined I could experience the fear that soon hit me like an avalanche. I had been through some tough times as a rancher, and as a marine in Viet Nam, but none of those experiences led to the fear that would soon consume my mind and body.

When I drilled the 2219 arrow with a four-bladed Satellite shaft into his chest, the bear rolled on his back, twisting to grab at the shaft of the arrow. But then, he ran straight toward me! Terror overpowered my body. I stood frozen to the spot, since I thought he was coming after *me*! But, he was not aware of my presence until he hit my scent at about 12 yards. Then, he stood on his hind feet, swinging his front legs wildly as he growled. My feet felt as if they were glued to the ground. "My God! What do I do now?" I thought.

I hesitate to say it, because you won't believe it, but that bear looked like he was over eight feet tall. Many times you can expect a black bear to run the other way, but a big, dominant boar who has been king of the mountain is not afraid of anything. He will avoid danger, but when he is provoked, he will not back down from anything.

My advice to other bow hunters about calling bears would be, "Don't do it alone!" Have a fellow hunter there to back you up, preferably with a big bore like a 44 Magnum, in the hands of someone who can shoot accurately under extreme pressure. I would not want a .357 Magnum behind me, since I've heard too many stories about the number of shots it takes to drop a bear with this gun. "Just do not hunt them alone, or it might be the last time you do anything."

In 1977, a rancher friend told me that he had seen a big bear track in the same country where a big buck pronghorn lived. Numerous trips failed to produce even one sighting of the trophy pronghorn, but I did see the tracks of a huge bear. I knew immediately this was the bear I wanted. A number of scouting and hunting trips were fruitless until 1979. I finally saw the big bear, after following his tracks from Aravaipa Canyon to the Muleshoe Ranch. The entire Galiuro Mountain range was his home.

Since bear tracks are fairly easy to see and follow, especially those of a big bear moving uphill or down, I found his sign marking the areas he frequented. I followed his tracks in manzanita berry country and lower on the mountain in oak country. Usually, during the season when the manzanita berries are ripe, bears can be found higher on the mountain, so I concentrated my hunting efforts there.

In the summer when prickly pear pods are ripe, bears will drop into the desert to enjoy the intoxicating fermented pods. But, there were not many prickly pears in this country, so the adage of "the bears are in the pears" did not apply to my hunt. I believed that persistence would eventually give me my chance, so I continued calling in the ripe manzanita berry country.

Five years of hunting with only one sighting would discourage many a hunter, but I believe that luck is part of every hunt. A hunter can force that luck some through knowledge and skill, so I was within a few hundred yards of my big bear. I felt confident that I would call him within bow range.

Every time I stopped to call, I looked for characteristics that would provide a good set up. Generally, I look for things that indicate good bear country, watching especially for high concentrations of foods currently being used by bears. Next, I look for an area that has either lots of dry oak leaves or small rocks, so that I can hear any animal approaching. I also look for an area that provides enough visibility for a shot. I used to look for visibility out to a few hundred yards so that I could see them coming in. But, experience taught me that even when I could see them early, I could not do anything until they were closer. Now, as long as I can see within my accurate shooting range, I have all the visibility I need. I prefer to shoot within 25 yards, so that I can be totally confident with my shot placement.

Another characteristic that I look for is an area that has no fresh tracks. Fresh tracks tell a hunter where a bear has been, not where he is now. When I find an area that has good (and current) feed, lots of leaves, visibility with good shooting lanes within my accuracy range, no fresh tracks, and good cover, I know that I have a good calling spot. Finally, I make sure that

I set up behind a large rock or thick bush. I need the cover in front of me to hide any movement while drawing my bow. I don't worry about what is behind me, since my scent would alert any bear that might move onto my back trail.

With bears and lions, a hunter will almost always have plenty of time to get off a shot, since they tend to stand and look, trying to figure out what has invaded their territory. Deer and turkey move out when a hunter moves, but bears will stay around long enough for a shot if the hunter uses some cover to partially conceal movement.

Since I believe only one out of five bears that hear a call will come, either out of curiosity or hunger, I am not frustrated by calling stands that do not produce a shot. I also believe that a bear that hears a call from a long distance is less likely to respond, so I do not call loudly. I keep my calling soft and make each one softer as I repeat calls from the same stand. I always hope that I have set up within a few hundred yards of a bear that is feeding or has bedded for the day. Of course, I always keep the wind in my face, whether I am moving to a calling stand or on stand. Any human scent, and the bear is gone.

During my five years of chasing the big bear's track, a typical day would find me walking 10 to 12 miles. Within each day, I would call about 10 times. I would walk for 20 minutes to get into country that was beyond my last call, then move to the best vantage point I could find. Whenever I made a stand, I would call for 30 minutes. Some hunters have success calling bears from long distances and waiting much longer, up to two hours. But, my approach and experience has led me to believe that calling will be more productive with soft calls made from more spots, with less time on each stand. I have been known to cover as much as 25 miles in one day, but usually I try to circle out for five or six miles, then work back to where I began.

Some experts say that bears are nocturnal; others say that they feed a few hours in the early morning, then bed for the day. Somebody must be right, but I figure it doesn't make any difference with my hunting style. Whether a bear is "laid up" or not, he will respond to a call. My problem is to get on stand, when there's bear in the vicinity that is within range of my soft calls, without him knowing I am there. That is why I often call into side canyons.

Once on stand, I will normally call from 30 to 45 seconds, wait for 10 minutes and call again, softer, for about 30 seconds. I then wait another 10 minutes, then repeat the cycle using a Circe jackrabbit single-reed call. I do not think the sound made by the caller is that critical; a variety of sounds and calls have successfully called in bears.

I imagine a few bears have been collected by chance where someone stumbles blindly into a bear. To me, that is not bear hunting. Bears are not like other big game animals that have a limited home range of a few square miles in which they live their entire lives. Not only will a bear use an entire mountain, like my bear used the Galiuro Mountains, but they will travel from mountain range to mountain range. Consequently, a bear hunter has to be willing and able to cover ground, especially if he is pursuing one particular bear like I was.

On that eventful day in 1982 when my big bear finally responded to my call, my persistence paid off. The fear still haunts, and the details of that day linger. As he charged, it was little relief when I saw the red, bloody froth gushing from his mouth. As he came closer, all I could think was, "Get your knife. You've got a fight on your hands." I knew this bear was bigger than I first thought, but I was not excited yet, only terrified. I knew that I could not outrun his 35 mile-an-hour speed. I knew climbing a tree was out of the question since the tallest one around was a six-foot juniper. Anyway, I figured climbing a six-foot tree would put my belt buckle right at his nose. I wanted no part of that, so I stood my ground thinking, "Now, why did I do this?"

As he advanced on his hind legs, closing the last 12 yards, his growls contained a few gurgles. At five yards, the bear fell and rolled on his back, paws in the air. It was then, for the first time, that I realized I had shot the big bear that had left his tracks all over the Galiuro Mountains. Excitement began to mingle with the fear that overwhelmed my whole body.

His claws, just five yards in front of me, were huge. The bear stood and charged again, but fell and rolled over. Since he was on a slight incline, the bear lost with each fall the ground he gained with each charge. But he continued to struggle to get me! After five or six attempts, he fell for the last time, spread-eagle over a clump of Spanish dagger. Yet, he clawed forward, trying to reach me, refusing to give up. Even though he was a bag of bones, this king of the mountain fought, clawing forward, until his last breath. If I had not hit my bear solidly through the lungs, I probably would not be telling you this story.

It is not important what the final score of my bear was, or what rank in any book my bear maintains. The important thing is that I took the best bear I could hope to take. The value of records book programs is the objective picture they paint of the size of all animals in the field. A specific score is irrelevant, and who shoots the animal is even less important. I was hesitant to enter this bear in the various programs because of the false assumptions that are sometimes drawn and of the ego that is too often involved. I sometimes wish the trophy books did not list the hunter's name. Yet, I finally decided that the animal deserved his place in the books, and the validity of the listings would be more accurate if all trophy animals were listed including my bear. Only then will a true picture be painted of what size a big bear can and does obtain, making accurate comparisons possible.

BLACK BEAR 21 14/16

THIRD AWARD

Cecil W. Brown

At the beginning of the 1984 hunting season, I decided that the only bear I would take would have to be either big or off-color. At that time, we had a nice spring bear rug mounted on our living room wall.

It was late April, after opening day and the snow had melted enough to get in to the hunting area with the four-wheel drive. Together with two of my four kids, I took off for the back roads. After several hours of only spotting a few bears that we did not consider worth taking, the next one was a bit of a surprise.

A perfect spring bear of about 500 pounds popped out of the bush onto the road, about 50 yards in front of us. After we followed him up the road for a short distance, the bear stepped off the road into an old logged area. Pulling up a little closer, we jumped out of the truck, only to find that my nice big bear had disappeared down a draw, never to be seen again. For the next four months during the summer, we spotted the odd bear, but none that would be considered good enough to take.

In September, at the start of the regular fall hunting season, bears were put aside while my hunting partner, Rick Moon, and I looked for the winter's supply of meat. Both of us, being unemployed, devoted a fair amount of time to hunting. This did not please the wives very much, but you can't win them all.

On the first day of the moose season, about an hour before dark, Rick phoned and we were off to drag his moose in. He had taken a nice two-year-old bull. Finishing up around 11:00 p.m., we decided to finish the cleanup the next day. When we had completed that chore the next day, we decided to check out one of our favorite areas. About a half-hour before dark, the next freezer-full was spotted. A nice five-year-old bull was standing at the timber edge, about 500 yards up the hill from where we had stopped. With the 7mm finding its mark, the work of hunting started all over again.

During the next couple of weeks we took out various friends to see if more game could be spotted. We spotted only one small brown and a few black bears, but none worth the taking.

In the early afternoon of September 27th, Rick and I climbed into the truck and headed for one of our favorite areas. Going in for about 8 miles off the main road, we spotted what looked to be a nice big black bear. After getting a little closer, and watching for quite some time, we decided that this was the one I would take. I took a good, solid rest. When Rick hollered, the bear turned and raised up, and I placed a single shot through the bear's chest. After a 10 to

15-minute climb, we reached the approximate place where the bear had been. Placing another shell in the chamber, we started to look. We found the bear right where he dropped. Both Rick and I were amazed at the bear's size. As a rough guess, we figured his weight at somewhere around 650 to 700 pounds.

As the skinning progressed, we found my bear to be in prime shape. We did find numerous tooth and claw marks on his back and underside. After we packed out to the truck and drove home, it was around midnight. Weighing the hide, with the skull still attached, we found it tipped the bathroom scales at 107 pounds. When the hide was stretched out, it measured 7 feet, 7½ inches from the tip of his nose to the base of his tail.

With the coming of another hunting season, and this big black bear decorating a front room wall, I will have to start looking now for the next big bear. This one, though, will have to be big and brown.

BLACK BEAR 22 7/16

CERTIFICATE OF MERIT

Utah Division of Wildlife, owner

This huge bear was hit by a large coal truck on I-70 in Salinas Canyon area of Sevier County, Utah, approximately 13 miles east of Salinas. Salinas Canyon is a major coal-producing area of the state, with coal trucks passing through the canyon at three-minute intervals, 24 hours a day. The truck driver didn't even know that he had hit the bear. He was informed of the incident by CB radio by another truck driver who was following close behind and saw what happened. Both drivers stopped to view the bear.

The drivers noted that the bear was seriously injured with a broken back. They called Conservation Officer Fred Pannunzio on their CB radio and reported what had happened. Fred followed up the call and, using his service revolver, dispatched the largest black bear he had ever seen.

At that time, the bear became the property of the Utah Division of Wildlife. The officer skinned the bear out at the kill site, and the head and hide were placed in the hatchery freezer while the Department of Wildlife decided what to do with the bear.

Ultimately, it was decided to have a rug made of the hide and display it at the Cedar City office. The head and hide were delivered to a taxidermist. Dennis Shirley (a dept. employee and also a Boone and Crockett Club Official Measurer) got the skull and cleaned it. After the 60 day drying period, Dennis scored the bear officially for the Boone and Crockett Club records and entered it as a pick-up. At the time of this writing, the rug is on display at the Cedar City office.

The area this bear came from is noted for producing big bears. The current World's Record, also a pick-up, was found in this area, as was a bow-killed bear that scored 21 12/16 and took the first place award at the Pope and Young Club's 14th Awards Banquet.

Photo Courtesy of William Hellebrand

Fox Creek, Alberta, was the site of William Hellebrand's black bear hunt in 1985 that resulted in this fine trophy that scores 21 7/16 points.

Photo Courtesy of John C. Whyne

This huge black bear scores 22 6/16 points and was invited to the 19th Awards. Shot in Lycoming County, Pennsylvania, by John C. Whyne in 1983, it had a dressed weight of 580 pounds.

Photo Courtesy of Roger J. Pentecost

NEW WORLD'S RECORD GRIZZLY BEAR (TIE)
FIRST AWARD
SCORE: 27 2/16

Locality: Dean River, B. C.   Date: October 1982
Hunter: Roger J. Pentecost

GRIZZLY BEAR 27²/₁₆

Roger J. Pentecost

Jason, my son, was then 12 years old; this was to be our first "real" hunt. He had hunted since he was seven years old, around our ranch in southern B.C. We had decided on grizzly. I had always wanted a trophy grizzly. I had ranched some years before in the Anahim Lake area. We had friends there, and we knew there were large bears in the area.

With two weeks set-aside, we packed our guns. Jason chose a single-shot Savage Model 219L in .30-30 caliber, with a four-power Weaver scope. I chose my .270 caliber Husqvarna with a 2½ to 8 power Bausch & Lomb scope.

After arriving in the Anahim Lake area, we spent a few days visiting and talking about bears, and hunting moose. We contacted Wayne Escott, who had worked for me in the early 70's and was now a commercial bush pilot for Dean River Air. We made a deal to get the float plane from Monday, October 11th until the 16th. We had heard the stories of big bear down on the Bella Coola River, but some of the Indians talked of "Good Bear" along the nearly inaccessible Dean River mouth where it meets the Dean Channel.

On Monday morning, we left Nimpo Lake and flew down southwest over Charlotte Lake, then heading west to Lonesome Lake, circling to take photos of the very impressive Hunlen Falls that drop straight down about 1,000 feet and flow into the Atnarko river. I had wanted to see these falls for a long time.

We then headed north, stopping for lunch and so Jason could fish at Squiness Lake, named after an old-time Indian family of the area.

We arrived late that afternoon in the Dean Channel. Pulling up on a sandbar at the river mouth, we unloaded the plane and made camp right there. We had already found tracks, so our excitement was starting to build. Next day (the 12th), we moved the plane along the river bank about 300 yards and on the south side, so as to be beside our camp. Starting out, we got across the river and worked our way up the shoreline. Wayne knew Felix, an 80-year old Swedish recluse, who had been living in almost isolation for many years there.

We took Felix a moose meat roast as a gift, and got into a long conversation with him about life, bears, etc. He told of mushroom hunters landing there by plane, and picking up to $1,000 per trip, each, with the mushrooms being sold in Japan. We scouted that area quite a bit, finding sign of bear but not seeing any of the real thing.

Wednesday the 13th, Jason and I left early, ready for bear. We went south, down the channel, finding sign but no bear. The banks along this channel were steep and made the going really tough. We saw seal out in the water, and a lot of eagles, but no bear. We worked our way back inland, arriving about a half-mile upriver from camp, where we found really promising sign and country, but that was all.

Thursday the 14th was cold and damp, but not freezing, yet. We had made up our minds that we would go up river on the south side. Wayne, our pilot, was going to come along, having fiddled enough with the plane the day before. The going was really slow and tough. It seemed that for every 10 feet forward, we would also go 10 feet sideways, first down into the river edge, which was usually covered with masses of tangled logs, then up along the very steep banks above the river. There we were, climbing over dead trees and inching our way along. The thought never really occurred to me as to how I would get back with a bear, if we got "lucky".

About mid-morning, we stopped to snack. Jason had found a simply enormous bear track in a sandy bay area tucked into the river edge, and we speculated over lunch at the size of the bear that made that track. It was surely a "good bear". We could not see up or down the river more than 100 yards.

About then, we heard a Super Cub drifting low and slow, as they are so good at. for a brief moment, it flashed in front of us, coming down-stream and passing out toward where our plane sat. I cursed under my breath, thinking that I had come all this way to have any bear spooked right out of the area by people when we were 100 miles from a village and even farther from a town.

With a little more uncertainty, but still the same enthusiasm, we started off, crossing a small side channel and re-wetting ourselves for at least the 10th time (or so it seemed). After a while, I decided to move away from the river's main course. Soon we were walking in a succession of semi-clearings, under some enormous cedar trees that shut out most of the direct sunlight. The flickering shadows across the leafy carpet gave a shady, peaceful look to the area.

Suddenly, off to our left side about 70 feet away and partly obscured by a cedar, something started to move slowly up out of the ground. It was a massive head in profile, followed by an enormous shoulder hump. We froze. Here was what we had come all this way for, "a good bear". But really, I never wanted it quite so close. As I readied my Husqvarna, I heard Jason close his gun.

For what seemed to be a long time, I had an excellent side shot. I squeezed the shot off. But, the bear, instead of falling over dead, rose up out of the hollow in the ground and turned towards us. Here it was, coming right at us. I aimed at his shoulder, still hardly believing he wasn't down. This next shot hit his side, I had gut shot him. This turned him, and he plunged off sideways into a real thick area of alders, windfalls and devils club. As he was going in, I placed a third shot.

All hell seemed to break loose in that small wooded area. It was too thick to see what was happening, but boy, could we hear the bear snorting, growling, grunting and gasping draughts of breath. It was a simply enormous and rather frightening sound. I looked back at Jason and Wayne. They looked as apprehensive as I felt. I knew a grizzly could explode out of that cover like an "express train", with none of the bush slowing him down at all, and leap 15 feet in a bound.

I indicated to the others that I was going to circle around, hoping I could get to a point for a fatal shot. Using some of the larger trees as cover, I circled from tree to tree in the best John Wayne style, but without his air of confidence. Jason and Wayne were following me. All of us were feeling very naked, only knowing where the bear was by that noise. At last, I could see part of the bear's rear.

At this point, I swapped guns with Jason for the final shot as I had used three of my five bullets. He had all six that he carried left. I was finally about 20 ft. away from the bear, feeling, to be honest, quite scared, before I could place the fatal shot into his neck with Jason's .30-30. As it lay dead, I could see that we had a very "good bear" indeed. But why had my first shot not killed it?

When I skinned it out later, I could see the bullet hole in the exact spot I had aimed, but the Nosler bullet had shattered before getting deep enough in such a large bear. I also found a tight, leather radio collar around his neck. It was well into his fur, and had rubbed sore marks on either side of his neck. I felt bad now, knowing that the bear I had shot was part of a study. But, what was it doing here, 50 miles from any closed area? Thinking back on this, I did not see the collar, even when close to the bear. Plus, with us walking up on him, I don't know if the bear would have given us the choice of letting him, or us, walk away.

We started the task of skinning, still in awe of this great trophy bear. The skinning went slowly, and we were only about half-finished when Wayne pointed out that it was about an hour before sunset. So, with great apprehension, we left the partially finished bear. With some knowledge of the best route back, we made it to camp just at darkness. We had nervously picked our way, expecting to meet another bear at every turn.

That night, I had many mixed thoughts. Some were good and some terrible. I'd really shot a "good bear", but there was the matter of the number of shots, the collar, and worst of all, leaving him there. What if coyote, fox, wolf, wolverine, eagle got to him? All these "what ifs" kept coming back to me. We consoled ourselves that at least another grizzly would not eat it.

That night, we had entertainment of a nature that we didn't need. It started with some splashing and grunts that sounded all too close. Were they just trying to find salmon carcasses, or were they looking for us? We built the fire up high, and in the light of it, pulled in some more of the washed-up logs scattered around real close. Supper was welcome, but the food seemed to dry out and stick as it went down my throat. Even Jason noticed the tension. Normally, good food and sleep would be the only thing on his mind by now, but that night he was making sure that he could sleep in the middle of the tent.

It seemed that all through the night, the bears were getting closer. Wayne and I agreed that we would take turns to keep the fire going. Morning drifted in, as a cold, damp blanket of mist, leaving everything dripping. Jason walked over toward the river, about 20 ft. from the tent area where we were preparing breakfast and coffee. His face told us that he had seen something. "Look! Quick, over there in the river are three more bears, not 200 yards from our camp", he said. They were poking around in the river, looking for their breakfast. We could have shot any one of them, with one looking as big as ours, right in camp!

We didn't discuss it, but I was feeling worried as to what would await us back at the bear site. Soon, we had the pack board, rope and some lunch ready and we were off. Wayne felt he should carry his .30-30 Winchester, "just in case". We set out up the river, with the three bears noted earlier no where to be seen. We tried to make quite a bit of noise and took our path out in the open as much as possible. Things had done a 180 degree turn from yesterday. I really hoped that our furry friends would stay away today.

A couple of ravens flew up as we approached the bear, but no eagles were in evidence. A quick examination showed the hide to be perfect, so we got down to work. Only now was the size of this bear really impacting on me. Just lifting his paws, and looking around at the havoc he had wrought, made me even more respectful of their massive power.

I had skinned out many moose while I was guiding, and also cows on the ranch, but trying to turn over and move 1,000 pounds of grizzly is tough. We pushed, pulled, shoved and did just about everything we could think of to turn him over. Boy, what a job. I had cut the skull off at the neck joint, and the paws at the wrist bones, thinking that I would do the rest in Anahim Lake the next day. We rolled up the skin, with the feet, paws and head inside, and proceeded to rope it onto the pack board. Then I tried to lift it and get it on my back. That didn't work. Wayne and I carried the pack board over to a large cedar, lifted it up to shoulder height, and with Wayne's help, I swung it on. Hell, it just about swung me down with it. I tightened the waist belt, and with Jason carrying my .270, we started back.

Things went well, until we came to the first downed tree. As I tried to get over, the pack and bear skin pulled me backward. It was no use, I couldn't hike out with this massive weight. I decided the only way was to skin the head and paws out, and generally flesh-out the hide. Two hours later, we were ready to continue. We had lost at least 50 pounds from the load, and when re-packed, I felt that I could just manage it. Boy, what a journey back to camp. I was glad we were only three miles in.

After a quick lunch, we broke camp and loaded the plane. This is when our next excitement began. The tide in the inlet was down; consequently, the river level at the mouth had fallen. It was too shallow for take-off with all the weight, so we unloaded the plane. I waded out into the river, holding the plane straight up stream as I stumbled around in the ice water. With the plane as light as possible and the motor warm, Wayne gave it full throttle. My heart was in my mouth as Wayne, in his expert manner, bounced the plane up the river, until first one and then the other float lifted and he disappeared round the bend. Moments later, we were pleased to see the plane lift up above the trees, as it wheeled round grabbing for height to get over the trees. It was then I realized my legs were damned cold, I was still standing out in the cold, rushing water.

Wayne landed out in the channel, then taxied in to the sandbar that we had started this hunt from. Packing our equipment on the plane went well, as I thought of warm baths and scotch whiskey that was waiting at Anahim Lake. A half-hour later, we were skimming over the lake infested timber. We landed at Nimpo Lake. We were soon at Darcy Christensen's village store, where we related the story for the first of many times.

Darcy, our host, had a country butchers shop out back, and a 500 pound scale with a meat hook hung high. Two of us hoisted up my grizzly and watched as the needle pointed to 148 pounds. Next, we weighed the undressed skull; it was 45 pounds, so we assumed that with the paws, etc., the hide had weighed over 200 pounds. No wonder it was so impossible to pack any distance over that rough going.

We got to work, spreading out the bear and then working coarse salt into the hide. We spent lots of time on the ears, releasing the cartilage right up to the tips and getting the salt in. From the measurements that we took, we worked out that the bear stood over 10 feet, six inches high and could have reached over 13 feet. The rug has a 9 foot, six inch spread, with claws longer than my fingers.

This was far more of a grizzly than I had ever dreamed of getting. As we retired that night, we went over bear stories such as the Anahim Lake rancher and neighbor, Cony King, who had been attacked by a grizzly sow and now sports a blank eye socket and massive scars from this near fatal encounter.

It was April 1983 when I got an excited phone call from Helmut Schold, a young German emigre taxidermist who had impressed me with his skill and artistic ability. He had been so shocked by the finished size of the skull that he had taken it to Helmut Cofmeister, a Government Wildlife Technician. They had measured a skull length of 17 inches and a skull width of $10^{5/16}$ inches, giving a total score of $27^{5/16}$ that put it well over the existing World's Record. On June 21, 1983, Jack Graham and Jim Laughton, both Boone & Crockett Official Measurers, met with grizzly and me for an official measuring. They recorded a final score for entry of $27^{4/16}$.

Jason and I have reflected on this hunt on several occasions, still only half believing that his first major hunt could end this way. For us, it simply remains "our grizzly hunt".

Photo Courtesy of Roger L. Pock

Roger L. Pock was hunting north of Motase Peak, B. C., when he shot this fine grizzly bear in 1984. It scores 24 9/16 points.

Photo Courtesy of Gary K. Engebretsen

This grizzly bear scores 23 2/16 points to qualify for the Awards records book. Gary Engebretsen shot it in 1982 in the Wrangell Mountains of Alaska.

GRIZZLY BEAR 26 9/16

SECOND AWARD

Stanley F. Smith, hunter
Stanley F. Smith and Gary Fait, owners

Stanley F. Smith makes his home in Rockville, Maryland, a suburb of metropolitan Washington, D.C. In those concrete environs, a hunter's thoughts often turn to the out-of-doors and big game trophies. Stanley's thoughts often turned to a big grizzly bear, a trophy he had long coveted.

Stan's dream finally came true in 1984 on a hunting trip with guide Gary Fait. Gary Fait operates out of Anchorage, Alaska, and he hunts a wide area of Alaska. He's a good bear guide, and he felt he could find the big trophy that Stan Smith wanted.

Smith arrived in Anchorage, Alaska, in early September of 1984. He had made his preparations well, and he was ready for a good hunt. They flew to the hunting area on the 22nd.

The next several days were spent in hunting, without finding that big bear. But their luck was due for a change, and it happened quickly.

It was the 26th, and it was only 7:30 a.m. Already the hunting day was well underway. They had found the big trophy that Stan Smith had been looking for, and at a distance of 75 yards, Smith took careful aim. His .338 Winchester Magnum did its job efficiently and well. The huge trophy was now his.

It was a sunny and clear day, made all the more beautiful by a spectacular trophy that would give Stan Smith many wonderful memories of his grizzly hunt.

Photo Courtesy of Thomas C. Roberson

GRIZZLY BEAR
THIRD AWARD
SCORE: 26 6/16

Locality: Cluculz Creek, B. C.   Date: September 1983
Hunter: Thomas C. Roberson

GRIZZLY BEAR 26 6/16

Thomas C. Roberson

Conditions were perfect, light rain overnight and a slight breeze this morning. I knew these factors would be helpful in allowing me to get close to my prey. And, after scouting it out the day before, I knew I would have to get within 25 to 30 yards for a good shot.

I saw something move. I jacked a shell into my .444. At this sound, the grizzly looked up and I found myself staring at him, face to face.

I knew I had to shoot, so I pulled over his left shoulder and fired. The impact rolled the bear off the moose he had killed. Then, he was gone.

I heard roaring, and the smashing of small bushes as he circled around to my right. Silence. I was certain he was going to charge. I waited, ready, but nothing happened.

About an hour later and after a half mile of slowly working my way down his trail, I could see where he had lain down three times within 30 yards. He wasn't moving fast, and he was in pain; he therefore would be extremely dangerous.

Carefully, I started into the dense bush. There he was, about 40 yards to my right, lying down.

I started working my way closer for a better shot. He heard my approach and started to get up, which turned him toward me. I fired. He wheeled around and moved further into the bush. I still had him within range, so I fired three more shots, each bullet pushing him forward, but not down.

I kept following for about 50 yards. He then stopped and turned towards me. I fired three more times, each shot smashing him backwards, but again, not down.

The bear stopped and stared at me. He then turned and bit a three-inch chunk out of a spruce tree. I fired again and he went down. When I finally walked to where he lay, I was 16 paces from him.

Photo Courtesy of DeVern Gardner

GRIZZLY BEAR
FOURTH AWARD
SCORE: 26 3/16

Locality: Bear Lake, B. C.   Date: May 1984
Hunter: DeVern Gardner

GRIZZLY BEAR 26³⁄₁₆

DeVern Gardner

The hunt booked for grizzly/black bear, from May 15 to 30, 1984, had been plagued with problems. The weather had been abysmal: rain in the valleys and snow on the mountains was an almost daily occurrence. While waiting for decent weather, we hunted for black bear from the outfitter's cabin. Blacks were everywhere. We would see one or two every day, and as a result, we were very selective. Finally, a large boar took a second look before he dived into the bush, which collected a bullet in the base of his skull. I believe he would have made the records book if his skull had not been shattered. Well, this occurrence was in keeping with the other events encountered so far during this hunt.

Flying weather, when it was available, found the lakes up country to be ice-covered. During one of the infrequent flights, two grizzlies were seen on the sunny side of a mountain near Lake Tetina. However, ice covered the lake and we were unable to land to set up camp. Upon returning to the cabins on Driftwood river, north of Takla Lake, magneto problems with the aircraft grounded us. While waiting for the aircraft to be repaired, Ray Polard (the outfitter who was guiding me) decided that we would take a boat up the river, which was swollen with spring runoff and free of ice, to where we could hunt for the grizzlies seen from the air.

We arrived at the south end of Lake Tetina one week after the initial sighting of the bears. Needless to say, I had no confidence that they would be within a hundred miles of where we had originally seen them. Ray assured me they would be there. So, without much enthusiasm on my part, we set out to see if we could find them.

Things were getting tight. It was the 29th of May, with only one more day left to hunt, as we started up the steep slope of the mountain. Approximately halfway up the mountain, we could see a small blonde bear digging roots in a clearing. While stalking this bear to get a better look, we heard a loud roar off to our left. I would judge that it was 100-150 yards in the timber. Ray, who was slightly ahead of me, turned, pointing in the direction of the noise, and mouthed, "Grizzly." The bear roared two or three more times at 30-60 second intervals. From the sound, we could tell he was slightly above us and moving our way. Approximately 50 yards up the mountain was a thicket of willows. Ray told me to watch there, as he thought that was where the bear would appear.

There had been no sound from the bear for about five minutes (it seemed much longer), when I saw movement in the willows. I looked through the scope and saw the bear moving slowly through the willows from left to right.

He would stop every four or five steps and look around with his head up, as though he was smelling the air. I tracked him until he passed through the willows and entered the clearing, about 80 yards away. Upon reaching the clearing, he turned to look up the mountain toward the smaller grizzly.

Thoughts at this time that were running through my mind were: don't shoot a bear when he is directly above you; break a big bear's shoulder; etc. Well, in order for me to break this one's shoulder, I would have to shoot through his right flank and into his left shoulder, with the bullet passing through him lengthwise. I was shooting a .338 Winchester Magnum with 250 grain Nosler handloads at 2,850 feet/second, and I had no doubt the gun was capable. So, lining up his off shoulder through his body, I let fly. The bear roared, reared up, slapping at his left shoulder, and came rolling down the mountain toward me. I reloaded as the bear came to rest in the willows about 50 yards away, still struggling to get up. I placed another round in his neck, at which he went limp and did not move.

Ray and I stayed where we were, watching the bear for 15 minutes. Since he had not moved after the second shot, we cautiously approached him with guns at the ready. Closer examination, and a poke with the rifle barrel, convinced us he was dead.

Ray jumped astride the bear and let out a war whoop almost as loud as mine. We rolled the huge carcass down onto a rock slide, where we skinned him. Between the two of us, we managed to carry the massive head and hide back to camp. When we got back to Ray's cabin, the aircraft had been repaired and was ready to take me back to civilization. I departed the next day with the trophy of a lifetime.

Photo Courtesy of K. James Malady, III

This beautifully furred grizzly bear was taken by James Malady in 1985 at Koyuk, Alaska. It scores 24 8/16 points.

Photo Courtesy of Vernon D. Holleman

This fine grizzly bear qualified for the Awards records book with a score of 23 1/16 points. It was killed by Vernon D. Holleman in 1983 in the Brooks Range of Alaska.

Photo Courtesy of Anthony Gioffre

ALASKA BROWN BEAR
FIRST AWARD
SCORE: 29 8/16

Locality: Sturgeon River, Alaska   Date: April 1984
Hunter: Anthony Gioffre

ALASKA BROWN BEAR 29⁸⁄₁₆

Anthony Gioffre

My first hunt for Kodiak bear was April 14 through May 1, 1983, on Kodiak Island in the Sturgeon River area. After seven or eight years of dreaming and talking about Kodiak bear hunting, my brother Carl and I decided to go on a hunt. We called a number of guides in Alaska, and then narrowed our list down to three.

We were looking for a backpack, Fair Chase hunt, so we chose Joe Want, who has 17 years of hunting experience in the Sturgeon River area. We immediately started our preparations, knowing we had to be in top physical condition. We were told that Kodiak Island was a very rugged terrain to hunt in. Joe sent lists of items we would need, and he gave us instructions for preparing ourselves for the hunt. We knew we would have to walk a number of hours each day, and we would be wearing hip boots the entire hunt because of the wet and soggy terrain. After two years of intensive physical preparation, my brother and I were ready to go.

Like all newcomers to Alaska, we were totally excited. We were going after the largest land animal in North America. During our 20-hour trip there, our dreams were to step off the plane right in the middle of the wilderness. To our surprise, Anchorage looked just about the same as any other American city. A few hours later, we boarded a prop plane for Kodiak Island. Once again we were looking for rugged wilderness; Kodiak Island looked like a small fishing village. So here we were, 7,000 miles from home and going after the brown bear of our dreams. Reality was finally starting to set in.

The next day, we boarded a float plane that took us 90 miles into the hunting area. After loading all of our gear, we wondered if the plane would get off the water. Two hours later, we landed in a lagoon, where we "checked in" at an old fishing cabin that was covered with very old metal siding and looked as if the first heavy rain storm would blow it over. (Little did we think that 14 days later, after back-packing and sleeping in spike camps for 14 days, this shack would look like the Hilton to us.)

The first day, after packing only the essentials, we then waited for low tide so we could cross the lagoon. This was the beginning of a new, 14-day experience of living and hunting in hip boots. After crossing the lagoon and walking on sandy beaches, my brother and I immediately thought, "This hunt's going to be easy"! At the mouth of the river, everything changed. The ground was soggy, and with each step we sank into tundra. There were small mountain ranges on both sides.

After two hours of walking, we started glassing for bear. Later, we set up spike camp. During this hunt, we saw 24 bears and had two opportunities to take a bear. But, my mind was made up; I would take nothing less than a trophy. My brother, however, took a nice 8½ foot bear on the last day of the hunt. Even though I did not get my prize on this trip, I knew that I had seen enough animals to possibly get a trophy if I decided to come back to Kodiak.

Three months after we returned home, and after much consideration and reflection, I had made up my mind. I was going back after a trophy. I called Joe Want, and expressed my desire for an early hunt the following year. Joe did not recommend an April 1 hunt, because it would still be cold in Alaska and many bears would still be in hibernation. However, he added that big boars would probably be out. This looked to me like a better chance of getting a large bear. I said, "Let's go for it." So, seven months later, here I was getting ready for Kodiak Island again, more determined than ever to get a world class bear.

Three weeks before the hunt, a bullet casing ruptured and scarred the chamber of my .375 Remington. I quickly called Remington, and was reassured by them that it could be repaired and returned to me in time for the trip. I air-freighted the gun to them; Remington, in turn, put a new barrel on the gun, rechambered it and air-freighted it back to me in six days. Everyone thought that would be impossible, but Remington really came through for me. This left only two weeks to re-sight and get the gun ready to go. I was still determined to be on that plane to Kodiak.

I again landed in Kodiak, ready to start hunting when the plane touched the ground. You can imagine my dismay when it rained solidly for three whole days, and the fog was so heavy on the fourth day that we could not get to our hunting area. The fifth day, we finally left for base camp (the shack again). This time, "The Hilton" somehow wasn't as horrible looking as the first time we saw it.

The next day, instead of us leaving for the hunt, would you believe that a snow storm set in. So there we were, in the cabin for another two days, with only seven days left of my 14-day hunt, wondering if I'd ever get a chance at a trophy.

The morning of the eighth day, the sun came up, beginning a picture perfect day for hunting. Our spirits were high and we were soon off. The first few hours, we glassed the snowy mountain sides, but still saw nothing at all. After setting up camp farther up river, we glassed for a few more hours and saw nothing. So, we went back to the spike camp.

The following morning, with nothing but wind and heavy rain, we cancelled the hunt for the day. The next two days, we glassed and walked for miles in canyons in heavy wind, not seeing one bear nor even a sign of a bear. Joe commented that we might be just a little early in the season. We set up spike camp a number of miles from base camp, and Joe went into one of his thinking modes to determine how we could get a bear in the four or five remaining days we had left to hunt.

The winds increased the following day, and were accompanied by snow. We decided not to go out. The following morning, there was three or four inches of snow, and you guessed it, the winds were blowing as strong as ever. That afternoon, the sun came out and the wind died down to a "small tornado". We said, "This is it, let's get the glasses and head out". To our astonishment, there were actual bear tracks in the snow.

We had only two days left. The following day, we packed up and headed for a canyon about three miles away. We spent the rest of our time there. Joe had seen big bear there the previous fall.

The next day produced nothing. It was now our final day, and we were walking through the canyon. This canyon was so huge that we had walked a half-day, and we still had not reached the middle of it. At mid-day, we decided to have something warm to drink. The winds were still blowing, and the temperature was approximately 18 to 20 degrees. While taking shelter on an embankment and drinking some hot tea, Joe asked me if I'd like to extend my hunt three more days since time was running out and we were getting nowhere. After not seeing a bear for 14 days, the decision was a tough one. I wanted a trophy-sized Kodiak bear, and I knew I was not going to give up at this point. My decision was quickly made and then it was time to get going again.

After glassing for about three or four hours, I saw something out of the corner of my eye on the mountainside. As I turned to say something to Joe, I realized he was already motioning for me to grab my backpack and go. Then, the adrenalin started flowing and the hunt was on. The bear was about a mile away, across some pretty rugged terrain. We were trying to make our way to the base of the mountain. When we got there, we quickly unloaded our gear and started making plans for stalking the bear. At that time, Joe said to me, "From this point on, there will be no conversation, we'll use only hand signals." As we started toward the bear, we knew it was a big one. But, we had no idea just how large it really was.

About 45 minutes later, we were within 500 yards of the bear. Joe had to make the decision as to whether we should go directly toward the bear or circle around and come out above it. It was getting late in the day, and to go around the mountain to get above the bear would take us about three hours. There was not enough time to do that, so we decided to go straight toward him. When we got to within approximately 300 yards, the bear stood up on the back side of the alders. Joe and I froze. The bear had not seen us and had gone back down on his fours to feed again. Even though the alders were nine feet high, the bear still towered over them. I knew this was my bear!

We slowly started our final stalk. We stopped when we were within 150 yards. At that point, we could not see nor hear the bear, he just seemed to disappear into thin air. We decided to let him make the next move, so we waited. We spotted him about 15 minutes later, coming out of the alders. I let him clear the alders, and as he approached a grassy area about 30-40 yards beyond the alders, I fired my first shot. I hit him just behind his front shoulder, which flipped him over on his back, and he started rolling down the mountain. I thought at this point the hunt was over, the bear was mine. But, while I was chambering my next shell into the gun, I realized the bear was running back up the mountain.

I fired again, and my second shot hit him in the same shoulder area as before. As the bear fell, it started sliding down the mountain again. He was very disoriented. I realized as I was chambering my next shot that the bear was running straight toward me. I put my scope directly on his chest area and fired the third time. The bear fell over on his back. Surely, he was finished at this point. I was out of shells anyway.

The next thing I knew, Joe was yelling, "Shoot!" The bear had gotten back up on his feet and was running back into the alders. While I was digging into my pockets for more shells, I was thinking, "This animal has three shots in him that no animal on earth should be able to withstand and here he is, actually running back up the mountain." By the time I loaded up, he was already back in the alders.

The bear was in a full rage. He sounded like a freight train, with his huge body parting the alders as he moved in our direction. For seemingly no reason, he just stopped. At that point, it seemed like everything else also stopped—the wind, the snow, everything except my heart, it was really pounding.

The next 20 minutes of waiting in complete silence seemed like days. I asked Joe, "What now?" He said "We are going to walk up to within 75-100 yards of the alders." He was to go above the alders, upwind of the bear, and start downward toward the bear. If the bear was still alive, it would come toward him. As Joe started into the alders 20 minutes later, the bear picked up his scent and, again in a rage, started toward Joe.

For some strange reason the bear at this point turned and started back down the mountain. I could see his shadow in the alders, but I couldn't get a good shot. I decided that when he approached the clearing on his way into another alder patch, that I would take my next shot. Just as he approached the clearing, he decided not to come out into the clearing but was making his way up the edge and around the alders. My gun was on the bear the whole time, and I followed him through my sights all around the alders. He must have caught my movement. He turned and looked directly at me. At that point, he stepped out toward me and I decided to take my shot. I hit him through the front shoulder and he flipped over on his back. I could not believe it for the life of me; he had actually gotten up and was running back into the alders! Joe yelled for me to come up to where he was above the alders. Once there, we both went in after him. By this time, I was stunned. I was wondering what on earth it would take to kill this bear.

In the alders, we found the dead giant. I knew then my dreams had come true; my trophy was finally a reality.

Photos Courtesy of Jack D. Revelle and William Kemp, Jr.

(l) Jack Revelle killed his Alaska brown bear, score 28 3/16 points, on Kodiak Island, Alaska, in 1984. (r) William Kemp hunted Bond Sound, B. C., in 1985 to take this grizzly bear that scores 25 12/16 points.

Photo Courtesy of Lonnie W. McCurry

Famed Cold Bay, Alaska, was the site of Lonnie McCurry's 1984 hunt that resulted in this Alaska brown bear that scores 28 2/16 points.

Photo Courtesy of George Caswell

ALASKA BROWN BEAR
SECOND AWARD
SCORE: 29 1/16

Locality: Cold Bay, Alaska   Date: May 1984
Hunter: George Caswell

ALASKA BROWN BEAR 29 1/16

George Caswell

Tomorrow, May 16, 1984, my flight out of Cold Bay, Alaska, was leaving at 3 p.m. This was my last day to hunt for an Alaskan brown bear in this remote area of the Alaskan Peninsula. It was late afternoon, and my guide and outfitter, Brent Jones, was feeling as disappointed as me. We had hunted this valley four straight days, after spending the first days several miles up the beach. Every day seemed promising, as new tracks were found high on the snow. But, not a sighting in four days. The area we had left earlier had produced five bears, but they were all high and very distant.

Time was against us. It was 6 p.m., and I had given in to the bears of Cold Bay. A lot of things passed through my mind; the distance traveled, the time and effort, and of course the expense. I felt good about the effort we gave and thought if I could do it again I'd come back to this area. This area has an excellent track record for large bodied bears. This was a late spring with few bears out, however the porcupines were active.

We had glassed every inch of that valley. So, I walked off about 50 yards to take a few pictures of the porcupine. I was about to touch the shutter release, when Brent yelled at the top of his lungs, "We have a bear". I rushed over to Brent to use my glasses. Brent assured me, with absolute confidence, "I guarantee that is a 10 foot bear".

It was after 7 p.m., and the bear was about a mile off in solid alders, very low, about 200 feet above sea level. Luckily, he broke into an opening not over 20 feet wide, where he laid down. We left the ridge about 7:45 p.m.

As most coastal bear hunters know, hip boots are a must. On our first leg of the hunt, we had a spike camp two miles in from the coast, and we walked as far as five miles in boots and back packs. We were on the Izembek Wildlife Refuge the first six days. It is a very remote wilderness, with wide valleys, many salmon streams, and majestic peaks on the back of the area we were to hunt. Caribou were a common sight, and cross fox, wolves, wolverine, ptarmigan, and porcupine were all sighted. Moose are found farther up the Peninsula, but not in this area. Cold Bay is near the Aleutian chain. Our camps were two Eureka tents, staked solid because of the strong winds. We usually left camp about 10 a.m., then hunting until 10 or 11 p.m. We seldom turned in before 1 a.m.

As we left the ridge, we knew we would loose sight of the bear. About 200 yards away, out of the alders, busted an 8 to 8½ foot bear within distance to shoot. I shouldered my .338, but Brent said nothing. We glassed her until she got clear of the alders. Another few minutes, and a 9 to 9½ foot bear left the alder patch and headed up the hill. I brought my gun up again, and I kept repeating, "What do you think?" Brent didn't answer! If it had been my decision, I would have tried. After all, it's eight o'clock and tomorrow the hunt would be over. I respect a guide's decision, and that had to be as tough as they come.

The two bears were within 200-300 yards of us all day. We never knew they were there. They were considerably lower than us, as the ridge gave us that advantage. I was beginning to believe my luck was rapidly changing. The larger bear broke out of the alders and headed inland. Brent was hurrying me along, as time was important. I couldn't help watching that last bear, but walking conditions didn't allow enough time to go after him. He was considerably higher than us. Then, he came to a water fall that we judged to be 40-50 feet high. It was not very wide, but as he crossed he fell all the way down and out of sight. He rolled over at least three times as his lighter-colored belly was displayed. What a sight! We stopped to glass the hole he fell into, but nothing showed up. My thoughts were obviously on the 10-foot bear, but here was an ace-in-the-hole. Maybe the bear broke his back; I couldn't believe what we had seen.

Brent kept pushing on, as we had a good ways to go. I kept looking back, while Brent broke trail. Finally, the fallen bear came up and out of the water fall. He appeared as though he had just left the shower. The last we saw of him, he was walking rather slow. Brent commented that he was most likely one mad bear.

We got downwind and to within 100 yards of where we had marked the 10-footer. We were on a side hill that worked down toward the final drainage to the sea. The stream was a tremendous roar, so if the wind cooperated, we should find the bear. It was 8:45 p.m. As we moved slowly down the hill, the alders kept getting thicker. By 9:40, there was still no sight of the bear. That 9-foot bear was starting to haunt my thoughts. The alders were so thick we had to walk back and forth to get any lower. That stream sounded like a jet engine. At exactly 9:45 p.m., over to my right, the bear appeared. I doubt that he heard or smelled us, as he appeared to be just walking up the hill with no sign of concern. I yelled at Brent, he acknowledged that I should fire. The bear stopped and looked, then I fired . He again stopped and looked, and I fired the second shot. He fell on his back and started sliding down hill toward the heavier alders. My next recollection was a swift slap on the back and a statement of assurance that I had taken an absolute 10-foot bear.

The 200 grain bonded core bullet apparently did an excellent job, as he never attempted to get to his feet. Pictures, with a lot of smiles, were then taken. At 10:30 p.m., we started the chore of skinning, finishing well after dark. We didn't make it to camp that night; we headed for the shore to try and get some sleep.

The next day, we made the trip back to the village of Cold Bay. The Alaska Fish and Game office there confirmed my bear as the largest of 224 bear taken on the Peninsula in the spring of 1984, and also the largest since that office was opened in 1961.

Brent and I were both very pleased and felt the wait for an eleventh hour bear was certainly worth it.

Photograph by Charlie Crunden

At the 19th Awards (Las Vegas, 1986), George Caswell accepts Second Award for his Alaska brown bear from Dr. Philip L. Wright, Chairman of the Records Committee.

Photograph by Charlie Crunden

At the 19th Awards (Las Vegas, 1986), Michael F. Short accepts Third Award for his Alaska brown bear from Dr. Philip L. Wright, Chairman of the Records Committee.

Photo Courtesy of Michael F. Short

ALASKA BROWN BEAR
THIRD AWARD
SCORE: 28 13/16

Locality: Herring Bay, Alaska   Date: May 1983
Hunter: Michael F. Short

ALASKA BROWN BEAR 28¹³⁄₁₆

Michael F. Short

Arriving in Kodiak from Anchorage on the morning of the 29th of April, 1983 with my good friend and hunting partner, Jim McMilin from Belgrade, Montana, I thought back over the events that had brought us there.

Jim and I had been planning this hunt with the help of J & B Safaris of Denver for some time. I had twice exchanged letters with Andy Runyan and his wife Ruthie. Andy's letters had said that bear hides should be good for our hunt dates of May 1 through 15, and that there was a reasonable chance for a really nice trophy. He wrote about a huge bear he had been seeing for the past five years, one that so far none of his hunters had been fortunate enough to catch up with. Andy often used descriptive nicknames to identify the larger bears in his area; he named this one simply "B.B." for "Big Bear." Andy estimated that he would square better than 10 feet. I had written Andy that Jim and I were in our early 30's, and we were willing to do our part to hold out for good bears. Although I said we would like to try for B.B., I knew how unlikely it really was.

After picking up licenses in Kodiak, we were off in the charter plane for Andy's camp at Herring Bay. The landscape was unlike any I had ever seen. Its stark beauty was fascinating, with steep hills and mountains devoid of trees, save scattered thickets of willow and alder brush. On our way, we flew over a cattle ranching operation on the north end of the island. I couldn't help wondering about the extreme optimism of such a venture in a land ruled by the huge carnivores.

Camp consisted of a two-room cabin, just off the beach, with glass around one end that provided a view on three sides of the bay and the hills rising almost vertically from the water's edge. Andy had the lean and somewhat weathered look that you would expect of an Alaskan professional who has spent nine months out of the year for the past 35 years in the bush running hunting camps and trap lines. He had guided sheep hunters until recently, then deciding to concentrate on his bear and trophy caribou camps. One of his clients held the record for the number one barren ground caribou for many years.

Charlie, Jim's guide, was a tall, friendly Hungarian who had been in the States for 17 years, and had guided for Andy for several seasons. He told Jim about the area they would be hunting. He explained that while it would require a tent camp, the area had not been hunted in the past three years and looked very promising. After checking our rifle sights, using a bench rest Andy keeps set-up, Charlie and Jim immediately began gathering supplies and making preparations for the charter flight into their area the next day.

The next morning, the charter service stopped on their way to another hunting camp to pick up Jim and Charlie for a short hop over a couple of drainages to another bay where they would set up their camp to begin hunting the next day. We wished them luck, kidding that it wouldn't be long before we had two 10-footers down. The funny thing about our "prediction" was that Andy's two previous hunters had taken bears 10 feet or better. Since some years there is not a single bear taken from the island that will reach that mark, we knew that the odds were against either of us taking such a trophy.

After seeing Jim and Charlie off, Andy and I took his small skiff out on the bay to glass some slopes above the opposite beach. Andy's nine-month-old golden labrador retriever, Curry, accompanied us, as he did throughout the hunt. It was obvious that the long months of total solitude spent running trap lines prior to the hunting season had formed a close bond between Andy and Curry. Although still a pup and full of enthusiasm, not once did Curry bark or cause the slightest disturbance, nor did Andy ever have a harsh word for him.

We spent the rest of the afternoon glassing the hillsides and watching the Sitka blacktail deer and bald eagles, but no bears appeared.

The next two days were the same, with the only excitement coming from the periodic visits of a beautiful red fox that prowled the beach in front of camp. It was obviously unaccustomed to the sight of man. It didn't seem to mind my following along to take pictures, as long as I didn't get closer than about 20 yards. The fox, like the bears, searches the beaches for dead fish, or even whales, that have been washed ashore.

The following day, we decided to try a new area, straight uphill from camp. We climbed for more than two hours before Andy spotted some tracks coming over a ridge, through a patch of snow, about a mile away. The tracks seemed to be headed down into a draw, where we couldn't see, so we worked our way over to the ridge overlooking the draw. There, on the opposite side, we spotted a dark-colored bear of about 8 to 8½ feet. As we waited, two small cubs came out of a small depression near their mother and began to play and roll about on the hillside. Andy set up the spotting scope, and we had lunch while we watched them for the next couple of hours. They scuffled with each other, rolling down the slope like a ball before bouncing up and running back up to Mom to do it all over again. Even though the rest of the day was uneventful, the fun of watching those cubs play made it a successful one.

Up well before dawn on the 4th, we began making preparations for an early start to what we suspected would be a special day. It was Andy's birthday: for the past two years, his clients had taken good bears on this day. So, we took the skiff up the bay several miles before heading inland for about five miles. Curry went along with us, as always, but the going was as tough for him as it was for us. The muskeg formed small mounds about three feet across, alternating with depressions of equal size and about two feet deep. Since it was too far to step from one mound to another, traversing this marshy ground involved one step up, followed by one step down, made all the more difficult by the hip boots we were wearing. After a couple of miles of this, we reached more solid ground. There, we began following the bear trails, some of which had been worn as much as two feet deep by thousands of years of travel by the big bears.

From the top of a small knoll, a wide valley opened up before us, reaching from the snow-lined ridges down to the shoreline, and punctuated only occasionally by small alder thickets. It wasn't long before we started to spot bears. First, a light-colored one that was too far away to tell much about; then, a smaller bear towards the head of the valley.

We were watching what appeared to be about a nine-footer, looking for fish along the beach, when two more bears suddenly appeared together, about 1,000 yards distant. One of the two was about nine feet, while the other was slightly smaller. What made them all the more fascinating to watch was that as the larger bear followed the smaller, they would stop every few yards, rise up on their hind legs, and swipe at each other with those powerful front paws. Andy said that the smaller one was probably a female just coming into season, and that this fighting was just part of their courtship. The two continued to work from our left to right, with the wind at their backs, when another bear came out about 300 yards away.

We could tell at once that this was an exceptional trophy by the way he moved with a lumbering gait. He was quartering into the wind, on a course that ultimately crossed the trail of the other two. He immediately picked up their trail, turned, and began following them. But, since the two were traveling with the wind at their backs, they caught the big male's scent 500 yards to their rear. It was comical to see the two take off at a dead run up the slope, as if they could tell that this was one bear they wanted nothing to do with. The big male followed them across the flat, through a narrow alder patch, and part of the way up the slope. There he stopped, took one look around the open slope, and returned to the alders.

During all this, Andy had said very little other than that it looked like a "good bear." But, it didn't take me long to answer when Andy asked whether I wanted to try for him. As we started down the hill, we knew the stalk would be a bit tricky. The big male had not emerged from the narrow but long alder thicket, and the other two bears remained on the hillside above him. We had to pass through several of these thickets on our way. I could see that we wouldn't want to go in one of them after a bear, especially a wounded one.

I was carrying a fiberglass-stocked .375 H & H Improved, on a pre-1964 Winchester Model 70 action. Andy was backing me up with a .404. We had our rifles at the ready as we climbed a small knoll above and downwind of the alders. The other two bears were about 75 yards farther up the slope. They caught our scent just as we moved into position. Andy was keeping an eye on them to see what their reaction would be; fortunately, they just milled around nervously. Meanwhile, I had spotted our bear just 30 yards below us, in a small opening in the thicket. The opening was only about 15 feet across. It was obvious that I would need to break him down on the spot.

Andy very calmly whispered that I should break the bear's spine at the hump in his back. Andy even went so far as to discuss the peculiar angle, with the bear head-on, below and to one side of us, before shaking my hand for luck. As Andy continued watching the two up on the hill, Curry sat perfectly still at his side without making a sound. Even with the scope set at two power, the bear looked huge as I touched off a shot. Fortunately, he went down immediately. I put two more rounds in him just to be sure.

After a careful approach, and a closer look, Andy slapped me on the back and congratulated me. Only then did I learn that I had taken B.B. I could hardly believe my luck, or the enormous size of this great animal. We did a good deal of handshaking and picture-taking before a steadily increasing rain, and the late hour, forced us to reluctantly leave for the long walk back without skinning him out.

It was an anxious night before our early start the next morning. The wind dictated a cautious approach from below, through the brush, to be sure that another bear had not found B.B. ahead of us. Then, we could start the skinning chores. I could not believe the massive physique of this animal. With the hide removed, I could see that he had the musculature of a heavyweight boxer. The back side of his hide had long scars from the many fights over the years in which he had established dominance of his territory. We found rock chips, and one small caliber bullet, that were likely the result of harassment from local fishing boats rather than sportsmen.

We had been working a couple of hours when Curry, who had never before made a sound in the field, suddenly started barking and growling wildly. We had a few tense minutes in the small opening before resuming our work without seeing the source of Curry's irritation. It is likely that he saved us from what might have been an embarrassing situation.

The pack out, with over 100 pounds of hide on one frame, and the head and our gear in the other, was a difficult race against an approaching storm. But, we made it back before the worst of it.

Over a hot meal, we toasted B.B. and his kind, and told and retold the story to each other. We laughed at the way Curry had only gotten excited after the shooting stopped and he thought that two of them were getting away. Andy made the comment that all we needed now was for Jim to show up with a 10-footer.

The next morning, with the hide laid out loose on the beach, it squared just two inches shy of 11 feet by averaging the distance between the front pads with that from nose to tail. Andy had already confirmed that the skull should place well in the records after drying.

A little later that day, Jim and Charlie returned with the incredible news that they too had taken a 10-foot bear. Jim had made a fine stalk and a good shot to drop his bear where it stood on the tidal flats. The hide on his bear was as free from rubs as was B.B.'s, but was even more luxurious in the quality of the hair. They were both super trophies, and we were as happy for each other as we were for ourselves.

TABULATIONS OF RECORDED TROPHIES

19TH AWARDS ENTRY PERIOD

1983—1985

The trophy data shown herein have been taken from score charts in the Records Archives of the Boone and Crockett Club for the 19th Awards entry period, 1983-1985. Trophies listed are those that meet minimum score and other stated requirements of trophy entry for the period. The final scores and rank shown are official, except for trophies shown with an asterisk. The asterisk is assigned to trophies whose entry scores are subject to certification by an Awards Panel of Judges. The asterisk can be removed (except in the case of a potential World's Record) by the submitting of two additional, independent scorings by Official Measurers of the Boone and Crockett Club. The Records Committee of the club will review the three scorings available (original, plus two additional) and determine which, if any, will be accepted in lieu of the judges panel measurement. When the score has been accepted as final by the Records Committee, the asterisk will be removed in future editions of the records book, *Records of North American Big Game*, and other publications. In the case of a potential World's Record trophy, the trophy *must* come before a Judges Panel at the end of an entry period. Only a Judges Panel can certify a World's Record and finalize its score.

Asterisked trophies are shown at the end of the listings for their category. They are *not* ranked, as their final score is subject to revision by a Judges Panel or by the submission of additional, official scorings, as described above.

The scientific and vernacular names, and the sequence of presentation, follows that suggested in the Revised Checklist of North American Mammals North of Mexico, 1979 (J. Knox Jones, *et al*; Texas Tech University, 14 December 1979.)

TROPHY BOUNDARIES

Many of the categories recognized in the records keeping are based upon subspecies differences. In nature, subspecies freely interbreed where their ranges overlap, thus necessitating the setting of geographic boundaries to keep them separate for records keeping purposes.

Geographic boundaries are described for a number of categories. These include: brown and grizzly bear; American and Roosevelt's elk; mule, Columbia, and Sitka blacktail deer; whitetail and Coues' deer; moose; and caribou. Pertinent information is included in the trophy data listings that follow, but the complete, detailed description for each is to be found in the latest edition (8th., 1981) of the records book, *Records of North American Big Game*, and also in the "how-to" book, *Measuring and Scoring North American Big Game Trophies*.

In addition to category specific boundaries, all trophies must be from North America, north of the south border of Mexico, to be eligible. For pelagic trophies, such as walrus and polar bear, they must be from the U. S. side of the International Date Line to be eligible.

Trophy boundaries are set by the Boone and Crockett Club's Records of North American Big Game Committee, working with the latest and best available information from scientific researchers, guides, hunters, and other parties with serious interest in our big game resources. In general, boundaries are set so that it is highly unlikely that specimens of the larger category can be taken within the boundary set for the smaller category, thus upsetting the rankings of the smaller category. Trophy boundaries are revised as necessary to maintain this separation of the categories.

Black Bear

Ursus americanus americanus and related subspecies

Minimum Score 20 — World's Record 23 10/16

Score	Greatest Length of Skull Without Lower Jaw	Greatest Width of Skull	Sex	Locality Killed	By Whom Killed	Owner	Date Killed	Rank
22 8/16	14 1/16	8 7/16	M	Gila Co., Ariz.	John F. Peters	John F. Peters	SE 1985	1
22 7/16	13 11/16	8 12/16	M	Sevier Co., Utah	Picked Up	Utah Div. of Wildl. Resc.	AG 1982	2
22 2/16	13 13/16	8 5/16	M	Graham Co., Ariz.	Peter C. Knagge	Peter C. Knagge	SE 1982	3
21 14/16	13 12/16	8 2/16	M	Hirsch Creek, B. C.	Cecil W. Brown	Cecil W. Brown	SE 1984	4
21 13/16	13 6/16	8 7/16	M	Carbon Co., Pa.	Robert F. Kulp	Robert F. Kulp	NO 1983	5
21 13/16	13 7/16	8 6/16	M	Big River, Sask.	William Dear	William Dear	MY 1985	5
21 12/16	13 8/16	8 4/16	M	Gila Co., Ariz.	Mike Lisk	Mike Lisk	SE 1984	7
21 12/16	13 10/16	8 2/16	M	Garfield Co., Utah	Clint Mecham	Clint Mecham	MY 1985	7
21 11/16	13 5/16	8 8/16	M	Menominee Co., Mich.	Ray Bray	Andy Bray	NO 1984	9
21 10/16	13 4/16	8 8/16	M	Grande Cache, Alta.	Laurier Adam	Laurier Adam	AP 1984	10
21 10/16	13 8/16	8 5/16	M	Gila Co., Ariz.	Harold W. Mosser	Harold W. Mosser	MY 1985	10
21 9/16	13 4/16	8 5/16	M	Zeballos, B. C.	Gary M. Biggar	Gary M. Biggar	MY 1983	12
21 9/16	13 5/16	8 3/16	M	Catron Co., N. M.	Sam Ray	Sam Ray	OT 1983	12
21 8/16	13 6/16	8 2/16	M	Gila Co., Ariz.	Rick Corven	R. Corven & R. Gifford	AP 1983	14
21 8/16	13 5/16	8 3/16	M	Bonneville Co., Idaho	George R. Adams	George R. Adams	JN 1982	14
21 8/16	13	8 8/16	M	Pike Co., Pa.	Paul D. Longenbach	Paul D. Longenbach	NO 1983	14
21 8/16	13 6/16	8 2/16	M	Marshall Co., Minn.	James E. Kelley	J. Zimpel & B. Zimpel	OT 1984	14
21 7/16	13 4/16	8 3/16	M	Gila Co., Ariz.	D. Highly Falkner	D. Highly Falkner	MY 1984	18
21 7/16	13 3/16	8 4/16	M	Cholmondeley Sound, Alaska	Philip A. Indovina	Philip A. Indovina	MY 1984	18
21 7/16	13 10/16	7 13/16	M	Flat Lake, Alta.	Dale T. Loosemore	Dale T. Loosemore	NO 1983	18
21 7/16	13 11/16	7 12/16	M	Peesane, Sask.	Peter Janzen	Peter Janzen	JN 1984	18
21 6/16	13 3/16	8 4/16	M	Fox Creek, Alta.	William Hellebrand	William Hellebrand	AP 1985	18
21 6/16	13 2/16	8 4/16	M	Thorne Bay, Alaska	Tod L. Reichert	Tod L. Reichert	MY 1985	23
21 5/16	13 3/16	8 2/16	M	Rockbridge Co., Va.	Richard L. Merchant	Richard L. Merchant	JN 1953	24
21 4/16	13 2/16	8 2/16	M	Sawyer Co., Wisc.	Harvey W. Klein	Harvey W. Klein	SE 1982	25
21 4/16	12 12/16	8 8/16	M	Mendocino Co., Calif.	Miles Dupret	M. Dupret & H. Gray	DC 1984	25
21 3/16	12 11/16	8 8/16	M	Yolo Co., Calif.	Walter D. Foster	Walter D. Foster	DC 1983	27
21 3/16	13 1/16	8 2/16	M	Neck Lake, Alaska	F. A. Lonsway, Jr.	F. A. Lonsway, Jr.	MY 1983	27
21 2/16	13	8 2/16	M	Goose River, Alta.	T. Barker & R. Mompere	Thomas Barker	MY 1983	29
21 2/16	12 12/16	8 6/16	M	Marquette Co., Mich.	Gerald J. Isetts, Sr.	Gerald J. Isetts, Sr.	SE 1984	29
21 2/16	13 8/16	7 10/16	M	Graham Island, B. C.	Roger Britton	Roger Britton	MY 1982	29
21 2/16	13	8 2/16	M	Terra Nova River, Nfld.	James A. Young	James A. Young	JN 1984	29
21 2/16	13 3/16	7 15/16	M	Hudson Bay, Sask.	Neil Southam	Neil Southam	SE 1984	29
21 1/16	13 10/16	7 7/16	M	Graham Island, B. C.	Roger Britton	Roger Britton	OT 1980	34

Black Bear—Continued

Ursus americanus and related subspecies

Score	Greatest Length of Skull Without Lower Jaw	Greatest Width of Skull	Sex	Locality Killed	By Whom Killed	Owner	Date Killed	Rank
21 1/16	12 13/16	8 4/16	M	Apache Co., Ariz.	William J. Morris	William J. Morris	SE 1985	34
21	13	8	M	Ft. Assiniboine, Alta.	George Plashka	George Plashka	AG 1982	36
21	13	8	M	Routt Co., Colo.	Jerome W. Keyes, Jr.	Jerome W. Keyes, Jr.	SE 1980	36
21	13 4/16	7 12/16	M	Wasatch Co., Utah	Picked Up	Utah Div. of Wildl. Resc.	DC 1980	36
21	12 14/16	8 2/16	M	Macon Co., N. C.	C. Rick Jones	C. Rick Jones	NO 1983	36
21	13	8	M	Cholmondely Sound, Alaska	Gerry D. Downey	Gerry D. Downey	MY 1985	36
21	12 10/16	8 5/16	M	Echouani Lake, Que.	Collins F. Kellogg	Collins F. Kellogg	JL 1985	36
21	13 3/16	7 13/16	M	Wild Goose, Ont.	William G. Tellijohn	William G. Tellijohn	MY 1985	36
20 14/16	13	7 14/16	M	Ministikwan Lake, Sask.	George F. Galler	George F. Galler	MY 1985	43
20 13/16	12 12/16	8 3/16	M	Eagle Co., Colo.	Terry L. Pierce	Terry L. Pierce	JN 1982	44
20 12/16	12 15/16	7 13/16	M	Navajo Co., Ariz.	James D. Borel	James D. Borel	MY 1985	45
20 11/16	12 9/16	8 2/16	M	McKean Co., Pa.	David H. Hanes	David H. Hanes	NO 1983	46
20 10/16	12 12/16	7 14/16	M	Mendocino Co., Calif.	Joseph A. Cantaroni, Sr.	Joseph A. Cantaroni, Sr.	DC 1982	47
20 9/16	13 5/16	7 8/16	M	Durban, Man.	David H. Boland	David H. Boland	SE 1985	48
20 7/16	12 10/16	7 13/16	M	York Co., N. B.	Charles A. Wallace	Charles A. Wallace	MY 1984	49
20 6/16	12 8/16	7 14/16	M	Piwei River, Sask.	William E. Butler	William E. Butler	MY 1982	50
20 6/16	12 9/16	7 13/16	M	Warren Co., Va.	Samuel Cooksey	Samuel Cooksey	DC 1984	50
20 5/16	12 12/16	7 9/16	M	Cameron Co., Pa.	John R. Bieniek	John R. Bieniek	NO 1984	52
20 4/16	12 12/16	7 8/16	M	Fremont Co., Colo.	Carl B. Mockensturm	Carl B. Mockensturm	JN 1985	53
20 3/16	12 6/16	7 13/16	M	Mesa Co., Colo.	Robert Keck	Robert Keck	JN 1984	54
20 1/16	12 6/16	7 12/16	M	Lake Dasserat, Que.	Richard J. Stadler	Richard J. Stadler	MY 1985	55
20 1/16	12 6/16	7 12/16	M	Skiff Lake, N. B.	Ronald A. Benner	Ronald A. Benner	MY 1984	56
20 1/16	12 6/16	7 8/16	M	Arntfield, Que.	John K. Deveney	John K. Deveney	JN 1983	56
20	12 6/16	7 9/16	M	Iron Co., Mich.	George J. Hronkin	George J. Hronkin	SE 1982	58
20	12 6/16	7 10/16	M	Kuiu Island, Alaska	Anthony Koutroumanis	Anthony Koutroumanis	MY 1985	58
20	12 5/16	7 11/16	M	Park Co., Wyo.	Loren M. Grosskopf	Loren M. Grosskopf	MY 1985	58
22 6/16*	13 11/16	8 11/16	M	Lycoming Co., Pa.	John C. Whyne	John C. Whyne	NO 1983	58

*Final Score subject to revision by additional verifying measurements.

Grizzly Bear
Ursus arctos horribilis

Minimum Score 23   **World's Record 27 5/16**

Score	Greatest Length of Skull Without Lower Jaw	Greatest Width of Skull	Sex	Locality Killed	By Whom Killed	Owner	Date Killed	Rank
27 5/16	16 14/16	10 4/16	M	Dean River, B. C.	Roger J. Pentecost	Roger J. Pentecost	OT 1982	1
26 9/16	16 4/16	10 5/16	M	Ungalik River, Alaska	Stanley F. Smith	S. Smith & G. Fait	SE 1983	2
26 6/16	16 5/16	10 1/16	M	Cluculz Creek, B. C.	Thomas C. Roberson	Thomas C. Roberson	SE 1983	3
26 2/16	16 12/16	9 7/16	M	Bear Lake, B. C.	DeVern Gardner	DeVern Gardner	MY 1984	4
25 14/16	16 5/16	9 9/16	M	Gardner Canal, B. C.	Steven B. Garland	Steven B. Garland	MY 1984	5
25 13/16	16 7/16	9 9/16	M	Spatsizi River, B. C.	Howard W. Gambrell	Howard W. Gambrell	SE 1985	6
25 12/16	16	9 12/16	M	Hanna Ridge, B. C.	Dale T. Dean	Dale T. Dean	MY 1984	7
25 12/16	16	9 12/16	M	Bond Sound, B. C.	William Kemp, Jr.	William Kemp, Jr.	MY 1985	7
25 10/16	15 14/16	9 12/16	M	Sheslay River, B. C.	John Welsh	John Welsh	MY 1983	9
25 9/16	16 3/16	9 6/16	M	Carpenter Lake, B. C.	Jim Sprangers	Jim Sprangers	JN 1982	10
25 8/16	15 12/16	9 12/16	M	Kuskokwim River, Alaska	Bernard V. Davis	Bernard V. Davis	MY 1983	11
25 7/16	15 13/16	9 10/16	M	Wedeene River. B. C.	Stuart Haslett	Stuart Haslett	AP 1983	12
25 6/16	15 12/16	9 10/16	M	Bond Sound, B. C.	James H. Garner	James H. Garner	OT 1982	13
25 5/16	15 7/16	9 14/16	M	Tonzona River, Alaska	George G. Houser	George G. Houser	MY 1985	14
25 4/16	15 10/16	9 10/16	M	Gisasa River, Alaska	Billy R. Deligans, Jr.	Billy R. Deligans, Jr.	AP 1985	15
25 3/16	15 9/16	9 10/16	M	Kingcome River, B. C.	Graydon A. Peat	Graydon A. Peat	NO 1983	16
25 2/16	16	9 2/16	M	Cluculz Creek, B. C.	Ed Roberson	Ed Roberson	AP 1978	17
25 2/16	15 10/16	9 8/16	M	Blue Ridge, Alta.	Thomas E. Deacon	Thomas E. Deacon	MY 1983	17
25 1/16	15 2/16	9 15/16	M	Pikmiktalik River, Alaska	Donald B. Huffines	Donald B. Huffines	SE 1984	19
25	15 13/16	9 3/16	M	Bella Coola River, B. C.	James G. Shelton	James G. Shelton	SE 1983	20
25	15 9/16	9 10/16	M	Koyuk River, Alaska	John Macaluso	John Macaluso	AP 1985	20
24 15/16	15 13/16	9 2/16	M	Nusatsum River, B. C.	Picked Up	Randy Svisdahl	SE 1980	22
24 14/16	15 15/16	8 15/16	M	Barney Creek, B. C.	Roy Pattison	Roy Pattison	MY 1984	23
24 13/16	15 15/16	8 14/16	M	Kilbella River, B. C.	Larry Sawchuk	Larry Sawchuk	AP 1984	24
24 13/16	15 14/16	8 15/16	M	Burnt Trail Creek, B. C.	Tom Housh	Tom Housh	MY 1985	24
24 12/16	15 15/16	8 13/16	M	Toklat River, Alaska	George P. Mann	George P. Mann	MY 1971	26
24 11/16	15 9/16	9 2/16	M	Kwatna Bay, B. C.	Norm Roettger	Norm Roettger	OT 1982	27
24 10/16	14 12/16	9 14/16	M	John River, Alaska	Rick J. Schikora	Rick J. Schikora	OT 1982	28
24 10/16	15 3/16	9 7/16	M	Pilgrim River, Alaska	Karen J. Chadwick	Karen J. Chadwick	SE 1982	28
24 6/16	15 7/16	9 2/16	M	Motase Peak, B. C.	Roger L. Pock	Roger L. Pock	MY 1984	30
24 5/16	15	9 8/16	M	Terminus Mt., B. C.	William E. Greehey	William E. Greehey	SE 1982	31
24 5/16	15 5/16	9 2/16	M	Koyuk, Alaska	K. James Malady, III	K. James Malady, III	MY 1985	31
24 7/16	15 5/16	9 2/16	M	Wood River, Alaska	Kerry Q. Gronewold	Kerry Q. Gronewold	SE 1984	33
24 6/16	15 10/16	8 12/16	M	Clyak River, B. C.	Marvin Opp	Marvin Opp	MY 1983	34

Grizzly Bear—Continued
Ursus arctos horribilis

Score	Greatest Length of Skull Without Lower Jaw	Greatest Width of Skull	Sex	Locality Killed	By Whom Killed	Owner	Date Killed	Rank
24⁶⁄₁₆	15⁵⁄₁₆	9²⁄₁₆	M	Nalbeelah Creek, B. C.	Wayne Moon	Wayne Moon	OT 1983	34
24⁶⁄₁₆	15²⁄₁₆	9⁴⁄₁₆	M	Tagagawik River, Alaska	Roland L. Quimby	Roland L. Quimby	SE 1983	34
24⁶⁄₁₆	15⁵⁄₁₆	9¹⁄₁₆	M	Knight Inlet, B. C.	Norman W. Dougan	Norman W. Dougan	OT 1984	34
24⁴⁄₁₆	15⁴⁄₁₆	9	M	Trout Lake, B. C.	Paul L. Reese	Paul L. Reese	OT 1982	38
24³⁄₁₆	15⁸⁄₁₆	8¹¹⁄₁₆	M	Nusatsum River, B. C.	Randy Svisdahl	Randy Svisdahl	SE 1983	39
24³⁄₁₆	15	9³⁄₁₆	M	White Creek, Alaska	J. H. Harvey & V. Landt	John H. Harvey, Jr.	SE 1985	39
24²⁄₁₆	15⁶⁄₁₆	8⁹⁄₁₆	M	Koeye River, B. C.	William H. Dunstan, IV	William H. Dunstan, IV	NO 1983	41
24²⁄₁₆	15¹⁹⁄₁₆	8⁸⁄₁₆	M	Kuskokwim River, Alaska	Anthony J. Bianchi	Anthony J. Bianchi	MY 1984	41
24¹⁄₁₆	15⁵⁄₁₆	9	M	Noatak River, Alaska	Stephen P. Connell	Stephen P. Connell	SE 1984	43
24¹⁄₁₆	14¹¹⁄₁₆	9⁹⁄₁₆	M	Pine River, B. C.	Brian R. Goates	Brian R. Goates	MY 1985	43
24	15⁵⁄₁₆	8¹¹⁄₁₆	M	Kitsumkalum River, B. C.	Bill Gourlie	Bill Gourlie	AP 1984	45
24	14⁵⁄₁₆	8¹²⁄₁₆	M	Ram River, Alta.	Howard Bugg	Howard Bugg	MY 1976	45
23¹⁵⁄₁₆	14¹⁵⁄₁₆	9	M	Hinton, Alta.	Roy Young	Roy Young	MY 1984	47
23¹⁴⁄₁₆	15⁷⁄₁₆	8⁷⁄₁₆	M	Entiako River, B. C.	Phillip G. Harrison	Phillip G. Harrison	MY 1985	48
23³⁄₁₆	14¹³⁄₁₆	8⁵⁄₁₆	M	Chisana Glacier, Alaska	Gary K. Engebretsen	Gary K. Engebretsen	SE 1982	49
23¹⁄₁₆	14⁵⁄₁₆	8¹²⁄₁₆	M	Wind River, Alaska	Vernon D. Holleman	Vernon D. Holleman	MY 1983	50
26³⁄₁₆*	16	10³⁄₁₆	M	Tok River, Alaska	Garlen Keen	Garlen Keen	SE 1983	

*Final Score subject to revision by additional verifying measurements.

Alaska Brown Bear

Ursus arctos middendorffi and certain related subspecies

Minimum Score 26   World's Record 30 2/16

Score	Greatest Length of Skull Without Lower Jaw	Greatest Width of Skull	Sex	Locality Killed	By Whom Killed	Owner	Date Killed	Rank
30 2/16	18	12 2/16	M	Uyak Bay, Alaska	Walter H. White	Walter H. White	JN 1954	1
29 6/16	17 2/16	11 12/16	M	Sturgeon River, Alaska	Anthony Gioffre	Anthony Gioffre	AP 1984	2
29 1/16	17 15/16	11 2/16	M	Cold Bay, Alaska	George Caswell	George Caswell	MY 1983	3
28 13/16	17 8/16	11 5/16	M	Herring Bay, Alaska	Michael F. Short	Michael F. Short	MY 1983	4
28 13/16	17 9/16	11 3/16	M	Deadman Bay, Alaska	Michael R. Anderson	Michael R. Anderson	OT 1971	4
28 10/16	17 14/16	10 12/16	M	Long Bay, Alaska	Delbert E. Starr	Delbert E. Starr	MY 1984	6
28 8/16	17 10/16	10 14/16	M	Karluk Lake, Alaska	Paul W. Hansen	Paul W. Hansen	AP 1983	7
28 8/16	17 2/16	11 4/16	M	Larsen Bay, Alaska	Sherron G. Perry	Sherron G. Perry	OT 1983	8
28 8/16	17 13/16	10 8/16	M	Cold Bay, Alaska	Timothy Orton	Timothy Orton	MY 1984	9
28 8/16	17 9/16	10 11/16	M	Cold Bay, Alaska	Kenneth C. Hayden	Kenneth C. Hayden	MY 1984	9
28 4/16	17 9/16	10 11/16	M	Unimak Island, Alaska	John D. Frost	John D. Frost	MY 1985	11
28 3/16	17 13/16	10 6/16	M	Volcano Bay, Alaska	L. Clark Kiser	L. Clark Kiser	MY 1984	12
28 3/16	16 13/16	11 6/16	M	Kaguyak Bay, Alaska	Jack D. Revelle	Jack D. Revelle	AP 1984	12
28 3/16	17 4/16	11 2/16	M	Red Lake, Alaska	Richard H. Neville	Richard H. Neville	MY 1984	12
28 2/16	17	11 2/16	M	Spiridon Lake, Alaska	Chris T. Hinchey	Bear Arms	AP 1983	15
28 2/16	17 7/16	10 1/16	M	Cold Bay, Alaska	Lonnie W. McCurry, Sr.	Lonnie W. McCurry, Sr.	MY 1984	15
28 1/16	17 9/16	10 8/16	M	Olga Bay, Alaska	Robert N. Wainscott	Robert N. Wainscott	MY 1982	17
28 1/16	18	10 4/16	M	Port Heiden, Alaska	William H. F. Wiltshire	William H. F. Wiltshire	MY 1984	17
28	17 2/16	10 4/16	M	Windy Bay, Alaska	Archie H. Stevens, Sr.	Archie H. Stevens, Sr.	MY 1982	19
28	16 5/16	11 1/16	M	Skilak Glacier, Alaska	Richard W. Carlock	Richard W. Carlock	MY 1983	19
28	17 5/16	10 1/16	M	Copper River, Alaska	Roger R. Card	Roger R. Card	AP 1985	19
27 14/16	17 5/16	9 15/16	M	Painter Creek, Alaska	John D. McCartt	John D. McCartt	MY 1984	22
27 13/16	17 3/16	10 4/16	M	Ramsey Bay, Alaska	Leonard O. Wallace	Leonard O. Wallace	MY 1984	23
27 6/16	16 9/16	10 12/16	M	Naugolka Point, Alaska	Scott S. Jury	Scott S. Jury	MY 1984	24
27 1/16	16 1/16	11	M	Uganik Bay, Alaska	F. Barry Shaw	F. Barry Shaw	MY 1985	25
27	17 4/16	9 12/16	M	Cold Bay, Alaska	Charles J. Folkman	Charles J. Folkman	SE 1985	26
26 2/16	16 2/16	10	M	Red Lake, Alaska	Earl R. Hossman	Earl R. Hossman	OT 1977	27
29*	17 9/16	11 6/16	M	Kaguyak Bay, Alaska	Ronald L. Winstead	Ronald L. Winstead	AP 1983	
28 12/16*	17 4/16	11 8/16	M	Kaiugnak Bay, Alaska	Dale E. Machacek	Dale E. Machacek	MY 1984	

*Final Score subject to revision by additional verifying measurements.

Cougar or Mountain Lion
Felis concolor hippolestes and related subspecies

Minimum Score 14$^{4}/_{16}$ World's Record 16$^{4}/_{16}$

Score	Greatest Length of Skull Without Lower Jaw	Greatest Width of Skull	Sex	Locality Killed	By Whom Killed	Owner	Date Killed	Rank
15$^{11}/_{16}$	9$^{9}/_{16}$	6$^{2}/_{16}$	M	Okanagan Lake, B. C.	D. Cooper & M. Hubbard	Dusty R. Cooper	JA 1985	1
15$^{9}/_{16}$	9	6$^{9}/_{16}$	M	Gallatin Co., Mont.	Tracy J. Peterson	Tracy J. Peterson	DC 1984	2
15$^{9}/_{16}$	9$^{2}/_{16}$	6$^{7}/_{16}$	M	Carbon Co., Utah	Robert F. McLawhorn	Robert F. McLawhorn	MY 1985	2
15$^{8}/_{16}$	9	6$^{8}/_{16}$	M	Idaho Co., Idaho	Jerry J. James	Jerry J. James	JA 1982	4
15$^{8}/_{16}$	9$^{2}/_{16}$	6$^{6}/_{16}$	M	Rio Blanco Co., Colo.	Robert L. Raley	Robert L. Raley	JA 1985	4
15$^{8}/_{16}$	9	6$^{8}/_{16}$	M	Bannock Co., Idaho	Frank N. Hough	Frank N. Hough	JA 1985	4
15$^{8}/_{16}$	9$^{3}/_{16}$	6$^{5}/_{16}$	M	Rio Arriba Co., N. M.	Dick Ray	Dick Ray	JA 1985	4
15$^{7}/_{16}$	9$^{2}/_{16}$	6$^{5}/_{16}$	M	Lemhi Co., Idaho	David W. Thompson	David W. Thompson	DC 1983	8
15$^{7}/_{16}$	9$^{1}/_{16}$	6$^{6}/_{16}$	M	Rio Blanco Co., Colo.	Ronald D. Vincent	Ronald D. Vincent	DC 1970	8
15$^{6}/_{16}$	9$^{5}/_{16}$	6$^{1}/_{16}$	M	Socorro Co., N. M.	Edwin E. Finkbeiner	Edwin E. Finkbeiner	JA 1984	10
15$^{6}/_{16}$	9	6$^{6}/_{16}$	M	Missoula Co., Mont.	Bruce E. Parker	Bruce E. Parker	DC 1984	10
15$^{6}/_{16}$	8$^{4}/_{16}$	6$^{8}/_{16}$	M	Lewis & Clark Co., Mont.	Wayne L. Beach	Wayne L. Beach	DC 1983	10
15$^{6}/_{16}$	9$^{1}/_{16}$	6$^{5}/_{16}$	M	Benewah Co., Idaho	Kurt R. Morris	Kurt R. Morris	DC 1984	10
15$^{5}/_{16}$	8$^{5}/_{16}$	6$^{6}/_{16}$	M	Pend Oreille Co., Wash.	Jack Schulte	Jack Schulte	DC 1981	14
15$^{4}/_{16}$	8$^{4}/_{16}$	6$^{6}/_{16}$	M	Broadwater Co., Mont.	Ray Toombs	Ray Toombs	DC 1982	15
15$^{4}/_{16}$	8$^{13}/_{16}$	6$^{7}/_{16}$	M	Wallowa Co., Oreg.	Donna Lancaster	Donna Lancaster	DC 1983	15
15$^{4}/_{16}$	9$^{2}/_{16}$	6$^{2}/_{16}$	M	Mill Creek, Alta.	Warren R. Burton	Warren R. Burton	JA 1984	15
15$^{4}/_{16}$	8$^{15}/_{16}$	6$^{5}/_{16}$	M	Lewis & Clark Co., Mont.	Robert A. Soukkala	Robert A. Soukkala	DC 1983	15
15$^{4}/_{16}$	8$^{15}/_{16}$	6$^{5}/_{16}$	M	Idaho Co., Idaho	Ralph E. Close	Ralph E. Close	FE 1980	15
15$^{4}/_{16}$	9$^{2}/_{16}$	6$^{2}/_{16}$	M	Colfax Co., N. M.	L. Profazi & R. Troyer	Louie Profazi	DC 1984	15
15$^{4}/_{16}$	9	6$^{4}/_{16}$	M	Coconino Co., Ariz.	Gregg A. Thurston	Gregg A. Thurston	NO 1984	15
15$^{4}/_{16}$	9	6$^{4}/_{16}$	M	Sevier Co., Utah	John R. Blanton	John R. Blanton	JA 1985	15
15$^{4}/_{16}$	8$^{4}/_{16}$	6$^{6}/_{16}$	M	Dolores Co., Colo.	Bruce Nay	Bruce Nay	FE 1984	15
15$^{3}/_{16}$	8$^{14}/_{16}$	6$^{5}/_{16}$	M	Rio Blanco Co., Colo.	Robert L. Raley	Robert L. Raley	JA 1983	24
15$^{2}/_{16}$	8$^{12}/_{16}$	6$^{6}/_{16}$	M	Garfield Co., Colo.	Leslie H. Brewster	Leslie H. Brewster	DC 1983	25
15$^{2}/_{16}$	8$^{13}/_{16}$	6$^{5}/_{16}$	M	Archuleta Co., Colo.	Judd Cooney	Judd Cooney	DC 1982	25
15$^{2}/_{16}$	8$^{11}/_{16}$	6$^{7}/_{16}$	M	Gallatin Co., Mont.	David M. Tofte	David M. Tofte	DC 1984	25
15$^{2}/_{16}$	8$^{12}/_{16}$	6$^{6}/_{16}$	M	Wallowa Co., Oreg.	Samuel E. Briscoe	Samuel E. Briscoe	JA 1984	25
15$^{2}/_{16}$	8$^{14}/_{16}$	6$^{4}/_{16}$	M	Sanders Co., Mont.	Conrad P. Anderson	Conrad P. Anderson	DC 1984	25
15$^{1}/_{16}$	9	6$^{1}/_{16}$	M	Wallowa Co., Oreg.	William E. Hosford	William E. Hosford	DC 1982	30
15$^{1}/_{16}$	8$^{13}/_{16}$	6$^{4}/_{16}$	M	Erickson Creek, B. C.	R. John Kovak	R. John Kovak	DC 1982	30
15$^{1}/_{16}$	8$^{13}/_{16}$	6$^{4}/_{16}$	M	Whitney Creek, Alta.	Bryne J. Lengyel	Bryne J. Lengyel	JA 1985	30
15	8$^{14}/_{16}$	6$^{2}/_{16}$	M	Gila Co., Ariz.	William T. Haney	William T. Haney	FE 1983	33

				Location	Hunter	Owner	Date	
15	8¹⁰/16	6⁶/16	M	Teton Co., Mont.	Richard Klick	John F. Sulik	JA 1982	33
15	8⁸/16	6⁶/16	M	Sheridan Co., Wyo.	Toby J. Johnson	Toby J. Johnson	FE 1984	33
15	8¹²/16	6⁴/16	M	Rio Arriba Co., N. M.	Michael Ray	Michael Ray	JA 1982	33
15	8¹¹/16	6⁵/16	M	Nine Mile Creek, B. C.	Ray Carry	Ray Carry	JA 1980	33
15	8⁹/16	6⁶/16	M	Wallowa Co., Oreg.	Edward Cranston	Edward Cranston	DC 1984	33
15	8³/16	6³/16	M	Mesa Co., Colo.	Lawrence C. Glass	Lawrence C. Glass	JA 1985	33
14¹³/16	8³/16	6	M	Montezuma Co., Colo.	George Wells	George Wells	JA 1985	40
14¹²/16	8²/16	6	M	Kittitas Co., Wash.	Gary R. Fountain	Gary R. Fountain	DC 1984	41
14¹⁰/16	8²/16	5¹⁴/16	M	Rio Arriba Co., N. M.	Dick Ray	Dick Ray	JA 1982	42
14¹⁰/16	8⁹/16	6	M	Lemhi Co., Idaho	Robert L. Highfill	Robert L. Highfill	DC 1984	42
14¹⁰/16	8⁹/16	6	M	Archuleta Co., Colo.	M. Howard Payne	M. Howard Payne	JA 1985	42
14⁹/16	8⁹/16	6	M	Garfield Co., Colo.	Douglas E. Starks	Douglas E. Starks	DC 1984	45
14⁸/16	8⁵/16	6³/16	M	Johnson Co., Wyo.	Hugh Jennings	Hugh Jennings	JA 1982	46
15¹⁰/16*	9¹/16	6⁹/16	M	Lincoln Co., Mont.	Bill Reynolds	Bill Reynolds	FE 1983	
15¹⁰/16*	9¹/16	6⁹/16	M	Lincoln Co., Mont.	W. Nixon & A. Kimberlin	Anthony Kimberlin	DC 1983	

*Final Score subject to revision by additional verifying measurements.

Jaguar
Felis onca hernandesii and related subspecies

World's Record 18 7/16

Minimum Score 14 8/16

Score	Greatest Length of Skull Without Lower Jaw	Greatest Width of Skull	Sex	Locality Killed	By Whom Killed	Owner	Date Killed	Rank
15 15/16	9 6/16	6 9/16	M	Tamaulipas, Mexico	Patrick W. Frederick	Patrick W. Frederick	AP 1983	1

326

Pacific Walrus
Odobenus rosmarus divergens

Minimum Score 100 — World's Record 145⁵⁄₈

Score	Entire Length of Loose Tusk R.	Entire Length of Loose Tusk L.	Circumference of Base R.	Circumference of Base L.	Circumference at Third Quarter R.	Circumference at Third Quarter L.	Sex	Locality Killed	By Whom Killed	Owner	Date Killed	Rank
133⁶⁄₈	32⁶⁄₈	32	9¹⁄₈	9¹⁄₈	7⁵⁄₈	7¹⁄₈	M	Port Heiden, Alaska	Picked Up	John T. Taylor	PU 1980	1
133⁴⁄₈	37³⁄₈	37⁷⁄₈	7⁴⁄₈	7⁵⁄₈	6¹⁄₈	6³⁄₈	M	Cape Seniavin, Alaska	Picked Up	Patrick C. Martin	PU 1985	2
132⁶⁄₈	36³⁄₈	37³⁄₈	8¹⁄₈	8	6⁵⁄₈	6	M	Port Moller, Alaska	Picked Up	R. Hammack & J. Hammack	PU 1984	3
130⁶⁄₈	31⁵⁄₈	32⁴⁄₈	8⁷⁄₈	9¹⁄₈	6⁷⁄₈	7	M	Port Moller, Alaska	Picked Up	John Sarvis	PU 1980	4
129⁴⁄₈	32	32	9	8⁶⁄₈	6⁷⁄₈	6⁴⁄₈	M	Izembek Lagoon, Alaska	Picked Up	John Sarvis	PU 1981	5
129⁴⁄₈	32⁵⁄₈	32⁷⁄₈	8⁵⁄₈	8⁵⁄₈	6²⁄₈	6³⁄₈	M	Port Heiden, Alaska	Picked Up	Donald R. Warren	PU 1982	5
126⁴⁄₈	31⁵⁄₈	31⁶⁄₈	8⁶⁄₈	8⁷⁄₈	6¹⁄₈	6¹⁄₈	M	Gambell, Alaska	Eskimo	Mike W. Millar	MY 1982	7

Wapiti or American Elk
Cervus elaphus nelsoni and related subspecies

Minimum Score 360 — World's Record 442 3/8

Score	Length of Main Beam R.	L.	Inside Spread	Circumference at Smallest Place Between First and Second Points R.	L.	Number of Points R.	L.	Locality Killed	By Whom Killed	Owner	Date Killed	Rank
418 7/8	58	55	43 3/8	10 5/8	11 3/8	6	7	Wyo.	J. G. Millais	G. Kenneth Whitehead	1886	1
400	56 7/8	57	49	9 1/8	9 1/8	7	7	Crook Co., Oreg.	Picked Up	Randall L. Ryerse	SE 1984	2
398	50 3/8	53 3/8	46 5/8	8 4/8	8 4/8	6	6	Pincher Creek, Alta.	Monty F. Adams	Pat Adams	NO 1977	3
394 1/8	58	58 3/8	46 7/8	9 5/8	10 2/8	6	6	Lincoln Co., Wyo.	Roland Smith	Leon C. Smith	1930	4
390 3/8	57 1/8	54 4/8	40 3/8	9 2/8	9 1/8	6	7	Hoback Canyon, Wyo.	Picked Up	Spanky Greenville	PU 1977	5
388 3/8	53 5/8	55	47 1/8	9	9 3/8	7	7	Coconino Co., Ariz.	Picked Up	Tim Cotten	PR 1982	6
386 7/8	58 4/8	61 3/8	41 7/8	8 7/8	8 7/8	6	6	Otero Co., N. M.	Picked Up	William M. Wheless, III	PU 1981	7
386 5/8	59 3/8	60	52 3/8	9 9/8	9 1/8	6	7	Panther River, Alta.	Leonard L. Hengen	Leonard L. Hengen	OT 1977	8
385 3/8	51 1/8	54 2/8	41 5/8	10 7/8	10 5/8	6	6	Otero Co., N. M.	Gregory C. Saunders	Gregory C. Saunders	SE 1985	9
385 3/8	55 4/8	55 3/8	47 3/8	10 1/8	10 5/8	6	6	Teton Co., Wyo.	Gene J. Riordan	Timothy D. Riordan	OT 1960	9
384 7/8	60	60 3/8	44 3/8	9 5/8	10	7	7	Apache Co., Ariz.	H. C. Meyer & J. T. Caid	Herman C. Meyer	OT 1982	11
384	53 3/8	51 1/8	48 3/8	8 5/8	8 2/8	6	6	Meagher Co., Mont.	Frank W. Fuller	Frank W. Fuller	NO 1963	12
383	52 1/8	52 3/8	51 1/8	9 5/8	9	6	6	Panther River, Alta.	Thomas Coupland	Echoglen Taxidermy	OT 1984	13
382 6/8	56 7/8	55 3/8	48	9 3/8	10 2/8	6	6	Apache Co., Ariz.	William E. Moss	William E. Moss	OT 1985	14
382 4/8	54	55 3/8	40 3/8	8 4/8	9 1/8	7	7	Cascade Co., Mont.	Robert J. Gliko	Robert J. Gliko	NO 1983	15
381 3/8	53 4/8	53 7/8	43 7/8	9 5/8	8 5/8	6	6	White Pine Co., Nev.	Michael N. Kalafatic	Michael N. Kalafatic	SE 1985	16
380 5/8	54 3/8	53 4/8	42 3/8	10 3/8	9 3/8	6	6	Apache Co., Ariz.	Don L. Corley	Don L. Corley	SE 1984	17
379 6/8	58 2/8	58 3/8	46 3/8	8 5/8	8 5/8	6	7	Grant Co., N. M.	Tony R. Grijalva	Tony R. Grijalva	OT 1983	18
379 3/8	60 1/8	61 1/8	45 3/8	8 7/8	8 3/8	6	6	Coconino Co., Ariz.	Tammy J. Otero	Tammy J. Otero	NO 1984	19
379	50 7/8	51	44 3/8	9 7/8	10 2/8	6	6	Petroleum Co., Mont.	Lana J. Sluggett	Lana J. Sluggett	NO 1984	20
377 6/8	53 3/8	53 4/8	41 7/8	9	9 5/8	9	9	Mistatim, Sask.	Peter Hrbachek	Peter Hrbachek	DC 1984	21
377 4/8	52 2/8	54	41 1/8	8 7/8	8 3/8	6	7	Park Co., Wyo.	Jon M. Mekeal	Jon M. Mekeal	OT 1984	22
377 2/8	54 2/8	54 2/8	44 2/8	8 2/8	8 1/8	7	7	Apache Co., Ariz.	Donald E. Franklin	Donald E. Franklin	OT 1981	23
377	49 4/8	48 1/8	39	7 1/8	7 4/8	7	7	Clearwater River, Alta.	Don H. Grimes	Don H. Grimes	SE 1985	24
376 6/8	59 3/8	59 7/8	45 4/8	10	9 2/8	8	7	Crook Co., Oreg.	Picked Up	Larry E. Miller	PU 1983	25
375 5/8	52 1/8	50 4/8	37 4/8	8 4/8	7 7/8	7	7	Shoshone Co., Idaho	Ralph H. Brandvold, Jr.	Ralph H. Brandvold, Jr.	OT 1983	26
375 5/8	55 3/8	55 3/8	41 3/8	8 3/8	8 3/8	6	6	Colfax Co., N. M.	Slim Pickens	Margaret M. Lindley	OT 1981	27
375	59	58 5/8	42 3/8	9 7/8	9 2/8	6	6	Lewis & Clark Co., Mont.	James Bollinger	James Bollinger	NO 1982	28
370 6/8	56	55 5/8	47 5/8	8 2/8	8 3/8	6	6	Grant Co., Oreg.	Lawrence E. Mayfield	Lawrence E. Mayfield	NO 1984	29
399 4/8*	57 3/8	58 2/8	44 4/8	8 1/8	8 1/8	6	6	Apache Co., Ariz.	T. R. Tidwell	T. R. Tidwell	SE 1983	
390 2/8*	52 5/8	52	39 2/8	10 2/8	10 2/8	6	6	Gila Co., Ariz.	Fred B. Dickey	Fred B. Dickey	OT 1984	
389*	45 3/8	46	46	7 1/8	7 1/8	6	7	Navajo Co., Ariz.	Melvin Nolte, Jr.	Melvin Nolte, Jr.	SE 1983	

*Final Score subject to revision by additional verifying measurements.

Roosevelt's Elk
Cervus elaphus roosevelti

Minimum Score 275
World's Record 384 3/8

The Roosevelt's elk category was established on 1 January 1980. Roosevelt's elk includes trophies from: west of Highway 1-5 in Oregon and Washington; Del Norte and Humboldt Counties, California; Afognak and Raspberry Islands, Alaska; and Vancouver Island, B.C.

Score	Length of Main Beam R.	L.	Inside Spread	Circumference at Smallest Place Between First and Second Points R.	L.	Number of Points R.	L.	Locality Killed	By Whom Killed	Owner	Date Killed	Rank
384 3/8	48 3/8	49	41 1/8	8 7/8	9 4/8	9	8	Clatsop Co., Oreg.	Robert Sharp	Harold E. Stepp	1949	1
380 6/8	52 3/8	52 6/8	45 3/8	8 3/8	8 1/8	8	8	Jefferson Co., Wash.	Sam Argo	Sam Argo	NO 1983	2
353 6/8	52	53 3/8	38 5/8	8 5/8	9 1/8	6	7	Washington Co., Oreg.	Kenneth R. Adamson	Kenneth R. Adamson	SE 1985	3
343 7/8	41 3/8	42 3/8	46 7/8	8 2/8	8	7	7	Tillamook Co., Oreg.	Bud Davis	Herb W. Davis	NO 1957	4
337 1/8	49 6/8	52	30 7/8	9 1/8	8 4/8	7	6	Wahkiakum Co., Wash.	E. L. McKie & T. Faubian	E. L. McKie	NO 1962	5
336 6/8	50 4/8	47 6/8	39	8	8 6/8	6	6	Tillamook Co., Oreg.	Gary L. Cox	Gary L. Cox	NO 1965	6
332 2/8	51 4/8	51 1/8	41 2/8	8 6/8	9 1/8	8	6	Humboldt Co., Calif.	Picked Up	Leo Prshora	PU 1955	7
332	49	48 4/8	45	8 1/8	8 5/8	7	6	Tillamook Co., Oreg.	Robert B. Thornton	Robert B. Thornton	NO 1984	8
327 4/8	47 7/8	46	44 7/8	10 3/8	11	6	6	Clallam Co., Wash.	Daniel D. Hinchen	Daniel D. Hinchen	NO 1976	9
327 3/8	48 5/8	50 5/8	42 3/8	8 3/8	8 1/8	8	7	Tillamook, Co., Oreg.	Dave Griffith	Dave Griffith	PU 1958	10
327 1/8	50 5/8	50	40 5/8	8 7/8	9 1/8	7	6	Clatsop Co., Oreg.	Billy L. Jasper	Billy L. Jasper	NO 1946	11
326 1/8	49 6/8	49 3/8	33 5/8	8 1/8	8 1/8	7	7	Wahkiakum Co., Wash.	Otis E. Wright	Otis E. Wright	NO 1966	12
320 4/8	47 1/8	51 1/8	32 5/8	8 5/8	8 8/8	7	6	Tillamook Co., Oreg.	Stanley E. Kephart	Stanley E. Kephart	NO 1964	13
316 5/8	51 3/8	49	39	8 5/8	9 7/8	6	7	Columbia Co., Oreg.	Harry Olsen	Harry Olsen	NO 1969	14
316 5/8	41 5/8	41 5/8	38 5/8	9 1/8	8 5/8	6	6	Clallam Co., Wash.	Daniel M. Hilt	Daniel M. Hilt	NO 1982	15
310 5/8	43 4/8	44 6/8	38 5/8	7 7/8	7 3/8	7	7	Clallam Co., Wash.	Daniel M. Hilt	Daniel M. Hilt	NO 1958	16
310 4/8	44 3/8	44	33 5/8	9 5/8	9 6/8	7	7	Clatsop Co., Oreg.	Elman Peterson, Jr.	Elman Peterson, Jr.	NO 1968	17
309 6/8	43 1/8	48 1/8	31 5/8	9 2/8	9 4/8	7	7	Clatsop Co., Oreg.	Terry E. Andrews	Terry E. Andrews	NO 1984	18
307 4/8	46 1/8	45 6/8	40 6/8	7 7/8	7 7/8	7	7	Tillamook Co., Oreg.	John A. Wehinger	John A. Wehinger	NO 1964	19
306	40 4/8	39 3/8	40 4/8	9 1/8	9 4/8	7	7	Washington Co., Oreg.	Michael R. Jamieson	Michael R. Jamieson	NO 1982	20
302 6/8	45 4/8	44 3/8	37 7/8	8 5/8	9	6	6	Grays Harbor Co., Wash.	Donald M. Vestal	Dean Vestal	NO 1981	21
296 6/8	43 1/8	42 2/8	34 7/8	9 3/8	9 2/8	6	6	Clallam Co., Wash.	Randy F. Mesenbrink	Randy F. Mesenbrink	OT 1977	22
296 6/8	46 5/8	48 3/8	47 5/8	8 4/8	8 5/8	5	7	Clallam Co., Wash.	Aubrey F. Taylor	Aubrey F. Taylor	NO 1984	22
373 3/8*	57 4/8	55 7/8	44 5/8	7 3/8	7 7/8	7	7	Wahkiakum Co., Wash.	William Williams	William Williams	OT 1968	
370 7/8*	50 6/8	49	35 4/8	8 3/8	8 3/8	9	9	Ucona River, B. C.	David R. Summers	David R. Summers	OT 1978	
356 2/8*	46	46 5/8	39 5/8	11 3/8	9 5/8	8	7	White River, B. C.	George Korhonen	George Korhonen	OT 1982	
341 2/8*	46 1/8	47 7/8	40 7/8	9	9 2/8	9	7	Moakwa Creek, B. C.	Harry Whitehead	Harry Whitehead	OT 1982	

*Final Score subject to revision by additional verifying measurements.

Mule Deer (Typical Antlers)

Odocoileus hemionus hemionus and certain related subspecies

Minimum Score 185 — World's Record 225 6/8

Score	Length of Main Beam R.	Length of Main Beam L.	Inside Spread	Circumference at Smallest Place Between Burr and First Point R.	Circumference at Smallest Place Between Burr and First Point L.	Number of Points R.	Number of Points L.	Locality Killed	By Whom Killed	Owner	Date Killed	Rank
209	26 3/8	27	24 2/8	5 6/8	5 5/8	5	5	Boise Co., Idaho	Charles Root	Soron Root	NO 1970	1
208 5/8	27 7/8	27 7/8	28 7/8	5 5/8	5 5/8	5	7	Rio Arriba Co., N. M.	Kelly Baird	Kelly Baird	NO 1984	2
205 4/8	26 4/8	26 4/8	25 2/8	5 1/8	4 6/8	6	5	Lincoln Co., Nev.	Erich P. Burkhard	Erich P. Burkhard	OT 1983	3
204 5/8	25 5/8	24 3/8	19 4/8	5 5/8	5 4/8	7	5	Eagle Co., Colo.	Robert V. Doerr	Robert V. Doerr	NO 1982	4
203 5/8	28 5/8	30 2/8	30 1/8	5	5	5	5	Grand Co., Utah	Glen Dumas	S. Kim Bonnett	PR 1960	5
202 4/8	26 7/8	24 7/8	21 5/8	5 5/8	5	4	6	Garfield Co., Colo.	James S. Harden	James S. Harden	NO 1982	6
202 3/8	25 5/8	26 1/8	23 5/8	5 3/8	5 3/8	7	6	Boulder Co., Colo.	Bob Wallace	Bob Wallace	OT 1963	7
202	26 1/8	27 7/8	25 5/8	5 1/8	5 3/8	5	5	Unknown	Unknown	Dale Selby	PU 1982	8
202	26 1/8	26 4/8	21 4/8	5	4 7/8	5	5	Idaho Co., Idaho	John H. Davis	John H. Davis	NO 1981	8
201 7/8	27 7/8	27 3/8	27 3/8	6 1/8	5 5/8	6	6	Dagget Co., Utah	Earl Eldredge	Phil Brotherson	OT 1940	10
201 4/8	23	24	20	5 4/8	5 2/8	6	6	Moffat Co., Colo.	Carl E. Jacobson	Carl E. Jacobson	OT 1967	11
200 5/8	27	25 2/8	26 5/8	5	5 1/8	5	5	La Plata Co., Colo.	Unknown	Ronald F. Lax	NO 1979	12
199 3/8	29 1/8	29 2/8	31	5 2/8	5 3/8	7	8	Sanpete Co., Utah	Roger M. Allred	Roger M. Allred	OT 1958	13
199	27 2/8	28 1/8	31 3/8	5 2/8	5 2/8	10	7	Carbon Co., Utah	Robert R. Henderson	Robert R. Henderson	OT 1965	14
198 7/8	25 7/8	25	27 5/8	5 3/8	5	5	5	Yavapai Co., Ariz.	Joseph C. Pecha	Joseph C. Pecha	OT 1983	15
198 5/8	25	24 7/8	23 5/8	4 7/8	4 7/8	5	5	Elmore Co., Idaho	William Hartwig	William Hartwig	NO 1984	16
198	25 4/8	26 1/8	26 2/8	5 2/8	5 2/8	5	5	Natrona Co., Wyo.	Kerry J. Clegg	Kerry J. Clegg	OT 1983	17
197 7/8	28 3/8	28 2/8	25 7/8	5 5/8	5 5/8	7	6	Blaine Co., Idaho	James D. Scarrow	James D. Scarrow	NO 1983	18
197 5/8	25 1/8	26 1/8	19 5/8	5 2/8	5 2/8	5	5	Beechy, Sask.	Brett E. Seidle	Brett E. Seidle	NO 1983	19
197 5/8	28 5/8	27 4/8	23 5/8	5 1/8	5 1/8	5	5	Kootenay River, B. C.	Raymond Carry	Raymond Carry	NO 1982	19
197 4/8	27 1/8	27 1/8	23 6/8	4 3/8	4 3/8	4	5	Bonneville Co., Idaho	LaDon Harriell	LaDon Harriell	DC 1982	21
197 3/8	28 7/8	28 6/8	23 4/8	5 3/8	5 3/8	7	6	Garfield Co., Utah	James R. McCourt	James R. McCourt	OT 1985	22
197	28 3/8	29 2/8	34 2/8	5 3/8	5 5/8	4	5	Butte Co., Idaho	John A. Little	John A. Little	DC 1981	23
196 7/8	27 5/8	27	25 1/8	5 1/8	5 1/8	5	5	Scherf Creek, B. C.	Manuela Selby	Manuela Selby	NO 1984	24
196 4/8	23 5/8	23	23	5 2/8	5 2/8	5	5	Powell Co., Mont.	Raymond A. Fitzgerald	Raymond A. Fitzgerald	SE 1983	25
196 2/8	27 1/8	27 3/8	25 1/8	5 3/8	5 2/8	5	6	Sweetwater Co., Wyo.	Donald H. Pabst	Donald H. Pabst	NO 1962	26
196 1/8	25 3/8	25 3/8	25 5/8	4 6/8	4 7/8	5	5	Eagle Co., Colo.	Jeffery D. Harrison	Jeffery D. Harrison	OT 1981	27
196 1/8	25 4/8	24 4/8	26 1/8	5 1/8	4 6/8	5	5	Clackamas Co., Oreg.	Picked Up	Curt M. Funk	PU 1983	27
195 5/8	25 1/8	25 4/8	25 5/8	5 7/8	6	6	5	Ferry Co., Wash.	Owen R. Burgess	Owen R. Burgess	OT 1982	29
195 5/8	26 1/8	26 1/8	24	5	5	5	6	Washington Co., Utah	Scott M. Bulloch	Scott M. Bulloch	OT 1985	30
195 4/8	26 3/8	26 5/8	25 2/8	5 5/8	5 5/8	5	5	Sanders Co., Mont.	William B. Hart	William B. Hart	NO 1984	31
195 3/8	26 3/8	26	26 1/8	4 6/8	4 6/8	5	5	Frontier Co., Neb.	Brent S. Klein	Brent S. Klein	NO 1984	32

195⁴⁄₈	23³⁄₈	24⁶⁄₈	21⁴⁄₈	5¹⁄₈	5²⁄₈	5	5	Sublette Co., Wyo.	John R. Birchett	John R. Birchett	SE 1981	33
195²⁄₈	29¹⁄₈	27⁷⁄₈	25⁷⁄₈	5³⁄₈	5⁴⁄₈	7	6	Gunnison Co., Colo.	Herman F. Tomky	Russell J. Tomky	OT 1937	33
195¹⁄₈	27¹⁄₈	26³⁄₈	29³⁄₈	5⁴⁄₈	5⁵⁄₈	5	5	Jackson Co., Colo.	Alvin Bush	Jerry Haldeman	NO 1961	35
192	25¹⁄₈	25⁴⁄₈	27⁴⁄₈	5⁴⁄₈	5⁴⁄₈	5	5	Rio Arriba Co., N. M.	C. J. McElroy	C. J. McElroy	DC 1970	36

Mule Deer *(Non-Typical Antlers)*

Odocoileus hemionus hemionus and certain related subspecies

Minimum Score 225 — World's Record 355⅞

Score	Length of Main Beam R.	Length of Main Beam L.	Inside Spread	Circumference at Smallest Place Between Burr and First Point R.	Circumference at Smallest Place Between Burr and First Point L.	Number of Points R.	Number of Points L.	Locality Killed	By Whom Killed	Owner	Date Killed	Rank
274²⁄₈	24⁴⁄₈	25⁷⁄₈	24⁵⁄₈	5⁶⁄₈	5³⁄₈	14	13	Fremont Co., Idaho	David L. Maurer	David L. Maurer	OT 1979	1
273⁷⁄₈	27⁷⁄₈	29²⁄₈	26⁶⁄₈	6¹⁄₈	6	8	12	Kane Co., Utah	Waldon Ballard	Alice Ballard	OT 1950	2
268⁴⁄₈	21³⁄₈	23⁶⁄₈	17⁴⁄₈	6⁵⁄₈	6⁵⁄₈	17	16	Cascade Co., Mont.	Unknown	Tom Williams	PR 1980	3
263⁶⁄₈	26⁵⁄₈	26⁵⁄₈	22²⁄₈	5	5	16	14	Sanpete Co., Utah	Wayne Dwyer	John E. Braithwaite	OT 1974	4
263⁴⁄₈	25³⁄₈	24²⁄₈	27⁷⁄₈	5⁶⁄₈	5⁵⁄₈	16	20	Grant Co., Oreg.	Harold T. Oathes	Harold T. Oathes	OT 1965	5
262	25⁷⁄₈	23⁷⁄₈	21	4⁷⁄₈	5	14	15	Utah Co., Utah	Michael D. Atwood	Michael D. Atwood	NO 1967	6
257¹⁄₈	25²⁄₈	24⁷⁄₈	19	5⁶⁄₈	5³⁄₈	10	8	Juab Co., Utah	P. L. Jones	Nelson L. Jones	1949	7
252⁵⁄₈	24²⁄₈	23²⁄₈	24⁶⁄₈	5⁴⁄₈	5¹⁄₈	16	12	Sweetwater Co., Wyo.	John C. Erickson	M. Painovich & J. Etcheverry	1932	8
250¹⁄₈	22⁷⁄₈	22¹⁄₈	24⁶⁄₈	5⁴⁄₈	5⁴⁄₈	18	16	Grease Creek, Alta.	Jack McCallum	J. H. Fry		9
247⁶⁄₈	24⁷⁄₈	23⁵⁄₈	22²⁄₈	5	5¹⁄₈	11	16	Shoshone Co., Idaho	Gary J. Finney	Gary J. Finney	NO 1983	10
247³⁄₈	22⁵⁄₈	22⁶⁄₈	22⁵⁄₈	4⁴⁄₈	4⁴⁄₈	11	9	Fremont Co., Idaho	Donald R. Craig	Donald R. Craig	NO 1982	11
245¹⁄₈	24	23²⁄₈	20²⁄₈	5³⁄₈	5⁴⁄₈	12	9	Power Co., Idaho	Mark B. Cooper	Mark B. Cooper	OT 1984	12
244⁵⁄₈	25¹⁄₈	25³⁄₈	22¹⁄₈	5¹⁄₈	5²⁄₈	9	10	Park Co., Mont.	Unknown	Larry F. Dvorak	PR 1968	13
244²⁄₈	25¹⁄₈	24⁵⁄₈	22⁵⁄₈	5	5	12	13	Wasatch Co., Utah	Unknown	Ted Clegg	1938	14
243⁶⁄₈	27³⁄₈	29²⁄₈	29⁶⁄₈	5²⁄₈	5⁵⁄₈	9	9	Montrose Co., Colo.	Jim Herndon	Mrs. Jim Herndon	OT 1974	15
241	26²⁄₈	27³⁄₈	26³⁄₈	4⁶⁄₈	4⁶⁄₈	11	11	Lewis & Clark Co., Mont.	Mike Filcher	Mike Filcher	NO 1972	16
240⁵⁄₈	27	25⁶⁄₈	27¹⁄₈	5⁷⁄₈	5¹⁄₈	10	8	Eagle Co., Colo.	Steve B. Humann	Steve B. Humann	NO 1982	17
240⁴⁄₈	23⁶⁄₈	23⁵⁄₈	23²⁄₈	5¹⁄₈	5²⁄₈	11	14	Morgan Co., Utah	Pietro De Santis	Pietro De Santis	OT 1982	18
240⁴⁄₈	23	24⁴⁄₈	21⁵⁄₈	5²⁄₈	5²⁄₈	15	14	Garfield Co., Colo.	James E. Powell, Jr.	James E. Powell, Jr.	NO 1983	18
237⁵⁄₈	26⁴⁄₈	26²⁄₈	30⁶⁄₈	4⁵⁄₈	4⁶⁄₈	10	9	La Plata Co., Colo.	Randall N. Bostick	Randall N. Bostick	NO 1984	20
229	23²⁄₈	21⁷⁄₈	19²⁄₈	4⁷⁄₈	5	9	11	Ravalli Co., Mont.	James Milleson	James Milleson	NO 1984	21
268⁴⁄₈*	25⁶⁄₈	23	22⁷⁄₈	5⁴⁄₈	5⁶⁄₈	17	14	Deschutes Co., Oreg.	Devon Talley	Devon Talley	OT 1983	
262⁷⁄₈*	27⁴⁄₈	27⁵⁄₈	25¹⁄₈	5	4⁷⁄₈	12	15	Teton Co., Wyo.	Thomas R. Ford	Thomas R. Ford	OT 1984	
256²⁄₈*	25³⁄₈	26	27²⁄₈	5⁴⁄₈	5⁴⁄₈	9	14	Blaine Co., Idaho	Philip T. Homer	Philip T. Homer	NO 1983	
252⁷⁄₈*	22⁴⁄₈	18⁶⁄₈	19¹⁄₈	5⁴⁄₈	5⁴⁄₈	11	22	Boise Co., Idaho	Dennis D. Snider	Dennis D. Snider	NO 1983	

*Final Score subject to revision by additional verifying measurements.

Columbia Blacktail Deer

Odocoileus hemionus columbianus

Minimum Score 120 | **World's Record 182 2/8**

Score	Length of Main Beam R.	Length of Main Beam L.	Inside Spread	Circumference at Smallest Place Between Burr and First Point R.	Circumference at Smallest Place Between Burr and First Point L.	Number of Points R.	Number of Points L.	Locality Killed	By Whom Killed	Owner	Date Killed	Rank
159 4/8	24 4/8	23 6/8	14 7/8	4 5/8	4 4/8	6	6	Mendocino Co., Calif.	Russ McLennan	Russ McLennan	SE 1984	1
158 2/8	22 4/8	23 7/8	19 6/8	4 6/8	4 6/8	5	5	Josephine Co., Oreg.	James E. Brierley	James E. Brierley	OT 1983	2
158	21 7/8	21 7/8	18 2/8	4 4/8	4 4/8	5	5	Trinity Co., Calif.	Charles A. Strickland	Charles A. Strickland	SE 1984	3
155 7/8	23 1/8	23 7/8	16 2/8	4 6/8	4 7/8	5	6	Pierce Co., Wash.	J. Bennett & F. Duell	J. Bennett & F. Duell	OT 1983	4
154 5/8	24 7/8	24 3/8	21	4 7/8	4 6/8	6	7	Siskiyou Co., Calif.	Darrell R. Jones	Darrell R. Jones	SE 1984	5
153 7/8	21 4/8	21 6/8	18 1/8	4 2/8	4 2/8	5	5	Cultus Lake, B. C.	Steven R. Rupp	Steven R. Rupp	SE 1983	6
153 4/8	21 3/8	20 7/8	17 6/8	4 6/8	4 7/8	5	5	Linn Co., Oreg.	Greg L. Anderson	Greg L. Anderson	NO 1983	7
151 3/8	23 1/8	22 6/8	19 4/8	5	5	5	6	Josephine Co., Oreg.	E. McKie & S. McKie	Ernie L. McKie	OT 1977	8
151 1/8	21 5/8	21 5/8	16 1/8	4	4	4	4	Josephine Co., Oreg.	Jim Wineteer	Jim Wineteer	OT 1980	9
149 2/8	21 6/8	22 6/8	19 4/8	4 4/8	4 2/8	5	5	Lane Co., Oreg.	Richard C. MacKenzie	Richard C. MacKenzie	OT 1983	10
149 2/8	20 2/8	20 3/8	14 6/8	4 2/8	4	5	5	Clackamas Co., Oreg.	Lance V. Bentz	Lance V. Bentz	OT 1980	10
148 4/8	21 6/8	22 5/8	15 6/8	5 3/8	5 6/8	5	5	Linn Co., Oreg.	Marlin D. Brinkley	Marlin D. Brinkley	OT 1982	12
146 4/8	21 2/8	21 2/8	17 2/8	4 6/8	4 7/8	5	5	Glenn Co., Calif.	Lawrence E. Germeshausen	Lawrence E. Germeshausen	OT 1983	13
145 1/8	19 6/8	19 5/8	15 1/8	4 6/8	4 5/8	5	5	Lane Co., Oreg.	Boyd Iverson	Boyd Iverson	NO 1982	14
144 6/8	22 2/8	22 1/8	17 7/8	4 4/8	4 3/8	6	6	Skamania Co., Wash.	Melvin D. Robertson	Melvin D. Robertson	NO 1983	15
144 6/8	21 3/8	22 4/8	19 5/8	6	6	5	4	Lincoln Co., Oreg.	William D. Harmon	Merle W. Emmert	OT 1976	15
143 4/8	22	23	16 4/8	3 7/8	4	5	5	Josephine Co., Oreg.	Virgil Welch	Virgil Welch	NO 1983	17
143 4/8	21	20 4/8	17	4 6/8	4 6/8	5	5	Trinity Co., Calif.	Barry Griffin	Barry Griffin	OT 1983	17
142 6/8	21 2/8	21 7/8	19 4/8	4 6/8	5	5	4	Linn Co., Oreg.	R. Reid & D. Liles	R. Reid & D. Liles	OT 1982	19
142 6/8	23 2/8	22	17 2/8	3 7/8	4	4	4	Linn Co., Oreg.	Kenneth W. Wegner	Kenneth W. Wegner	OT 1982	19
142 2/8	20 7/8	20 4/8	16 2/8	4 3/8	4 6/8	5	5	Jackson Co., Oreg.	Eileen F. Damone	Eileen F. Damone	NO 1976	21
142	23	20 7/8	21 4/8	4 4/8	4 4/8	5	5	Skamania Co., Wash.	Herbert P. Roberts	Herbert P. Roberts	NO 1983	22
141 6/8	20 2/8	20 7/8	18 2/8	4 5/8	4 4/8	5	5	Linn Co., Oreg.	Eugene L. Wilson	Eugene L. Wilson	OT 1982	23
140 7/8	23 3/8	22	16 5/8	3 7/8	4	5	5	Mendocino Co., Calif.	Douglas W. Lim	Douglas W. Lim	OT 1981	24
140 7/8	23 7/8	23 7/8	18 6/8	5	5	10	8	Polk Co., Oreg.	Gale A. Draper	Gale A. Draper	NO 1984	24
140 4/8	21 1/8	20 7/8	18 2/8	4 7/8	4 6/8	6	5	Yamhill Co., Oreg.	Richard Watts	Richard Watts	OT 1981	26
140 2/8	21 4/8	21 4/8	19 6/8	3 7/8	3 7/8	5	5	Mendocino Co., Calif.	Earl E. Hamlow, Jr.	Earl E. Hamlow, Jr.	1977	27
140 1/8	20 7/8	22 1/8	16 5/8	4 3/8	4 3/8	5	5	Lincoln Co., Oreg.	Darrel R. Grishaber	Darrel R. Grishaber	OT 1984	28
140 1/8	19	19 6/8	16 5/8	4 5/8	4 6/8	5	5	Snohomish Co., Wash.	Kenneth A. Peterson	Kenneth A. Peterson	NO 1985	28
139	21 2/8	21 3/8	16 4/8	3 7/8	3 7/8	5	5	Marion Co., Oreg.	Gene Collier	Gene Collier	OT 1983	30
138 6/8	22	21 4/8	23 4/8	4 3/8	4 3/8	4	5	Trinity Co., Calif.	Charles E. Davy	Charles E. Davy	SE 1983	31
138 2/8	21 5/8	22	17 6/8	3 6/8	3 6/8	5	5	Trinity Co., Calif.	Thomas A. Pettigrew, Jr.	Thomas A. Pettigrew, Jr.	SE 1972	32

Columbia Blacktail Deer—*Continued*

Odocoileus hemionus columbianus

Score	Length of Main Beam R.	Length of Main Beam L.	Inside Spread	Circumference at Smallest Place Between Burr and First Point R.	Circumference at Smallest Place Between Burr and First Point L.	Number of Points R.	Number of Points L.	Locality Killed	By Whom Killed	Owner	Date Killed	Rank
138 2/8	18 6/8	18 6/8	15 6/8	4 1/8	4 3/8	5	5	Marion Co., Oreg.	Gene Collier	Gene Collier	OT 1974	32
138 2/8	18	18	14 4/8	4 4/8	4 1/8	5	5	Mendocino Co., Calif.	Kenzia L. Drake	Kenzia L. Drake	OT 1985	32
137 4/8	21 1/8	21 1/8	19	4 1/8	4 3/8	5	5	Trinity Co., Calif.	Picked Up	C. Brown & J. Brown	PU 1982	35
136 3/8	20 2/8	19 7/8	15 7/8	4 3/8	4 2/8	5	5	Tillamook Co., Oreg.	Guy L. Thompson	Guy L. Thompson	OT 1983	36
136 2/8	20 4/8	21	21 6/8	3 7/8	3 6/8	5	5	Siskiyou Co., Calif.	Shirley Eastlick	Shirley Eastlick	OT 1962	37
135 7/8	20 3/8	21 1/8	16 7/8	5	5	5	5	Snohomish Co., Wash.	Edmund L. Hurst	Edmund L. Hurst	NO 1984	38
135 2/8	19 1/8	19 4/8	13 2/8	3 4/8	3 4/8	4	4	Humboldt Co., Calif.	Christopher A. Umbertus	Christopher A. Umbertus	SE 1981	39
134 5/8	20 4/8	20 3/8	15 5/8	4 5/8	4 6/8	5	5	Siskiyou Co., Calif.	Roy Eastlick	Roy Eastlick	SE 1965	40
134 4/8	22	21 4/8	18 4/8	5 2/8	5 1/8	5	4	Sonoma Co., Calif.	Richard O'Farrell	Richard O'Farrell	SE 1984	41
134 2/8	24 1/8	23 6/8	22 4/8	4 3/8	4 4/8	4	4	Colusa Co., Calif.	Gregory R. Bonetti	Gregory R. Bonetti	SE 1983	42
133 7/8	20 4/8	21 3/8	13 5/8	3 6/8	3 5/8	5	5	Siskiyou Co., Calif.	William E. Turner	William E. Turner	OT 1982	43
133 4/8	21	22 4/8	17 4/8	4 6/8	5	6	5	Trinity Co., Calif.	Barry Griffin	Barry Griffin	OT 1976	44
133 3/8	21 4/8	20 5/8	16 5/8	4 1/8	4 1/8	5	5	Marion Co., Oreg.	Gene Collier	Gene Collier	OT 1984	45
133 2/8	19 1/8	18 5/8	16	3 2/8	3 2/8	5	5	Trinity Co., Calif.	Kirk Finch	Kirk Finch	NO 1975	46
133 1/8	19 4/8	19 2/8	15 5/8	4 2/8	4 2/8	5	5	Josephine Co., Oreg.	Michael J. Collins	Michael J. Collins	OT 1983	47
133 1/8	18 2/8	18 5/8	13 5/8	4 2/8	4 1/8	5	5	Langley, B. C.	Frank Jackson	Brooke Whitelaw	1935	47
133 1/8	23 2/8	23	20 3/8	3 7/8	4 6/8	4	5	Lane Co., Oreg.	Picked Up	Wayne E. Everett	PU 1971	47
132 6/8	22	22 6/8	21 6/8	4 4/8	4 6/8	5	4	Mendocino Co., Calif.	Jay M. Gates, III	Jay M. Gates, III	NO 1984	50
132 4/8	19 5/8	20 7/8	16 2/8	4 2/8	4 4/8	5	5	Linn Co., Oreg.	Gene Collier	Gene Collier	OT 1964	51
132 4/8	20 4/8	19 7/8	15 2/8	4	3 7/8	5	5	Clackamas Co., Oreg.	Katherine M. Searls	Katherine M. Searls	NO 1982	51
132 3/8	18 7/8	19 7/8	18 1/8	4	4 1/8	5	5	Siskiyou Co., Calif.	Lawrence F. Weckerle	Lawrence F. Weckerle	OT 1982	53
132 2/8	21 3/8	19 3/8	14 6/8	4 6/8	4 1/8	5	4	Humboldt Co., Calif.	Guy Hooper	Guy Hooper	OT 1977	54
130 7/8	20 7/8	20 4/8	16 5/8	3 7/8	3 7/8	5	5	Tehama Co., Calif.	James D. Fiske	James D. Fiske	SE 1956	55
130 6/8	22	22	16 6/8	4 4/8	4 4/8	5	5	Linn Co., Oreg.	Gene Collier	Gene Collier	OT 1967	56
130 6/8	19 4/8	19 3/8	14 4/8	4 1/8	4 3/8	5	5	Yamhill Co., Oreg.	Picked Up	John N. Washburn	PU 1984	56
130 6/8	19 4/8	20 4/8	16 2/8	4 2/8	4 2/8	5	6	Jackson Co., Oreg.	Roy D. Hugie	U. of Mont. Mus.	OT 1983	56
130 4/8	19	19 5/8	15 4/8	4 2/8	4 2/8	4	4	Santa Cruz Co., Calif.	William J. McGrath	William J. McGrath	AG 1982	59
125 5/8	21 3/8	20 7/8	16 1/8	3 6/8	3 1/8	4	5	Marion Co., Oreg.	Douglas G. Ellis	Douglas G. Ellis	NO 1984	60
122 3/8	18	16 6/8	14 1/8	5	4 6/8	5	5	Pierce Co., Wash.	Guy A. Hanson	Guy A. Hanson	NO 1984	61
122 2/8	19	18 5/8	17	4 2/8	5	5	4	Sonoma Co., Calif.	Richard O'Farrell	Richard O'Farrell	SE 1983	62
122 2/8	19	20	15 4/8	4 4/8	4 1/8	5	5	Humboldt Co., Calif.	Don L. Corley	Don L. Corley	OT 1982	62

Sitka Blacktail Deer
Odocoileus hemionus sitkensis

Minimum Score 100   **World's Record 123 3/8**

Sitka blacktail deer includes trophies from coastal Alaska and Queen Charlotte Islands of British Columbia.

Score	Length of Main Beam R.	Length of Main Beam L.	Inside Spread	Circumference at Smallest Place Between Burr and First Point R.	Circumference at Smallest Place Between Burr and First Point L.	Number of Points R.	Number of Points L.	Locality Killed	By Whom Killed	Owner	Date Killed	Rank
123 3/8	21 1/8	20 3/8	17 6/8	3 6/8	3 6/8	4	4	Uganik Bay, Alaska	Donna D. Braendel	Donna D. Braendel	NO 1983	1
117 1/8	16 4/8	16 4/8	13 1/8	4 1/8	4 2/8	5	6	Baird Peak, Alaska	William C. Dunham	William C. Dunham	AG 1984	2
116	17 2/8	16 5/8	16	4 1/8	3 6/8	5	5	Kiliuda Bay, Alaska	Timothy Tittle	Timothy Tittle	OT 1984	3
114 7/8	15 7/8	16 1/8	14 3/8	3 7/8	4	5	6	Control Lake, Alaska	Timothy C. Winsenberg	Timothy C. Winsenberg	AG 1985	4
113 4/8	18 4/8	18 1/8	15 4/8	3 5/8	3 4/8	4	4	Viekoda Bay, Alaska	Edward R. Hajdys	Edward R. Hajdys	NO 1980	5
113 1/8	17 5/8	18 7/8	16 1/8	3 6/8	3 7/8	5	5	Wadding Cove, Alaska	Kurt W. Kuehl	Kurt W. Kuehl	OT 1984	6
109 6/8	17 5/8	17 3/8	14 4/8	4 3/8	4 4/8	5	5	Cleveland Pen., Alaska	Dennis E. Northrup	Dennis E. Northrup	OT 1983	7
109 4/8	19	17 7/8	17 2/8	3 6/8	3 7/8	4	4	Uganik Bay, Alaska	Harvey D. Harms	Harvey D. Harms	OT 1982	8
109 1/8	18 3/8	18	16 7/8	4	3 6/8	5	5	Ugak Bay, Alaska	Donald H. Tetzlaff	Donald H. Tetzlaff	NO 1984	9
109	17 4/8	16 6/8	16 3/8	4	4	5	5	Uganik Bay, Alaska	Karl G. Braendel	Karl G. Braendel	NO 1982	10
108 5/8	17 2/8	17 3/8	15 4/8	3 5/8	3 6/8	5	5	Barling Bay, Alaska	Guy C. Powell	Guy C. Powell	DC 1984	11
108 3/8	18 7/8	19 2/8	15 7/8	4 4/8	4 7/8	7	5	Whale Passage, Alaska	Howard W. Honsey	Howard W. Honsey	NO 1985	12
104 2/8	15 4/8	15 4/8	15 4/8	4	3 7/8	5	5	Uganik Bay, Alaska	John A. Miller	John A. Miller	NO 1984	13
120 3/8 *	17 5/8	17 4/8	15 7/8	4 4/8	4 3/8	5	5	Boulder Bay, Alaska	Ronald D. Swingle	Ronald D. Swingle	OT 1983	
118 3/8 *	17 5/8	19 2/8	17 3/8	4 1/8	4 2/8	5	5	Uganik Lake, Alaska	Robert D. Gilliland	Robert D. Gilliland	OT 1983	
118 1/8 *	16 7/8	17 2/8	14 4/8	4	4 2/8	5	5	Long Island, Alaska	Daniel G. Bowden	Daniel G. Bowden	SE 1981	
112 7/8 *	17	18	15 1/8	3 6/8	3 6/8	5	5	Kodiak Island, Alaska	Gene Coughlin	Gene Coughlin	OT 1984	

*Final Score subject to revision by additional verifying measurements.

Whitetail Deer *(Typical Antlers)*

Minimum Score 160 — ***Odocoileus virginianus virginianus*** **and certain related subspecies** — World's Record 206 1/8

Score	Length of Main Beam R.	Length of Main Beam L.	Inside Spread	Circumference at Smallest Place Between Burr and First Point R.	Circumference at Smallest Place Between Burr and First Point L.	Number of Points R.	Number of Points L.	Locality Killed	By Whom Killed	Owner	Date Killed	Rank
204 2/8	26 4/8	22 6/8	25 1/8	5 1/8	5 1/8	7	10	Beaverdam Creek, Alta.	Stephen Jansen	Stephen Jansen	OT 1967	1
200 2/8	26 3/8	27 1/8	24	5	4 7/8	6	7	Whitkow, Sask.	Peter J. Swistun	Peter J. Swistun	NO 1983	2
195 5/8	28 4/8	27 6/8	22 1/8	5 6/8	5 7/8	6	7	Marshall Co., Minn.	Robert Sands	Robert Sands	NO 1960	3
194 2/8	30 6/8	30 3/8	24 7/8	5 3/8	5 2/8	9	7	Vigo Co., Ind.	D. Bates & S. Winkler	D. Bates & S. Winkler	NO 1983	4
193 3/8	28 6/8	28 6/8	21 2/8	4 4/8	4 4/8	5	7	Itasca Co., Minn.	Picked Up	Paul M. Shaw	PU 1935	5
193	25 6/8	26	25	5 3/8	5 5/8	6	6	S. D.	Unknown	Eugene J. Lodermeier	NO 1964	6
192 7/8	27 4/8	27 2/8	19 3/8	4 3/8	4 5/8	8	9	York Co., Maine	Alphonse Chase	Earl Taylor	NO 1920	7
190 5/8	22 4/8	23 5/8	19 5/8	4 4/8	4 4/8	7	6	Buffalo Lake, Alta.	Eugene L. Boll	Eugene L. Boll	OT 1969	8
189 5/8	28 7/8	27 6/8	21 3/8	4 7/8	4 6/8	5	5	St. Landry Parish, La.	Leonce Mallet	Johnny M. Hollier	N0 1965	9
189 3/8	28 2/8	27 2/8	20 1/8	4 1/8	4 1/8	5	5	McKenzie Co., N. D.	Gene Veeder	McLean Bowman	1972	10
189 1/8	28	28 1/8	23 5/8	4 4/8	4 5/8	5	7	Blaine Co., Mont.	Kenneth Morehouse	Kenneth Morehouse	OT 1959	11
187 6/8	25 5/8	26 4/8	19	4 6/8	5 1/8	5	5	Johnson Co., Iowa	Gregg R. Redlin	Gregg R. Redlin	DC 1983	12
187 5/8	26 5/8	26 3/8	15 6/8	5 5/8	5 6/8	6	6	Mont.	Unknown	Johnny M. Hollier	PR 1984	13
187 1/8	26 6/8	26 4/8	18 7/8	4 6/8	4 7/8	6	6	Pulaski Co., Ky.	Scott Abbott	Scott Abbott	NO 1982	14
186 7/8	27 7/8	27 2/8	19 1/8	5	5 2/8	7	8	Atchison Co., Mo.	Mike Moody	Mike Moody	NO 1968	15
186 3/8	26 2/8	27 2/8	20 4/8	5 2/8	5 2/8	8	7	Ontonagon Co., Mich.	Unknown	Mac's Taxidermy		16
186 3/8	30 2/8	29	22 5/8	4 4/8	4 5/8	5	5	Flathead Co., Mont.	Unknown	Wayne D. Williamson	1973	16
186 2/8	28 6/8	29 1/8	19	5 2/8	5 1/8	8	5	Hancock Co., Maine	Gerald C. Murray	Gerald C. Murray	NO 1984	18
185 3/8	26 4/8	27	19 4/8	5 1/8	5 2/8	7	10	Marshall Co., Minn.	Donald W. Wilkens	Donald W. Wilkens	NO 1973	19
185 3/8	27 6/8	28	20 5/8	4 7/8	4 7/8	5	5	Canwood, Sask.	Clark Heimbechner	Clark Heimbechner	NO 1984	19
185 1/8	26 2/8	27 4/8	23 1/8	4 5/8	5 1/8	6	7	Franklin Co., Ind.	Gayle Fritsch	Gayle Fritsch	DC 1972	21
184 4/8	30 3/8	30 4/8	20 4/8	5	5 1/8	7	7	Chase Co., Kan.	Thomas D. Mosher	Thomas D. Mosher	DC 1984	22
184 4/8	26 5/8	28 3/8	22 4/8	5 3/8	5 1/8	6	5	Bossier Co., La.	Earnest O. McCoy	Lucille McCoy	DC 1961	22
184 3/8	26	26 6/8	20 6/8	5 3/8	5 6/8	5	6	Paulding Co., Ga.	Floyd Benson	Floyd Benson	NO 1962	24
182 7/8	27 1/8	26 4/8	24	5 4/8	5 4/8	6	7	Mont.	Unknown	Johnny M. Hollier	PR 1983	25
182 4/8	24 2/8	23 6/8	18	5 4/8	5 4/8	6	6	Menominee Co., Wisc.	Unknown	John L. Stein		26
182 3/8	28 3/8	27 3/8	19 1/8	4 3/8	4 4/8	5	6	Buffalo Co., Wisc.	Anthony F. Wolfe	Anthony F. Wolfe	NO 1984	27
182 2/8	27 3/8	27	20 4/8	4 7/8	5	7	5	Sullivan Co., Pa.	Floyd Reibson	Maynard Reibson	1930	28
182 2/8	26	26 4/8	18 1/8	5 2/8	5 1/8	5	5	Park Co., Mont.	Jim Whitt	Jim Whitt	NO 1983	28
182 2/8	27 1/8	26 4/8	19 6/8	5 1/8	5 2/8	5	5	Claiborne Co., Miss.	R. L. Bobo	R. L. Bobo	NO 1955	28
182 1/8	25 6/8	25 2/8	22 7/8	5 6/8	5 5/8	5	5	Round Lake, Sask.	Jesse Bates	Jesse Bates	NO 1984	31
181 7/8	26 4/8	26 2/8	21 3/8	4 6/8	4 6/8	5	5	Hotchkiss, Alta.	Andy G. Petkus	Andy G. Petkus	NO 1984	32

181 7/8	27 4/8	27 5/8	20 5/8	4 4/8	4 4/8	5	6	Whitman Co., Wash.	George A. Cook, III	George A. Cook, III	OT 1985	32
181 4/8	28 4/8	27 7/8	22	5 1/8	5 3/8	5	5	Wadena Co., Minn.	Lester Zentner, Jr.	E. E. Patson	NO 1962	34
181 2/8	25 2/8	25 7/8	25 7/8	5 1/8	5 4/8	5	6	Hardin Co., Ky.	Thomas L. House	Thomas L. House	NO 1963	35
181 2/8	25	25 2/8	21	4 3/8	4 3/8	6	6	Lafayette Co., Wisc.	Michael Morrissey	Michael Morrissey	NO 1982	35
181 1/8	27 6/8	26 2/8	17 3/8	5 4/8	5 4/8	5	5	Waldo Co., Maine	Clarendon Pomeroy	Larry C. Pomeroy	NO 1946	37
181	25 6/8	26 5/8	19	5 6/8	5	5	5	Langlade Co., Wisc.	Elroy W. Timm	Elroy W. Timm	NO 1959	38
180 7/8	27 7/8	28 4/8	21 6/8	5 2/8	5	5	7	Unknown	Unknown	Johnny M. Hollier		39
180 6/8	30	29 4/8	23 4/8	5 6/8	5 6/8	5	6	Hancock Co., Maine	Cyrus H. Whitaker	Orrin W. Whitaker	NO 1912	40
180 5/8	25	23 4/8	19 2/8	4 4/8	4 4/8	7	7	Maverick Co., Texas	Jim Webb	Richard H. Bennett	1912	41
180 4/8	30	29 1/8	24 5/8	4 7/8	4 7/8	8	8	Okanogan Co., Wash.	Joe Peone	Joe Peone	NO 1983	42
180 3/8	25 4/8	25 2/8	23 6/8	4 6/8	4 7/8	6	5	Union Parish, La.	Picked Up	Johnny M. Hollier	1963	43
180 2/8	27 1/8	27 1/8	19 4/8	4 4/8	4 4/8	5	5	Iowa	Unknown	Tom Williams	PR 1984	44
180 1/8	24	24 7/8	19 4/8	5 1/8	5	7	5	Hubbard Co., Minn.	Larry D. Dierks	Larry D. Dierks	NO 1984	45
180 1/8	25 1/8	25 1/8	19 1/8	5 2/8	5 2/8	6	6	Cottonwood Co., Minn.	Charles C. Burnham	Charles C. Burnham	DC 1983	45
179 7/8	25 3/8	27 1/8	19	5	5 1/8	9	6	Hancock Co., Maine	Butler B. Dunn	Butler B. Dunn	1930	47
179 6/8	27 1/8	29 3/8	21 2/8	4 7/8	5	7	7	Steele Co., Minn.	Elmer Janning	Elmer Janning	NO 1972	48
179 6/8	25 6/8	26 6/8	21 5/8	5 2/8	5 3/8	6	5	Penobscot Co., Maine	Dale Rustin	Dale Rustin	NO 1984	48
179 3/8	26 1/8	26 2/8	17 7/8	4 7/8	4 6/8	6	6	Vernon Co., Wisc.	Alois V. Schendel	Alois V. Schendel	NO 1966	50
179 2/8	24 2/8	24 2/8	19 4/8	4 4/8	4 5/8	6	6	Dimmit Co., Texas	William M. Knolle	William M. Knolle	DC 1982	51
179 2/8	23 6/8	25 1/8	19 2/8	5 5/8	5 5/8	7	7	Buffalo Co., Wisc.	Jerome Kulig	Jerome Kulig	NO 1984	51
179 1/8	28 6/8	27 1/8	18 2/8	4 4/8	4 4/8	6	6	Twiggs Co., Ga.	Cy Smith	Duncan A. Dobie	DC 1970	53
179	26 6/8	26 2/8	21 4/8	4 4/8	4 6/8	5	6	Jasper Co., Ga.	Hubert R. Moody	Hubert R. Moody	NO 1957	54
179	27 4/8	29 4/8	20 2/8	4 6/8	4 6/8	6	7	Logan Co., Ohio	Gregory K. Snyder	Greta J. Snyder	NO 1982	54
178 7/8	28 1/8	26 2/8	19 5/8	4 6/8	4 6/8	6	6	Van Buren Co., Iowa	Noel E. Harlan	Noel E. Harlan	DC 1984	56
178 6/8	26 2/8	27 2/8	20 6/8	5	5	6	6	Aroostook Co., Maine	John R. Hardy	John R. Hardy	NO 1983	57
178 5/8	24 1/8	24 7/8	20 4/8	4 7/8	5 1/8	6	7	Pincher Creek, Alta.	Unknown	H. Bruce Freeman	1973	58
178 5/8	25 6/8	27 2/8	20 2/8	5 4/8	5 4/8	6	5	Bolivar Co., Miss.	Grady Robertson	Merigold Hunting Club	NO 1951	58
178 4/8	26 2/8	25 3/8	21	5 3/8	5 3/8	5	5	Scotland Co., Mo.	Picked Up	Roland E. Meyer	PU 1984	60
178 3/8	27	27 3/8	17 5/8	4 3/8	4 4/8	5	7	Queens Co., N. B.	Bert Bourque	Bert Bourque	NO 1970	61
178 2/8	27 4/8	27	19 6/8	4 3/8	4 4/8	5	5	Tuscarawas Co., Ohio	Raymond D. Gerber, Jr.	Raymond D. Gerber, Jr.	DC 1983	62
178 2/8	27 6/8	27 3/8	24 6/8	4 3/8	4 3/8	6	6	Wallowa Co., Oreg.	Sterling K. Shaver	Sterling K. Shaver	OT 1982	62
178 2/8	26 5/8	26 1/8	20 6/8	4 6/8	4 6/8	5	5	Pawnee Co., Neb.	Picked Up	Gale Sup	1960	62
178 1/8	27 4/8	27 4/8	21 1/8	5 5/8	5 4/8	5	5	Price Co., Wisc.	Terry Staroba	Terry Staroba	NO 1983	65
178 1/8	27 5/8	27 4/8	17 4/8	4 7/8	4 7/8	8	7	Iron Co., Wisc.	DuWayne A. Weichel	Robert G. Steidtmann	NO 1957	65
178	27	27 2/8	17 4/8	4 6/8	5	7	6	Price Co., Wisc.	Emery Swan	Emery Swan	NO 1949	67
178	25 1/8	26 2/8	22 6/8	6	6	5	5	Union Co., Ky.	Gary L. Gibson	Gary L. Gibson	NO 1983	67
177 7/8	26 4/8	27 4/8	23	5 5/8	5	7	9	Jefferson Co., Mont.	Tracy Forcella	Tracy Forcella	OT 1983	69
177 5/8	26 2/8	26 6/8	22 6/8	4 7/8	4 7/8	7	6	Wabasha Co., Minn.	Bruce J. Hall	Bruce J. Hall	NO 1972	70
177 5/8	25	24 3/8	17 6/8	4 1/8	4 1/8	6	8	Macon Co., Ga.	James W. Athon	Mike's Gun Shop	NO 1976	70
177 5/8	29	28 2/8	22	4 4/8	4 4/8	7	8	Harrison Co., Ohio	Mark Dulkoski	Mark Dulkoski	NO 1984	70
177 5/8	25 5/8	25 5/8	19 5/8	5 3/8	5 3/8	5	5	Washburn Co., Wisc.	Patrick Henk	Patrick Henk	NO 1984	70
177 4/8	26	26 4/8	24	5	5	6	6	McMullen Co., Texas	Unknown	Ken Mamatz	1983	74
177 3/8	25 3/8	25 1/8	16 7/8	6 2/8	6	10	7	Unknown	Unknown	Johnny M. Hollier		75

Whitetail Deer (Typical Antlers)—Continued
Odocoileus virginianus virginianus and certain related subspecies

Score	Length of Main Beam R.	L.	Inside Spread	Circumference at Smallest Place Between Burr and First Point R.	L.	Number of Points R.	L.	Locality Killed	By Whom Killed	Owner	Date Killed	Rank
177 3/8	27	26 6/8	23 1/8	5	5 1/8	5	5	Menominee Co., Wisc.	William Matchapatow, Sr.	William Matchapatow, Sr.	NO 1981	75
177 2/8	29 2/8	30 2/8	18 2/8	6 5/8	6 3/8	6	6	Geary Co., Kan.	Kelly D. Gulker	Kelly D. Gulker	NO 1982	77
177 2/8	25 5/8	25 7/8	18 2/8	4 5/8	4 5/8	6	6	Richland Co., Wisc.	Dewitt S. Pulham	Dewitt S. Pulham	NO 1982	77
177 2/8	27 5/8	29	21 7/8	6	6	5	6	Litchfield Co., Conn.	Picked Up	Rickey A. Vincent	PU 1984	77
177 1/8	27 2/8	27	21 7/8	4 4/8	4 4/8	5	5	Walworth Co., Wisc.	Daniel J. Brede	Daniel J. Brede	NO 1984	80
177	28 1/8	26 1/8	20 7/8	5 4/8	5 5/8	7	6	Innisfree, Alta.	Donald M. Baranec	Donald M. Baranec	NO 1984	81
176 7/8	25 3/8	25 5/8	22 1/8	4 5/8	5	5	5	Butler Co., Kan.	Craig D. Waltman	Craig D. Waltman	DC 1982	82
176 7/8	28	26 7/8	16 7/8	3 7/8	3 6/8	5	5	Day Co., S. D.	William B. Davis	William B. Davis	NO 1959	82
176 7/8	27 3/8	27 7/8	20 3/8	4 5/8	4 5/8	5	5	Pierce Co., Wisc.	John M. Oelke	John M. Oelke	NO 1984	82
176 5/8	26 7/8	26	20 6/8	4 4/8	4 4/8	6	6	Tensas Parish, La.	Sam Barber	Johnny M. Hollier	DC 1974	85
176 4/8	27 3/8	28	21 2/8	4 3/8	4 4/8	5	5	Sanders Co., Mont.	Dallas J. C. Nelson	Dallas J. C. Nelson	NO 1983	86
176 4/8	26 5/8	27	26 6/8	4 2/8	4 4/8	6	6	Houston Co., Minn.	James L. Reinhart	James L. Reinhart	NO 1971	86
176 4/8	24 5/8	24 5/8	19 4/8	4 5/8	4 5/8	6	7	Charlotte Co., N. B.	Albert E. Dewar	Albert E. Dewar	OT 1960	86
176 3/8	26 1/8	25 5/8	22 4/8	5 7/8	5 5/8	6	6	Koochiching Co., Minn.	Picked Up	James R. Smith	PU 1957	89
176 2/8	24 7/8	25 4/8	20 6/8	4 5/8	4 7/8	6	6	Troup Co., Ga.	James E. Lasater	James E. Lasater	NO 1984	90
176 1/8	25 1/8	23 7/8	24 1/8	5 5/8	5 5/8	6	6	Assiniboine River, Man.	G. G. Graham	G. G. Graham	NO 1984	91
176	28 5/8	29 5/8	17 5/8	5 3/8	5 3/8	8	7	Florence Co., Wisc.	John G. Kozicki	Vernon J. Kozicki	DC 1936	92
175 7/8	26 5/8	27	21 7/8	4 3/8	4 3/8	5	6	Swift Co., Minn.	Kim Manska	Kim Manska	NO 1982	93
175 7/8	27	26 4/8	22 5/8	4 4/8	4 4/8	5	5	Sundre, Alta.	Russell D. Holmes	Russell D. Holmes	NO 1984	93
175 6/8	24 5/8	24 5/8	17 7/8	6 2/8	6 3/8	8	10	Marshall Co., Minn.	Ell-Kay B. Foss	Ell-Kay B. Foss	1974	95
175 5/8	25 5/8	25	17 7/8	4 5/8	4 5/8	6	7	Benewah Co., Idaho	Carl Groth	Carl Groth	NO 1982	96
175 5/8	24 5/8	25	17 1/8	5 1/8	5 2/8	5	5	Unknown	Unknown	Brad Lewis		96
175 4/8	26 7/8	27 7/8	21	5 1/8	5 1/8	5	5	Renville Co., Minn.	Larry D. Youngs	Larry D. Youngs	NO 1973	98
175 3/8	28 7/8	28 3/8	19 6/8	5 1/8	5 2/8	7	5	Fulton Co., Ind.	Larry A. Croxton	Larry A. Croxton	NO 1984	99
175 2/8	27 1/8	27	19	6	6 1/8	5	5	Union Co., Ill.	Randy Edmonds	Randy Edmonds	DC 1984	99
175 2/8	26 7/8	26 3/8	20 4/8	4 3/8	4 5/8	5	5	Claiborne Parish, La.	Picked Up	Johnny M. Hollier	NO 1982	99
175 1/8	22 3/8	22 7/8	20 5/8	5	5 2/8	6	6	Marinette Co., Wisc.	John Nielson	John Nielson	NO 1983	102
175 1/8	28	27 5/8	25	4 7/8	4 6/8	8	7	Waldo Co., Maine	Unknown	Kenneth T. Winters	NO 1924	102
175 1/8	27 3/8	27 1/8	21 2/8	5 7/8	6	6	5	Wetzel Co., W. Va.	Matthew Scheibelhood	Matthew Scheibelhood	NO 1984	102
175	26	27 4/8	21	5 1/8	5 1/8	6	5	Jim Hogg Co., Texas	Carl D. Ellis	Lee H. Lytton, Jr.	DC 1984	105
175	25 3/8	25 4/8	19 7/8	5 5/8	5 4/8	5	5	Itasca Co., Minn.	David A. Frandsen	David A. Frandsen	NO 1982	105
174 7/8	25 5/8	25 7/8	21 3/8	4 7/8	4 4/8	5	6	Jo Daviess Co., Ill.	W. V. Patrick	Jerry Patrick	DC 1983	107
174 6/8	28 7/8	27 7/8	21	4 6/8	4 5/8	5	6	Maine	Unknown	Warren H. Delaware	PR 1977	108

174 5/8	25	25 2/8	24 3/8	4 3/8	4 2/8	7	7	Kleberg Co., Texas	C. T. Burris	Darrell Pitts	1959	109
174 4/8	28 2/8	27 5/8	17	5 2/8	5 3/8	5	7	Boone Co., Iowa	Curtis A. Lind	Curtis A. Lind	DC 1982	110
174 3/8	25 2/8	25 3/8	20 1/8	4 5/8	4 6/8	5	5	Goshen Co., Wyo.	Casey L. Hunter	Casey L. Hunter	NO 1984	111
174 2/8	23 3/8	23 6/8	15 6/8	4 4/8	4 5/8	10	9	La Salle Co., Texas	Walter L. Taylor	Walter L. Taylor	DC 1979	112
174 1/8	27	26 1/8	21 1/8	5 2/8	5 5/8	7	6	Aroostook Co., Maine	Unkown	Vern Black	1930	113
174 1/8	23 2/8	24 5/8	20 6/8	5 1/8	5 2/8	5	5	Johnson Co., Kan.	Ralph E. Schlagel	Ralph E. Schlagel	DC 1984	113
173 6/8	25 2/8	25 3/8	18 2/8	4 3/8	4 4/8	7	7	Carroll Co., Ga.	Ken Yearta	Ken Yearta	NO 1983	115
173 6/8	24 1/8	24 1/8	17 6/8	4 6/8	4 6/8	6	6	Regina, Sask.	Don Wolk	Don Wolk	NO 1982	115
173 6/8	24 5/8	24 4/8	23 4/8	5 2/8	5 4/8	5	5	Hart Creek, B. C.	Greg Lamontange	Greg Lamontange	SE 1984	115
173 5/8	25	25 6/8	22 5/8	4 2/8	4 4/8	6	6	Lowndes Co., Miss.	Geraline Holliman	Geraline Holliman	NO 1982	118
173 5/8	27 5/8	28 1/8	22 6/8	5 3/8	5 3/8	4	7	Woods Co., Okla.	Jack Clover	Jack Clover	NO 1983	118
173 5/8	28 3/8	28 5/8	20 7/8	5 2/8	5 4/8	6	7	Flathead Co., Mont.	Mike J. Beaty	Mike J. Beaty	NO 1984	118
173 4/8	27 6/8	28	26 1/8	5 5/8	5 5/8	7	9	Marengo Co., Ala.	Picked Up	L. M. Cabiniss	PU 1960	121
173 3/8	26 1/8	25 5/8	18 6/8	5	5	5	5	Keya Paha Co., Neb.	Gene F. Pool	Gene F. Pool	NO 1980	122
173 3/8	27 4/8	27 4/8	17 1/8	4 5/8	4 6/8	7	5	Clay Co., Kan.	Charles A. Hammons	Charles A. Hammons	DC 1984	122
173 2/8	27 3/8	25 3/8	18 4/8	4	4 1/8	6	6	Decatur Co., Tenn.	Glen D. Odle	Glen D. Odle	DC 1972	124
173 2/8	26 4/8	26 5/8	19	4 1/8	4	5	5	Chisago Co., Minn.	Roger A. Peterson	Roger A. Peterson	NO 1984	124
173 1/8	26	26 6/8	18 5/8	4 1/8	3 7/8	6	6	White Co., Tenn.	Sam H. Langford	Sam H. Langford	DC 1980	126
173 1/8	29 3/8	28 7/8	25 1/8	5 2/8	5 1/8	4	4	Fillmore Co., Minn.	Gerry D. Arnold	Gerry D. Arnold	NO 1973	126
173 1/8	24 4/8	25 3/8	16 3/8	4 3/8	4 3/8	5	5	Big Muddy Valley, Sask.	Lyndon T. Ross	Lyndon T. Ross	NO 1984	126
173	25 4/8	25 1/8	19 4/8	4 5/8	4 5/8	4	4	Sullivan Co., Tenn.	C. Alan Altizer	C. Alan Altizer	OT 1984	129
173	27	27 2/8	23 5/8	5 7/8	6 1/8	6	7	Doniphan Co., Kan.	Charles A. Staudenmier	Charles A. Staudenmier	DC 1983	129
173	24 5/8	24 7/8	16 4/8	5 3/8	5 2/8	5	5	Bonnyville, Alta.	Lionel P. Tercier	Lionel P. Tercier	NO 1983	129
173	23 2/8	25 5/8	19 5/8	4 6/8	4 6/8	7	8	Bunder Lake, Alta.	Steve Swinhoe	Steve Swinhoe	NO 1983	129
173	24 4/8	25 5/8	16 7/8	3 7/8	3 6/8	6	7	Trinity Co., Texas	Don Knight	Don Knight	NO 1983	129
172 7/8	26	27 3/8	22 5/8	4 4/8	4 6/8	7	10	Heard Co., Ga.	Keith McCullough	Keith McCullough	NO 1982	134
172 6/8	27 3/8	27 5/8	24	5	5	5	5	Waldo Co., Maine	Wallace Humphrey	Arthur Humphrey	NO 1963	135
172 5/8	28 4/8	28	22	6 2/8	6 3/8	8	8	Adams Co., Miss.	Adrian L. Stallone	Adrian L. Stallone	DC 1983	136
172 5/8	24 7/8	25 7/8	25 1/8	4 7/8	4 7/8	5	5	Barren Co., Ky.	Billy N. Short	Billy N. Short	NO 1984	136
172 4/8	24 3/8	25 2/8	23 4/8	5 6/8	5 4/8	8	7	Muhlenberg Co., Ky.	Dennis Nolen	Dennis Nolen	NO 1982	138
172 4/8	26 4/8	26 2/8	21 7/8	5 2/8	5 2/8	6	6	Muskingum Co., Ohio	Michael Wilson	Michael Wilson	DC 1982	138
172 4/8	23 5/8	25 2/8	20	6 1/8	5 7/8	6	5	Franklin Co., Ill.	Joseph S. Smothers	Joseph S. Smothers	NO 1984	138
172 3/8	27 6/8	28 2/8	17 2/8	4 6/8	4 5/8	6	5	Decatur Co., Tenn.	Danny Pope	Danny Pope	NO 1982	141
172 3/8	24 5/8	24 3/8	18	4 6/8	4 7/8	8	7	Rusk Co., Wisc.	Randy A. Jochem	Randy A. Jochem	NO 1984	141
172 3/8	30 1/8	30 3/8	22 3/8	5 4/8	5 4/8	9	9	Porcupine Plain, Sask.	Kim Mikkonen	Kim Mikkonen	OT 1985	141
172 2/8	25 7/8	25 6/8	20 2/8	4 4/8	4 4/8	5	5	Cattaraugus Co., N. Y.	Thomas J. Hinchey	Thomas J. Hinchey	NO 1982	144
172 2/8	26 2/8	25 1/8	22	5	5	7	5	Pendleton Co., Ky.	Kevin L. Galloway	Kevin L. Galloway	NO 1983	144
172 2/8	26 2/8	25	18 7/8	5	5	6	6	Stewart Co., Tenn.	Joe K. Sanders	Joe K. Sanders	NO 1984	144
172 2/8	31 4/8	30 7/8	23 5/8	4 7/8	5 1/8	6	5	Perry Co., Ill.	Raymond E. Haertling	Raymond E. Haertling	DC 1968	144
172 1/8	24	24 4/8	20 6/8	5 1/8	5 1/8	8	7	Fillmore Co., Minn.	Murrel Mathison	Murrel Mathison	DC 1977	148
172	24 6/8	25 6/8	22 6/8	5 3/8	5 3/8	5	6	Miami Co., Kan.	Dan R. Moore	Dan R. Moore	NO 1982	149
172	24	25 7/8	18	4 2/8	4 2/8	6	5	Tift Co., Ga.	Mayo Tucker	Mayo Tucker	NO 1982	149
172	25 7/8	25 2/8	19	4 5/8	4 5/8	5	5	Waukesha Co., Wisc.	Donald R. Friedlein	Donald R. Friedlein	NO 1983	149

Whitetail Deer *(Typical Antlers)*—*Continued*

Odocoileus virginianus virginianus and certain related subspecies

Score	Length of Main Beam R.	Length of Main Beam L.	Inside Spread	Circumference at Smallest Place Between Burr and First Point R.	Circumference at Smallest Place Between Burr and First Point L.	Number of Points R.	Number of Points L.	Locality Killed	By Whom Killed	Owner	Date Killed	Rank
172	27 3/8	28 3/8	18 2/8	5	5 1/8	5	5	Westmoreland Co., N. B.	Edgar Cormier	Edgar Cormier	NO 1983	149
171 7/8	25	24 4/8	20	5	5	5	6	Washington Co., Ohio	Thomas E. Burnette	Thomas E. Burnette	DC 1982	153
171 7/8	26 2/8	26 4/8	24 1/8	4 4/8	4 4/8	5	5	Scotland Co., Mo.	David R. Smith	David R. Smith	OT 1984	153
171 6/8	26 6/8	26 3/8	19 7/8	5 3/8	5 3/8	7	10	Perry Co., Ill.	Daniel P. Hollenkamp	Daniel P. Hollenkamp	DC 1982	155
171 6/8	25 5/8	25 6/8	24 1/8	5 6/8	5 6/8	6	6	Clinton Co., N. Y.	William J. Branch	William J. Branch	NO 1982	155
171 6/8	24 4/8	23 2/8	19 4/8	4 5/8	4 5/8	10	8	Gray Creek, B. C.	Ross Oliver	Ross Oliver	MR 1982	155
171 6/8	26 3/8	26 3/8	20 4/8	4 5/8	4 6/8	4	5	Van Buren Co., Mich.	Ronald E. Eldred	Ronald E. Eldred	NO 1983	155
171 5/8	27 3/8	27 4/8	18 3/8	5	4 6/8	6	5	Riley Co., Kan.	Mick McCallister	Mick McCallister	DC 1980	159
171 5/8	25 1/8	26 1/8	16 7/8	4	4	6	7	Baldwin Co., Ga.	Picked Up	E. Donald Graham	PU 1977	159
171 5/8	25 4/8	26 5/8	19 3/8	5 5/8	5 6/8	7	7	Bonnell Brook, N. B.	Steve R. McCutcheon	Steve R. McCutcheon	NO 1984	159
171 4/8	25	24 4/8	20 4/8	4 3/8	4 4/8	6	6	Rusk Co., Wisc.	Luke Dernovsek, III	Luke Dernovsek, III	NO 1983	162
171 4/8	24 5/8	21 7/8	21 3/8	5	4 7/8	8	6	Crooked Lake, Alta.	Bruce J. Ferguson	Bruce J. Ferguson	NO 1984	162
171 4/8	25 6/8	24 5/8	19 6/8	4 4/8	4 3/8	5	5	Clearwater Co., Minn.	Peter Tranby	Peter Tranby	NO 1978	162
171 4/8	27 1/8	26 7/8	18 6/8	4 5/8	4 5/8	5	6	Becker Co., Minn.	Kraig J. Ketter	Kraig J. Ketter	NO 1983	162
171 3/8	27 2/8	27 2/8	21 2/8	5	4 7/8	7	6	Boyd Co., Neb.	Scott A. Sperling	Scott A. Sperling	NO 1982	166
171 3/8	28	27 1/8	18 4/8	4 4/8	4 7/8	5	6	Kalamazoo Co., Mich.	Harvey B. Braden	Harvey B. Braden	NO 1984	166
171 3/8	25 7/8	26 3/8	21 3/8	5 1/8	5 1/8	8	10	Douglas Co., Minn.	Gregory A. Dropik	Gregory A. Dropik	NO 1984	166
171 3/8	27 2/8	28 2/8	18 1/8	4 4/8	4 4/8	5	5	Sumner Co., Kan.	Jeff D. Ehlers	Jeff D. Ehlers	DC 1984	166
171 2/8	27	26 4/8	21 4/8	5 3/8	5 2/8	6	6	Waldo Co., Maine	Paul K. Nickerson	Paul K. Nickerson	NO 1957	170
171 2/8	25 6/8	25 7/8	19 4/8	5	5	5	6	Bayfield Co., Wisc.	Lawrence Stumo	Lawrence Stumo	NO 1956	170
171 1/8	24 7/8	25	20 6/8	6	6	5	5	Penobscot Co., Maine	Kenneth Scott	Kenneth W. Bennett	NO 1960	172
171	26 2/8	25 6/8	20 5/8	4 1/8	4 1/8	6	6	Buffalo Co., Wisc.	Clarence H. Castleberg, Jr.	Clarence H. Castleberg, Jr.	NO 1964	173
171	25 2/8	24	15 6/8	5 1/8	5 2/8	5	5	Christian Co., Mo.	Melba J. Herndon	Melba J. Herndon	NO 1983	173
171	26	26	20	5	4 6/8	5	5	Aroostook Co., Maine	Roland L. Demers	Roland L. Demers	NO 1983	173
171	25 2/8	25 4/8	19 2/8	4 7/8	4 7/8	5	6	Okanagan Range, B. C.	Picked Up	Dennis A. Dorholt	PU 1984	173
170 7/8	25 5/8	24 6/8	22 5/8	5	5 7/8	6	7	Burleigh Co., N. D.	Ronald C. Wagner	Ronald C. Wagner	NO 1982	177
170 7/8	28 1/8	27 1/8	19 2/8	5	5	5	4	Issaquena Co., Miss.	Warren A. Miller	L. M. Cooley & A. M. Cooley	1920	177
170 7/8	25 7/8	25 5/8	17 5/8	5 4/8	5 4/8	5	5	Washington Co., Maine	Merle G. Michaud	Merle G. Michaud	1979	177
170 6/8	25 7/8	25 6/8	20	4 6/8	4 6/8	5	5	Carroll Co., Md.	Wes McKenzie	Wes McKenzie	NO 1971	180
170 6/8	24 4/8	24 1/8	16 4/8	4	4	7	7	Harris Co., Ga.	Gorman S. Riley	Gorman S. Riley	OT 1983	180
170 6/8	23 3/8	23 3/8	19 5/8	4 6/8	4 5/8	5	6	Great Sand Hills, Sask.	Ralph Cervo	Ralph Cervo	NO 1984	180

170 6/8	28 4/8	28 1/8	24 6/8	4 2/8	4 1/8	6	8	Zapata Co., Texas	G. O. Elliff	Michael Elliff	1926	180
170 5/8	27 1/8	26 1/8	19 3/8	4 6/8	4 5/8	6	5	Jasper Co., Ga.	Gordon W. Cown	Gordon W. Cown	NO 1961	184
170 5/8	26 5/8	27 2/8	21	6	5 3/8	6	7	Lyon Co., Kan.	Bill D. Hollond	Bill D. Hollond	DC 1984	184
170 5/8	25 5/8	26	20 3/8	4 4/8	4 5/8	5	6	Berrien Co., Mich.	G. Steven Abdoe	G. Steven Abdoe	NO 1982	184
170 5/8	25 6/8	25 5/8	18 3/8	4 5/8	4 6/8	6	6	Lake Co., Minn.	Unknown	George W. Flaim	1960	184
170 4/8	26 1/8	25 4/8	18	4 4/8	4 4/8	5	5	Marshall Co., Ind.	Alan R. Collins	Alan R. Collins	NO 1982	188
170 4/8	28 5/8	28	20	5	5	8	8	Todd Co., Minn.	Freddie H. Peterson	Freddie H. Peterson	NO 1982	188
170 4/8	24	24 2/8	19 2/8	4 5/8	4 6/8	5	5	Day Co., S. D.	Credan Ewalt	Credan Ewalt	NO 1982	188
170 4/8	24 7/8	24 1/8	21	4 7/8	5	5	5	Chippewa Co., Mich.	Paul Slawski	Paul Slawski	NO 1984	188
170 4/8	25 2/8	24 2/8	16 4/8	5	5	7	7	Oneida Co., Wisc.	Leonard E. Westberg	Leonard E. Westberg	NO 1981	188
170 3/8	25 5/8	25 2/8	22 6/8	5 2/8	5 4/8	7	8	Lac qui Parle Co., Minn.	Paul W. Hill	Paul W. Hill	NO 1974	193
170 3/8	25 2/8	25 4/8	18 6/8	5 2/8	4 7/8	6	6	Wilkinson Co., Ga.	James W. Whitaker	James W. Whitaker	OT 1982	193
170 3/8	25 5/8	25 1/8	16 4/8	4 7/8	5	9	9	Price Co., Wisc.	N. J. Groelle	Melvin Guenther	NO 1905	193
170 3/8	23 1/8	23 2/8	19 5/8	4 6/8	4 5/8	6	6	Niobrara Co., Wyo.	Joseph A. Perry, III	Joseph A. Perry, III	OT 1985	193
170 2/8	28 6/8	29 1/8	19 5/8	4 5/8	4 4/8	9	5	Blue Earth Co., Minn.	Roland Bode	Roland Bode	NO 1967	197
170 2/8	23 7/8	22 4/8	17 4/8	4 4/8	4 6/8	5	5	Hopkins Co., Ky.	Michael E. Dillingham	Michael E. Dillingham	NO 1977	197
170 2/8	25 1/8	26	20 4/8	6 7/8	6 7/8	5	5	Ribstone Creek, Alta.	David H. Crum	David H. Crum	NO 1984	197
170 2/8	26 6/8	26 7/8	22 2/8	5 6/8	5 6/8	5	6	Riley Co., Kan.	Paul K. Byarlay	Paul K. Byarlay	DC 1983	197
170 2/8	23 6/8	26 4/8	18 2/8	5 2/8	5 4/8	5	5	Oglethorpe Co., Ga.	H. D. Cannon	H. D. Cannon	NO 1971	197
170 1/8	25 3/8	24 6/8	16 5/8	4 7/8	5	6	7	St. Louis Co., Minn.	Allan Ramstad	Allan Ramstad	NO 1959	202
170 1/8	24 3/8	22 6/8	18 3/8	5	5 1/8	8	6	Sanders Co., Mont.	Richard Lukes	Richard Lukes	NO 1984	202
170 1/8	25 6/8	25 2/8	21 3/8	4 4/8	4 5/8	5	5	Mower Co., Minn.	Robert D. Plumb	Robert D. Plumb	NO 1984	202
170 1/8	27	27 1/8	19	4 6/8	4 6/8	7	6	Cook Co., Minn.	William Bohnen	William Bohnen	NO 1984	202
170 1/8	25 4/8	25 7/8	22 2/8	4 5/8	4 3/8	6	7	Winona Co., Minn.	Roger J. Traxler	Roger J. Traxler	NO 1980	202
170	26 2/8	26 6/8	20 2/8	4 7/8	4 5/8	5	7	Wapello Co., Iowa	George C. Ellis	George C. Ellis	DC 1984	207
170	28 3/8	27 4/8	21	4 6/8	5	4	6	Androscoggin Co., Maine	Ricky D. Cavers	Ricky D. Cavers	NO 1981	207
169 6/8	25 4/8	26 5/8	17 3/8	5	5	6	6	Wadena Co., Minn.	Keith Van Orsdel	Keith Van Orsdel	NO 1984	209
169	24 3/8	24 6/8	18 4/8	4	4 2/8	5	5	Colquitt Co., Ga.	Timothy G. Huffman, Sr.	Timothy G. Huffman, Sr.	NO 1984	210
168 2/8	26 7/8	26	19	5 4/8	5 5/8	4	4	Licking Co., Ohio	David J. Alexander	David J. Alexander	NO 1984	211
168 1/8	24 6/8	24 6/8	19 1/8	5 2/8	5	5	5	Wadena Co., Minn.	Don Carter	Don Carter	NO 1984	212
167 6/8	26 3/8	26 6/8	21 2/8	4 5/8	4 5/8	5	5	Piscataquis Co., Maine	Robert Collura	Robert Collura	NO 1981	213
167	26 3/8	25 2/8	18 1/8	4 4/8	4 3/8	6	6	Crooked Creek, Sask.	Robert J. Hurry	Robert J. Hurry	NO 1984	214
166 6/8	25 1/8	27	20 6/8	5 2/8	5 3/8	5	7	Blue Earth Co., Minn.	Jesse L. Cornish	Jesse L. Cornish	NO 1983	215
166 6/8	28 6/8	28 5/8	20 6/8	5 1/8	5 3/8	5	5	Gallia Co., Ohio	Rodger D. Kern	Rodger D. Kern	NO 1982	215
165 4/8	24 6/8	24 2/8	21 4/8	4 3/8	4 3/8	9	8	Maverick Co., Texas	Robert L. Parker, Jr.	Robert L. Parker, Jr.	DC 1982	217
164 2/8	26	27 4/8	22 1/8	4 6/8	5	8	6	Somerset Co., Maine	James A. Stevens	James A. Stevens	NO 1983	218
163 6/8	24 1/8	24 5/8	18 2/8	4 3/8	4 4/8	5	5	Durham Co., N. C.	Harvey Garrett	Harvey Garrett	NO 1984	219
163 2/8	27 1/8	26	20 4/8	5	4 7/8	8	11	Union Co., Ark.	Johnny Gathright	Johnny Gathright	NO 1983	220
162 6/8	26 1/8	26 1/8	21 3/8	6	6	6	7	Otter Tail Co., Minn.	Mark M. Gontarek	Mark M. Gontarek	NO 1983	221
162 5/8	25 1/8	23 6/8	17 5/8	4 5/8	4 7/8	6	5	Shelby Co., Ala.	Gary L. Dimon	Gary L. Dimon	DC 1976	222
162 2/8	23	23 1/8	18 4/8	4 6/8	4 6/8	5	5	Sutton Co., Texas	Linda Corley	Linda Corley	DC 1983	223
162 1/8	25 1/8	25 5/8	17 7/8	4 6/8	5	5	6	Dewey Co., Okla.	Ronald B. Hall	Ronald B. Hall	NO 1982	224
162	23 2/8	22 4/8	17 4/8	5 4/8	5 1/8	5	6	Jackson Co., Ga.	Teddy Parker	Teddy Parker	NO 1984	225
162	24	25	19 2/8	4 4/8	4 3/8	7	6	Henderson Co., Ill.	Robert G. Hosford	Robert G. Hosford	DC 1984	225

Whitetail Deer *(Typical Antlers)—Continued*

Odocoileus virginianus virginianus and certain related subspecies

Score	Length of Main Beam R.	Length of Main Beam L.	Inside Spread	Circumference at Smallest Place Between Burr and First Point R.	Circumference at Smallest Place Between Burr and First Point L.	Number of Points R.	Number of Points L.	Locality Killed	By Whom Killed	Owner	Date Killed	Rank
161 7/8	22 1/8	22 7/8	18 7/8	4 1/8	4 1/8	6	6	Powell Co., Mont.	Neil Midtlyng	N. Midtlyng & P. Haviland	NO 1984	227
161 5/8	24 5/8	25 7/8	19 6/8	6 2/8	6 4/8	4	4	Avoyelles Parish, La.	M. J. Hartley	M. J. Hartley	JA 1980	228
161 5/8	22	22	19 5/8	4 5/8	4 6/8	5	5	Jo Daviess Co., Ill.	Bradley E. Giertz	Bradley E. Giertz	DC 1983	228
160	24 7/8	25 1/8	16	5 1/8	5	5	5	Dodge Co., Ga.	Jay Mullis	Jay Mullis	DC 1984	230
199 2/8*	31 7/8	31 7/8	24 4/8	5 3/8	5 3/8	5	5	Saunders Co., Neb.	Vernon A. Virka	Vernon A. Virka	NO 1983	
190 5/8*	28 4/8	27 2/8	18 5/8	5 6/8	6	6	8	Clinton Co., Ind.	Alan W. Brannan	Alan W. Brannan	DC 1982	
188 4/8*	27 2/8	28 7/8	20 1/8	5	4 7/8	8	8	Riley Co., Kan.	Robert E. Luke	Robert E. Luke	NO 1984	

*Final Score subject to revision by additional verifying measurements.

Whitetail Deer (*Non-Typical Antlers*)

Odocoileus virginianus virginianus and certain related subspecies

Minimum Score 185 — World's Record 333 7/8

Score	Length of Main Beam R.	L.	Inside Spread	Circumference at Smallest Place Between Burr and First Point R.	L.	Number of Points R.	L.	Locality Killed	By Whom Killed	Owner	Date Killed	Rank
328 2/8	25 5/8	24 4/8	24 3/8	6 3/8	5 5/8	23	22	Portage Co., Ohio	Picked Up	Dick Idol	PU 1940	1
277 5/8	27 5/8	28 4/8	24 6/8	6	6 1/8	17	16	Hardisty, Alta.	Doug Klinger	Doug Klinger	NO 1976	2
267 3/8	25 4/8	28 3/8	20	6 5/8	6 3/8	18	7	Peoria Co., Ill.	Richard A. Pauli	Richard A. Pauli	NO 1983	3
255 4/8	23 5/8	22 7/8	18 1/8	5 5/8	5 5/8	18	15	Pigeon Lake, Alta.	Leo Eklund	Leo Eklund	NO 1973	4
245 2/8	22 1/8	22 2/8	24 6/8	5 2/8	6 6/8	9	17	Nez Perce Co., Idaho	John D. Powers, Jr.	Zeke West	OT 1983	5
241 7/8	29 2/8	25 7/8	19 3/8	5 2/8	5	9	11	Wisc.	Unknown	Robert Kietzman	1940	6
241 1/8	26 4/8	26 1/8	18 1/8	6 1/8	6	19	18	Bighill Creek, Alta.	Donald D. Dwernychuk	Donald D. Dwernychuk	SE 1984	7
239 5/8	24 2/8	24 1/8	18 6/8	6 1/8	5 5/8	20	14	N. B.	Unknown	Johnny M. Hollier		8
235 1/8	24	23 7/8	21 2/8	5	4 7/8	14	15	Frio Co., Texas	C. J. Stolle	John F. Stolle	DC 1919	9
234 2/8	27 3/8	26 5/8	20 1/8	7	7 1/8	10	12	Alfalfa Co., Okla.	Loren Tarrant	Loren Tarrant	NO 1984	10
232	25 1/8	25	17	6	6	18	11	Waukesha Co., Wisc.	John Herr, Sr.	Mac's Taxidermy	NO 1955	11
231 5/8	26 1/8	25 3/8	23 3/8	6	6 1/8	11	13	Peace River, Alta.	Terry Doll	Terry Doll	OT 1978	12
230 7/8	24 5/8	24 4/8	15 3/8	6 3/8	5 4/8	24	13	Sumter Co., Ala.	James L. Spidle, Sr.	James L. Spidle, Sr.	PR 1942	13
229 2/8	27	28 5/8	21 1/8	6 3/8	7	8	15	Linn Co., Kan.	Merle C. Beckman	Merle C. Beckman	DC 1984	14
226 6/8	26 2/8	26	18 7/8	6	5 5/8	7	9	Pulaski Co., Ky.	H. C. Sumpter	H. C. Sumpter	NO 1984	15
225	25 4/8	25 6/8	21 7/8	5 5/8	6	15	12	Nipawin, Sask.	Picked Up	John L. Stein	PU 1981	16
224	23 5/8	23 2/8	22 2/8	4 4/8	4 7/8	13	14	N. Y.	Unknown	Johnny M. Hollier	PR 1983	17
223 7/8	25 1/8	24 2/8	16 3/8	4 3/8	4 3/8	10	13	Nuevo Leon, Mexico	Ron Kolpin	Ron Kolpin	JA 1983	18
223 3/8	28	28	25 3/8	7 1/8	6 4/8	10	11	Greene Co., Ill.	Terry L. Walters	Terry L. Walters	NO 1982	18
223	21 3/8	23	23 4/8	4 1/8	4 2/8	19	11	Hawkins Co., Tenn.	Luther E. Fuller	Luther E. Fuller	NO 1984	20
222 7/8	21 4/8	22 7/8	16 1/8	5 7/8	5 3/8	11	10	Itasca Co., Minn.	Picked Up	James R. Smith	PU 1936	21
222 5/8	24 6/8	23 7/8	18 5/8	5 1/8	5 5/8	9	9	Edgerton, Alta.	Nick Leskow	Russell Thornberry	NO 1964	22
222 4/8	25 4/8	23 5/8	21 1/8	5 3/8	5 2/8	14	11	Richland Co., Wisc.	Janice K. Beranek	Janice K. Beranek	NO 1983	23
222 3/8	25 3/8	25 5/8	19 5/8	5 5/8	5 5/8	14	12	Itasca Co., Minn.	Lumie Jackson	Rick Ferguson	1942	24
221 7/8	25 4/8	26 4/8	16 4/8	5 5/8	5 4/8	12	14	Trigg Co., Ky.	Bill McWhirter	Bill McWhirter	NO 1982	25
221 5/8	23 7/8	25 7/8	21 5/8	5 4/8	5 5/8	13	10	Snipe Lake, Alta.	Robert Dickson, Sr.	Robert Dickson, Sr.	NO 1984	26
220 7/8	28 7/8	28 4/8	21	5	5	9	8	Zavala Co., Texas	J. D. Jarratt	J. D. Jarratt	DC 1930	27
219 5/8	24 5/8	25 1/8	21 1/8	5 7/8	6 3/8	13	12	Warren Co., Mo.	James E. Williams	James E. Williams	NO 1959	28
218 7/8	29 2/8	28 6/8	21	5 4/8	5 5/8	6	8	Waldo Co., Maine	Roy C. Guse	J. Bruce Probert	NO 1957	29
218 3/8	23 4/8	22 7/8	15 7/8	5 5/8	5 5/8	11	7	Sumter Co., Ala.	Josh Jones	Harrison H. Perry	PR 1952	30
215	23 7/8	25 4/8	15 5/8	5 5/8	5 4/8	17	13	Fergus Co., Mont.	Robert D. Fleherty	Robert D. Fleherty	NO 1958	31
214 5/8	25 1/8	25 7/8	16 5/8	5	4 7/8	15	14	Koochiching Co., Minn.	Unknown	Wilbur Tilander	1956	32

Whitetail Deer *(Non-Typical Antlers)—Continued*

Odocoileus virginianus virginianus and certain related subspecies

Score	Length of Main Beam R.	Length of Main Beam L.	Inside Spread	Circumference at Smallest Place Between Burr and First Point R.	Circumference at Smallest Place Between Burr and First Point L.	Number of Points R.	Number of Points L.	Locality Killed	By Whom Killed	Owner	Date Killed	Rank
214	28 7/8	28 6/8	23 1/8	4 5/8	4 4/8	10	9	Clay Co., Minn.	Dean Klemetson	Dean Klemetson	NO 1984	33
213 5/8	24 2/8	24 2/8	17 1/8	5 6/8	5 5/8	12	6	Beltrami Co., Minn.	Unknown	Jim Smith	1924	34
213	24 4/8	24	17 5/8	4 7/8	4 5/8	10	10	Kinney Co., Texas	Rankin F. O'Neill	John L. Stein	DC 1960	35
212 5/8	24 6/8	25 2/8	17 6/8	5	5	11	13	Glentworth, Sask.	Garnet Fortnum	Garnet Fortnum	NO 1984	36
212 2/8	21	19	24	4	4	9	16	Parker Co., Texas	Pleasant Mitchell	Pleasant Mitchell	NO 1982	37
212 2/8	25	25 4/8	19 4/8	5 2/8	5 2/8	11	13	Webb Co., Texas	Claude W. King	Claude W. King	DC 1949	37
212	26 7/8	25	16 7/8	4 7/8	5 1/8	14	13	Becker Co., Minn.	Unknown	George W. Flaim	1922	39
211 4/8	23 2/8	23 2/8	13 6/8	6 2/8	5 6/8	12	10	Dodge Co., Wisc.	Michael A. Koehler	Michael A. Koehler	NO 1984	40
211 2/8	27 7/8	27	19 2/8	6 2/8	6 1/8	8	9	Marshall Co., Minn.	Picked Up	Robert Sands	PU 1959	41
210 3/8	24 3/8	25	19 2/8	5	5	13	12	Lyon Co., Ky.	Roy D. Lee	Roy D. Lee	NO 1975	42
210	23 4/8	23 6/8	20 3/8	5 7/8	6 2/8	9	8	Gregory Co., S. D.	Richard C. Berte	Richard C. Berte	NO 1982	43
209 7/8	20 6/8	19 7/8	19 6/8	4 7/8	4 6/8	13	11	Hawkins Co., Tenn.	Johnny W. Byington	Johnny W. Byington	NO 1982	44
209 6/8	23 2/8	24 1/8	22 6/8	4 4/8	4 6/8	8	10	Edwards Co., Kan.	Tim C. Schaller	Tim C. Schaller	DC 1984	45
209 6/8	27	27 2/8	17 1/8	5 2/8	5 1/8	11	10	Koochiching Co., Minn.	Harry Van Keuren	Louis E. Muench	NO 1929	45
209 3/8	23 5/8	21 6/8	16 6/8	4 3/8	4 4/8	11	10	Grant Co., Wisc.	Tim Yanna	Tim Yanna	NO 1982	47
209	26 7/8	28 2/8	23 6/8	5 4/8	5 4/8	8	9	Lee Co., Iowa	Glenn L. Carter, II	Glenn L. Carter, II	DC 1984	48
208 7/8	26 7/8	26 7/8	26 6/8	5 3/8	5 3/8	10	8	Charles Co., Md.	Robert A. Boarman	Robert A. Boarman	NO 1984	49
208 5/8	27 4/8	28	22	6	5 7/8	10	8	Taylor Co., Wisc.	Unknown	Mac's Taxidermy	PR 1945	50
208 2/8	26 5/8	24	19 3/8	5 3/8	7 3/8	10	10	Chauvin, Alta.	Picked Up	Shane Hansen	PU	51
208 2/8	24 3/8	23 4/8	19	5	5	7	11	Monona Co., Iowa	Rob L. Cadwallader	Rob L. Cadwallader	DC 1984	51
208 2/8	27	26 1/8	20 4/8	4 7/8	4 6/8	11	11	St. Louis Co., Minn.	Walter H. Enzenauer	Walter H. Enzenauer	NO 1961	51
208 1/8	25 6/8	24 2/8	18 2/8	4 7/8	5	12	12	Mexico	Unknown	William M. Day	1959	54
207 7/8	23 7/8	23 5/8	21 3/8	4 5/8	4 7/8	13	19	Suffolk Co., N. Y.	George Hackal	Gary C. Boyer	1950	55
207 5/8	27 1/8	26 5/8	22 2/8	6 6/8	7	11	9	Lincoln Co., Minn.	Joe Ness	Joe Ness	NO 1961	56
207 5/8	24	23 6/8	23 6/8	6 3/8	6 2/8	10	8	Buffalo Co., Wisc.	Dennis M. Eberhart	Dennis M. Eberhart	NO 1984	56
207 1/8	22	23 7/8	19 2/8	8	8 5/8	14	13	Buffalo Co., Neb.	Unknown	John L. Stein	1978	58
207	23 4/8	23 1/8	18 4/8	5 6/8	6 4/8	16	13	Bayfield Co., Wisc.	Francis F. Zifko	Francis F. Zifko	NO 1954	59
206 7/8	26 2/8	29 5/8	27 7/8	5 2/8	5 4/8	11	10	Wright Co., Minn.	Richard A. Erickson	Richard A. Erickson	NO 1983	60
206 5/8	26	24 2/8	19 6/8	5 3/8	5 2/8	7	12	Chase Co., Kan.	Jay A. Talkington	Jay A. Talkington	DC 1983	61
206 4/8	23 2/8	23 1/8	16 4/8	5 4/8	5 4/8	14	8	Norman Co., Minn.	Unknown	Tom Williams	1950	62
206 3/8	22 7/8	23 2/8	19	4 7/8	4 5/8	11	11	Webb Co., Texas	Willard V. Brenizer	Gerry Elliff	1942	63
206 2/8	28 4/8	28 5/8	25	5 5/8	5 6/8	9	11	Cortland Co., N. Y.	Hank Hayes	Interlaken Sportsmans Club	1947	64

Score								Locality	Hunter	Owner		Date	Rank
206 1/8	31 1/2	24 3/8	22 7/8	6	5 5/8	9	7	Piscataquis Co., Maine	Ralph E. Dow	Ralph E. Dow	NO	1964	64
206 1/8	31	25 3/8	18 7/8	5 5/8	5 1/8	8	9	Dunn Co., N. D.	Kenneth E. DeLap	Kenneth E. DeLap	NO	1982	66
205 7/8	27 7/8	28 7/8	19 7/8	5	5 1/8	10	8	Switzerland Co., Ind.	Paul Graf	Paul Graf	NO	1981	67
205 7/8	23 7/8	23 7/8	17 5/8	5 4/8	5 4/8	9	13	Clark Co., Mo.	Allen L. Courtney	Allen L. Courtney	NO	1983	67
205 7/8	25	23 3/8	20 2/8	6	5 4/8	13	12	Missoula Co., Mont.	Unknown	John L. Stein		1973	67
205 5/8	23 3/8	23	20 3/8	5 4/8	5 3/8	9	10	Cloud Co., Kan.	Gary G. Pingel	Gary G. Pingel	DC	1982	70
205 5/8	24 3/8	24	21	5	5 2/8	9	9	Ritchie Co., W. Va.	Ed Bailey	Ed Bailey	NO	1979	70
205 5/8	23 1/8	21 1/8	18 1/8	4 7/8	4 4/8	12	12	Lowndes Co., Miss.	Joe W. Shurden	Joe W. Shurden	JA	1976	70
205 5/8	25 3/8	26 1/8	18 1/8	4 5/8	4 4/8	11	9	Minn.	Unknown	Greg Jensen		1965	70
205	26 3/8	26 3/8	16 7/8	6 1/8	5 7/8	12	9	St. Louis Co., Minn.	Ed Nelson	George W. Flaim	NO	1964	74
204 7/8	26 2/8	26 3/8	18 5/8	5 1/8	5	9	7	Nemaha Co., Kan.	Unknown	John L. Stein			75
204 3/8	23 4/8	24	20 3/8	5 5/8	5 5/8	10	12	Waukesha Co., Wisc.	Unknown	Mac's Taxidermy			76
204 2/8	25 5/8	23 3/8	17 7/8	5 1/8	5 4/8	7	15	Silver Lake, Alta.	Edwin Nelson	Gary Padleski	NO	1980	77
204 1/8	28 5/8	25 7/8	22 7/8	6 1/8	6 1/8	12	9	Charlotte Co., N. B.	Gary L. Lister	Gary L. Lister	NO	1984	78
204	23 3/8	23 6/8	18 3/8	5 5/8	5 5/8	13	14	Holbein, Sask.	Jesse Bates	Jesse Bates	NO	1981	79
204	26 5/8	27 1/8	21 7/8	5 1/8	5 4/8	9	11	Webster Co., Ky.	Jeff Robinson	Jeff Robinson	NO	1982	79
204	26 1/8	26 1/8	16 2/8	5 1/8	5 3/8	10	8	Carlton Co., Minn.	Erick Zack	Glen Van Guilder	NO	1964	79
203 7/8	27 7/8	27 7/8	17 4/8	4 7/8	4 7/8	11	8	Eastland Co., Texas	Picked Up	William B. Wright, Jr.	PU	1920	82
203 6/8	24 2/8	25 3/8	16 5/8	4	3 7/8	8	8	Maverick Co., Texas	Picked Up	Richard H. Bennett	PU	1941	83
203 3/8	28	27 3/8	20	5 1/8	5 3/8	7	10	George Lake, N. B.	Henry Kirk	Ron Kirk		1903	83
203 5/8	24 3/8	26 3/8	21 7/8	5 5/8	5 7/8	12	11	St. Louis Co., Minn.	Picked Up	Phillip A. Roalstad	PU	1981	85
203 3/8	25 1/8	24 4/8	21	5 4/8	5 3/8	8	10	Olmsted Co., Minn.	Logan Behrens	Logan Behrens	NO	1961	86
203 1/8	23 7/8	24 4/8	19 5/8	5 4/8	5 7/8	10	12	Wetzel Co., W. Va.	Tom Kirkhart	Tom Kirkhart	NO	1981	87
203 1/8	23 5/8	25 1/8	16	4 7/8	4 4/8	11	10	Koochiching Co., Minn.	Unknown	George W. Flaim		1934	87
203	26 1/8	27 5/8	17 7/8	4 5/8	4 5/8	9	8	Jefferson Co., Kan.	Dale Heston	Dale Heston	DC	1982	89
202 5/8	23	24	14 7/8	5 4/8	5	9	9	McMullen Co., Texas	Picked Up	Patrick L. Seals	PU	1984	90
202 4/8	24 4/8	24 6/8	16 6/8	5	4 7/8	13	12	Missoula Co., Mont.	Unknown	Robert A. Bracken		1962	91
202 3/8	26 1/8	27	20 6/8	5 1/8	5 1/8	10	10	Aitkin Co., Minn.	Joe Clarke	Joe Clarke	NO	1960	92
202 1/8	28 7/8	28 1/8	16 7/8	5 4/8	5 4/8	11	15	Oktibbeha Co., Miss.	Oliver H. Lindig	Oliver H. Lindig	NO	1983	93
202 1/8	25 4/8	25 4/8	19 1/8	4 5/8	4 5/8	10	10	Pennington Co., Minn.	R. Scott Sorvig	R. Scott Sorvig	NO	1980	93
202	26 6/8	28 6/8	26 6/8	5	5	7	7	Knox Co., Maine	Skip Black	Skip Black	NO	1981	95
201 7/8	28 2/8	27	17 2/8	6	7 2/8	11	11	Itasca Co., Minn.	Picked Up	J. Gorden & G. Dopp	PU	1981	96
201 5/8	26 1/8	23 3/8	26 2/8	5 2/8	4 5/8	8	9	Waldo Co., Maine	James A. Tripp, Sr.	James A. Tripp, Sr.	NO	1959	97
201 3/8	26 3/8	27 3/8	16 5/8	5	5 4/8	10	7	Itasca Co., Minn.	Cecil L. Johnson	Cecil L. Johnson	NO	1976	98
201 3/8	26 7/8	26 3/8	16	5 3/8	5 5/8	17	14	Pennington Co., Minn.	Glenn Tasa	Glenn Tasa		1940	98
201	23 3/8	21 7/8	19 3/8	6 2/8	7 2/8	8	11	Anoka Co., Minn.	Unknown	John L. Stein		1977	100
200 7/8	23 4/8	24 3/8	21	4 4/8	4 5/8	11	10	Kleberg Co., Texas	Picked Up	John A. Larkin	PU	1982	101
200 6/8	24 7/8	25 7/8	25 1/8	6 4/8	6 6/8	8	11	Wapello Co., Iowa	Rod A. McKelvey	Rod A. McKelvey	DC	1983	102
200 3/8	24 4/8	25 1/8	18	5 1/8	5 5/8	9	11	Butler Co., Neb.	Joyce L. Novak	Joyce L. Novak	NO	1983	103
200 3/8	27	23 3/8	24 5/8	5 2/8	5	10	12	Knox Co., Ohio	Albert Hall	Albert Hall	NO	1983	103
200 3/8	23 5/8	24	18 3/8	4 5/8	4 4/8	8	8	Lake of the Woods Co., Minn.	Mark H. Hagen	Mark H. Hagen	NO	1974	103
200 1/8	24 3/8	24 5/8	20 3/8	5	5	9	8	Blaine Co., Neb.	Pauline C. Sander	Pauline C. Sander	NO	1983	106
199 7/8	23 3/8	23 5/8	17 5/8	5 5/8	5 5/8	10	10	Flathead Co., Mont.	Unknown	Tom Williams	PR	1980	107

Whitetail Deer (*Non-Typical Antlers*)—Continued
Odocoileus virginianus virginianus and certain related subspecies

Score	Length of Main Beam R.	L.	Inside Spread	Circumference at Smallest Place Between Burr and First Point R.	L.	Number of Points R.	L.	Locality Killed	By Whom Killed	Owner	Date Killed	Rank
199 4/8	25 6/8	25 4/8	21 2/8	5 6/8	5 6/8	9	9	Wilcox Co., Ala.	Billy W. Morton	Billy W. Morton	NO 1975	107
199 2/8	28 6/8	27 6/8	23 6/8	5 2/8	5 2/8	7	9	Winston Co., Ala.	James W. Huckbay	James W. Huckbay	DC 1973	109
199 1/8	25 2/8	25 6/8	17 4/8	5 1/8	5 2/8	10	13	St. Louis Co., Minn.	Orville Schultz	Orville Schultz	NO 1978	110
199	24 6/8	27 6/8	19 6/8	5	5	8	7	Westaskiwin, Alta.	John Miller	John Miller	NO 1984	111
199	22 6/8	21	17 6/8	5 3/8	5	13	7	Clark Co., Wisc.	George Mashin	Douglas Wampole	NO 1946	111
199	26 3/8	25	19 1/8	5 1/8	5	10	8	Yellow Medicine Co., Minn.	William A. Botten	William A. Botten	NO 1976	111
198 7/8	29 3/8	28 3/8	24	4 6/8	4 6/8	8	7	Ripley Co., Ind.	William L. Wagner	William L. Wagner	NO 1982	114
198 6/8	29 1/8	27 1/8	15 7/8	5 3/8	5 3/8	11	7	Fillmore Co., Minn.	Phillip Hansen	Phillip Hansen	NO 1973	115
198 5/8	26 1/8	25 7/8	22 4/8	5	4 7/8	8	7	Webb Co., Texas	Larry Bickham	Larry Bickham	DC 1962	116
198 4/8	22 6/8	26	21 1/8	5 2/8	4 5/8	12	8	Wheeler Co., Ga.	David Frost	David Frost	NO 1983	117
198 4/8	25	26 2/8	23 6/8	4 6/8	4 6/8	7	8	Webb Co., Texas	Alvin C. Santleben, Jr.	Alvin C. Santleben, Jr.	DC 1983	117
198 3/8	26 3/8	26 1/8	17 5/8	4 2/8	4 2/8	8	10	Montgomery Co., Tenn.	Clarence McElhaney	Clarence McElhaney	OT 1978	119
197 7/8	27 1/8	28 1/8	25	5 4/8	5 2/8	9	8	Cheyenne Co., Neb.	Reid Block	Reid Block	NO 1984	120
197 6/8	20 7/8	22 6/8	22 6/8	5	5	8	11	Unknown	Unknown	John L. Stein	PR 1984	121
197 5/8	25 1/8	24 6/8	22 4/8	5 4/8	5 4/8	10	8	Blue Earth Co., Minn.	Daniel R. Nelson	Daniel R. Nelson	NO 1981	122
197 5/8	20	24	18	8 4/8	4 7/8	12	8	Luce Co., Mich.	Sid Jones	Jim Deavereaux	NO 1917	122
197 4/8	24 4/8	24 6/8	21 6/8	7	6 6/8	8	10	Chippewa Co., Minn.	Dean D. Anspach	Dean D. Anspach	NO 1973	124
197 4/8	25 3/8	26 3/8	16 6/8	5 1/8	5 3/8	6	8	Lyon Co., Kan.	John R. Clifton	John R. Clifton	NO 1984	124
197 4/8	26 3/8	27 3/8	18	4 6/8	4 5/8	10	12	Dooly Co., Ga.	Wayne Griffin	Wayne Griffin	DC 1984	124
197 3/8	27 3/8	26 3/8	20 4/8	5 2/8	5 2/8	8	9	Faribault Co., Minn.	Randy L. Sandt	Randy L. Sandt	NO 1982	127
197 3/8	22 3/8	23 7/8	21 6/8	5 5/8	5 1/8	14	10	Marshall Co., Kan.	Lloyd Wenzl	Lloyd Wenzl	DC 1983	127
197 3/8	25	26	17 4/8	5 5/8	5 5/8	9	9	Stevens Co., Wash.	Coulston W. Drummond	Coulston W. Drummond	OT 1948	127
197 2/8	27 1/8	26 5/8	21	5	5	8	8	Hancock Co., Maine	Hollis Patterson	Reginald R. Clark	PR 1950	130
197 2/8	24 5/8	24 3/8	18 5/8	4 4/8	4 3/8	9	14	Redvers, Sask.	Eugene M. Gazda	Eugene M. Gazda	NO 1984	130
197 1/8	25 3/8	25 4/8	21	5 1/8	5 7/8	10	10	Jefferson Co., Ill.	Unknown	Jeff Sartaine	PU 1983	132
197 1/8	28 5/8	26 6/8	18 7/8	5	5 1/8	9	11	Worth Co., Mo.	Gary G. Kinder	Gary G. Kinder	NO 1982	132
197 1/8	23	22 7/8	17 7/8	5 1/8	4 6/8	10	9	Noble Co., Okla.	Kenneth R. Bright	Kenneth R. Bright	NO 1982	132
197 1/8	26 1/8	26 3/8	17 3/8	5 2/8	4 6/8	8	7	Jackson Co., Mo.	Jim Martin	Jim Martin	DC 1984	132
197	21 4/8	22 1/8	15 4/8	5 4/8	5	11	11	Rosebud Co., Mont.	Mark D. Holmes	Mark D. Holmes	NO 1983	136
196 7/8	24 5/8	24 7/8	19	5	5	10	8	Edmunds Co., S. D.	Melvin Borkirchert	Melvin Borkirchert	DC 1983	137
196 6/8	25 5/8	25 1/8	20 6/8	5 7/8	5 5/8	9	9	Van Buren Co., Iowa	Kenneth R. Barker	Kenneth R. Barker	DC 1984	138
196 3/8	24 3/8	18 3/8	24	5 4/8	5 3/8	9	10	Clark Co., Ill.	Mary K. LeCrone	Mary K. LeCrone	NO 1982	139

Score								Locality	Hunter	Owner	Date	Rank
196 1/8	24 3/8	24 1/8	19 3/8	5 4/8	5 6/8	8	11	Nemaha Co., Neb.	Picked Up	Gale Sup	PU 1975	140
196	28 7/8	30 2/8	25 1/8	5 4/8	5 2/8	12	10	Annapolis Valley, N. S.	David Cabral	David Cabral	NO 1984	141
195 7/8	26 3/8	26 2/8	19 2/8	6	6	10	7	Beltrami Co., Minn.	Ollie Jamtaas	James Gorden	1938	142
195 6/8	25 4/8	26 4/8	19 4/8	6 6/8	7	11	12	Roseau Co., Minn.	George H. Tepley	George H. Tepley	NO 1984	143
195 5/8	26 7/8	26 1/8	21 3/8	5 3/8	5 2/8	8	7	Story Co., Iowa	Jordan L. Larson	Jordan L. Larson	DC 1983	144
195 4/8	25 5/8	16 2/8	20 6/8	6	6	7	7	Bureau Co., Ill.	Picked Up	John Cotter	PU 1976	145
195 4/8	26	25 3/8	16 5/8	4 7/8	4 6/8	10	7	Winona Co., Minn.	Patrick Bartholomew	Patrick Bartholomew	NO 1976	145
195 3/8	27 3/8	29 7/8	20 5/8	6	5 5/8	6	7	Colquitt Co., Ga.	Olen P. Ross	Olen P. Ross	NO 1976	147
195 3/8	25 5/8	25 4/8	22 4/8	5	4 5/8	9	12	Webb Co., Texas	Sidney A. Lindsay, Jr.	Sidney A. Lindsay, Jr.	DC 1983	147
195	22 4/8	23 5/8	20 3/8	5 4/8	5 2/8	8	9	Calhoun Co., Ill.	Roger F. Becker	Roger F. Becker	NO 1983	149
193 3/8	22	23 5/8	14 2/8	7	6 5/8	10	15	Trinity Co., Texas	Earl Smith	Syble Smith	NO 1960	150
193 2/8	24 4/8	23 5/8	16 5/8	5 4/8	5 2/8	10	7	Coahuila, Mexico	H. Kent Hill	H. Kent Hill	JA 1985	151
192	23 3/8	23 5/8	18 5/8	5 3/8	5 4/8	9	8	McLeod Co., Minn.	Leonard Krulikosky, Jr.	Leonard Krulikosky, Jr.	NO 1982	152
190 3/8	24 5/8	22 5/8	23 5/8	5	5	11	10	Coahuila, Mexico	Picked Up	Javier de los Santos	PU 1983	153
189 3/8	20 6/8	21 1/8	16 5/8	5	4 7/8	9	11	Carroll Co., Ill.	Thomas D. Drish	Thomas D. Drish	NO 1984	154
189 1/8	25 5/8	26 5/8	17 7/8	4 5/8	4 5/8	9	9	Wilcox Co., Ga.	Ronnie Wilcox	Ronnie Wilcox	NO 1984	155
267 7/8 *	25	24 5/8	22 5/8	6 1/8	6 2/8	20	18	Shoal Lake, Alta.	Jerry Froma	Jerry Froma	NO 1984	
259 *	25 4/8	26 7/8	19 5/8	6 1/8	5 7/8	15	16	Washington Co., Maine	Hill Gould	Charles T. Arnold	OT 1910	

*Final Score subject to revision by additional verifying measurements.

Coues' Whitetail Deer *(Typical Antlers)*

Odocoileus virginianus couesi

Minimum Score 100 | **World's Record 143**

Score	Length of Main Beam R.	Length of Main Beam L.	Inside Spread	Circumference at Smallest Place Between Burr and First Point R.	Circumference at Smallest Place Between Burr and First Point L.	Number of Points R.	Number of Points L.	Locality Killed	By Whom Killed	Owner	Date Killed	Rank
118	18 2/8	19 2/8	12 6/8	3 5/8	3 7/8	4	4	Santa Cruz Co., Ariz.	Michael L. Valenzuela	Michael L. Valenzuela	NO 1982	1
113 2/8	19 3/8	18 5/8	16	4 3/8	4 4/8	4	4	Gila Co., Ariz.	David W. Miller, Jr.	David W. Miller, Jr.	DC 1984	2
112 5/8	18 6/8	19 1/8	13 1/8	3 4/8	3 5/8	5	6	Sonora, Mexico	William W. Sharp	William W. Sharp	NO 1968	3
112 2/8	16 2/8	16	13 2/8	4 6/8	4 6/8	4	5	Pima Co., Ariz.	William W. Sharp	William W. Sharp	NO 1981	4
112	15 4/8	15 6/8	12 4/8	3 6/8	3 7/8	5	5	Greenlee Co., Ariz.	Jerald S. Wager	Jerald S. Wager	NO 1982	5
111 3/8	17 6/8	18 5/8	16 5/8	4 1/8	4 1/8	4	4	Santa Cruz Co., Ariz.	Frank Yubeta, III	Frank Yubeta, III	DC 1983	6
111 2/8	16 4/8	16 4/8	15 2/8	3 4/8	3 4/8	5	5	Santa Cruz Co., Ariz.	Robert L. Rabb	Robert L. Rabb	NO 1977	7
110 7/8	16 6/8	16 5/8	13 1/8	4	4	6	4	Pima Co., Ariz.	William W. Sharp	William W. Sharp	NO 1974	8
110 2/8	18 6/8	18	16	4 1/8	4	4	5	Pima Co., Ariz.	David G. Mattausch	David G. Mattausch	DC 1984	9
109 4/8	18 3/8	18 4/8	12 4/8	4 1/8	4 1/8	4	5	Pima Co., Ariz.	William W. Sharp	William W. Sharp	NO 1982	10
107 2/8	17 4/8	17 2/8	16 5/8	4 1/8	4 1/8	5	5	Pima Co., Ariz.	William W. Sharp	William W. Sharp	OT 1961	11
107 1/8	17 3/8	16	12 1/8	4	3 6/8	5	6	Santa Cruz Co., Ariz.	Richard G. Acedo, Jr.	Richard G. Acedo, Jr.	DC 1984	12
106 2/8	16 6/8	16 4/8	15	4 3/8	4 3/8	4	4	Santa Cruz Co., Ariz.	Jack K. Rouge	Jack K. Rouge	DC 1984	13
104 1/8	17 6/8	17 6/8	13 4/8	4 1/8	3 7/8	4	6	Santa Cruz Co., Ariz.	Warren A. Cartier	Warren A. Cartier	DC 1984	14
120 5/8*	20 1/8	19 2/8	16 3/8	3 5/8	3 6/8	4	4	Cochise Co., Ariz.	Becki D. Goffrier	Becki D. Goffrier	DC 1984	
115 4/8*	18 6/8	18 2/8	15	4	4	5	4	Cochise Co., Ariz.	Bill Byrd	Bill Byrd	NO 1983	
115*	17 2/8	17 1/8	17	3 5/8	3 4/8	5	5	Yavapai Co., Ariz.	Jim D. Snodgrass	Jim D. Snodgrass	DC 1983	

*Final Score subject to revision by additional verifying measurements.

Coues' Whitetail Deer (Non-Typical Antlers)
Odocoileus virginianus couesi

Minimum Score 105 — World's Record 151 5/8

Score	Length of Main Beam R.	L.	Inside Spread	Circumference at Smallest Place Between Burr and First Point R.	L.	Number of Points R.	L.	Locality Killed	By Whom Killed	Owner	Date Killed	Rank
143 6/8	17 3/8	16 5/8	14 5/8	4 2/8	5	6	9	Pima Co., Ariz.	Oscar C. Truex	Oscar C. Truex	DC 1983	1
125 7/8	16 7/8	16 2/8	13 4/8	4 4/8	4 2/8	6	8	Pima Co., Ariz.	Fred W. Havens	Fred W. Havens	OT 1966	2
124 5/8	20	18 4/8	17 7/8	3 7/8	4	6	6	Pinal Co., Ariz.	C. J. Adair	C. J. Adair	OT 1966	3
121	16 6/8	16 5/8	14	3 5/8	3 5/8	8	6	Gila Co, Ariz.	James E. Stinson	James E. Stinson	OT 1983	4
120 7/8	17 2/8	17 6/8	15 5/8	5 1/8	4 7/8	6	6	Gila Co., Ariz.	David M. Conrad	David M. Conrad	NO 1982	5
128 5/8 *	16 4/8	17 1/8	12 5/8	4 3/8	4 4/8	6	6	Hidalgo Co., N. M.	Jack Samson	Jack Samson	NO 1984	
127 6/8 *	17 2/8	17 3/8	13 5/8	4 1/8	4 2/8	6	6	Hidalgo Co., N. M.	Michael C. Finley	Michael C. Finley	NO 1983	

*Final Score subject to revision by additional verifying measurements.

Canada Moose

Alces alces americana and *Alces alces andersoni*

Minimum Score 185 **World's Record 242**

Three categories of moose are recognized for records keeping, with boundaries based on geographic lines. Canada moose includes trophies from Newfoundland and Canada (except for the Yukon and Northwest Territories), Minnesota, and Maine.

Score	Greatest Spread	Length of Palm		Width of Palm		Circumference of Beam at Smallest Place		Number of Normal Points		Locality Killed	By Whom Killed	Owner	Date Killed	Rank
		R.	L.	R.	L.	R.	L.	R.	L.					
223 5/8	64 7/8	46 1/8	47 1/8	17 4/8	14	7 4/8	7 2/8	12	12	Island Lake, Man.	Indian	Jack E. Dunn	1980	1
218 6/8	58 2/8	42 6/8	40 4/8	15	15 4/8	8 7/8	8 6/8	16	16	Kennicott Lake, B.C.	Mike Popoff	Mike Popoff	SE 1984	2
217 1/8	63 1/8	40 4/8	43 6/8	14 3/8	15	8 2/8	8 1/8	14	15	Liard River, B.C.	Wayne E. Dalgleish	Wayne E. Dalgleish	OT 1984	3
216 2/8	62 4/8	46 7/8	43 6/8	14 4/8	13 4/8	7 7/8	7 5/8	15	12	Cassiar Mts., B.C.	Don L. Corley	Don L. Corley	NO 1984	4
215	57 4/8	43	45 1/8	15 5/8	14	7 6/8	7 6/8	15	14	Ice Mt., B.C.	David H. Hilsberg	David H. Hilsberg	AG 1985	5
214 4/8	62	42 2/8	38 6/8	15 7/8	17	7 5/8	7 5/8	14	16	Piscataquis Co., Maine	Desmond Harvey	Desmond Harvey	OT 1984	6
212	54	39 4/8	39	16 4/8	17 4/8	7 4/8	7 4/8	16	18	Grayling River, B.C.	Arnold E. Dado	Arnold E. Dado	OT 1984	7
208 6/8	61	41 2/8	41 1/8	14 7/8	14 5/8	7 1/8	7 2/8	11	13	Ketchum Lake, B.C.	Gailand K. Hann	Gailand K. Hann	SE 1985	8
207 5/8	52 7/8	44 2/8	44	15 7/8	13 6/8	7 5/8	7 5/8	16	12	Ash Mt., B.C.	Robert E. Rabon	Robert E. Rabon	SE 1984	9
206 7/8	62 5/8	41	40 3/8	13 3/8	13 2/8	7 4/8	7 4/8	11	13	Somerset Co., Maine	Stephen D. Cole	Stephen D. Cole	OT 1984	10
205 6/8	54 2/8	42	41 4/8	14 1/8	16 6/8	7 6/8	7 5/8	14	13	Turnagain River, B.C.	Audrey E. Crabtree	Audrey E. Crabtree	SE 1984	11
204 2/8	65	41 6/8	39 5/8	15 1/8	13	7 1/8	7	11	10	Peace River, Alta.	Wilbur C. Savage	Wilbur C. Savage	OT 1984	12
203 5/8	59 5/8	39 2/8	41 7/8	13 5/8	13 1/8	7 5/8	7 6/8	12	12	Gladys Lake, B.C.	Harry Hoeft	Harry Hoeft	SE 1984	13
203 5/8	56 3/8	43 1/8	45	13 1/8	13 2/8	7 4/8	7 3/8	16	10	Surmont Lake, Alta.	Daryl Goodine	Daryl Goodine	SE 1984	13
203 2/8	59 6/8	39 3/8	38 3/8	13 4/8	15 7/8	8	7 7/8	12	12	Wapiti River, Alta.	David L. Savage	David L. Savage	OT 1984	15
202 6/8	58	43 1/8	40 3/8	11 4/8	11 7/8	7 4/8	7 4/8	14	13	Bee Peak, B.C.	Dennis J. Eakin	Dennis J. Eakin	SE 1984	16
201 6/8	54 6/8	41 1/8	40 2/8	13 2/8	12	7 2/8	7 4/8	14	15	Toad River, B.C.	Dennis R. Gustafson	Dennis R. Gustafson	NO 1982	17
200 5/8	59 5/8	40 2/8	41 6/8	14	13 2/8	8 2/8	8	9	14	Robb Lake, B.C.	Richard L. Bostrom	Richard L. Bostrom	SE 1985	18
200 3/8	53 1/8	40 6/8	38 6/8	13 7/8	14 3/8	7	7 1/8	16	14	Cypress Creek, B.C.	Raymond A. Racette	Raymond A. Racette	SE 1984	19
199 4/8	58 6/8	40 1/8	40 4/8	12 2/8	14 1/8	7	7	11	11	Aroostook Co., Maine	Richard Neal	Richard Neal	SE 1983	20
199 1/8	51 5/8	43 4/8	43 4/8	11 6/8	13 3/8	7 4/8	7 5/8	11	12	Coutts River, Alta.	George J. Thimer	George J. Thimer	DC 1983	21
199	51 4/8	41 6/8	44 1/8	17 6/8	15 3/8	7 5/8	7 7/8	14	9	Fox Creek, Alta.	Ken McDonald	Merv Zaddery	1969	22
198 6/8	53 4/8	40 6/8	40 7/8	13 6/8	17	7 3/8	7 1/8	11	11	Mt. Laurier, B.C.	Don Miller	Don Miller	OT 1985	23
198 1/8	50 5/8	39 5/8	41	16	13 6/8	7 3/8	8 1/8	14	13	Fraser River, B.C.	J. Henry Scown	J. Henry Scown	NO 1973	24
198 1/8	55 7/8	42 4/8	42 7/8	12	13 2/8	7 5/8	7 5/8	9	9	Hluey Lakes, B.C.	Dale Campbell	Dale Campbell	OT 1982	24
196 7/8	62 3/8	38 3/8	43	13 6/8	12	7 3/8	7 4/8	14	10	Pink Mountain, B.C.	Tony J. Farace	Tony J. Farace	SE 1984	26

Score									Locality	Hunter	Owner	Date	Rank
196 6/8	57 6/8	36	38 2/8	16 4/8	16 3/8	7 3/8	7 1/8	10	12	Wapiti River, Alta.	John J. Seeliger	John J. Seeliger	OT 1985	27
196 2/8	56 2/8	35 4/8	37	14	13 7/8	7 4/8	7 3/8	14	13	Aroostook Co., Maine	R. E. Gatchell & C. Dole	Robert E. Gatchell	SE 1982	28
196 1/8	51 1/8	41 3/8	42 4/8	12 4/8	12 3/8	8 1/8	7 7/8	13	11	Penobscot Co., Maine	Richard A. Record	Richard A. Record	SE 1982	29
195 7/8	57 4/8	37 7/8	40 6/8	11 3/8	16	7 3/8	7 2/8	13	13	Somerset Co., Maine	Frank White	Frank White	SE 1983	30
195 4/8	55 4/8	41 4/8	41 7/8	14 2/8	12 6/8	6 6/8	6 6/8	9	9	Turnagain Lake, B.C.	Fenton C. Carter	Fenton C. Carter	SE 1985	30
195 3/8	55 7/8	39 1/8	43 5/8	15	13 7/8	6 6/8	7	10	13	Chip Lake, Alta.	Elon Johnson	Elon Johnson	NO 1984	32
195 2/8	57 3/8	41 2/8	42	12	12 3/8	7 3/8	7 3/8	8	8	Nuthinaw Mt., B.C.	Robert S. Curtis	Robert S. Curtis	SE 1984	33
195 1/8	61 3/8	39	34 2/8	14 1/8	15 1/8	6 4/8	5 7/8	13	14	Terminus Mt., B.C.	Modesta S. Williams	Modesta S. Williams	SE 1982	34
195 1/8	58 7/8	38 3/8	38 3/8	11 5/8	12 2/8	7 2/8	7 3/8	11	11	Ash Mt., B.C.	H. Frank Grainger	H. Frank Grainger	SE 1984	34
195	61 4/8	37 7/8	36 6/8	16 7/8	14 3/8	7 5/8	8	10	8	Aroostook Co., Maine	Sterling W. Waterman	Sterling W. Waterman	SE 1982	36
195	53 3/8	40 1/8	40	12 4/8	13 7/8	7 2/8	7 2/8	11	11	Piscatiquis Co., Maine	Lester Whitten	Cecile D. Therrien	SE 1982	36
194 5/8	55 1/8	38	38	14	15 1/8	7 2/8	6 2/8	11	11	Robb Lake, B.C.	James A. Askins	James A. Askins	SE 1985	38
189 3/8	61 3/8	37 1/8	39 4/8	13 1/8	13 2/8	7	6 2/8	13	7	Graham Inlet, B.C.	William V. Comn, Jr.	William V. Comn, Jr.	OT 1983	39
228 3/8*	62 2/8	48 2/8	46 3/8	17 1/8	15 1/8	7 4/8	7 3/8	17	14	Buffalo Lake, Man.	Pierre A. Lachance	Pierre A. Lachance	SE 1985	
219 1/8*	65 3/8	41	40 1/8	13	13 5/8	7 5/8	7 3/8	18	16	Carrot River, Sask.	Stewart Hilliar	James Hilliar	NO 1984	

*Final Score subject to revision by additional verifying measurements.

Alaska-Yukon Moose
Alces alces gigas

Minimum Score 210   **World's Record 255**

Alaska-Yukon moose includes trophies from Alaska, the Yukon Territory, and the Northwest Territories.

Score	Greatest Spread	Length of Palm R.	Length of Palm L.	Width of Palm R.	Width of Palm L.	Circumference of Beam at Smallest Place R.	Circumference of Beam at Smallest Place L.	Number of Normal Points R.	Number of Normal Points L.	Locality Killed	By Whom Killed	Owner	Date Killed	Rank
249⁵/₈	69⁵/₈	46⁵/₈	43³/₈	21²/₈	22	8²/₈	8⁴/₈	22	17	Granite Mt., Alaska	David B. Parent	Earl D. Hahn	SE 1982	1
230⁶/₈	67⁵/₈	53⁵/₈	52⁶/₈	13¹/₈	14²/₈	7⁷/₈	7⁶/₈	9	8	Innoko River, Alaska	Leslie R. Hunter	Leslie R. Hunter	SE 1983	2
230⁵/₈	64¹/₈	46⁷/₈	48³/₈	15³/₈	16⁴/₈	8	8²/₈	13	14	Alaska Pen., Alaska	Lucky Christoph	Carl V. Christoph	SE 1981	3
228⁶/₈	63⁴/₈	47²/₈	44⁷/₈	15⁵/₈	15³/₈	7	6⁵/₈	19	16	Holitna River, Alaska	Scott R. Sexson	Scott R. Sexson	SE 1978	4
228⁴/₈	71	47²/₈	47³/₈	15⁴/₈	15¹/₈	7³/₈	7⁵/₈	12	10	Tagagawik River, Alaska	Jesse C. Sprague	Jesse C. Sprague	DC 1983	5
227⁴/₈	65⁵/₈	46²/₈	49¹/₈	17¹/₈	18³/₈	7⁷/₈	8²/₈	10	10	Dog Salmon River, Alaska	John C. Davis	John C. Davis	SE 1984	6
227⁵/₈	67⁵/₈	45	46³/₈	14⁵/₈	17⁵/₈	7²/₈	8	13	13	Susitna River, Alaska	Darryl G. Sanford	Darryl G. Sanford	SE 1981	7
227⁴/₈	66	44²/₈	42⁵/₈	16³/₈	16¹/₈	7⁴/₈	7⁵/₈	15	15	Elliott Lake, Yukon	Paul E. Wollenman	Paul E. Wollenman	SE 1984	8
227³/₈	67⁵/₈	48	49⁵/₈	17	13²/₈	8⁴/₈	8⁴/₈	13	10	Bonnet Plume Lake, Yukon	A. H. Clise	A. H. Clise	SE 1982	9
227¹/₈	74³/₈	46¹/₈	44⁴/₈	14	15²/₈	7⁷/₈	8¹/₈	10	11	Aniak Lake, Alaska	Michael L. Caverly	Michael L. Caverly	SE 1982	10
227	62²/₈	47⁷/₈	47⁷/₈	14⁴/₈	14⁵/₈	7²/₈	7³/₈	13	13	South Macmillan River, Yukon	Louis T. Hill	Louis T. Hill	SE 1973	11
226⁶/₈	58³/₈	52⁵/₈	50⁷/₈	13⁵/₈	15¹/₈	7⁵/₈	7⁵/₈	14	12	Camp Creek, Alaska	Michael E. Carter	Michael E. Carter	SE 1982	12
225⁴/₈	66²/₈	43⁵/₈	43	17	16²/₈	8⁴/₈	8³/₈	12	12	Wernecke Mt., Yukon	David V. Collis	David V. Collis	SE 1984	13
224⁴/₈	63⁵/₈	45²/₈	45	16⁴/₈	16⁵/₈	7⁴/₈	7⁷/₈	12	13	Hess River, Yukon	Richard B. Limbach	Richard B. Limbach	SE 1985	14
233³/₈*	66¹/₈	48	48	15⁵/₈	16³/₈	8⁷/₈	8⁷/₈	12	11	Worm Lake, Yukon	James E. Nelson	James E. Nelson	SE 1985	
231⁷/₈*	69⁵/₈	43⁵/₈	44	22⁴/₈	18	8⁵/₈	8¹/₈	13	15	Red Paint Creek, Alaska	Larry D. Kropf	Larry D. Kropf	SE 1983	

*Final Score subject to revision by additional verifying measurements.

Wyoming or Shiras Moose
Alces alces shirasi

Minimum Score 140
World's Record 205 5/8

Wyoming (Shiras) moose includes trophies taken in Utah, Idaho, Montana, Wyoming, and Washington.

Score	Greatest Spread	Length of Palm R.	Length of Palm L.	Width of Palm R.	Width of Palm L.	Circumference of Beam at Smallest Place R.	Circumference of Beam at Smallest Place L.	Number of Normal Points R.	Number of Normal Points L.	Locality Killed	By Whom Killed	Owner	Date Killed	Rank
182 6/8	48 3/8	34 6/8	38 3/8	12 3/8	13	6	6	14	15	Caribou Co., Idaho	Patricia A. Wood	Patricia A. Wood	OT 1983	1
177 5/8	51 7/8	38 1/8	35 3/8	11 5/8	11 7/8	6 6/8	6 7/8	10	11	Teton Co., Wyo.	John R. Blanton	John R. Blanton	SE 1985	2
177 2/8	51 4/8	33 3/8	33 2/8	11 4/8	11 4/8	6 4/8	6 1/8	12	12	Park Co., Mont.	Lawrence A. Allestad	Lawrence A. Allestad	SE 1961	3
176 2/8	50 5/8	33 3/8	35	12 1/8	12 4/8	6 3/8	6 3/8	12	11	Bonneville Co., Idaho	Steven A. Barnard	Steven A. Barnard	OT 1985	4
174 4/8	46	35 1/8	33 3/8	11	11 4/8	7	7	13	13	Park Co., Wyo.	Walter L. Gale	Walter L. Gale	OT 1983	5
170 6/8	45 7/8	37 2/8	38 3/8	10 2/8	10 3/8	7 1/8	7	8	10	Lincoln Co., Mont.	Bruce C. Todd	Bruce C. Todd	SE 1982	6
170 3/8	47 7/8	35 4/8	34 4/8	10 4/8	8 4/8	7 4/8	7	13	11	Sublette Co., Wyo.	Don L. Corley	Don L. Corley	SE 1983	6
167 3/8	49 1/8	36 5/8	30 5/8	12	12	6 4/8	6 4/8	12	10	Bonneville Co., Idaho	John K. Ryan	John K. Ryan	SE 1984	8
167	44 5/8	33 5/8	32 5/8	11 1/8	11 5/8	6 3/8	6 3/8	11	12	Lincoln Co., Mont.	Jeff Wisehart	Jeff Wisehart	OT 1983	9
166 5/8	50	28 5/8	28 3/8	13 4/8	15 4/8	6 4/8	6 4/8	10	11	Bonneville Co., Idaho	Daniel J. Duggan	Daniel J. Duggan	SE 1982	10
164 2/8	51 3/8	34	34 5/8	7 7/8	7 7/8	6 4/8	6 6/8	8	9	Park Co., Wyo.	Burton H. Ward	Burton H. Ward	SE 1984	11
164 2/8	40	35 7/8	37 7/8	10 2/8	11 5/8	6 5/8	6 4/8	10	10	Teton Co., Wyo.	Don L. Corley	Don L. Corley	SE 1985	11
164	43 3/8	30 4/8	31 3/8	11 4/8	13 2/8	6 2/8	6 3/8	12	12	Teton Co., Wyo.	Clifford H. Rockhold	Clifford H. Rockhold	SE 1984	13
163 6/8	45 2/8	32 4/8	30 4/8	11 5/8	12	6	6	11	11	Teton Co., Wyo.	Robert D. Rice	Robert D. Rice	SE 1982	14
163 5/8	51 3/8	30 5/8	35 5/8	11 5/8	10 4/8	6 6/8	6 4/8	10	10	Lincoln Co., Mont.	Alfred E. Journey	Alfred E. Journey	NO 1983	15
163 3/8	44 6/8	37 1/8	35 5/8	11 7/8	11 3/8	6 6/8	6 6/8	6	10	Bonneville Co., Idaho	Gerald E. Hill	Gerald E. Hill	OT 1981	16
162	48 7/8	29 6/8	34	10 3/8	10 7/8	6 4/8	6 7/8	10	10	Lincoln Co., Wyo.	Joan Burnett	Dee J. Burnett	OT 1963	17
162	42	33	34 4/8	9 6/8	11 5/8	6 2/8	6 2/8	13	11	Madison Co., Mont.	Joseph A. Aanes	Joseph A. Aanes	NO 1984	17
161 2/8	50	34 4/8	27 4/8	11 3/8	11 4/8	6 6/8	6 6/8	11	10	Lincoln Co., Mont.	Stanley J. Evans	Stanley J. Evans	OT 1982	19
160 7/8	46 3/8	30	30 2/8	10 3/8	10 6/8	6	6	12	11	Lincoln Co., Wyo.	Hugh E. Taylor	Hugh E. Taylor	OT 1976	20
159 4/8	46	32	32 4/8	10 3/8	9 5/8	6 1/8	6	9	10	Fremont Co., Idaho	Lennard C. Bradley	Lennard C. Bradley	OT 1983	21
159 3/8	55 3/8	26 5/8	28	10	10 5/8	6 4/8	6 5/8	9	11	Idaho Co., Idaho	Rick E. Kramer	Rick E. Kramer	SE 1980	22
159 3/8	46 7/8	31 7/8	31 7/8	11 4/8	9 2/8	6 2/8	6 1/8	10	9	Teton Co., Wyo.	Tony D. Poulos	Tony D. Poulos	OT 1983	22
159 3/8	41 5/8	30 5/8	30 6/8	10 7/8	11	6 5/8	6 2/8	11	13	Weber Co., Utah	Carl O. Berube	Carl O. Berube	NO 1983	22
158 5/8	46 3/8	30 4/8	31 7/8	8 7/8	10 3/8	6 4/8	6 4/8	10	10	Teton Co., Wyo.	Fred L. Eales	Fred L. Eales	SE 1984	25
157 6/8	43 7/8	31 7/8	31 7/8	9 4/8	8 4/8	6 6/8	6 6/8	10	10	Teton Co., Wyo.	Willard H. Leedy	Willard H. Leedy	OT 1982	26
157 5/8	47 7/8	35 4/8	33	8 4/8	9 7/8	6 6/8	6 6/8	7	8	Sublette Co., Wyo.	Mrs. Kenneth Fortuna	Mrs. Kenneth Fortuna	OT 1984	27
157 3/8	51 3/8	31 3/8	28	10	9 5/8	6 5/8	6 4/8	9	9	Sublette Co., Wyo.	Teressa Ennis	Teressa Ennis	OT 1983	28
157 3/8	41 3/8	28 5/8	28 5/8	12 2/8	12	6 2/8	6 3/8	12	11	Idaho Co., Idaho	Norman R. Fuchs	Norman R. Fuchs	OT 1984	28
156 6/8	43 3/8	31	29 4/8	10 3/8	11	6 7/8	6 6/8	10	10	Fremont Co., Wyo.	Jan Liggett	J. Liggett & L. Liggett	SE 1985	30
155 6/8	52 2/8	36 4/8	33 6/8	7 3/8	6 2/8	5 7/8	5 5/8	8	6	Summit Co., Utah	Monika M. Anderson	Monika M. Anderson	NO 1982	31

Wyoming or Shiras Moose—*Continued*

Alces alces shirasi

Score	Greatest Spread	Length of Palm R.	Length of Palm L.	Width of Palm R.	Width of Palm L.	Circumference of Beam at Smallest Place R.	Circumference of Beam at Smallest Place L.	Number of Normal Points R.	Number of Normal Points L.	Locality Killed	By Whom Killed	Owner	Date Killed	Rank
155 3/8	49 5/8	23 4/8	29	13 3/8	14 7/8	6 4/8	6 5/8	10	11	Pend Oreille Co., Wash.	Thomas F. Kneeshaw	Thomas F. Kneeshaw	NO 1983	32
155 2/8	47	28 3/8	29 4/8	10	9 4/8	6 2/8	6 2/8	11	10	Teton Co., Wyo.	Clarence Harris	David M. Clark	1947	33
147	47 6/8	36 4/8	28 2/8	7 2/8	6 1/8	6 4/8	6 2/8	10	9	Morgan Co., Utah	Craig Cross	Craig Cross	NO 1982	34
179*	50 4/8	34	38	13 4/8	14 1/8	6 6/8	6 6/8	12	10	Bonneville Co., Idaho	Michael B. Whitfield	Michael B. Whitfield	OT 1982	
176 3/8*	42 1/8	37 3/8	37 5/8	12 6/8	12 5/8	6 6/8	6 5/8	13	11	Bonneville Co., Idaho	Karen Kopinski	Karen Kopinski	SE 1984	
175 4/8*	46 4/8	35	34 7/8	13 7/8	12	6 5/8	6 7/8	11	12	Teton Co., Wyo.	Richard D. Oster	Richard D. Oster	SE 1985	

*Final Score subject to revision by additional verifying measurements.

Mountain Caribou

Rangifer tarandus caribou

Minimum Score 360 **World's Record 452**

Five categories of caribou are recognized for records keeping, with boundaries based on geographic lines. Mountain caribou includes trophies from British Columbia, Alberta, southern Yukon, and the Mackenzie Mountains of the Northwest Territories.

Score	Length of Main Beam R.	Length of Main Beam L.	Inside Spread	Circumference at Smallest Place Between Brow and Bez Points R.	Circumference at Smallest Place Between Brow and Bez Points L.	Length of Brow Points R.	Length of Brow Points L.	Width of Brow Points R.	Width of Brow Points L.	Number of Points R.	Number of Points L.	Locality Killed	By Whom Killed	Owner	Date Killed	Rank
444	52	52 1/8	38 2/8	6	6 1/8	8 6/8	20 2/8	1/8	15 7/8	16	25	Mountain River, N.W.T.	John A. Kolar	John A. Kolar	SE 1984	1
442 7/8	44 2/8	46 2/8	37 2/8	7	6 7/8	15 6/8	17 1/8	11 6/8	4 6/8	24	23	Spatsizi Plateau, B.C.	Jay L. Brasher	Jay L. Brasher	OT 1984	2
416 6/8	53 1/8	52 1/8	38 7/8	7 3/8	7 5/8	15 2/8	19 7/8	1/8	14 5/8	14	20	Little Dal Lake, N.W.T.	Patricia M. Dreeszen	Patricia M. Dreeszen	SE 1984	3
416 4/8	50 1/8	47 2/8	46	6 3/8	6 4/8	14 7/8	12 3/8	10 3/8	1/8	14	18	Redstone River, N.W.T.	David D. Hill	David D. Hill	AG 1980	4
416 3/8	52 6/8	51 2/8	47 6/8	7 4/8	7 2/8	17 6/8	18 5/8	2 3/8	11 3/8	12	13	Mountain Lake, N.W.T.	Stewart N. Shaft	Stewart N. Shaft	OT 1985	5
414 4/8	48 3/8	48 2/8	40 2/8	7 1/8	7 2/8	3 1/8	16 1/8	1 2/8	10 4/8	16	21	Hoole River, Yukon	Kris M. Gustafson	Kris M. Gustafson	SE 1984	6
413 4/8	42 3/8	39 6/8	35 1/8	6 2/8	7	18 3/8	18 4/8	1 6/8	15 4/8	17	27	Livingstone Creek, Yukon	Lawrence W. Dossman	Lawrence W. Dossman	SE 1984	7
412 4/8	51 6/8	50	37 2/8	7 4/8	7 2/8	14 7/8	21 7/8	4 2/8	15 6/8	16	17	Ross River, Yukon	Barry E. Enders	Barry E. Enders	SE 1984	8
411 1/8	48 6/8	49 4/8	43	6 4/8	6 5/8	18 1/8	10	13 3/8	1/8	22	13	Norman Wells, N.W.T.	Elmer R. Kochans	Elmer R. Kochans	AG 1981	9
407 3/8	54 7/8	56 2/8	37 4/8	6 2/8	6	2 7/8	17 4/8	1/8	13 3/8	14	15	Keele River, N.W.T.	Roland Schwengler	Roland Schwengler	SE 1984	10
406 5/8	50 3/8	51 5/8	39 4/8	8 4/8	8 4/8	17 7/8	17 3/8	12 6/8	1 5/8	18	19	Mountain River, N.W.T.	Grover F. Glasner	Grover F. Glasner	SE 1985	11
400 3/8	41 7/8	42 5/8	28 5/8	7 6/8	6 7/8	18 5/8	18 3/8	6 2/8	9 2/8	16	17	Caribou Mt., Yukon	Charles B. Heuring	Charles B. Heuring	SE 1984	12
400	54	53 6/8	37 4/8	6 4/8	6 4/8	17	14 4/8	6 4/8	5 4/8	18	14	Nahanni River, N.W.T.	Kevin Davidson	Kevin Davidson	SE 1977	13
399 6/8	47 2/8	49 2/8	33 2/8	8 4/8	8 6/8	14 4/8	17 3/8	3	14 3/8	20	27	Divide Lake, N.W.T.	Brooks Carmichael	Brooks Carmichael	SE 1984	14
399 4/8	45 1/8	45 1/8	38 1/8	5 6/8	5 7/8	15 1/8	3 1/8	8 2/8	1/8	19	16	Turnagain River, B.C.	Gerald L. Simpson	Gerald L. Simpson	SE 1984	15
398	47 1/8	44 2/8	36 5/8	6 3/8	6 2/8	19 5/8	18 6/8	10 2/8	12 6/8	22	18	Pelly Mts., Yukon	Michael F. Short	Michael F. Short	SE 1982	16
395 7/8	46	42 4/8	40 5/8	6 7/8	6 7/8	4	19	1/8	15 7/8	18	21	Ice Lake, Yukon	Tadeus S. Konieczka	Tadeus S. Konieczka	SE 1982	17
395	56 5/8	54 7/8	46 7/8	5 6/8	5 7/8	19 5/8	15 5/8	18 1/8	1 4/8	17	9	Mountain River, N.W.T.	Robert L. Williamson	Robert L. Williamson	SE 1983	18
392 6/8	46 3/8	44 3/8	36	6 7/8	6 7/8	16 7/8	17 4/8	9 7/8	5	18	20	Little Dal Lake, N.W.T.	Douglas M. Dreeszen	Douglas M. Dreeszen	SE 1984	19
392 3/8	44 1/8	44	34 7/8	6 3/8	6 3/8	16 4/8	17 2/8	10 3/8	6 5/8	18	16	Dease Lake, B.C.	Ross H. Mann	Ross H. Mann	SE 1984	20
392 2/8	45 6/8	43 1/8	30 7/8	5 2/8	5 2/8	16 3/8	17	8 4/8	11 6/8	18	22	Keele River, N.W.T.	Dale R. Hill	Dale R. Hill	AG 1980	21
392	42 4/8	47 4/8	32 4/8	5 6/8	6 4/8	19 2/8	5 2/8	13 2/8	1	19	15	Twopete Mt., Yukon	David H. Crum	David H. Crum	SE 1984	22
391 7/8	44 6/8	44 4/8	30 2/8	6 3/8	6 4/8	15 1/8	15 6/8	9	7 4/8	19	18	Mt. Rognaas, B.C.	Michael D. Miklosi	Michael D. Miklosi	OT 1983	23
391 2/8	49	52 5/8	40 4/8	5 6/8	5 5/8	22	21 2/8	5 3/8	11 3/8	14	13	Ruby Range, Yukon	William K. Hilton	William K. Hilton	OT 1985	24
389 1/8	42 1/8	42 2/8	34	6 4/8	6	16 7/8	16 6/8	3 3/8	10 1/8	15	15	Cypress Creek, B.C.	Kay Fries	Kay Fries	SE 1984	25
360 2/8	40 2/8	39 4/8	33 1/8	6	6	8 2/8	19	6/8	14 7/8	14	19	Rabbit River, B.C.	Earl Womble	Earl Womble	SE 1985	26
360	46 1/8	45 1/8	35 5/8	6	6 3/8	14 1/8		8		15	15	Arctic Red River, N.W.T.	Fred Tarran	Fred Tarran	SE 1984	27

Mountain Caribou—Continued
Rangifer tarandus caribou

Score	Length of Main Beam		Inside Spread	Circumference at Smallest Place Between Brow and Bez Points		Length of Brow Points		Width of Brow Points		Number of Points		Locality Killed	By Whom Killed	Owner	Date Killed	Rank
	R.	L.		R.	L.	R.	L.	R.	L.	R.	L.					
436 3/8*	57	54 4/8	46 4/8	6 5/8	6 7/8	20 7/8	16 7/8	10 7/8	8	17	14	St. Cyr Range, Yukon	Randall W. Lawton	Randall W. Lawton	AG 1985	
421 5/8*	51	52	31 1/8	6 7/8	6 1/8	15 1/8	6	11	1 1/8	22	14	Cry Lake, B.C.	Gordon W. Heenan	Gordon W. Heenan	SE 1985	

*Final Score subject to revision by additional verifying measurements.

Woodland Caribou

Minimum Score 265

Rangifer tarandus caribou

World's Record 419 5/8

Woodland caribou includes trophies from Nova Scotia, New Brunswick, and Newfoundland.

Score	Length of Main Beam R.	Length of Main Beam L.	Inside Spread	Circumference at Smallest Place Between Brow and Bez Points R.	Circumference at Smallest Place Between Brow and Bez Points L.	Length of Brow Points R.	Length of Brow Points L.	Width of Brow Points R.	Width of Brow Points L.	Number of Points R.	Number of Points L.	Locality Killed	By Whom Killed	Owner	Date Killed	Rank
347	45 3/8	43 1/8	33 3/8	5 5/8	5 4/8	14	19	13 1/8	3	15	12	Rocky Pond, Nfld.	Gordon J. Birgbauer, Jr.	Gordon J. Birgbauer, Jr.	OT 1984	1
334 1/8	39 6/8	39 6/8	31	5 1/8	4 7/8	17 2/8	16 7/8	17 4/8	16	15	18	King George Lake, Nfld.	John R. Blanton	John R. Blanton	OT 1984	2
320 2/8	39 4/8	39 4/8	34	4 6/8	5 1/8	15 5/8	17 3/8	12	6 4/8	12	17	Top Pond, Nfld.	Donald F. Senter	Donald F. Senter	OT 1984	3
306 4/8	37 1/8	42 2/8	29	5 1/8	5 1/8	14 7/8	14 1/8	10 4/8	10 4/8	11	11	Grand Lake, Nfld.	Theodore R. Greenwood	Theodore R. Greenwood	OT 1983	4
297 5/8	32 4/8	33 3/8	29 7/8	5 5/8	5 4/8	13 4/8	12 5/8	9 1/8	6 4/8	17	14	Buchans Plateau, Nfld.	Morton J. Greene	Morton J. Greene	SE 1983	5
294 6/8	41 4/8	40	35	6 1/8	5 6/8	9 4/8	13 6/8	4 5/8	11 3/8	18	14	Avalon Pen., Nfld.	W. James & W. Noftall	Wayne M. James	SE 1983	6
278 6/8	32 6/8	34 6/8	25 3/8	4 4/8	4 6/8	12 4/8	12 4/8	12 3/8	11	16	15	Buchans Plateau, Nfld.	Don B. Skidmore	Don B. Skidmore	SE 1983	7
277 4/8	36 4/8	36 7/8	22 2/8	5 3/8	5 2/8	11 2/8	11 7/8	4 7/8	8 2/8	12	15	Ironbound Hill, Nfld.	George Dempsey	George Dempsey	OT 1982	8
334 7/8*	48 6/8	44 7/8	37 3/8	5 7/8	6	16 4/8	13 7/8	8 2/8	3 7/8	18	16	Burnt Pond, Nfld.	E. B. Pannkuk, Jr.	E. B. Pannkuk, Jr.	SE 1983	
324 4/8*	40 1/8	37 7/8	31 6/8	6 1/8	5 7/8	12	12	6 2/8	1 2/8	21	16	Long Range Mts., Nfld.	William H. Taylor	William H. Taylor	SE 1983	
321 1/8*	44	44 6/8	34 6/8	6 3/8	6 3/8	14 1/8	13 1/8	12 2/8	4 1/8	18	15	Dashwoods Pond, Nfld.	Daniel P. Amatuzzo	Daniel P. Amatuzzo	OT 1983	

*Final Score subject to revision by additional verifying measurements.

Barren Ground Caribou
Rangifer tarandus granti

Minimum Score 375
World's Record 463 3/8

Barren ground caribou includes trophies from Alaska, northern Yukon Territory, Saskatchewan, Manitoba, and Ontario.

Score	Length of Main Beam R.	L.	Inside Spread	Circumference at Smallest Place Between Brow and Bez Points R.	L.	Length of Brow Points R.	L.	Width of Brow Points R.	L.	Number of Points R.	L.	Locality Killed	By Whom Killed	Owner	Date Killed	Rank
453	50 6/8	51 3/8	35 5/8	11 2/8	6 5/8	20 5/8	15 7/8	20 6/8	5 2/8	36	18	Alaska Pen., Alaska	Ken Higginbotham	Ken Higginbotham	OT 1984	1
449 5/8	49 7/8	48 7/8	40 5/8	9 5/8	8 3/8	19 2/8	20	17	8 5/8	25	23	Lake Clark, Alaska	Dennis Burdick	Dennis Burdick	AG 1984	2
448 5/8	54 7/8	56 4/8	42	6 5/8	6 3/8	16 7/8	24 2/8	4 2/8	21 1/8	18	20	Dog Salmon River, Alaska	Picked Up	Butch Hautanen	PU 1982	3
432 5/8	55 5/8	55 4/8	48 3/8	5 5/8	5 4/8	7	21 1/8	17 7/8	1/8	23	15	Hick Creek, Alaska	Justin D. Hall	Justin D. Hall	AG 1984	4
431 5/8	51 1/8	51 5/8	55 1/8	6 1/8	6 2/8	22 5/8	20 7/8	3 4/8	12 5/8	23	15	King Salmon, Alaska	Warren F. Phillips	Warren F. Phillips	SE 1983	5
430 7/8	49	48 3/8	40 5/8	7 4/8	7 2/8	15 5/8	14	8	7 7/8	18	19	Susitna River, Alaska	James I. Roland	James I. Roland	SE 1983	6
428 5/8	57	54 1/8	41	6 3/8	6 5/8	21 3/8	7	16 6/8	1/8	20	12	Iliamna Lake, Alaska	Linda J. Corley	Linda J. Corley	AG 1983	7
425 3/8	55 5/8	56 2/8	41	6 6/8	7 2/8	17 7/8	18 2/8	5 4/8	9 5/8	17	17	Moody Creek, Alaska	Ervin Hostetler	Ervin Hostetler	AG 1983	8
425 3/8	56 5/8	59	43 3/8	7 1/8	7	20 5/8	19 5/8	8	10 3/8	20	14	Iliamna Lake, Alaska	A. A. Bishop	A. A. Bishop	SE 1982	8
423	47 5/8	50	48	6 4/8	6 3/8	18 2/8	16 3/8	9 2/8	8 7/8	15	16	Panorama Mt., Alaska	Ronald R. Minard	Ronald R. Minard	SE 1985	10
422 5/8	44 2/8	44 5/8	35 5/8	5 5/8	5 7/8	22	4 3/8	13 5/8	1 2/8	23	16	Snipe Lake, Alaska	Steven S. Lambe	Steven S. Lambe	AG 1983	11
422 5/8	50 4/8	45 4/8	34 3/8	9 5/8	6 6/8	20 4/8	17	15	5 5/8	16	19	Mt. Sanford, Alaska	John J. Heidel	John J. Heidel	SE 1982	11
420 6/8	56 5/8	57 4/8	46 5/8	5 4/8	6	20 1/8	23	5 5/8	5	18	14	Becharof Lake, Alaska	Steven H. Schaust	Steven H. Schaust	SE 1983	13
420 1/8	50 3/8	55 3/8	41 7/8	6 5/8	6 4/8	21			16 1/8	14	20	King Salmon River, Alaska	Frank N. Rome	Frank N. Rome	OT 1983	14
420 1/8	56 3/8	54 2/8	37 7/8	7 3/8	7 2/8	20	17 5/8	13 4/8	1/8	18	15	Yanert Fork, Alaska	Michael H. Werner	Michael H. Werner	SE 1984	14
417 7/8	50 3/8	54 2/8	38 5/8	7 3/8	7 3/8	19 1/8	1 5/8	17	1/8	20	14	Tonzona River, Alaska	Fred T. Hecox	Fred T. Hecox	AG 1983	16
417 5/8	56 5/8	56 4/8	43 3/8	5 7/8	6 1/8	19 2/8	4 7/8	11	1 1/8	11	14	Tangle Lakes, Alaska	Kurt C. Dunn	Kurt C. Dunn	AG 1981	17
417 3/8	50 6/8	50 4/8	36 6/8	6 4/8	6	17 5/8	16 4/8	6	12 5/8	19	22	Mt. Sanford, Alaska	Dennis Brieske	Dennis Brieske	SE 1984	18
417 3/8	47 5/8	50 6/8	38 7/8	5	5	19 4/8	19	16 1/8	5 5/8	23	21	Fracture Creek, Alaska	L. Irvin Barnhart	L. Irvin Barnhart	OT 1983	18
416 5/8	59 5/8	57 5/8	45 5/8	5 4/8	5 4/8	4 2/8	21 3/8	1/8	17	11	17	King Salmon, Alaska	F. Robert Bell	F. Robert Bell	OT 1983	20
416 3/8	56 5/8	54 2/8	48 5/8	5 5/8	6	15	19 5/8	3 6/8	10 4/8	13	18	Mulchatna River, Alaska	Willard L. Hubbard	Willard L. Hubbard	AG 1983	21
416 3/8	49 5/8	52	44 3/8	6 4/8	6 3/8	16 7/8	17 5/8	12	10	18	20	American Pass, Alaska	Brett G. Alexander	Brett G. Alexander	SE 1984	21
416 3/8	56 5/8	56 7/8	35 1/8	5 3/8	5 4/8	20 1/8	19	6 3/8	14 4/8	13	18	Blackstone River, Yukon	Ken Vickerman	Ken Vickerman	OT 1983	23
416	50 7/8	50 7/8	40 5/8	9 7/8	7 4/8	18 6/8	6 3/8	15 4/8	1/8	19	16	Stony River, Alaska	Charles F. Nadler	Charles F. Nadler	AG 1985	24
415 5/8	50 4/8	47 5/8	40 7/8	5 1/8	5 1/8	19 4/8	16 3/8	13 5/8	12 2/8	19	19	Monsoon Lake, Alaska	Paul A. Szopa	Paul A. Szopa	AG 1983	25
415 3/8	50 2/8	50 3/8	43 3/8	6 5/8	6 4/8	6 2/8	17 4/8	4 5/8	13 3/8	15	20	Whitefish Lake, Alaska	Jeffrey S. Sorg	Jeffrey S. Sorg	AG 1982	26
415 3/8	49 5/8	50 1/8	41 2/8	5 5/8	5 5/8	17 5/8	13 5/8	14 3/8	1/8	14	15	Nenana River, Alaska	James H. Hunt	James H. Hunt	OT 1983	27
413 6/8	48 2/8	52	42 1/8	5	5 1/8	17 4/8	20 1/8	11 2/8	14 2/8	12	15	Alaska Pen., Alaska	Robert C. Kaufman	Robert C. Kaufman	SE 1978	28
413 3/8	55 1/8	57 3/8	44 3/8	6 3/8	6 5/8	18	5 7/8	13 5/8		19	14	Whitefish Lake, Alaska	Larry D. Domson	Larry D. Domson	SE 1984	29

358

Score											Locality	Hunter	Owner	Date Killed	Rank
412 6/8	50 3/8	46 3/8	38 5/8	5 1/8	5 2/8	17 6/8	20 4/8	12 3/8	19	23	Port Moller, Alaska	Billy W. Green	Billy W. Green	SE 1983	30
412 3/8	61 1/8	62 2/8	50 1/8	5 5/8	5 5/8	22 2/8	8 7/8	14	1/8	18	King Salmon, Alaska	Larry Spiva	Larry Spiva	OT 1983	31
411 7/8	45 1/8	44 2/8	40	5 3/8	5 3/8	17	17 7/8	11 7/8	14 2/8	23	Dog Salmon River, Alaska	Benny B. Kerns	Benny B. Kerns	SE 1983	32
411 4/8	56 3/8	57	42 2/8	6 3/8	6 1/8	16 1/8	10 4/8	10 4/8	1/8	12	Wood River, Alaska	Carol L. Schwabland	Carol L. Schwabland	AG 1981	33
411 1/8	53 3/8	55 5/8	46 4/8	9 9/8	9 9/8		16 4/8		7 3/8	13	Wood River, Alaska	Luther W. Palmer	Luther W. Palmer	AG 1984	34
410 5/8	49 2/8	47 7/8	35	6 4/8	6	15 5/8	15 2/8	14 2/8	9 2/8	18	Hunt River, Alaska	James W. Styler	James W. Styler	SE 1981	35
409 6/8	54 2/8	52 7/8	27 5/8	7 4/8	6 5/8	15	15 3/8	5 7/8	10 7/8	19	Wood River, Alaska	Stuart L. G. Rees	Stuart L. G. Rees	SE 1983	36
408 6/8	52 2/8	51	39 3/8	6 1/8	9 1/8	4	18 7/8	1	12 2/8	14	Red Paint Creek, Alaska	Larry D. Kropf	Larry D. Kropf	SE 1983	37
408 3/8	52 3/8	53 6/8	44 3/8	5 5/8	5 4/8	3	22 5/8	1/8	16 2/8	15	Becharof Lake, Alaska	Pete M. Baughman, Jr.	Pete M. Baughman, Jr.	SE 1984	38
408 2/8	52 1/8	51 7/8	37 7/8	7 1/8	6 2/8	15 3/8	18 6/8	7 4/8	9 1/8	14	Bruskasna Creek, Alaska	Rod Boertje	Rod Boertje	SE 1984	39
408 2/8	58 4/8	59 5/8	48 5/8	6 3/8	6 7/8	18	20 3/8	8 5/8	8 2/8	19	Dog Salmon River, Alaska	Arlington F. Svoboda	Arlington F. Svoboda	SE 1983	39
407 7/8	58 5/8	56	37 1/8	7 2/8	6 5/8	19 2/8	19 4/8	10 2/8	12 5/8	18	Kuskokwim River, Alaska	Robert Jacobsen	Robert Jacobsen	SE 1982	41
406 7/8	50 2/8	52	45 7/8	5 5/8	5	21 1/8	17 2/8	17 4/8	13 3/8	16	Ugashik Lake, Alaska	John A. Moody	John A. Moody	OT 1983	42
405 7/8	57 2/8	58 5/8	57	6	6	19	11 1/8	11 5/8	1/8	15	Becharof Lake, Alaska	Max E. Chittick	Max E. Chittick	SE 1983	43
405 5/8	60 1/8	62 2/8	42 2/8	5 7/8	5 5/8	19 4/8	16 2/8	14 1/8	1 4/8	20	Joseph Creek, Alaska	Madeline M. Kelleyhouse	Madeline M. Kelleyhouse	AG 1984	44
405 2/8	47 3/8	48 7/8	36 2/8	7 4/8	6 7/8	15 5/8	14 2/8	8 3/8	5 2/8	22	Mulchatna River, Alaska	Thomas J. Gallo	Thomas J. Gallo	AG 1983	45
405 1/8	51 1/8	56 3/8	39 4/8	6 1/8	6 1/8	13 1/8	18 4/8	1/8	10 5/8	15	Bear Lake, Alaska	Ruth S. Kennedy	Ruth S. Kennedy	OT 1983	46
404 5/8	46 1/8	47 1/8	39 4/8	8 5/8	6 6/8	17 5/8	2 1/8	11 1/8	1/8	17	Becharof Lake, Alaska	Dan M. Rudanovich	Dan M. Rudanovich	OT 1983	47
404 5/8	53 3/8	51 1/8	39 5/8	6 3/8	6 3/8	22 2/8	18 3/8	1/8	15 2/8	13	Wood River, Alaska	Robert D. Hancock, Jr.	Robert D. Hancock, Jr.	SE 1983	48
404 3/8	52 7/8	52 1/8	34	6 7/8	5 7/8	20 1/8	17 5/8	10 2/8	9 2/8	16	Tyone Creek, Alaska	Frederick W. Fernelius	Frederick W. Fernelius	SE 1981	49
404 2/8	57 2/8	54 7/8	38 2/8	7 1/8	7	23	19 4/8	1/8	16 6/8	13	Post Lake, Alaska	John T. Holzschuh	John T. Holzschuh	AG 1983	50
402	51 7/8	52 7/8	43 1/8	4 7/8	5 1/8	22 5/8	23 2/8	12 5/8	9 3/8	14	Talkeetna Mts., Alaska	Clyde A. McLeod	Clyde A. McLeod	AG 1983	51
401 7/8	47 7/8	48 7/8	44 1/8	5 5/8	6 1/8	15 4/8	6 2/8	12 1/8	1/8	15	Mt. Sanford, Alaska	Harold R. Clark	Harold R. Clark	SE 1981	52
401 3/8	49 3/8	49	38 5/8	5 5/8	5 4/8	19 5/8	20 7/8	16 5/8	6 5/8	23	Becharof Lake, Alaska	Bill D. Reed	Bill D. Reed	SE 1983	53
401 1/8	61 3/8	59 5/8	39 2/8	7 4/8	7	17 7/8	18 1/8	2 4/8	9 4/8	13	Little Delta River, Alaska	Danny R. Hart	Danny R. Hart	SE 1983	53
401 1/8	61 1/8	63 5/8	48 4/8	7 2/8	7 1/8	17 4/8	6	10 7/8		17	Stuyahok River, Alaska	Fred A. Wright	Fred A. Wright	AG 1982	53
401 1/8	50 5/8	54 3/8	42 4/8	6 6/8	6 4/8	17 3/8		11 1/8		16	Wood River, Alaska	William P. Ghiorso	William P. Ghiorso	SE 1983	56
401	60 5/8	53 5/8	43 5/8	6 2/8	7	19 3/8		16/8		20	King Salmon, Alaska	Edward W. Ratcliff	Edward W. Ratcliff	OT 1984	57
401	55 2/8	56 3/8	37	8 5/8	7 3/8	18 3/8	19 4/8	11 7/8	4	18	Red Devil, Alaska	Joseph L. LaNou	Joseph L. LaNou	AG 1984	58
400 4/8	48 1/8	49 4/8	29 1/8	7	6 6/8	22 3/8	21 2/8	16 4/8	4 5/8	16	Fortymile River, Alaska	Arnold O. Burton	Arnold O. Burton	SE 1985	59
400	54 3/8	53 3/8	31 1/8	6 3/8	7	6	17	1/8	9	18	White Fish Lake, Alaska	Thomas K. Willard	Thomas K. Willard	AG 1984	60
400	48	50	39 5/8	6 4/8	6	15 3/8	17 1/8	12	1 4/8	19	Caribou Lake, Alaska	Donald J. Giottonini, Jr.	Donald J. Giottonini, Jr.	AG 1983	60
399 7/8	45 7/8	47 1/8	33 1/8	5 7/8	5 7/8	2 4/8	17 5/8	1/8	13 7/8	15	Resurrection Creek, Alaska	John H. Stuckey, III	John H. Stuckey, III	SE 1983	62
395 5/8	53	53	44	6 4/8	6 4/8	15 3/8	14 1/8	10 5/8	5 4/8	16	Tanana Hills, Alaska	Stephen J. Zolczynski	Stephen J. Zolczynski	SE 1983	63
377 7/8	48 5/8	48 7/8	34	6 5/8	6 3/8	16 5/8	15 2/8	11 5/8	1 5/8	14	Alaska Range, Alaska	Randall E. Biggerstaff	Randall E. Biggerstaff	SE 1985	64
376 5/8	53 1/8	55 3/8	37 1/8	6 1/8	6 1/8	12 2/8	1 7/8	10 7/8	1/8	21	Nushagak River, Alaska	Theresa M. Patterson	Theresa M. Patterson	SE 1984	65
459 3/8*	60 5/8	57 3/8	57 3/8	6 4/8	6 4/8	5 4/8	21	1/8	14 5/8	17	Becharof Lake, Alaska	Gordon G. Chittick	Gordon G. Chittick	SE 1983	
441 4/8*	53 2/8	51 1/8	42 2/8	6 7/8	6 7/8	19 4/8		14 5/8		19	Stephans Lake, Alaska	Timothy J. Schrage	Timothy J. Schrage	AG 1984	
439 1/8*	55 5/8	56 5/8	41 5/8	5 5/8	6 3/8	20 1/8	18 3/8	10 5/8	8 1/8	17	Alaska Pen., Alaska	Rodney D. Fulcher	Rodney D. Fulcher	SE 1984	

*Final Score subject to revision by additional verifying measurements.

Central Canada Barren Ground Caribou

Minimum Score 330

Rangifer tarandus groenlandicus

World's Record 408 6/8

Central Canada barren ground caribou occur in the mainland of N.W.T., with geographic boundaries of the Mackenzie River to the west; the north edge of the continent to the north (excluding any islands); Hudson's Bay to the east; and the southern boundary of Northwest Territories to the south.

Score	Length of Main Beam		Inside Spread	Circumference at Smallest Place Between Brow and Bez Points		Length of Brow Points		Width of Brow Points		Number of Points		Locality Killed	By Whom Killed	Owner	Date Killed	Rank
	R.	L.		R.	L.	R.	L.	R.	L.	R.	L.					
408 6/8	52 2/8	51 1/8	38 7/8	4 6/8	4 6/8	21 2/8	18 2/8	8 6/8	15 5/8	17	23	Rendez-vous Lake, N.W.T.	Picked Up	Tom W. Barry	OT 1982	1
408 2/8	46 4/8	47	39 1/8	4 2/8	4 4/8	16 3/8	19	10 7/8	18 3/8	20	25	Courageous Lake, N.W.T.	Raymond H. Bonar	Raymond H. Bonar	AG 1985	2
395 3/8	49 3/8	49 5/8	31 4/8	4 5/8	4 7/8	15 7/8	16 2/8	11 1/8	7 5/8	18	20	Courageous Lake, N.W.T.	George O. Poston	George O. Poston	SE 1985	3
382 2/8	56	56 1/8	37 1/8	6 4/8	6	16 2/8	16 3/8	8 6/8	9 2/8	17	15	Courageous Lake, N.W.T.	Earle H. Harder	Earle H. Harder	SE 1985	4
371 1/8	56 3/8	58	37 1/8	5 5/8	6	16	12 2/8	12 6/8	5	16	16	Courageous Lake, N.W.T.	Jon R. Stephens	Jon R. Stephens	SE 1984	5
369 1/8	50 3/8	51 4/8	43	5	5 4/8	14 5/8	14 2/8	9	7 6/8	15	14	Seahorse Lake, N.W.T.	Barry D. Taylor	Barry D. Taylor	SE 1985	6
361 1/8	49 4/8	49 5/8	29 4/8	5 4/8	5 6/8	6 5/8	18 6/8	2 3/8	14 1/8	17	23	Winter Lake, N.W.T.	Warren D. St. Germaine	Warren D. St. Germaine	SE 1984	7
357 5/8	48	47	27 5/8	5 2/8	5	19	13 5/8	7 2/8	11 3/8	17	18	Undine Lake, N.W.T.	Barry D. Taylor	Barry D. Taylor	SE 1985	8
357 1/8	49 3/8	48 7/8	33	4 4/8	4 5/8	16 5/8	18 4/8	13 2/8	7 4/8	16	18	Courageous Lake, N.W.T.	Kaye Poston	Kaye Poston	SE 1983	9
351 1/8	48 4/8	48 4/8	31	5 2/8	5 4/8		16 1/8		11 6/8	11	14	Robin Lake, N.W.T.	Gary D. Cooney	Gary D. Cooney	SE 1981	10
350 4/8	46 6/8	43 5/8	31 2/8	5 3/8	5 1/8	13	8 1/8	10	1/8	20	15	Perry Pen., N.W.T.	Donald F. Senter	Donald F. Senter	OT 1985	11
344 6/8	44 6/8	47 1/8	32 7/8	5 2/8	5	14 3/8	13 3/8	10 5/8	8 2/8	22	18	Jolly Lake, N.W.T.	Barry D. Taylor	Barry D. Taylor	SE 1985	12
391 5/8*	49	54 6/8	41 2/8	5 6/8	5 4/8	5 5/8	15 6/8	1/8	10 3/8	14	16	Winter Lake, N.W.T.	William M. Leschasin	William M. Leschasin	SE 1985	
390 4/8*	59	57	41 6/8	5 3/8	5 1/8	20 6/8	17 2/8	10 6/8	10 4/8	16	13	Grizzle Bear Lake, N.W.T.	Douglas C. Heard	Douglas C. Heard	SE 1978	
388 3/8*	52 3/8	50 1/8	30 4/8	5 7/8	5 6/8	17 4/8	19 7/8	3 2/8	17	12	23	Courageous Lake, N.W.T.	James E. Nelson	James E. Nelson	SE 1984	
377 5/8*	47 2/8	48 6/8	31 2/8	5 5/8	5 2/8	17 3/8	18 5/8	12	16 7/8	17	18	Winter Lake, N.W.T.	Warren D. St. Germaine	Warren D. St. Germaine	SE 1985	

*Final Score subject to revision by additional verifying measurements.

Quebec-Labrador Caribou
Rangifer tarandus from Quebec and Labrador

Minimum Score 365   World's Record 474 6/8

Score	Length of Main Beam R.	L.	Inside Spread	Circumference at Smallest Place Between Brow and Bez Points R.	L.	Length of Brow Points R.	L.	Width of Brow Points R.	L.	Number of Points R.	L.	Locality Killed	By Whom Killed	Owner	Date Killed	Rank
460 6/8	59 4/8	56 5/8	49 2/8	5 1/8	5 3/8	16 5/8	21 1/8	13 5/8	18 4/8	22	24	Ungava Bay, Que.	Lynn D. McLaud	Lynn D. McLaud	SE 1978	1
439 4/8	56 5/8	59 1/8	42	6 7/8	5 7/8	17 7/8	20 3/8	12 3/8	13 7/8	11	22	Ungava Bay, Que.	Don Tomberlin	Don Tomberlin	SE 1985	2
434 7/8	51 7/8	52	44 7/8	4 7/8	5 1/8	16 3/8	20 5/8	14 7/8	8 5/8	25	22	Mistinibi Lake, Que.	Don L. Corley	Don L. Corley	OT 1983	3
410 7/8	57 7/8	55 5/8	49	5 2/8	5 3/8	20 5/8	16 3/8	17	10 4/8	21	21	Mistinibi Lake, Que.	Picked Up	Toby J. Johnson	PU 1984	4
408 4/8	53 5/8	53 1/8	46 5/8	6	6 7/8	18	13 4/8	12 2/8	1/8	19	19	Ungava Bay, Que.	Richard H. Propp	Richard H. Propp	SE 1985	5
403 5/8	51 2/8	51 1/8	48 5/8	5 1/8	5 3/8	18 2/8	19 1/8	11	13 5/8	15	16	Thibault Lake, Que.	Ralph Cervo	Ralph Cervo	SE 1983	6
402 5/8	49 7/8	50 3/8	51 7/8	5 4/8	5 3/8	16 5/8	17 3/8	14 3/8	8 5/8	20	17	Sagler Fiord, Lab.	Ernest W. Foster, Jr.	Ernest W. Foster, Jr.	SE 1985	7
402	54 2/8	53 4/8	48 5/8	5 7/8	6 1/8	15 5/8	16	6 3/8	10 4/8	18	18	Mistinibi Lake, Que.	Theodore L. Greenwood	Theodore L. Greenwood	SE 1981	8
394 3/8	54 2/8	53	57 1/8	5 5/8	5 7/8	9 4/8	16 4/8	1/8	11 2/8	12	20	George River, Que.	Stanley M. Boots	Stanley M. Boots	SE 1983	9
392 7/8	48	47	35 5/8	4 7/8	4 4/8	17 3/8	17 4/8	14	13 3/8	24	25	George River, Que.	Kerry W. Blanton	Kerry W. Blanton	OT 1983	10
392 4/8	55	53 4/8	41	5 5/8	5 5/8	12 4/8	16 4/8	3 7/8	14	15	18	George River, Que.	Donald F. Senter	Donald F. Senter	OT 1983	11
389 7/8	54 2/8	56 3/8	48 7/8	5 7/8	5 7/8	15 5/8	12 4/8	9 5/8	1 5/8	18	16	Ford Lake, Que.	Carl F. Gernold	Carl F. Gernold	SE 1982	12
389 4/8	48 5/8	49 4/8	40 5/8	5	5 4/8	13 4/8	18 1/8	6 5/8	14	16	21	Mistinibi Lake, Que.	Don L. Corley	Don L. Corley	OT 1983	13
387 7/8	53 5/8	53 7/8	47	5 7/8	5 7/8	1	17	1/8	11 4/8	14	18	Tunulik River, Que.	Larry Hoff	Larry Hoff	SE 1984	14
386 3/8	49 5/8	49 4/8	44 1/8	5	5 3/8	12 7/8	18 3/8	2 7/8	12 1/8	17	17	Mistinibi Lake, Que.	Watson T. Yoshimoto	Watson T. Yoshimoto	SE 1980	15
385 5/8	57 7/8	56	50 2/8	5 1/8	5	20 5/8	20 7/8	6	5	13	15	George River, Que.	Daniel B. Kahle	Daniel B. Kahle	SE 1983	16
383 2/8	53 5/8	53 3/8	53 3/8	5 5/8	5 5/8	4 2/8	15 1/8	1/8	12	17	23	Mistinibi Lake, Que.	Watson T. Yoshimoto	Watson T. Yoshimoto	SE 1979	17
380 5/8	47 5/8	48 7/8	44 3/8	6	6	14 7/8	12	8 2/8	1 6/8	14	18	Mistinibi Lake, Que.	Paul F. Barnhart	Paul F. Barnhart	SE 1980	18
380 4/8	51 6/8	52 2/8	47 1/8	5 5/8	5 7/8	16	20 3/8	1	14 5/8	16	18	Mistinibi Lake, Que.	Toby J. Johnson	Toby J. Johnson	SE 1984	19
380	51 3/8	50 7/8	55	5 5/8	5 5/8	19 3/8	17 7/8	10 5/8	2	12	12	Tunulic River, Que.	Peter Smith	Peter Smith	SE 1982	20
378 5/8	54	52 4/8	40 5/8	4 4/8	4 5/8	17 3/8	15 1/8	7	9 2/8	15	14	Tunulliq Lake, Que.	Scott M. Schowalter	Scott M. Schowalter	SE 1982	21
377 7/8	45 5/8	45 4/8	40 5/8	4 4/8	4 7/8	16 6/8	16 2/8	10 6/8	12 6/8	20	17	Lake Brisson, Que.	David Read	David Read	SE 1983	22
376 5/8	50 5/8	50 6/8	45 5/8	5 5/8	5 4/8	16 7/8	15 5/8	13 4/8	10 2/8	18	13	Ungava Bay, Que.	John D. Powers	John D. Powers	SE 1981	23
375	46 5/8	44	49 2/8	6 5/8	6 2/8	14	13 7/8	9 5/8	4/8	16	16	Ungava Pen., Que.	Theodore M. Schall	Theodore M. Schall	SE 1985	24
373 6/8	52	52 3/8	60	5 5/8	5	2 4/8	14 3/8	4/8	14 5/8	11	15	Ungava Bay, Que.	Edward J. Pallay	Edward J. Pallay	SE 1982	25
368	49 4/8	47 3/8	51 1/8	5 3/8	5	15 2/8	14 4/8	12	6 3/8	16	15	Ford Lake, Que.	Willard L. Divine	Willard L. Divine	SE 1985	26
468*	61 1/8	53 4/8	54 4/8	5 5/8	5 7/8	19 1/8	19 3/8	6 5/8	14 2/8	18	24	Tunulic River, Que.	James A. DeLuca	James A. DeLuca	SE 1983	
446 4/8*	61 4/8	60 7/8	67 1/8	5 5/8	5 5/8	23 4/8	22 5/8	16 5/8	4 2/8	20	15	Ungava Bay, Que.	Leonard M. Clarke	Leonard M. Clarke	AG 1983	

*Final Score subject to revision by additional verifying measurements.

Pronghorn
Antilocapra americana americana and related subspecies

Minimum Score 80   World's Record 93 4/8

Score	Length of Horn R.	Length of Horn L.	Circumference of Base R.	Circumference of Base L.	Circumference at Third Quarter R.	Circumference at Third Quarter L.	Inside Spread	Tip to Tip Spread	Length of Prong R.	Length of Prong L.	Locality Killed	By Whom Killed	Owner	Date Killed	Rank
93 4/8	17 6/8	17 4/8	6 7/8	7	3 1/8	3 3/8	12 4/8	8 3/8	8	8 2/8	Coconino Co., Ariz.	Michael J. O'Haco, Jr.	Michael J. O'Haco, Jr.	SE 1985	1
90 4/8	18 1/8	18 3/8	6 5/8	6 5/8	2 5/8	2 7/8	10 3/8	2 7/8	7	6 4/8	Yavapai Co., Ariz.	Joe P. Fornara	Joe P. Fornara	SE 1984	2
89 4/8	17 1/8	17 1/8	7	7	3 1/8	3	7 4/8	1 5/8	6	6	Moffat Co., Colo.	Gerald Scott	Gerald Scott	SE 1982	3
89	17	16 3/8	7 2/8	7 1/8	3	3 3/8	11	5 3/8	6 5/8	6 5/8	Lassen Co., Calif.	Picked Up	George W. Conant	PU 1985	4
89	18	18 1/8	6 7/8	7	2 5/8	2 5/8	10 3/8	3 5/8	6 2/8	6	Lincoln Co., N. M.	Arthur E. Long	Arthur E. Long	SE 1985	4
88 7/8	17 7/8	17 5/8	7	7	3	3	15 5/8	11 5/8	5	5 1/8	Humboldt Co., Nev.	Clifford J. Heaverne	Clifford J. Heaverne	AG 1983	6
88 4/8	19 2/8	18 6/8	6 5/8	6 5/8	2 5/8	2 6/8	13 4/8	10 4/8	5 4/8	5 3/8	Coconino Co., Ariz.	Harold R. Edgemon	Harold R. Edgemon	SE 1984	6
88 3/8	18 2/8	18 2/8	6 6/8	6 6/8	3 1/8	3 3/8	11 4/8	8 4/8	5	5 3/8	Navajo Co., Ariz.	John M. Griffith, Jr.	John M. Griffith, Jr.	SE 1983	8
88 2/8	16 7/8	16 7/8	7	6 7/8	2 7/8	2 7/8	10 5/8	5 5/8	5 3/8	5 7/8	Yavapai Co., Ariz.	Larry D. Saylor	Larry D. Saylor	SE 1984	8
87	16 3/8	16 4/8	6 5/8	6 4/8	2 5/8	2 6/8	11 4/8	7 4/8	7 2/8	6 5/8	Sweetwater Co., Wyo.	William S. Salisbury	William S. Salisbury	SE 1983	10
87	17	17	6 5/8	6 7/8	2 5/8	2 5/8	10 5/8	8 3/8	6 1/8	6 5/8	Millard Co., Utah	Duane Stanworth	Duane Stanworth	SE 1984	10
86 5/8	15 5/8	15 3/8	7 3/8	7 3/8	2 5/8	2 5/8	11 3/8	10 5/8	6 5/8	7	Albany Co., Wyo.	Lloyd D. Kindsfater	Lloyd D. Kindsfater	SE 1983	12
86 3/8	18 3/8	18 1/8	6 5/8	6 5/8	3	3	8 7/8	5 5/8	4 4/8	5 3/8	Sublette Co., Wyo.	Glenn A. Eiden	Glenn A. Eiden	SE 1983	12
86 2/8	17 3/8	17 4/8	6 6/8	6 6/8	2 5/8	2 5/8	9 1/8	2	6 1/8	5 5/8	Washoe Co., Nev.	Bruce D. Gallio	Bruce D. Gallio	AG 1983	14
86 2/8	15 2/8	15	6 6/8	6 6/8	4	3 6/8	9 5/8	5 5/8	5	4 5/8	Hartley Co., Texas	Ernie Davis	Ernie Davis	OT 1983	15
86 1/8	15 5/8	15 5/8	6 3/8	6 2/8	2 5/8	2 6/8	11	5 7/8	8 3/8	8 4/8	Otero Co., N. M.	Robert B. West	Dorothy West	1957	15
86 1/8	17 2/8	17 1/8	6 4/8	6 4/8	2 5/8	2 6/8	11 3/8	7 3/8	5 2/8	5 3/8	Washoe Co., Nev.	Daniel E. Warren	Daniel E. Warren	AG 1983	15
86	16 1/8	16	7 1/8	7	3	2 7/8	9 2/8	4 2/8	5 7/8	5 5/8	Natrona Co., Wyo.	David H. Crum	David H. Crum	OT 1983	18
86	16 4/8	16 5/8	6 6/8	6 7/8	2 5/8	2 6/8	9 2/8	4 3/8	5 7/8	6	Wibaux Co., Mont.	Raymond G. Marciniak	Raymond G. Marciniak	OT 1984	18
86	16 3/8	16 4/8	6 6/8	7 1/8	4 1/8	4 3/8	6 5/8	2 2/8	4 3/8	3 5/8	Apache Co., Ariz.	Charles R. Sprung	Charles R. Sprung	OT 1984	18
86	16 4/8	16 4/8	6 6/8	6 5/8	3 1/8	2 7/8	14 3/8	12 4/8	6 1/8	5 5/8	Valley Co., Mont.	Ernie Freebury	Ernie Freebury	NO 1981	18
86	14 2/8	14 5/8	7 4/8	7 5/8	2 5/8	2 6/8	10 4/8	7 5/8	6 7/8	7	Lake Co., Oreg.	Frank Biggs	Frank Biggs	SE 1985	18
85 5/8	15 5/8	15 4/8	6 7/8	6 7/8	2 5/8	2 5/8	8 4/8	2 3/8	6 3/8	6 3/8	Fremont Co., Wyo.	Roger E. Udovich	Roger E. Udovich	SE 1982	23
85 5/8	17 3/8	17 3/8	6 3/8	6 1/8	2 7/8	2 5/8	9 1/8	4 2/8	6 3/8	5 7/8	Lemhi Co., Idaho	Michael Wolf	Michael Wolf	SE 1982	23
85 4/8	17	16 5/8	6 7/8	6 7/8	2 7/8	2 7/8	9 3/8	6	5 3/8	5 7/8	Sweetwater Co., Wyo.	E. Jay Dawson	E. Jay Dawson	SE 1983	23
85 1/8	16 3/8	15 7/8	7	7 1/8	2 4/8	2 4/8	10 4/8	5 5/8	7 1/8	6 7/8	Sioux Co., Neb.	John W. Hlavacek	John W. Hlavacek	SE 1983	23
85 1/8	17 7/8	17 3/8	7	7	2 7/8	2 4/8	14 1/8	12 5/8	5 3/8	6	Lake Co., Oreg.	Edna J. Kettenburg	Edna J. Kettenburg	AG 1985	23
85 1/8	18 1/8	18 4/8	6 4/8	6 4/8	2 4/8	2 5/8	17 4/8	13 5/8	5 4/8	5 5/8	Apache Co., Ariz.	Don L. Corley	Don L. Corley	SE 1985	23
85 2/8	17	17 1/8	6 4/8	6 4/8	2 6/8	2 6/8	14 1/8	13 2/8	5 1/8	5 1/8	Colfax Co., N. M.	S. X. Callahan, III	S. X. Callahan, III	SE 1983	29

85 2/8	17 3/8	17 3/8	7 2/8	7	2 7/8	2 6/8	12	7 2/8	5 2/8	5 3/8	Rosebud Co., Mont.	Dale R. Brauer	Dale R. Brauer	OT 1983	29
85 2/8	16 3/8	16 3/8	7	6 7/8	2 5/8	2 4/8	14 3/8	10 5/8	6 2/8	6 2/8	Carbon Co., Wyo.	Patrick R. Adams	Patrick R. Adams	SE 1982	29
85 2/8	16 7/8	16 7/8	6 6/8	6 6/8	3	3	11 6/8	6 5/8	5 1/8	5 3/8	Coconino Co., Ariz.	Philip S. Leiendecker	Philip S. Leiendecker	OT 1982	29
85 2/8	16 1/8	16 1/8	7	6 7/8	2 7/8	2 5/8	10 5/8	7 1/8	5 5/8	6 1/8	Sweetwater Co., Wyo.	L. Bill Miller	L. Bill Miller	SE 1982	29
85 1/8	17 4/8	16 5/8	6 6/8	6 5/8	3	2 6/8	20 5/8	20	7 2/8	6 4/8	Sweetwater Co., Wyo.	Annette D. Lynch	Annette D. Lynch	SE 1983	34
85	16 2/8	16	6 6/8	6 6/8	2 5/8	2 5/8	12 7/8	9 4/8	6 1/8	6 1/8	Carbon Co., Wyo.	Kelly W. Hepworth	Kelly W. Hepworth	OT 1982	35
85	17	17 2/8	6 2/8	6 2/8	2 6/8	2 5/8	11 7/8	8 4/8	6 1/8	6 3/8	Millard Co., Utah	Scott C. Rowley	Scott C. Rowley	SE 1984	35
85	16 6/8	16 6/8	6 3/8	6 3/8	2 7/8	2 7/8	10 2/8	3 5/8	6 2/8	5 5/8	Hudspeth Co., Texas	Vernon Dodd	Vernon Dodd	SE 1984	35
84 6/8	17	16 5/8	6 5/8	6 5/8	2 7/8	2 6/8	8	1 5/8	6	5 4/8	Lemhi Co., Idaho	Sherl L. Chapman	Sherl L. Chapman	OT 1983	38
84 6/8	15 4/8	15 4/8	7 3/8	7 2/8	2 4/8	2 4/8	11 5/8	7 6/8	6 5/8	6 5/8	Sweetwater Co., Wyo.	David L. Thompson	David L. Thompson	SE 1982	38
84 6/8	16 7/8	16 3/8	6 5/8	6 5/8	2 2/8	2 3/8	11 4/8	8 4/8	7 1/8	6 7/8	Carbon Co., Wyo.	Robb D. Hitchcock	Robb D. Hitchcock	OT 1981	38
84 4/8	15 4/8	15 2/8	7 4/8	7 4/8	3	3	13 6/8	10	5 6/8	5 5/8	Fremont Co., Wyo.	Michael P. Hauffe	Michael P. Hauffe	SE 1983	41
84 4/8	16 6/8	16 7/8	7 3/8	7 2/8	2 5/8	2 6/8	14 4/8	8 6/8	4 5/8	4 5/8	Fremont Co., Wyo.	William R. Suranyi	William R. Suranyi	SE 1983	41
84 4/8	16 1/8	16 4/8	6 6/8	6 5/8	2 6/8	3	15	12 2/8	5 5/8	5 5/8	Carbon Co., Wyo.	Jack A. Berger	Jack A. Berger	SE 1982	41
84 4/8	15	15	6 4/8	6 5/8	2 5/8	2 6/8	9 6/8	7 3/8	7	6 6/8	Carbon Co., Wyo.	William J. Stokes	William J. Stokes	SE 1982	41
84 4/8	17	17 4/8	7	6 7/8	2 5/8	2 3/8	15	11	5 2/8	5 2/8	Deschutes Co., Oreg.	Rick Ward	Rick Ward	AG 1985	41
84 4/8	16 4/8	16 2/8	6 3/8	6	2 5/8	2 4/8	9	5 1/8	7 1/8	7	Phillips Co., Mont.	Donald W. Hellhake	Donald W. Hellhake	OT 1984	41
84 2/8	16 5/8	16 4/8	7 4/8	7 4/8	3	3	9 2/8	5 1/8	5 1/8	4 6/8	Natrona Co., Wyo.	Allen J. Hogan	Allen J. Hogan	SE 1983	47
84 2/8	15 5/8	15 5/8	6 7/8	6 5/8	2 5/8	2 4/8	9 3/8	4 5/8	6 5/8	6 1/8	Carbon Co., Wyo.	Mike Clegg	Mike Clegg	SE 1983	47
84 2/8	17 2/8	17 3/8	6 4/8	6 6/8	2 4/8	2 5/8	8 5/8	2 2/8	5 6/8	5 4/8	Washoe Co., Nev.	Judy Taylor	Judy Taylor	AG 1983	47
84 2/8	16	16 2/8	6 5/8	6 5/8	3	3	13 2/8	11	5 6/8	5 6/8	Fremont Co., Wyo.	John Monje	John Monje	OT 1985	47
84 2/8	16 6/8	16 7/8	6 2/8	6 2/8	2 7/8	3	9 1/8	6 6/8	5 3/8	5 2/8	Coconino Co., Ariz.	William R. Vaughn	William R. Vaughn	OT 1983	47
84 2/8	15	15	6 7/8	6 6/8	2 6/8	3	12 5/8	10 2/8	6 2/8	6	White Pine Co., Nev.	Paul E. Podborny	Paul E. Podborny	AG 1985	47
84	17 2/8	17 2/8	6 5/8	6 4/8	3	2 7/8	9 3/8	5 4/8	4 5/8	5 7/8	Bennett Co., S. D.	Paul R. Nelson	Paul R. Nelson	OT 1983	53
84	16 7/8	16 3/8	7	6 6/8	2 5/8	2 5/8	10 4/8	6 4/8	5 2/8	5 4/8	Sweetwater Co., Wyo.	Richard H. Maddock	Richard H. Maddock	SE 1982	53
84	15 5/8	15 5/8	6 6/8	6 4/8	3 4/8	3 1/8	15 1/8	11 2/8	5 1/8	5 2/8	Coconino Co., Ariz.	Fred J. Nobbe, Jr.	Fred J. Nobbe, Jr.	OT 1982	53
84	14 6/8	14 5/8	7 2/8	7 2/8	3	3	11 1/8	7 5/8	6 1/8	5 5/8	Sheridan Co., Neb.	Wayne M. Kelly	Wayne M. Kelly	SE 1983	53
84	16 4/8	16 4/8	6 3/8	6 3/8	2 6/8	2 6/8	11 6/8	7 4/8	5 6/8	5 7/8	Sweetwater Co., Wyo.	Dennis W. Gallegos	Dennis W. Gallegos	SE 1983	53
84	16 7/8	16 6/8	6 5/8	6 5/8	2 4/8	2 3/8	10 4/8	6 4/8	6 3/8	6 3/8	Natrona Co., Wyo.	Dale A. Ableidinger	Dale A. Ableidinger	SE 1984	53
84	16 2/8	16 2/8	6 4/8	6 5/8	3	3 2/8	12	9 5/8	5 3/8	5 1/8	Mora Co., N. M.	Roger B. Coit	Roger B. Coit	SE 1983	53
84	16	16	6 4/8	6 5/8	2 7/8	2 7/8	10	7 6/8	5 7/8	6 1/8	Washoe Co., Nev.	Bert F. Carder	Bert F. Carder	AG 1984	53
84	17 4/8	16 2/8	6 7/8	6 6/8	3 1/8	3	10 3/8	4 6/8	5 7/8	5 2/8	Yavapai Co., Ariz.	Fredrick T. Lau	Fredrick T. Lau	SE 1985	53
83 6/8	15 6/8	16	7 4/8	7 5/8	2 3/8	2 4/8	15 5/8	11 6/8	5 6/8	6 3/8	Lake Co., Oreg.	Barbara J. Smallwood	Barbara J. Smallwood	AG 1983	62
83 6/8	15 7/8	15 7/8	6 6/8	6 6/8	2 3/8	2 3/8	12 5/8	11	6 5/8	6 4/8	Sweetwater Co., Wyo.	Robert Gilbert	Robert Gilbert	SE 1983	62
83 6/8	16 1/8	16 4/8	6 7/8	6 4/8	2 4/8	2 4/8	9 1/8	5 6/8	6 1/8	6 3/8	Humboldt Co., Nev.	Harold J. Ward	Harold J. Ward	SE 1981	62
83 6/8	16 3/8	16 7/8	6 2/8	6 1/8	2 6/8	2 6/8	8 5/8	2	6	6 5/8	Lincoln Co., N. M.	James R. Doverspike	James R. Doverspike	SE 1982	62
83 6/8	15 4/8	14 7/8	7 5/8	7 4/8	2 7/8	2 6/8	9 2/8	6	5 5/8	5 4/8	Carbon Co., Wyo.	Jack F. Schakel	Jack F. Schakel	SE 1981	62

Pronghorn—*Continued*

Antilocapra americana americana and related subspecies

Score	Length of Horn R.	Length of Horn L.	Circumference of Base R.	Circumference of Base L.	Circumference at Third Quarter R.	Circumference at Third Quarter L.	Inside Spread	Tip to Tip Spread	Length of Prong R.	Length of Prong L.	Locality Killed	By Whom Killed	Owner	Date Killed	Rank
83 6/8	16 2/8	16 5/8	7	6 6/8	2 5/8	2 6/8	12 6/8	8 4/8	5 6/8	5 5/8	Carbon Co., Wyo.	Douglas L. Hancock	Douglas L. Hancock	SE 1983	62
83 6/8	15 6/8	15 7/8	6 2/8	6 2/8	2 5/8	2 7/8	11	7 6/8	6	6 1/8	Jackson Co., Colo.	Cylestine A. Manguso	Cylestine A. Manguso	SE 1983	62
83 6/8	16 1/8	16 1/8	6 4/8	6 3/8	2 5/8	2 6/8	12 7/8	9 6/8	6 2/8	6	Washoe Co., Nev.	Arthur L. Biggs	Arthur L. Biggs	AG 1984	62
83 6/8	15 6/8	16 1/8	6 6/8	6 5/8	2 7/8	2 5/8	12	7 2/8	5 2/8	5 2/8	Millard Co., Utah	Mitchell S. Bastian	Mitchell S. Bastian	SE 1985	62
83 4/8	14 1/8	14 2/8	6 5/8	6 5/8	3 2/8	3 2/8	8 5/8	4	6 3/8	6 2/8	Jackson Co., Colo.	Cynthia L. Welle	Cynthia L. Welle	SE 1982	71
83 4/8	17 5/8	17 3/8	6 1/8	6 1/8	2 3/8	2 4/8	6 7/8	0	6 3/8	5 7/8	Natrona Co., Wyo.	Gerald J. Ahles	Gerald J. Ahles	OT 1982	71
83 4/8	15 4/8	15 5/8	6 6/8	6 7/8	3 1/8	3 1/8	13	10 1/8	5 1/8	5 3/8	Rosebud Co., Mont.	James D. Cameron	James D. Cameron	NO 1981	71
83 4/8	16 7/8	17	6 4/8	6 4/8	2 5/8	2 5/8	14 1/8	10 2/8	5 4/8	5 5/8	Lake Co., Oreg.	Donald R. Davidson	Donald R. Davidson	AG 1984	71
83 4/8	18	18	6 7/8	7	3 7/8	3 2/8	9 3/8	6 2/8	4 6/8	3 1/8	Carbon Co., Wyo.	Ronald K. Pettit	Ronald K. Pettit	SE 1983	71
83 4/8	17 3/8	17 4/8	6 4/8	6 4/8	3 2/8	3	13 3/8	11 2/8	4 4/8	4 4/8	Coconino Co., Ariz.	Duane D. Backhaus	Duane D. Backhaus	SE 1984	71
83 4/8	17 5/8	17 5/8	6	6	2 6/8	2 7/8	10 7/8	8	5 3/8	5	Coconino Co., Ariz.	Arthur A. Smith	Arthur A. Smith	SE 1984	71
83 4/8	16 2/8	16 3/8	6 4/8	6 4/8	2 7/8	2 7/8	13 2/8	8 5/8	5 4/8	5 1/8	Yavapai Co., Ariz.	Glenn E. Leslie, Jr.	Glenn E. Leslie, Jr.	SE 1984	71
83 4/8	17 4/8	17 2/8	6 7/8	6 7/8	3	2 6/8	18	14	4 5/8	4 5/8	Colfax Co., N. M.	David S. Dickenson	David S. Dickenson	SE 1984	71
83 2/8	15 2/8	15 7/8	7 1/8	6 7/8	2 4/8	2 6/8	11 6/8	6 5/8	5 5/8	5 5/8	Lake Co., Oreg.	Richard L. Smith	Richard L. Smith	AG 1983	80
83 2/8	17 3/8	17 4/8	7	6 6/8	2 6/8	2 6/8	12 3/8	7	5 1/8	3 6/8	Apache Co., Ariz.	Robert A. Stacy	Robert A. Stacy	SE 1983	80
83 2/8	16 6/8	17	6 6/8	6 4/8	2 6/8	2 6/8	9 5/8	3 7/8	5 2/8	5 3/8	Sweetwater Co., Wyo.	Donald W. Kramer	Donald W. Kramer	SE 1983	80
83 2/8	16 3/8	16 1/8	6 4/8	6 4/8	3 2/8	3 2/8	8 7/8	3 5/8	4 6/8	4 7/8	Brewster Co., Texas	Richard T. Delgado	Richard T. Delgado	OT 1982	80
83 2/8	17 1/8	17 3/8	6 2/8	6 3/8	3	3 1/8	12 4/8	6 6/8	4 5/8	4 6/8	Coconino Co., Ariz.	Delroy Western	Delroy Western	SE 1983	80
83 2/8	14 6/8	14 6/8	7 3/8	7 3/8	2 6/8	2 6/8	13 5/8	11 1/8	5 2/8	5 4/8	Lake Co., Oreg.	Clyde L. Dehlinger	Clyde L. Dehlinger	AG 1983	80
83 2/8	16 4/8	16 5/8	6 2/8	6	3 2/8	3 3/8	11 5/8	8 1/8	4 7/8	4 7/8	Coconino Co., Ariz.	Gilbert S. Garside	Gilbert S. Garside	OT 1982	80
83 2/8	15 2/8	15 2/8	7 4/8	7 4/8	2 7/8	3 1/8	12	11 2/8	4 5/8	5 3/8	Natrona Co., Wyo.	Gary A. Campbell	Gary A. Campbell	OT 1983	80
83 2/8	15 6/8	15 7/8	6 2/8	6 2/8	3 2/8	3 2/8	8 5/8	4 5/8	4 5/8	4 7/8	Coconino Co., Ariz.	Matthew Dominy	Matthew Dominy	SE 1984	80
83 2/8	16 4/8	16 2/8	6 5/8	6 5/8	2 2/8	2 2/8	8 6/8	3 4/8	6 6/8	6 2/8	Uinta Co., Wyo.	Earl H. Heninger	Earl H. Heninger	SE 1983	80
83 2/8	16 2/8	16 5/8	6	6	2 7/8	2 6/8	9 1/8	3 5/8	7	6 5/8	Carter Co., Mont.	Martin Crane	Martin Crane	NO 1983	80
83 2/8	15 3/8	15 2/8	7 1/8	7	3 2/8	3 1/8	15 3/8	14	4 4/8	4 6/8	Thomas Co., Kan.	Charles M. Barnett	Charles M. Barnett	OT 1985	80
83 2/8	16 2/8	15	6 6/8	6 4/8	3 3/8	3 1/8	11 4/8	7 3/8	6 1/8	6	Cochise Co., Ariz.	Jim Tomlin	Jim Tomlin	SE 1984	80
83 2/8	16 1/8	16 3/8	6 6/8	6 5/8	3	3 1/8	14 3/8	10 1/8	5	5 2/8	Mora Co., N. M.	James E. Davenport, Jr.	James E. Davenport, Jr.	SE 1983	80
83	15 7/8	15 7/8	7 1/8	7	2 6/8	2 6/8	13 6/8	9 3/8	5 6/8	5 4/8	Colfax Co., N. M.	John W. Ladd	John W. Ladd	SE 1983	94
83	16	15 7/8	7 1/8	7 1/8	2 4/8	2 5/8	10 1/8	8 4/8	5 6/8	5 4/8	Carbon Co., Wyo.	Frederick L. Proffit	Frederick L. Proffit	SE 1983	94
83	15 4/8	15 6/8	7 2/8	7	2 5/8	2 5/8	10 6/8	4 6/8	5 5/8	5 4/8	Humboldt Co., Nev.	Thomas S. Kelley	Thomas S. Kelley	AG 1983	94
83	15 2/8	15 3/8	6 4/8	6 2/8	3 4/8	3 2/8	11 5/8	7 2/8	5 4/8	5	Hartley Co., Texas	William G. Kendrick	William G. Kendrick	OT 1953	94

83	16⁴⁄₈	16⁵⁄₈	6⁴⁄₈	6²⁄₈	2⁴⁄₈	2⁴⁄₈	11⅛	5⁶⁄₈	6²⁄₈	6⁶⁄₈	Meade Co., S. D.	Randy A. Cammack	Randy A. Cammack	NO 1982	94
83	15⅜	15⅝	7	7	3	3⅛	9	7	5²⁄₈	5⁶⁄₈	Box Butte Co., Neb.	Lynda G. Sydow	Lynda G. Sydow	SE 1984	94
82⁶⁄₈	14⁶⁄₈	15	7⅝	7²⁄₈	2⅝	2⁶⁄₈	14⁶⁄₈	12⅜	6⅜	5⁶⁄₈	Carbon Co., Wyo.	Kenneth E. Grail	Kenneth E. Grail	OT 1983	100
82⁶⁄₈	15	15	7²⁄₈	6⅞	2⅝	2⅝	10	6	5⅜	5⅝	Carbon Co., Wyo.	Dailen R. Jones	Dailen R. Jones	SE 1982	100
82⁶⁄₈	15⅝	16	6⅝	6⁴⁄₈	2⅝	2⁶⁄₈	9²⁄₈	6⅜	6⅜	5⁶⁄₈	Natrona Co., Wyo.	Eugene Turner, Jr.	Eugene Turner, Jr.	OT 1982	100
82⁶⁄₈	16⅞	16⁶⁄₈	6²⁄₈	6²⁄₈	2⁶⁄₈	2⁶⁄₈	11⅜	8⅜	4⅞	5	Mora Co., N. M.	Donald R. Warren	Donald R. Warren	AG 1982	100
82⁶⁄₈	16⅜	16⁴⁄₈	6⅛	6	2⅝	2⁶⁄₈	13⅞	10⅛	5²⁄₈	5²⁄₈	Yellowstone Co., Mont.	Robert M. Labert	Robert M. Labert	SE 1984	100
82⁶⁄₈	17⅛	17⁴⁄₈	6⁶⁄₈	6⅝	2²⁄₈	2²⁄₈	11⅛	4⅝	5²⁄₈	5⅜	Washoe Co., Nev.	Michael J. Lange	Michael J. Lange	AG 1983	100
82⁶⁄₈	14⅝	14⅝	6⁶⁄₈	6⁶⁄₈	2²⁄₈	2⅛	11²⁄₈	7⅝	7²⁄₈	7²⁄₈	Grant Co., Oreg.	A. Paul Malstrom	A. Paul Malstrom	AG 1978	100
82⁶⁄₈	16⅜	16²⁄₈	6²⁄₈	6²⁄₈	2⁴⁄₈	2⁴⁄₈	8⁴⁄₈	2⅝	6⁴⁄₈	6²⁄₈	Sweetwater Co., Wyo.	Craig B. Argyle	Craig B. Argyle	SE 1985	100
82⁶⁄₈	17⅜	17	6	6	2⅝	2⁶⁄₈	9⅝	5⅛	5⁴⁄₈	5⅜	Custer Co., Idaho	William P. Benscoter	William P. Benscoter	OT 1985	100
82⅝	15⁶⁄₈	15⅝	6⅜	6²⁄₈	2⅝	2⁴⁄₈	15⅞	13	6⅜	6²⁄₈	Yavapai Co., Ariz.	Joseph C. Cancilliere	Joseph C. Cancilliere	SE 1984	109
82⁴⁄₈	16⁶⁄₈	16⅛	6⁶⁄₈	6⅝	2⁴⁄₈	2⅜	8⅛	2⁶⁄₈	5⅞	5⁴⁄₈	Washoe Co., Nev.	Vernon E. Benney	Vernon E. Benney	AG 1983	110
82⁴⁄₈	16²⁄₈	16⅛	6⁴⁄₈	6⁴⁄₈	3	2⁶⁄₈	9²⁄₈	4⅝	5⅝	5⅜	Natrona Co., Wyo.	Edgar M. Artecona	Edgar M. Artecona	OT 1982	110
82⁴⁄₈	15⅛	15⅛	6⁶⁄₈	6⁶⁄₈	2⅝	2⁶⁄₈	10⁶⁄₈	9⅛	5⅞	5⅞	Carbon Co., Wyo.	John T. Butters	John T. Butters	OT 1982	110
82⁴⁄₈	17⁶⁄₈	17⅜	6	6	2⅝	2⅝	11²⁄₈	6	5²⁄₈	5⁴⁄₈	Hudspeth Co., Texas	Ray A. Acker, Sr.	Ray A. Acker, Sr.	OT 1980	110
82⁴⁄₈	15⁶⁄₈	16⅜	6⁶⁄₈	6⁶⁄₈	2⁴⁄₈	2⁶⁄₈	9⁴⁄₈	5⅜	6	5⁶⁄₈	Sweetwater Co., Wyo.	Richard E. Knox, Jr.	Richard E. Knox, Jr.	SE 1983	110
82⁴⁄₈	16⅛	16⅛	7	7	2⁴⁄₈	2⁴⁄₈	5²⁄₈	2	5²⁄₈	5²⁄₈	Natrona Co., Wyo.	Bill E. Boatman	Bill E. Boatman	SE 1983	110
82⁴⁄₈	15⅝	15⅜	6⁴⁄₈	6⁴⁄₈	3	2⅞	8	3⁶⁄₈	6	5⁶⁄₈	Navajo Co., Ariz.	Perry H. Finger	Perry H. Finger	SE 1984	110
82⁴⁄₈	16⅜	15⁶⁄₈	6⁴⁄₈	6⅝	3	2⅝	14⅛	9⁶⁄₈	5⅜	6²⁄₈	Hudspeth Co., Texas	Ernest Elbert, Jr.	Ernest Elbert, Jr.	SE 1985	110
82⁴⁄₈	16⅝	16⅜	7	6⅞	2⁶⁄₈	2⁶⁄₈	8⅞	3⅛	5⁴⁄₈	5⁴⁄₈	Natrona Co., Wyo.	Toby J. Johnson	Toby J. Johnson	SE 1985	110
82⁴⁄₈	15⅝	16⅛	6⁴⁄₈	6⅝	2⁶⁄₈	2⅞	8⁶⁄₈	5²⁄₈	5⅜	5⁴⁄₈	Sweetwater Co., Wyo.	W. A. Chambers	W. A. Chambers	SE 1985	110
82⁴⁄₈	15⅝	16	6⁴⁄₈	6⅜	3	3	12	10⅝	5⁶⁄₈	5⁴⁄₈	Carbon Co., Wyo.	Merlyn J. Kiel	Merlyn J. Kiel	SE 1983	110
82²⁄₈	16²⁄₈	16²⁄₈	6⁴⁄₈	6⅜	2⅞	2⅞	13²⁄₈	11	5⅝	4⅞	Fremont Co., Wyo.	Michael C. Meeker	Mike Meeker	SE 1982	121
82²⁄₈	15⅞	15⁶⁄₈	6⁶⁄₈	6⅝	2⁶⁄₈	2⁶⁄₈	10⅜	10	5⁴⁄₈	5⁴⁄₈	Washakie Co., Wyo.	Carol Greet	Carol Greet	OT 1983	121
82²⁄₈	16⅝	16²⁄₈	6⁶⁄₈	6⁴⁄₈	2⅞	2⅞	15	11	5	5⅛	Navajo Co., Ariz.	A. T. Boultinghouse	A. T. Boultinghouse	SE 1983	121
82²⁄₈	16⅜	15⅞	6⅜	6⅜	2⁴⁄₈	2⅜	10⅝	6⅜	6⅛	5⅞	Butte Co., Idaho	Chris Tiller	Chris Tiller	NO 1983	121
82²⁄₈	16⁶⁄₈	16⁴⁄₈	6⁴⁄₈	6⅝	2⁴⁄₈	2⁶⁄₈	11⅝	8⁶⁄₈	4⅞	4⅞	Washoe Co., Nev.	Thomas O. Malone	Thomas O. Malone	AG 1982	121
82²⁄₈	16⁴⁄₈	16⁴⁄₈	6⁴⁄₈	6⅜	2⁴⁄₈	2⁴⁄₈	13⅛	9²⁄₈	5⅝	5⁶⁄₈	Fremont Co., Wyo.	Richard L. Bostrom	Richard L. Bostrom	SE 1983	121
82²⁄₈	16⅞	18	6⅛	6	2⁶⁄₈	2⁶⁄₈	11⅛	5⁶⁄₈	5⅛	5⅛	Brewster Co., Texas	McLean Bowman	McLean Bowman	OT 1982	121
82²⁄₈	15⅛	15⁴⁄₈	6⅜	6⁴⁄₈	2⅞	3	10	4⅞	6⅛	6	Fremont Co., Wyo.	Charles D. Day	Charles D. Day	SE 1984	121
82²⁄₈	15⅞	15⁶⁄₈	6⅛	6⅛	2⅝	2⅝	12⁶⁄₈	8⅞	6⅜	6⅜	Hartley Co., Texas	Ernie Davis	Ernie Davis	OT 1984	121
82²⁄₈	15⁶⁄₈	15⁶⁄₈	6⅜	6⅜	2⅝	2⅝	14⅛	13⁶⁄₈	5⁶⁄₈	5⁶⁄₈	Carbon Co., Wyo.	Larry J. Thoney	Larry J. Thoney	SE 1982	121
82²⁄₈	17⅜	16⅞	6²⁄₈	6	2⁴⁄₈	2²⁄₈	11⅞	9⁴⁄₈	6²⁄₈	5⅝	Siskiyou Co., Calif.	Laird E. Marshall	Laird E. Marshall	AG 1984	121
82²⁄₈	16²⁄₈	16²⁄₈	6⁴⁄₈	6⁴⁄₈	2⅞	2⁶⁄₈	9⅝	3⅝	5⁴⁄₈	5⁴⁄₈	Garfield Co., Mont.	William E. Butler	William E. Butler	OT 1983	121
82²⁄₈	14	14⅜	7⁶⁄₈	7⅞	2⁴⁄₈	2⁴⁄₈	10⁴⁄₈	8⁴⁄₈	6²⁄₈	6²⁄₈	Sweetwater Co., Wyo.	Peter B. Shaw	Peter B. Shaw	SE 1983	121
82²⁄₈	16	15⁶⁄₈	6²⁄₈	6⅜	2⅝	2⁶⁄₈	12⅛	8⁶⁄₈	6⅛	6²⁄₈	Natrona Co., Wyo.	Michael D. Samuelson	Michael D. Samuelson	OT 1984	121

Pronghorn—Continued
Antilocapra americana americana and related subspecies

Score	Length of Horn R.	L.	Circumference of Base R.	L.	Circumference at Third Quarter R.	L.	Inside Spread	Tip to Tip Spread	Length of Prong R.	L.	Locality Killed	By Whom Killed	Owner	Date Killed	Rank
82 2/8	16 3/8	16 5/8	6 2/8	6 2/8	2 4/8	2 5/8	13 3/8	8 3/8	5 6/8	5 6/8	Fremont Co., Wyo.	Evelyn A. Maxon	Evelyn A. Maxon	SE 1983	121
82	17	17	6 2/8	6 1/8	2 4/8	2 4/8	6 6/8	1 6/8	5 4/8	5 4/8	Lincoln Co., Wyo.	Tom Crank	Tom Crank	SE 1982	136
82	16 2/8	16 4/8	6 2/8	6 2/8	2 5/8	2 7/8	11 3/8	8 4/8	6	5 7/8	Carbon Co., Wyo.	David J. Schlosser	David J. Schlosser	SE 1982	136
82	15 2/8	15 2/8	6 5/8	6 4/8	3	3 1/8	10	6 4/8	5 2/8	5 4/8	Carbon Co., Wyo.	Eric J. Swanson	Eric J. Swanson	SE 1982	136
82	16 1/8	16	6 1/8	6 1/8	2 2/8	2 2/8	14	10 1/8	6 4/8	6 4/8	Washoe Co., Nev.	Jerry L. Nelms	Jerry L. Nelms	AG 1981	136
82	15	14 5/8	7	7 1/8	2 6/8	2 5/8	12	10 6/8	5 5/8	5 5/8	Carbon Co., Wyo.	Albert Gregg	Albert Gregg	OT 1983	136
82	16 2/8	15 6/8	6 5/8	6 5/8	2 4/8	2 4/8	7 4/8	1	5 7/8	5 7/8	Washoe Co., Nev.	Jack D. Bothwell	Jack D. Bothwell	AG 1984	136
82	17 1/8	17 4/8	6 4/8	6 3/8	3 1/8	3 1/8	0	0	4 2/8	4 4/8	Culberson Co., Texas	Charles Seidensticker	Charles Seidensticker	SE 1978	136
82	16	15 7/8	6 2/8	6 3/8	2 7/8	2 6/8	9 6/8	5	5	5 3/8	Coconino Co., Ariz.	Charles L. Holland	Charles L. Holland	SE 1984	136
82	16 5/8	16 3/8	6 1/8	6 1/8	2 3/8	2 4/8	14 1/8	10 1/8	5 6/8	5 5/8	Quay Co., N. M.	Donald E. Fritz	Donald E. Fritz	SE 1984	136
81 6/8	16 1/8	15 1/8	6	6 4/8	2 7/8	3	11 7/8	7 2/8	6	5 7/8	Hudspeth Co., Texas	Ken E. Moreland	Ken E. Moreland	OT 1984	145
81 2/8	15 1/8	15 1/8	6 5/8	6 5/8	2 4/8	2 4/8	11 5/8	6 3/8	6 2/8	6	Lake Co., Oreg.	Steve B. Laskey	Steve B. Laskey	AG 1985	146
81 2/8	15 5/8	15 5/8	6 1/8	6	3 1/8	3 2/8	11 2/8	6 5/8	5	4 4/8	Apache Co., Ariz.	Lloyd L. Parker	Lloyd L. Parker	SE 1985	146
81	16 3/8	16 2/8	6 2/8	6 1/8	2 5/8	2 4/8	10 6/8	6 3/8	5 5/8	5 5/8	Wayne Co., Utah	Ronald K. Lowe	Ronald K. Lowe	SE 1985	148
80 4/8	16	16 1/8	6 7/8	6 6/8	2 4/8	2 5/8	11 4/8	8	5 5/8	5 1/8	Niobrara Co., Wyo.	John E. Howard	John E. Howard	OT 1982	149
80	14 7/8	14 6/8	7 2/8	7 2/8	2 4/8	2 4/8	10 3/8	5	5 1/8	5 2/8	Natrona Co., Wyo.	John F. Druschba	John F. Druschba	SE 1983	150
80	16 1/8	15 7/8	6 2/8	6 2/8	2 4/8	2 4/8	11 3/8	11	5 4/8	5 4/8	Prairie Co., Mont.	Thomas G. Marallo	Thomas G. Marallo	OT 1984	150
80	15 3/8	15 3/8	5 7/8	5 7/8	2 6/8	2 6/8	11 5/8	6 5/8	4 5/8	4 4/8	Hudspeth Co., Texas	Will Ross	Will Ross	SE 1985	150
89 4/8*	17	16 7/8	7 1/8	7	2 5/8	2 5/8	11	6 5/8	6 3/8	6 5/8	Sweetwater Co., Wyo.	Richard D. Ullery	Richard D. Ullery	SE 1983	

*Final Score subject to revision by additional verifying measurements.

Bison

Minimum Score 115 — ***Bison bison bison* and *Bison bison athabascae*** — **World's Record 136⅛**

Beginning in 1977, hunter taken trophies from the lower 48 states are acceptable only for records, not awards, and only from states that recognize bison as wild and free-ranging and for which a hunting license and/or big game tag is required for hunting.

Score	Length of Horn R.	Length of Horn L.	Circumference of Base R.	Circumference of Base L.	Circumference at Third Quarter R.	Circumference at Third Quarter L.	Greatest Spread	Tip to Tip Spread	Sex	Locality Killed	By Whom Killed	Owner	Date Killed	Rank
124	18 6/8	18 4/8	14	14	6 4/8	7 6/8	33 2/8	27 6/8	M	Coconino Co., Ariz.	Philip A. Sturgill	Philip A. Sturgill	OT 1984	1
123 2/8	17 5/8	18	16 2/8	15 4/8	6	6	29 1/8	22 1/8	M	Custer Co., S. D.	Tim P. Matzinger	Tim P. Matzinger	JA 1983	2
121 6/8	18 2/8	18 2/8	14 3/8	14 3/8	7	7 2/8	29 3/8	23 7/8	M	Custer Co., S. D.	Jon R. Stephens	Jon R. Stephens	DC 1982	3
121	17 6/8	17 4/8	15 2/8	15 4/8	7 5/8	6 1/8	25 5/8	19 5/8	M	Custer Co., S. D.	Wilson W. Crook, III	Wilson W. Crook, III	DC 1982	4
120 6/8	18	18 3/8	15 6/8	15 3/8	5 1/8	5 3/8	29 1/8	26 4/8	M	Custer Co., S. D.	Lucky Simpson	Lucky Simpson	JA 1985	5
120	18 1/8	20 2/8	16	16 2/8	4 5/8	5 1/8	29 5/8	23	M	Big Delta, Alaska	Thomas B. Hite	Thomas B. Hite	SE 1983	6
119	16 7/8	16 7/8	14 5/8	14 6/8	6 5/8	6 4/8	27 2/8	18 7/8	M	Coconino Co., Ariz.	Melvin C. Kincaid	Melvin C. Kincaid	OT 1983	7
118	18 4/8	19 4/8	15 1/8	15 1/8	5	5 1/8	31 7/8	29 1/8	M	Custer State Park, S. D.	Harry T. Scharfenberg	Harry T. Scharfenberg	DC 1984	8
117	17 7/8	17 6/8	14 2/8	14 2/8	6 1/8	6 6/8	29	23 7/8	M	Delta Junction, Alaska	Elizabeth B. McConkey	Elizabeth B. McConkey	NO 1981	9
115 4/8	17 7/8	17 4/8	13 4/8	14 1/8	5 6/8	5 7/8	29 3/8	24 1/8	M	Garfield Co., Utah	Roger Stewart	Roger Stewart	NO 1984	10
115 2/8	18 2/8	19 1/8	14 7/8	15 2/8	4 3/8	5 6/8	28 6/8	21	M	Custer Co., S. D.	J. P. Moon, Jr.	J. P. Moon, Jr.	DC 1983	11
115	16	16 6/8	15	15	5 4/8	6 2/8	29 3/8	27 6/8	M	Custer Co., S. D.	Rodger E. Warwick	Rodger E. Warwick	DC 1982	12
115	18 1/8	18 6/8	14	14 2/8	5 6/8	5 3/8	30 3/8	25 6/8	M	Custer Co., S. D.	August Benz, Jr.	August Benz, Jr.	DC 1983	12

Rocky Mountain Goat

Oreamnos americanus americanus and related subspecies

World's Record 56 4/8
Minimum Score 47

Score	Length of Horn R.	L.	Circumference of Base R.	L.	Circumference at Third Quarter R.	L.	Greatest Spread	Tip to Tip Spread	Sex	Locality Killed	By Whom Killed	Owner	Date Killed	Rank
52 4/8	10 4/8	10 4/8	5 5/8	5 5/8	2 1/8	2 1/8	7 1/8	6 1/8	M	Reflection Lake, Alaska	Timothy F. McGinn	Timothy F. McGinn	SE 1985	1
52 2/8	9 5/8	9 7/8	6	5 7/8	2 1/8	2	8 1/8	7 5/8	M	Taku River, B.C.	Fritz Stork	Fritz Stork	SE 1985	2
52 2/8	10 2/8	10	6 2/8	6 1/8	2	2	7 5/8	7 1/8	M	Sheslay River, B.C.	Frank L. Stukel	Frank L. Stukel	AG 1984	3
52	10 2/8	10 2/8	5 5/8	5 7/8	2	2	8 1/8	7 4/8	M	Burnie Lake, B.C.	Paul R. Levan	Paul R. Levan	SE 1983	4
51 6/8	10 2/8	10 4/8	5 5/8	5 5/8	2	2 1/8	6 3/8	5 5/8	M	Lake Rowena, Alaska	George T. Law	George T. Law	SE 1983	5
51 6/8	10 2/8	10 3/8	6	6	1 5/8	1 5/8	7 7/8	7 4/8	M	Bonneville Co., Idaho	K. Rands Wiley	K. Rands Wiley	OT 1983	5
51 6/8	10 4/8	10 2/8	5 5/8	5 5/8	2 1/8	2 1/8	6 5/8	6	M	Tyee Lake, Alaska	Daniel G. Bowden	Daniel G. Bowden	AG 1982	5
51 6/8	10 6/8	10 5/8	5 3/8	5 3/8	2	2	7 1/8	6	M	Leduc Lake, Alaska	Steve Lepschat	Steve Lepschat	SE 1982	5
51 6/8	10 4/8	10 4/8	5 5/8	5 5/8	1 7/8	2	7 5/8	7 1/8	M	Kildala River, B.C.	Lorne Hallman	Lorne Hallman	NO 1966	5
51 6/8	9 7/8	9 6/8	5 5/8	5 5/8	2	2	6	4 4/8	M	Cleveland Pen., Alaska	Michael L. Ward	Michael L. Ward	OT 1983	5
51 4/8	10 4/8	10 4/8	5 5/8	5 5/8	1 7/8	1 7/8	7 1/8	6 1/8	M	Snohomish Co., Wash.	Edward M. Beitner	Edward M. Beitner	OT 1984	5
51 4/8	10 3/8	10 3/8	5 5/8	5 5/8	1 7/8	1 7/8	6 7/8	6 2/8	M	Chouteau Co., Mont.	Larry W. Lander	Larry W. Lander	NO 1983	12
51 4/8	10 7/8	10 7/8	5 4/8	5 4/8	1 7/8	1 7/8	7 2/8	7 1/8	M	Snohomish Co., Wash.	Theodore H. Kiser	Theodore H. Kiser	SE 1985	12
51 2/8	10 5/8	10 5/8	6	5 7/8	1 7/8	1 7/8	7 4/8	6 7/8	M	Kaustua Creek, B.C.	Duane Pankratz	Duane Pankratz	AG 1982	14
51 2/8	10	10 2/8	5 5/8	5 5/8	2 1/8	2 1/8	5 7/8	5	M	Tyee Lake, Alaska	David L. Bowden	David L. Bowden	AG 1982	14
51 2/8	10 6/8	10 1/8	5 5/8	5 5/8	1 7/8	1 7/8	6 6/8	6 2/8	M	Okanogan Co., Wash.	Richard D. Grant	Richard D. Grant	OT 1982	14
51 2/8	10 4/8	10	5 5/8	5 5/8	2	1 7/8	8 3/8	7 7/8	F	Glenallen, Alaska	Kirk Z. Smith	Kirk Z. Smith	SE 1982	14
51 2/8	9 4/8	9 1/8	5 5/8	5 5/8	2 4/8	2 4/8	7 4/8	6 6/8	M	Taku River, B.C.	Charles W. Schmidt	Charles W. Schmidt	SE 1985	14
51	9 7/8	9 5/8	5 7/8	5 7/8	1 7/8	1 7/8	6	4 4/8	M	Granite Basin, Alaska	Gerry D. Downey	Gerry D. Downey	SE 1983	19
51	10 7/8	10 7/8	5 3/8	5 4/8	1 6/8	1 7/8	6 6/8	5 5/8	M	Gallatin Co., Mont.	Ronald K. Lewis	Ronald K. Lewis	SE 1984	19
51	10 6/8	10 6/8	5 5/8	5 5/8	1 7/8	1 7/8	7 3/8	6 6/8	M	Snohomish Co., Wash.	John W. Lane	John W. Lane	OT 1982	19
51	10 6/8	10 3/8	5 5/8	5 5/8	1 7/8	1 7/8	7 3/8	6 7/8	M	Sheslay River, B.C.	Steven M. Sullivan	Steven M. Sullivan	OT 1985	19
50 6/8	10 6/8	10 4/8	5 5/8	5 5/8	2	2	7 4/8	7	M	Stewart, B.C.	Harry J. McCowan	Harry J. McCowan	OT 1983	23
50 6/8	10 3/8	10 5/8	5 7/8	5 7/8	1 6/8	1 5/8	7 1/8	6 1/8	M	Dutch Creek, B.C.	Tom Housh	Tom Housh	SE 1982	23
50 6/8	11 2/8	11 7/8	5 5/8	5 5/8	1 5/8	1 5/8	7 7/8	7	M	Beaverfoot Range, B.C.	Kelley Knight	Kelley Knight	OT 1984	23
50 4/8	11	10 6/8	6	5 7/8	2	1 7/8	7 3/8	6 2/8	M	Little Oliver Creek, B.C.	David J. Flemming	David J. Flemming	JA 1985	23

368

50 6/8	10	10	5 7/8	5 7/8	1 7/8	1 7/8	7 5/8	7 2/8	M	Okanogan Co., Wash.	Jerrel R. Harmon	Jerrel R. Harmon	OT 1984	23
50 6/8	10	10	5 6/8	5 7/8	1 7/8	1 7/8	6 5/8	6 3/8	M	Okanogan Co., Wash.	Susan M. Fletcher	Susan M. Fletcher	SE 1985	23
50 6/8	10 3/8	10 3/8	5 5/8	5 5/8	1 6/8	1 7/8	9 5/8	9 5/8	M	Day Harbor, Alaska	Steen Henriksen	Steen Henriksen	OT 1984	23
50 4/8	10	9 7/8	5 6/8	5 5/8	2	2	9 1/8	9	M	Stikine Canyon, B.C.	Reuben F. Gerecke	Reuben F. Gerecke	OT 1982	30
50 4/8	10 6/8	10 7/8	5 3/8	5 3/8	1 7/8	1 7/8	7 4/8	6 4/8	M	Leduc Lake, Alaska	James M. Judd	James M. Judd	AG 1985	30
50 4/8	10 4/8	10 3/8	5 7/8	5 7/8	1 6/8	1 6/8	7 7/8	7 3/8	M	Mt. Cummins, B.C.	Rod Aune	Rod Aune	NO 1984	30
50 2/8	10 1/8	10	5 6/8	5 6/8	1 7/8	1 7/8	6 6/8	5 5/8	M	Pemberton, B.C.	Weldon Talbot	Weldon Talbot	SE 1982	33
50 2/8	10 3/8	10 2/8	5 6/8	5 6/8	1 6/8	1 6/8	7 4/8	6 7/8	M	Chouteau Co., Mont.	Robert E. Young	Robert E. Young	NO 1983	33
50 2/8	10 1/8	10 1/8	5 5/8	5 4/8	2	2	8 1/8	7 3/8	M	Kildala River, B.C.	Philip Perrone	Philip Perrone	AG 1983	33
50 2/8	10 7/8	10 5/8	5 5/8	5 4/8	1 6/8	1 6/8	8	7 2/8	M	Skeena, B.C.	Clarence J. Fields	Clarence J. Fields	AG 1983	33
50 2/8	9 3/8	9 1/8	5 7/8	5 7/8	1 7/8	1 7/8	6 7/8	6 3/8	M	Okanogan Co., Wash.	Richard J. Wristen	Richard J. Wristen	SE 1982	33
50 2/8	10 3/8	10 3/8	5 5/8	5 5/8	1 6/8	1 6/8	7 6/8	7 4/8	M	Mt. Stockdale, B.C.	James C. King	James C. King	OT 1983	33
50 2/8	10 5/8	10 5/8	5 4/8	5 4/8	1 6/8	1 6/8	6 7/8	6 3/8	M	Bleasdell Creek, B.C.	Daniel Fediuk	Daniel Fediuk	OT 1984	33
50	9 2/8	9 2/8	5 2/8	5 2/8	1 7/8	1 7/8	7 1/8	7 1/8	M	Bonneville Co., Idaho	Charles E. Wood	Charles E. Wood	OT 1983	40
50	10 1/8	10 1/8	5 4/8	5 5/8	1 7/8	1 7/8	7 4/8	8	M	Inklin River, B.C.	John V. Macaluso	John V. Macaluso	SE 1984	40
50	10 3/8	10 2/8	5 5/8	5 5/8	1 7/8	2	8 2/8	7	M	Yeth Creek, B.C.	Michael Follett	Michael Follett	OT 1983	40
47	10 1/8	10 3/8	5	5 2/8	1 5/8	1 6/8	6 2/8	5 3/8	M	Chaix Hills, Alaska	Richard O. Burns, Jr.	Richard O. Burns, Jr.	SE 1984	43
52 6/8*	10 6/8	10 6/8	6	6 1/8	1 7/8	2	9	8 7/8	M	Similkameen River, B.C.	D. & J. Crossley	D. & J. Crossley	NO 1983	
52 6/8*	10 1/8	9 7/8	6	6	2 1/8	2 1/8	7 7/8	7 1/8	M	Nimbus Mt., B.C.	J. D. Souza	J. D. Souza	AG 1985	

*Final Score subject to revision by additional verifying measurements.

Muskox

Ovibos moschatus moschatus and certain related subspecies

Minimum Score 90 | **World's Record 122**

Score	Length of Horn R.	Length of Horn L.	Width of Boss R.	Width of Boss L.	Circumference at Third Quarter R.	Circumference at Third Quarter L.	Greatest Spread	Tip to Tip Spread	Sex	Locality Killed	By Whom Killed	Owner	Date Killed	Rank
121	28 2/8	29 6/8	9 7/8	9 7/8	5 5/8	6 4/8	31 4/8	31	M	Ellice River, N.W.T.	Picked Up	John G. Stelfox	PU 1983	1
112 4/8	27 5/8	27 5/8	8 2/8	8 2/8	5	5	31 1/8	30 2/8	M	Thirty Mile Lake, N.W.T.	Joe Scotti	Neale Wortley	MR 1983	2
110 4/8	27 6/8	26 6/8	9 3/8	9 4/8	5	4 5/8	28 1/8	27	M	Holman Island, N.W.T.	Adam Ovilek	Roger Britton	1981	3
110 4/8	25	25 1/8	10	10	5	5 4/8	28 3/8	27 2/8	M	Holman Island, N.W.T.	William M. Phillippe, Jr.	William M. Phillippe, Jr.	NO 1982	3
110 4/8	26	26	9 6/8	9 6/8	4 5/8	5	25 6/8	21 5/8	M	Banks Island, N.W.T.	David V. Collis	David V. Collis	MR 1985	3
110	26 6/8	26 4/8	8 5/8	8 6/8	5 4/8	5 1/8	27	26 1/8	M	Sadlerochit River, Alaska	Ronald L. Deis	Ronald L. Deis	MR 1985	6
109 4/8	25 4/8	26	9 7/8	9 4/8	5 2/8	5 3/8	28 1/8	27 5/8	M	Nunivak Island, Alaska	Carolyn Elledge	Carolyn Elledge	AG 1983	7
109 2/8	27	26 6/8	9 1/8	8 7/8	4 6/8	4 5/8	26 4/8	23 5/8	M	Parry Pen., N.W.T.	Douglas J. Dollhopf	Douglas J. Dollhopf	MR 1983	8
109 2/8	28	26 6/8	9 7/8	9 7/8	5 4/8	4 2/8	25 6/8	23	M	Banks Island, N.W.T.	Audrey E. Crabtree	Audrey E. Crabtree	OT 1985	8
108 6/8	25 3/8	25 7/8	8 7/8	8 3/8	5 7/8	5 7/8	27 7/8	27 6/8	M	Nunivak Island, Alaska	James P. Moon, Jr.	James P. Moon, Jr.	MR 1985	10
108	26 6/8	25 7/8	9 4/8	9 4/8	5 1/8	5	25 6/8	25 3/8	M	Paulatuk, N.W.T.	Don McVittie	Don McVittie	MR 1983	11
108	26 7/8	25 7/8	9 4/8	9 6/8	5	4 5/8	28	26 2/8	M	Sachs Harbour, N.W.T.	John G. Munsinger	John G. Munsinger	AP 1985	11
107 6/8	27 4/8	26 2/8	9 7/8	9 7/8	4 7/8	4 1/8	26 5/8	24 5/8	M	Victoria Island, N.W.T.	Picked Up	John Behrns	PU 1982	13
107 4/8	25 3/8	25 6/8	9 4/8	9 2/8	4 6/8	5	27 2/8	25 7/8	M	Banks Island, N.W.T.	Jack Fiske	Jack Fiske	OT 1981	14
106 6/8	26 1/8	26 3/8	9 3/8	9	4 7/8	5	27	25	M	Sachs Harbour, N.W.T.	John R. Blanton	John R. Blanton	MR 1984	15
106	26 1/8	25 2/8	8	8 2/8	5 3/8	5	27 4/8	27 2/8	M	Canning River, Alaska	Darrel W. Sauder	Darrel W. Sauder	MR 1983	16
105 4/8	25 3/8	26 3/8	8 7/8	8 6/8	5 1/8	4 3/8	29 4/8	29	M	Nunivak Island, Alaska	Joseph A. Carr	Joseph A. Carr	FE 1984	17
104 6/8	24 1/8	23 3/8	8 7/8	9 2/8	6 1/8	5 4/8	30 4/8	30	M	Banks Island, N.W.T.	Don L. Corley	Don L. Corley	AP 1983	18
104 4/8	28 4/8	26 1/8	8 2/8	8 4/8	4 7/8	4 2/8	28 3/8	27 1/8	M	Nunivak Island, Alaska	Lawrence T. Epping	Lawrence T. Epping	MR 1984	19
104 4/8	24 4/8	25 4/8	9	9 1/8	4 4/8	5 4/8	28 4/8	27 5/8	M	Banks Island, N.W.T.	Donald F. Senter	Donald F. Senter	OT 1985	19
103 6/8	24 6/8	24 6/8	9	9	5	5	23 7/8	23	M	Holman Island, N.W.T.	Thomas E. Phillippe, Sr.	Thomas E. Phillippe, Sr.	NO 1982	21

103 6/8	25 5/8	24 2/8	8 7/8	8 5/8	5 3/8	5	27 2/8	26 5/8	M	Nunivak Island, Alaska	Reginald W. Elkins	Reginald W. Elkins	FE 1984	21
103 2/8	25	24 7/8	8 6/8	8 4/8	4 6/8	4 4/8	26 4/8	25 4/8	M	Nunivak Island, Alaska	Bobby L. Graham	Bobby L. Graham	MR 1985	23
103	25	26 4/8	9 7/8	9 7/8	4	5 2/8	24 4/8	21 1/8	M	Prince Wales Island, N.W.T.	Jay R. Wolfenden	Jay R. Wolfenden	MR 1984	24
102 6/8	24 5/8	25 1/8	8 6/8	8 5/8	5	5 2/8	28	27 2/8	M	Nunivak Island, Alaska	David A. Widby	David A. Widby	MR 1983	25
102 4/8	25 6/8	25	8 2/8	8 3/8	4 6/8	4 4/8	26 6/8	25 3/8	M	Nunivak Island, Alaska	Edward L. Russell	Edward L. Russell	MR 1984	26
102 2/8	22 3/8	24 1/8	9 3/8	9 1/8	5 6/8	5 7/8	24 6/8	23 5/8	M	Victoria Island, N.W.T.	Dennis D. Schlafmann	Dennis D. Schlafmann	OT 1983	27
102	24 4/8	25	8	8 4/8	4 7/8	5 1/8	25 4/8	23 1/8	M	Nunivak Island, Alaska	Curtis W. Lynn	Curtis W. Lynn	MR 1984	28
101 6/8	24 5/8	24 7/8	8 1/8	8 3/8	4 6/8	4 7/8	29 7/8	29 5/8	M	Nunivak Island, Alaska	John R. Jameson	John R. Jameson	FE 1984	29
101 2/8	26 4/8	25 4/8	8 6/8	8 5/8	4 2/8	4 7/8	28 3/8	27 4/8	M	Nunivak Island, Alaska	Don B. Skidmore	Don B. Skidmore	MR 1983	30
100 6/8	23 4/8	25 1/8	9 1/8	8 7/8	4 5/8	5 4/8	27	26 6/8	M	Sabine Bay, N.W.T.	Picked Up	Ken Ryalls	AG 1976	31
100 6/8	26 6/8	25 1/8	8 1/8	8	5	3 7/8	27 2/8	26 4/8	M	Nunivak Island, Alaska	Carolyn Elledge	C. Elledge & G. Elledge	SE 1985	31
100 6/8	24 2/8	25 1/8	8 3/8	8 2/8	4 5/8	5 2/8	25 6/8	24 2/8	M	Barter Island, Alaska	John W. Sargent	John W. Sargent	MR 1985	31
99 6/8	26 1/8	26 7/8	7 4/8	7 4/8	4 1/8	4 5/8	27 6/8	26 7/8	M	Nunivak Island, Alaska	Harvey D. Harms	Harvey D. Harms	MR 1983	34
99 4/8	24 7/8	24 7/8	7 5/8	7 5/8	4 3/8	4 3/8	25 6/8	23 4/8	M	Banks Island, N.W.T.	Picked Up	L. Irvin Barnhart	MR 1981	35
98 6/8	22 7/8	23 5/8	9 4/8	9 4/8	4 3/8	4 5/8	24 4/8	20 5/8	M	Banks Island, N.W.T.	Gary Boychuk	Gary Boychuk	NO 1981	36
98 4/8	24 5/8	24 2/8	7 6/8	8	4 3/8	4 3/8	24 1/8	20 1/8	M	Banks Island, N.W.T.	L. Irvin Barnhart	L. Irvin Barnhart	MR 1981	37
97 4/8	23 4/8	23 6/8	7 3/8	7 2/8	5 2/8	5 6/8	27 2/8	25 2/8	M	Back Bay, N.W.T.	James W. Perkins	James W. Perkins	MR 1983	38
96 4/8	21 6/8	23 6/8	8 7/8	8 1/8	5	5 4/8	25 2/8	24 7/8	M	Nunivak Island, Alaska	Michael W. Elkins	Michael W. Elkins	FE 1984	39
96 2/8	23 3/8	24 7/8	7 7/8	7 4/8	4 7/8	5 1/8	23 4/8	23	M	Ellesmere Island, N.W.T.	Robert I. Michel	Robert I. Michel	MR 1984	40
96	24 4/8	24 2/8	7 1/8	7	4 5/8	4 6/8	25 1/8	23 4/8	M	Killinupak Mt., Alaska	Ray E. Stock	Ray E. Stock	FE 1984	41
90 2/8	22 4/8	21 6/8	7	7	4 7/8	4 4/8	23 6/8	22 7/8	M	Cambridge Bay, N.W.T.	Unknown	Jules Verquin		42
111 2/8*	26 6/8	28	10 2/8	10 1/8	4 6/8	5 4/8	25 6/8	25 1/8	M	Parry Pen., N.W.T.	Roy L. Mondike	Roy L. Mondike	MR 1985	
111*	24 6/8	24 4/8	9 6/8	9 6/8	5 2/8	5	26 7/8	26	M	Victoria Island, N.W.T.	William H. Taylor	William H. Taylor	MR 1985	

*Final Score subject to revision by additional verifying measurements.

Bighorn Sheep

Minimum Score 175

Ovis canadensis canadensis and certain related subspecies

World's Record 208 1/8

Score	Length of Horn R.	Length of Horn L.	Circumference of Base R.	Circumference of Base L.	Circumference at Third Quarter R.	Circumference at Third Quarter L.	Greatest Spread	Tip to Tip Spread	Locality Killed	By Whom Killed	Owner	Date Killed	Rank
196 4/8	40 6/8	40 2/8	15 4/8	15 4/8	12	12	24	19 2/8	Badlands Natl. Park, S. D.	Picked Up	Badlands Natl. Park	1984	1
191 7/8	41 3/8	40 4/8	16	15 7/8	10 1/8	9 5/8	24	24	Granite Co., Mont.	Steven L. Gingras	Steven L. Gingras	SE 1984	2
191 2/8	42	41	14 5/8	14 4/8	10 6/8	10 4/8	22 1/8	19 4/8	Leyland Mt., Alta.	Rick J. Tymchuk	Rick J. Tymchuk	OT 1982	3
190 5/8	43 5/8	43 2/8	15 6/8	15 5/8	8 6/8	8 4/8	24 5/8	24 5/8	Missoula Co., Mont.	John J. Ottman	John J. Ottman	OT 1985	4
189 3/8	40 7/8	40 4/8	16 6/8	16 4/8	8 4/8	8 5/8	23	19 1/8	Teton Co., Mont.	R. L. Kennedy	R. L. Kennedy	NO 1983	5
188 5/8	41	38 7/8	15 3/8	15 6/8	10 5/8	10 6/8	20 3/8	19	Simpson River, B. C.	Patrick Deuling	Patrick Deuling	OT 1985	6
188 3/8	39 3/8	39 6/8	15 3/8	15 3/8	11	10 4/8	22 1/8	14	Gibraltar Mt., Alta.	Leslie Kish	Leslie Kish	SE 1981	7
188 2/8	42 5/8	42 5/8	15 6/8	15 6/8	8 3/8	8 4/8	25 7/8	25 7/8	Spences Bridge, B. C.	Romeo Leduc	Romeo Leduc	OT 1982	8
188 1/8	38 5/8	39 4/8	16 6/8	16 5/8	9	9 2/8	26 4/8	21	Sanders Co., Mont.	Patti L. Lewis	Patti L. Lewis	NO 1984	9
187 6/8	39 4/8	42	15 6/8	15 6/8	8 7/8	8 7/8	23 2/8	23 1/8	Deer Lodge Co., Mont.	William H. Shurte	William H. Shurte	OT 1984	10
187 2/8	38 4/8	39 4/8	15 6/8	15 6/8	10	10 3/8	22 2/8	17 3/8	Plateau Mt., Alta.	Randy Jackson	Randy Jackson	OT 1984	11
187 1/8	41	38 5/8	15 6/8	15 7/8	9	9 3/8	22 6/8	15 2/8	Red Deer River, Alta.	Richard B. Smith	Richard B. Smith	OT 1984	12
187 1/8	40 7/8	40 4/8	14 5/8	14 4/8	10 5/8	10 3/8	23 4/8	23 4/8	Deer Lodge Co., Mont.	David J. Etzwiler	David J. Etzwiler	OT 1985	12
187	41 3/8	41 3/8	16	15 6/8	8 2/8	8 2/8	24 4/8	24 4/8	Sanders Co., Mont.	Mark S. Eaton	Mark S. Eaton	OT 1985	14
186 6/8	38 6/8	38 2/8	16 3/8	16 3/8	8 7/8	8 7/8	23 3/8	18 5/8	Highwood River, Alta.	Ross Nikonchuk	Ross Nikonchuk	OT 1984	15
186 6/8	41 7/8	42 7/8	15 7/8	15 7/8	7 3/8	7 4/8	22 3/8	21 6/8	Whitman Co., Wash.	Picked Up	Inland Empire Big Game Council		15
186 5/8	38 6/8	38 3/8	15 3/8	15 3/8	10 1/8	10	22	17 7/8	Blind Canyon, Alta.	Picked Up	Alberta Fish & Wildlife	PU 1983	17
186 2/8	40	41	16 1/8	16 1/8	8 5/8	8 1/8	20 7/8	13	Riverside Mt., B. C.	Paul A. Templin	Paul A. Templin	SE 1983	18
186 2/8	39 6/8	39 4/8	16 1/8	16 1/8	8 5/8	8 4/8	23 3/8	17 4/8	Little Elbow River, Alta.	John Liefso	John Liefso	SE 1982	18
186 2/8	40	41 4/8	16	16	8	8 3/8	22 2/8	22 2/8	Rabbit Creek, B. C.	Lanny E. Kniert	Lanny E. Kniert	OT 1982	18
186	40 2/8	40 2/8	15 2/8	15	9 7/8	9 3/8	22	18 6/8	Sparwood, B. C.	Unknown	H. Bruce Freeman		21
185 3/8	39 4/8	38 3/8	14 7/8	15 1/8	10 2/8	10 2/8	22	17 4/8	Lewis & Clark Co., Mont.	Richard Tyler	Richard Tyler	NO 1954	22
184 5/8	38 2/8	40 1/8	15 4/8	15 3/8	9 3/8	9 3/8	22 5/8	21 4/8	Ruby Lake, Alta.	Picked Up	John G. Stelfox	PU 1965	23
183 7/8	43 5/8	35 2/8	17	17	7 5/8	6 6/8	24 4/8	23	Beaverhead Co., Mont.	James C. Garrett	James C. Garrett	SE 1983	24
183 2/8	38 4/8	40 2/8	15 6/8	15 6/8	8	8 4/8	22 3/8	18 4/8	Granite Co., Mont.	John L. Wozniak	John L. Wozniak	OT 1984	25
183 2/8	39 6/8	40 4/8	14 6/8	15 1/8	9	8 6/8	23 1/8	18 2/8	Clearwater River, Alta.	Joseph C. Sellitti	Joseph C. Sellitti	SE 1981	25
183 2/8	41	42 6/8	15 2/8	15 2/8	7 4/8	7 7/8	23 7/8	23 7/8	Deer Lodge Co., Mont.	Phillip Demers	Phillip Demers	SE 1985	25
183 1/8	36 2/8	36 1/8	16 1/8	16 2/8	9 5/8	9 4/8	21 1/8	16 3/8	Mt. Sparrowhawk, Alta.	Randy Ward	Randy Ward	OT 1984	28
182 2/8	36 4/8	35 6/8	16 1/8	16 2/8	9 1/8	9 1/8	23 3/8	18 7/8	Rocky Creek, Alta.	Randy A. Desabrais	Randy A. Desabrais	OT 1982	29

Score							Locality	Hunter	Owner	Date Killed
182 2/8	37 5/8	39 3/8	14 5/8	14 7/8	10 1/8	10 1/8	22 5/8	21 3/8	Park Co., Mont.	Rodney W. Cole	Rodney W. Cole	SE 1985	29
182	37 4/8	39 2/8	15 3/8	15 3/8	8 6/8	8 7/8	20 3/8	17 1/8	Mt. Kidd, Alta.	Dwayne W. Oneski	Dwayne W. Oneski	SE 1982	31
182	38 3/8	38 4/8	14 3/8	14 3/8	10 3/8	10 4/8	19	17 4/8	Mt. Kidd, Alta.	Picked Up	Dirk Kieft	OT 1982	31
181 7/8	39 1/8	38 4/8	15 1/8	15 1/8	9	9 1/8	20	19	Kakwa River, Alta.	Donald C. Fobert	Donald C. Fobert	AG 1983	33
181 7/8	38	38 7/8	15 7/8	15 5/8	8 3/8	8 6/8	23 2/8	22 7/8	Cataract Creek, Alta.	Michael J. Hogan	Michael J. Hogan	OT 1984	33
181 6/8	38 1/8	38 5/8	15	15 1/8	9 6/8	10	20 6/8	16 3/8	Prospect Creek, Alta.	Wayne Tarnasky	Wayne Tarnasky	OT 1983	35
181 5/8	39 3/8	37	16 4/8	16 3/8	7 3/8	7 5/8	20	15 4/8	Fisher Range, Alta.	Reginald Zebedee	Reginald Zebedee	OT 1982	36
181 5/8	39 5/8	39 5/8	15 4/8	15 4/8	8 6/8	8 1/8	21 4/8	17 3/8	Goat Range, Alta.	Christian D. Pagenkopf	Christian D. Pagenkopf	SE 1984	36
181 5/8	38 1/8	34 4/8	16 2/8	16 2/8	9 4/8	9 3/8	23	18	Pigeon Mt., Alta.	Paul S. Inzanti, Jr.	Paul S. Inzanti, Jr.	NO 1984	36
181 2/8	41 2/8	40 5/8	14	13 7/8	10 3/8	9 5/8	21 2/8	19 3/8	Highwood River, Alta.	Ralph Rink	George Beach	1946	39
181 1/8	38 7/8	35	15 3/8	15 5/8	9 3/8	9	20 4/8	15	Spray Lakes Reservoir, Alta.	G. Robert Willows	G. Robert Willows	OT 1977	40
181 1/8	39 4/8	39 3/8	14 5/8	14 5/8	9 5/8	9 4/8	22 5/8	22 5/8	Deer Lodge Co., Mont.	Thomas R. Puccinelli	Thomas R. Puccinelli	NO 1984	40
180 6/8	39 5/8	39 4/8	15	15	8 7/8	8 4/8	22	19 1/8	Mineral Co., Mont.	Roberta A. Hartford	Roberta A. Hartford	NO 1982	42
180 6/8	37 1/8	37 7/8	15 7/8	15 7/8	8 4/8	8 7/8	21 4/8	17 7/8	Forbidden Creek, Alta.	Dennis H. Russell	Dennis H. Russell	SE 1984	42
180 5/8	37 3/8	36	15 3/8	15 3/8	9 5/8	9 1/8	22 1/8	16 2/8	Ghost River, Alta.	Robert W. Hodge	Robert W. Hodge	OT 1985	44
180 4/8	40 5/8	38 2/8	14 5/8	14 5/8	9 2/8	9 3/8	23 2/8	22 5/8	Deer Lodge Co., Mont.	Jan J. Henry	Jan J. Henry	SE 1983	45
180 3/8	40 7/8	40 7/8	14 6/8	14 5/8	8 2/8	8 3/8	22 7/8	22 7/8	Lemhi Co., Mont.	Picked Up	R. Munn & F. Porter	PU 1982	46
180 3/8	35 5/8	38 2/8	16 4/8	16 4/8	8 3/8	8 3/8	24 4/8	21 5/8	Silver Bow Co., Mont.	Robert C. Carlson	Robert C. Carlson	SE 1983	46
180 3/8	37	37 7/8	15 1/8	15 2/8	9 5/8	9 5/8	23	19	Park Co., Wyo.	Robert G. Curtis	Robert G. Curtis	OT 1984	46
180 3/8	39 4/8	39 7/8	15 3/8	15 3/8	8 5/8	8 1/8	22 5/8	19 5/8	Mineral Co., Mont.	J. Ray Lake	J. Ray Lake	OT 1984	46
180 1/8	37 6/8	37 7/8	16	16	7 7/8	8	21 4/8	14 4/8	Cougar Mt., Alta.	Norman Howg	Norman Howg	OT 1984	50
180 1/8	37 4/8	35 3/8	15 4/8	15 5/8	9 7/8	9 7/8	19 4/8	16	Coral Creek, Alta.	Leonard W. King	Leonard W. King	OT 1983	50
180	40 2/8	40 3/8	14 5/8	14 5/8	8 4/8	8 4/8	25	25	Wallowa Co., Oreg.	Jerome V. Epping	Jerome V. Epping	SE 1984	52
179 7/8	36	35 7/8	16 3/8	16 4/8	9 1/8	8 5/8	21 2/8	19	Wallowa Co., Oreg.	Jim A. Turcke	Jim A. Turcke	SE 1982	53
179 4/8	38 5/8	38 1/8	14 7/8	14 6/8	9	9	21 1/8	19	Park Co., Wyo.	Robert M. Anderson	Robert M. Anderson	SE 1983	54
178 7/8	37 5/8	38 4/8	15 4/8	16 3/8	7 5/8	7 7/8	23 2/8	23 3/8	Leyland Mt., Alta.	Walter E. Hartman	Walter E. Hartman	OT 1984	55
178 5/8	40 1/8	38 6/8	14	14	8 7/8	8 7/8	23 3/8	23 3/8	Park Co., Mont.	Craig L. Leerberg	Craig L. Leerberg	SE 1985	56
177 4/8	38 6/8	38 2/8	14 7/8	14 7/8	8 5/8	8 5/8	22 6/8	19 4/8	Valley Co., Idaho	R. Barry Wood	R. Barry Wood	SE 1985	57
199*	43 2/8	43 6/8	15 6/8	16 1/8	10 7/8	10 5/8	23 7/8	23 7/8	Granite Co., Mont.	Larry D. Smith	Larry D. Smith	SE 1984	
196*	44 7/8	41 3/8	15 7/8	16	10 1/8	9 7/8	22 7/8	20	Missoula Co., Mont.	Claude I. Burlingame	Claude I. Burlingame	OT 1984	
191 5/8*	41 7/8	42 2/8	16 2/8	16	8 6/8	8 2/8	23	22 2/8	Sanders Co., Mont.	Bryan G. Nelson	Bryan G. Nelson	NO 1982	
191 3/8*	42 3/8	42 2/8	15 4/8	15 4/8	9 1/8	9 1/8	24	20 1/8	El Paso Co., Colo.	Raymond E. Moore	Raymond E. Moore	SE 1983	

*Final Score subject to revision by additional verifying measurements.

Desert Sheep

Ovis canadensis nelsoni and certain related subspecies

Minimum Score 165 — World's Record 205 1/8

Score	Length of Horn R.	Length of Horn L.	Circumference of Base R.	Circumference of Base L.	Circumference at Third Quarter R.	Circumference at Third Quarter L.	Greatest Spread	Tip to Tip Spread	Locality Killed	By Whom Killed	Owner	Date Killed	Rank
201 3/8	45 5/8	46 2/8	15 5/8	15 5/8	11 2/8	11 5/8	20 4/8	20	Pima Co., Ariz.	Picked Up	Greg Koons	PU 1982	1
185 2/8	41	40 2/8	15 7/8	15 6/8	8 2/8	9	21 1/8	20 3/8	Graham Co., Ariz.	John W. Harris	John W. Harris	DC 1982	2
185	38 2/8	37 2/8	16 4/8	16 4/8	9	8 7/8	24 5/8	21	Baja Calif., Mexico	Miguel Zaldivar De Valasco	Miguel Zaldivar De Valasco	NO 1979	3
182 1/8	37 7/8	37	14 7/8	14 7/8	10 7/8	10 1/8	23	19 1/8	Baja Calif., Mexico	Jesus H. Garza-Villarreal	Jesus H. Garza-Villarreal	FE 1984	4
182 1/8	40 7/8	39 7/8	15 5/8	15 4/8	8 4/8	7 3/8	22 7/8	22 7/8	Graham Co., Ariz.	James W. Ferguson	James W. Ferguson	DC 1984	4
178 5/8	35 2/8	36 5/8	15 5/8	15 5/8	9 5/8	9 2/8	23 4/8	22	Lincoln Co., Nev.	William A. Bertelson	William A. Bertelson	DC 1984	6
177 7/8	37	37 7/8	14 7/8	15	9 5/8	9 5/8	21	19 5/8	Mohave Co., Ariz.	William C. Duffy, Jr.	William C. Duffy, Jr.	DC 1981	7
177 7/8	36 5/8	36	15 4/8	15 6/8	9 3/8	9 5/8	22 7/8	20 5/8	Yuma Co., Ariz.	J. Dorsey Smith	J. Dorsey Smith	DC 1983	7
176 7/8	37 4/8	38 2/8	15 4/8	15 6/8	8 2/8	8 5/8	23 5/8	21 5/8	Pinal Co., Ariz.	Travis R. Holder	Travis R. Holder	FE 1984	9
176 5/8	35 7/8	36 4/8	15 5/8	15 5/8	9 4/8	9 1/8	19 5/8	14 5/8	Baja Calif., Mexico	Douglas J. Dollhopf	Douglas J. Dollhopf	FE 1983	10
176 2/8	38 5/8	37 4/8	14 4/8	14 4/8	8 7/8	9	21	21	Pinal Co., Ariz.	D. Mark Exline	D. Mark Exline	DC 1982	11
176 2/8	34	37	15 2/8	15 2/8	9 1/8	9 5/8	23	21 7/8	Clark Co., Nev.	Jack Oberly	Jack Oberly	NO 1983	11
176	36	36	15 4/8	15 4/8	9	9 1/8	18 7/8	18 5/8	Baja Calif., Mexico	Paul S. Inzanti, Jr.	Paul S. Inzanti, Jr.	NO 1982	13
175 5/8	35 2/8	35 7/8	16	16	8 7/8	9 1/8	20	17 7/8	Baja Calif., Mexico	William C. Cloyd	William C. Cloyd	MR 1984	14
175 4/8	36 3/8	36 1/8	14 3/8	14 2/8	10 1/8	10 1/8	21 1/8	18	Yuma Co., Ariz.	Anton E. Rimsza	Anton E. Rimsza	DC 1982	15
175 3/8	38 5/8	38 3/8	14 5/8	14 5/8	8 5/8	8 5/8	22	19 5/8	Yuma Co., Ariz.	Patrick E. Hurley	Patrick E. Hurley	DC 1981	16
175 3/8	37 5/8	39 4/8	13 7/8	14	9 2/8	9 4/8	19 1/8	17 7/8	Baja Calif., Mexico	Isidro Lopez-Del Bosque	Isidro Lopez-Del Bosque	MR 1984	16
175	37 4/8	37 5/8	15	15	9 2/8	9 5/8	26 5/8	26 5/8	Clark Co., Nev.	Timothy P. Ryan	Timothy P. Ryan	DC 1983	18
175	37 4/8	33 5/8	15 5/8	15 3/8	8 4/8	8 7/8	20 4/8	18 5/8	Yuma Co., Ariz.	Harry B. Cook	Harry B. Cook	DC 1982	18
174 5/8	33 5/8	34 5/8	15	14 7/8	10 5/8	10 1/8	25 4/8	25 4/8	Clark Co., Nev.	Ron W. Biggs	Ron W. Biggs	NO 1980	20
174 5/8	36 4/8	37 5/8	14 6/8	14 4/8	8 7/8	9 3/8	25 1/8	25 1/8	Clark Co., Nev.	Roseanne K. Wilkinson	Roseanne K. Wilkinson	NO 1980	21
174 4/8	37 2/8	37 4/8	15 5/8	15 5/8	7 7/8	7 5/8	25 7/8	26 2/8	Clark Co., Nev.	Stanley R. Galvin, Jr.	Stanley R. Galvin, Jr.	DC 1983	22
174 4/8	36 5/8	37 2/8	14 2/8	14 2/8	9	9 1/8	21 4/8	18 5/8	Lincoln Co., Nev.	Larry G. Marshall	Larry G. Marshall	NO 1983	22
174 2/8	34 4/8	35 5/8	14 5/8	15 2/8	9 7/8	9 7/8	26	26	Lincoln Co., Nev.	Larry M. Evans	Larry M. Evans	DC 1982	24
174 2/8	35 4/8	40 4/8	14 4/8	14 5/8	8 1/8	8 3/8	30 3/8	30 3/8	Mohave Co., Ariz.	Howard Grounds	Howard Grounds	DC 1984	24
174	36 3/8	35 1/8	15 2/8	15 1/8	9 1/8	8 5/8	23	23	Baja Calif., Mexico	James W. Owens	James W. Owens	FE 1983	26
173 7/8	37	37 5/8	15	14 6/8	8 5/8	9 3/8	20	21 4/8	Yuma Co., Ariz.	John C. Marsalla	John C. Marsalla	DC 1982	27
173 5/8	37 1/8	34 2/8	15 2/8	15	9	9	19 1/8	15 1/8	Sonora, Mexico	Douglas G. Williams	Douglas G. Williams	NO 1983	28
173 5/8	36 5/8	34 5/8	15 2/8	15 1/8	9 3/8	8 7/8	24 4/8	19 7/8	Yuma Co., Ariz.	David C. Root	David C. Root	DC 1983	28
173 3/8	36	36 3/8	15 3/8	15 3/8	8 2/8	8 3/8	21 1/8	19 1/8	Mohave Co., Ariz.	Donald E. Franklin	Donald E. Franklin	DC 1982	30

Score									Locality	Hunter	Owner	Date Killed	Rank
172 4/8	40	36	14 4/8	14 5/8	8	7 6/8	25	25	Clark Co., Nev.	Scott D. Oxborrow	Scott D. Oxborrow	NO 1983	31
172 4/8	33 3/8	33 3/8	15 1/8	15 3/8	9 3/8	9 2/8	21 4/8	21	Baja Calif., Mexico	Hector Aguilar Parada	Hector Aguilar Parada	MR 1985	31
172 3/8	35 3/8	36	14 7/8	14 7/8	8 4/8	9 5/8	21 2/8	21 2/8	Clark Co., Nev.	John F. Lohse	John F. Lohse	NO 1982	33
171 3/8	37 5/8	38 1/8	14 1/8	14 2/8	9	9 2/8	26	25	Lincoln Co., Nev.	Roy F. Lerg	Roy D. Lerg	DC 1984	34
171 2/8	34 4/8	35	15 4/8	15 5/8	8 2/8	8 4/8	24	24	Baja Calif., Mexico	David L. Harshbarger	David L. Harshbarger	FE 1983	35
171 3/8	35 3/8	36 7/8	14 4/8	14 5/8	8 6/8	8 5/8	20 7/8	20 7/8	Clark Co., Nev.	Bill R. Balsi, Jr.	Bill R. Balsi, Jr.	NO 1979	35
171 3/8	38	38 2/8	14 6/8	14 3/8	9 3/8	9 4/8	21 6/8	21 4/8	Yuma Co., Ariz.	Lauren W. Hogan	Lauren W. Hogan	DC 1984	35
170 7/8	34 7/8	32 7/8	15	14 7/8	9 4/8	9 5/8	22 6/8	22 6/8	Clark Co., Nev.	George W. Wilkinson, Jr.	George W. Wilkinson, Jr.	NO 1976	38
170 5/8	35 1/8	35 6/8	13 6/8	14 6/8	9 5/8	9 5/8	23 6/8	19 3/8	Clark Co., Nev.	Tracy L. Wilkinson	Tracy L. Wilkinson	DC 1982	39
170 5/8	35	35 7/8	14 2/8	14 2/8	9 6/8	9 6/8	23 6/8	23 3/8	Lincoln Co., Nev.	Robert S. Mastronardi	Robert S. Mastronardi	NO 1982	39
170 4/8	34 5/8	33 7/8	14 6/8	14 6/8	9 2/8	9 1/8	21 2/8	16	Sonora, Mexico	Leonard E. Brewster	Leonard E. Brewster	DC 1982	41
170 2/8	35 5/8	35 4/8	14 2/8	14 2/8	8 7/8	9 4/8	20 4/8	19 5/8	Baja Calif., Mexico	Alfred Barone	Alfred Barone	NO 1984	42
169 7/8	35 3/8	36 1/8	15 5/8	15 4/8	7 5/8	7 5/8	20 4/8	18 4/8	Baja Calif., Mexico	Steve F. Reiter	Steve F. Reiter	JA 1984	43
168 7/8	36	35 4/8	14 2/8	14 5/8	7 7/8	7 7/8	18 7/8	18 7/8	Baja Calif., Mexico	John Whitcombe	John Whitcombe	FE 1983	44
168 7/8	35 7/8	37 1/8	14 3/8	14 4/8	8 2/8	8 2/8	25 3/8	25 3/8	Clark Co., Nev.	Ronald E. Brown	Ronald E. Brown	DC 1983	45
168 7/8	35 4/8	33 1/8	15 1/8	15 2/8	8 4/8	8 3/8	19 6/8	19	Baja Calif., Mexico	Roger R. Card	Roger R. Card	FE 1985	45
168 4/8	32 7/8	34 3/8	15 2/8	15 2/8	8 5/8	9	20	15 4/8	Sonora, Mexico	David V. Collis	David V. Collis	JA 1985	47
168	35 7/8	35	15 4/8	15 4/8	7 7/8	7 7/8	20	19 4/8	Baja Calif., Mexico	Carl E. Jacobson	Carl E. Jacobson	FE 1985	48
168	34	35	14 3/8	14 3/8	9 2/8	8 7/8	21	20	Mohave Co., Ariz.	Perry H. Finger	Perry H. Finger	OT 1985	48
168	36 4/8	35 4/8	14 2/8	14 4/8	8 4/8	8 1/8	23 5/8	22 2/8	Clark Co., Nev.	Dennis K. Evans	Dennis K. Evans	NO 1981	48
166 5/8	35 4/8	35 4/8	13 6/8	13 6/8	8 4/8	8 4/8	21 5/8	21 2/8	Clark Co., Nev.	Kirk R. Ostrom	Kirk R. Ostrom	DC 1983	48
191 1/8*	39 3/8	39 2/8	16 3/8	16 6/8	10	10	19 3/8	19 2/8	Baja Calif., Mexico	Bruno Scherrer	Bruno Scherrer	NO 1981	51

*Final Score subject to revision by additional verifying measurements.

Dall's Sheep
Ovis dalli dalli and *Ovis dalli kenaiensis*

Minimum Score 165 — World's Record 189⁶⁄₈

Score	Length of Horn R.	L.	Circumference of Base R.	L.	Circumference at Third Quarter R.	L.	Greatest Spread	Tip to Tip Spread	Locality Killed	By Whom Killed	Owner	Date Killed	Rank
172⁶⁄₈	40⁷⁄₈	41⁷⁄₈	15	15	5⁷⁄₈	6²⁄₈	29	28⁵⁄₈	Mountain River, N.W.T.	Edmond D. Henley	Edmond D. Henley	SE 1983	1
172⁴⁄₈	40⁶⁄₈	42	14⁶⁄₈	15	6⁰⁄₈	6³⁄₈	26⁶⁄₈	26⁶⁄₈	Mackenzie Mts., N.W.T.	Leslie C. Finger	Leslie C. Finger	AG 1985	2
172²⁄₈	45⁷⁄₈	44⁷⁄₈	13⁷⁄₈	13⁷⁄₈	5⁵⁄₈	6⁰⁄₈	32	32	Copper River, Alaska	C. J. McElroy	C. J. McElroy	AG 1977	3
171⁷⁄₈	40⁴⁄₈	40⁵⁄₈	14¹⁄₈	14²⁄₈	6³⁄₈	6³⁄₈	28²⁄₈	28²⁄₈	Wrangell Mts., Alaska	Brent R. Hanks	Brent R. Hanks	AG 1983	4
171⁵⁄₈	40³⁄₈	41	14⁴⁄₈	14⁴⁄₈	6⁵⁄₈	6⁷⁄₈	22¹⁄₈	22¹⁄₈	Nabesna Glacier, Alaska	John F. Saltz	John F. Saltz	AG 1983	5
170⁶⁄₈	44	44	13⁴⁄₈	13³⁄₈	5⁷⁄₈	5⁵⁄₈	30⁶⁄₈	30⁶⁄₈	Teepee Mt., B.C.	Steve Snider	Jon K. Mahoney	SE 1983	6
170	41⁷⁄₈	42	13³⁄₈	13³⁄₈	6⁴⁄₈	6⁵⁄₈	23⁵⁄₈	23⁵⁄₈	Farewell Lake, Alaska	Frank G. Merz	Frank G. Merz	SE 1983	7
170	41⁷⁄₈	42⁷⁄₈	13⁷⁄₈	14	5⁷⁄₈	5⁵⁄₈	24⁴⁄₈	24⁴⁄₈	Haley Creek, Alaska	Larry C. Munn	Larry C. Munn	AG 1985	7
187¹⁄₈*	45⁵⁄₈	47⁷⁄₈	14³⁄₈	14²⁄₈	7³⁄₈	7⁴⁄₈	25⁵⁄₈	25⁵⁄₈	Jacksina Creek, Alaska	Sherwin N. Scott	Sherwin N. Scott	AG 1984	
178⁴⁄₈*	42⁴⁄₈	43³⁄₈	14⁴⁄₈	14⁴⁄₈	6⁶⁄₈	7²⁄₈	27⁶⁄₈	27⁶⁄₈	Nabesna Glacier, Alaska	Floyd Saltz, Jr.	Floyd Saltz, Jr.	AG 1982	
176*	41⁴⁄₈	41⁶⁄₈	14⁷⁄₈	14⁷⁄₈	6²⁄₈	6³⁄₈	24²⁄₈	24²⁄₈	Nabesna Glacier, Alaska	Sandra T. Saltz	Sandra T. Saltz	AG 1982	
175⁷⁄₈*	39	39⁴⁄₈	15	15	7³⁄₈	7³⁄₈	26³⁄₈	26³⁄₈	Wrangell Mts., Alaska	Russell A. Reed	Russell A. Reed	AG 1983	

*Final Score subject to revision by additional verifying measurements.

Stone's Sheep

Ovis dalli stonei

Minimum Score 165 | **World's Record 196⅝**

Score	Length of Horn R.	Length of Horn L.	Circumference of Base R.	Circumference of Base L.	Circumference at Third Quarter R.	Circumference at Third Quarter L.	Greatest Spread	Tip to Tip Spread	Locality Killed	By Whom Killed	Owner	Date Killed	Rank
175	40 4/8	42	14	14 1/8	8 2/8	7 6/8	22 5/8	20 1/8	Toad River, B. C.	William E. Butler	William E. Butler	OT 1975	1
172 3/8	38 6/8	38 7/8	15 1/8	15 2/8	6 5/8	6 5/8	25 1/8	25 1/8	Muskwa River, B. C.	Ken W. Scheer	Ken W. Scheer	AG 1985	2
172 1/8	40 3/8	41	14 3/8	14 2/8	6 3/8	6 4/8	20 5/8	20 2/8	Muskwa River, B. C.	Greg L. Stires	Greg L. Stires	AG 1984	3
171 5/8	40 4/8	40 7/8	14 3/8	14 3/8	5 6/8	6	22 5/8	22 2/8	Pink Mt., B. C.	Paul V. Palmer, Jr.	Paul V. Palmer, Jr.	AG 1985	4
171 3/8	39 2/8	38 5/8	14 1/8	14	7 4/8	7 3/8	22 4/8	22 4/8	Besa River, B. C.	Dale Webber	Dale Webber	AG 1984	5
170 5/8	40 7/8	40 6/8	14	14	6 2/8	6 4/8	24 3/8	24 3/8	Prophet River, B. C.	Robert E. Speegle	Robert E. Speegle	AG 1983	6
170 2/8	41	39 2/8	14 5/8	14 3/8	6 1/8	6 1/8	24 2/8	24 2/8	Racing River, B. C.	Bill Stevenson	Bill Stevenson	SE 1983	7
170 2/8	40 4/8	39 2/8	14 5/8	14 5/8	6 1/8	6 1/8	25 3/8	25 3/8	Prophet River, B. C.	Steve J. Polich	Steve J. Polich	SE 1984	7
166 2/8	38 4/8	39 4/8	15	15 4/8	6	6 1/8	24 1/8	24 1/8	Graham River, B. C.	David V. Collis	David V. Collis	OT 1982	9
165	40 4/8	40 2/8	13 4/8	13 6/8	5 7/8	5 7/8	22 5/8	22 5/8	West Toad River, B. C.	Dennis C. Campbell	Dennis C. Campbell	SE 1982	10
174*	40 1/8	40 1/8	15 2/8	15 3/8	6 3/8	6 4/8	25 1/8	24 7/8	Muskwa River, B. C.	R. L. Gearhart	R. L. Gearhart	SE 1983	
173*	41 4/8	42 4/8	13 6/8	13 5/8	6 6/8	7	24	23 5/8	Rapid River, B. C.	Bill Silveira	Bill Silveira	SE 1983	

*Final Score subject to revision by additional verifying measurements.

Score Charts
of the
Official Scoring System
for
North American
Big Game Trophies

OFFICIAL SCORING SYSTEM FOR NORTH AMERICAN BIG GAME TROPHIES

Records of North American Big Game
BOONE AND CROCKETT CLUB
241 South Fraley Blvd.
Dumfries, Virginia 22026

BEAR

Minimum Score:
- Alaska brown 28
- black 21
- grizzly 24
- polar 27

Kind of Bear grizzly

Sex male

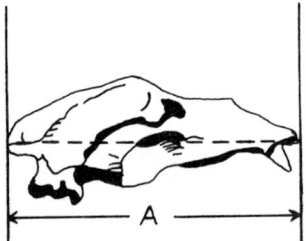
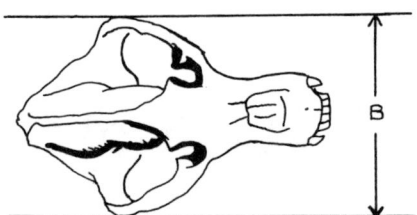

SEE OTHER SIDE FOR INSTRUCTIONS	Measurements
A. Greatest Length without Lower Jaw	16 14/16
B. Greatest Width	10 4/16
TOTAL AND FINAL SCORE	27 2/16
Exact locality where killed Dean River, B.C.	
Date killed 14 Oct. 82 By whom killed Roger J. Pentecost	
Present owner Roger J. Pentecost	
Address	
Guide's Name and Address	
Remarks: (Mention any abnormalities or unique qualities)	

I certify that I have measured the above trophy on 12 May 19 86
at (address) Nevada State Museum   City Las Vegas   State NV
and that these measurements and data are, to the best of my knowledge and belief, made in accordance with the instructions given.

Witness: Horace Gore

Signature: Frank Cook
Official Measurer

INSTRUCTIONS FOR MEASURING BEAR

Measurements are taken with calipers or by using parallel perpendiculars, to the nearest one-sixteenth of an inch, without reduction of fractions. Official measurements cannot be taken for at least sixty days after the animal was killed. All adhering flesh, membrane and cartilage must be completely removed before official measurements are taken.

A. Greatest Length is measured between perpendiculars parallel to the long axis of the skull, without the lower jaw and excluding malformations.

B. Greatest Width is measured between perpendiculars at right angles to the long axis.

* * * * * * * * * * * *

FAIR CHASE STATEMENT FOR ALL HUNTER-TAKEN TROPHIES

To make use of the following methods shall be deemed as UNFAIR CHASE and unsportmanlike, and any trophy obtained by use of such means is disqualified from entry for Awards.
- I. Spotting or herding game from the air, followed by landing in its vicinity for pursuit;
- II. Herding or pursuing game with motor-powered vehicles;
- III. Use of electronic communications for attracting, locating or observing game, or guiding the hunter to such game;
- IV. Hunting game confined by artificial barriers, including escape-proof fencing; or hunting game transplanted solely for the purpose of commercial shooting.

I certify that the trophy scored on this chart was not taken in UNFAIR CHASE as defined above by the Boone and Crockett Club. I further certify that it was taken in full compliance with local game laws of the state, province, or territory.
Date_____ Signature of Hunter_____
(Have signature notarized by a Notary Public)

Copyright © 1981 by Boone and Crockett Club
(Reproduction strictly forbidden without express, written consent)

OFFICIAL SCORING SYSTEM FOR NORTH AMERICAN BIG GAME TROPHIES

Records of North American Big Game

BOONE AND CROCKETT CLUB

241 South Fraley Blvd.
Dumfries, Virginia 22026

Minimum Score:
cougar 15
jaguar 14½

COUGAR and JAGUAR

Kind of Cat __cougar__

Sex __male__

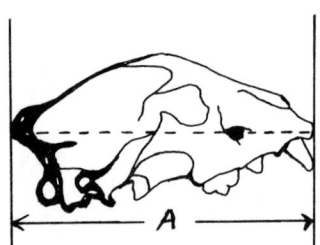 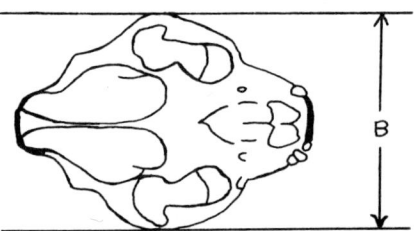

SEE OTHER SIDE FOR INSTRUCTIONS	Measurements
A. Greatest Length without Lower Jaw	9 2/16
B. Greatest Width	6 9/16
TOTAL AND FINAL SCORE	15 11/16

Exact locality where killed Okanagan Lake, B.C.
Date killed 27 Jan. 1985 By whom killed Dusty R. Cooper & Marc Hubbard
Present owner Dusty R. Cooper
Address
Guide's Name and Address
Remarks: (Mention any abnormalities or unique qualities)

I certify that I have measured the above trophy on 13 May 19 86
at (address) Nevada State Museum   City Las Vegas   State NV
and that these measurements and data are, to the best of my knowledge and belief, made in accordance with the instructions given.

Witness: __C. Randall Byers__   Signature: __Frank E. Bertoia__
                                             Official Measurer

INSTRUCTIONS FOR MEASURING COUGAR AND JAGUAR

Measurements are taken with calipers or by using parallel perpendiculars, to the nearest one-sixteenth of an inch, without reduction of fractions. Official measurements cannot be taken for at least sixty days after the animal was killed. All adhering flesh, membrane and cartilage must be completely removed before official measurements are taken.

A. Greatest Length is measured between perpendiculars parallel to the long axis of the skull, without the lower jaw and excluding malformations.

B. Greatest Width is measured between perpendiculars at a right angle to the long axis.

* * * * * * * * * * * *

FAIR CHASE STATEMENT FOR ALL HUNTER-TAKEN TROPHIES

To make use of the following methods shall be deemed as UNFAIR CHASE and unsportmanlike, and any trophy obtained by use of such means is disqualified from entry for Awards.
  I. Spotting or herding game from the air, followed by landing in its vicinity for pursuit;
  II. Herding or pursuing game with motor-powered vehicles;
  III. Use of electronic communications for attracting, locating or observing game, or guiding the hunter to such game;
  IV. Hunting game confined by artificial barriers, including escape-proof fencing; or hunting game transplanted solely for the purpose of commercial shooting.

I certify that the trophy scored on this chart was not taken in UNFAIR CHASE as defined above by the Boone and Crockett Club. I further certify that it was taken in full compliance with local game laws of the state, province, or territory.
Date_____Signature of Hunter_____
(Have signature notarized by a Notary Public)

Copyright © 1981 by Boone and Crockett Club
(Reproduction strictly forbidden without express, written consent)

OFFICIAL SCORING SYSTEM FOR NORTH AMERICAN BIG GAME TROPHIES

Records of North American Big Game

BOONE AND CROCKETT CLUB

241 South Fraley Blvd.
Dumfries, Virginia 22026

Minimum Score:
Atlantic 95
Pacific 100

WALRUS

Kind of Walrus __Pacific__

Sex __unknown__

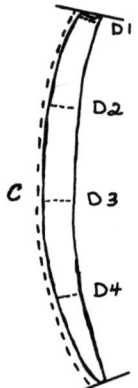
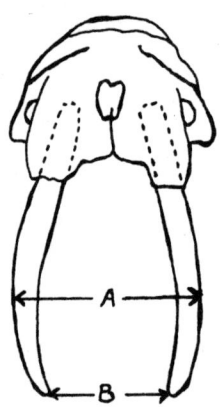

SEE OTHER SIDE FOR INSTRUCTIONS		Column 1	Column 2	Column 3
		Right Tusk	Left Tusk	Difference
A. Greatest Spread				
B. Tip to Tip Spread				
C. Entire Length of Loose Tusk		32 6/8	32	6/8
D-1. Circumference of Base		9 1/8	9 1/8	
D-2. Circumference at First Quarter		10 2/8	10 1/8	1/8
D-3. Circumference at Second Quarter		8 6/8	8 4/8	2/8
D-4. Circumference at Third Quarter		7 2/8	7 1/8	1/8
TOTALS		68 1/8	66 7/8	1 2/8

	Column 1	68 1/8	Exact locality where killed Port Heiden, Alaska
ADD	Column 2	66 7/8	Date killed 28 Jun 80 By whom killed Picked Up
	Total	135	Present owner John T. Taylor
SUBTRACT Column 3		1 2/8	Address
FINAL SCORE		133 6/8	Guide's Name and Address
			Remarks: (Mention any abnormalities or unique qualities)

I certify that I have measured the above trophy on 29 February 19 84
at (address) 109 West 6th Avenue   City Anchorage   State AK
and that these measurements and data are, to the best of my knowledge and belief, made in accordance with the instructions given.

Witness: __Craig Cook__

Signature: __Frank Cook__
Official Measurer

INSTRUCTIONS FOR MEASURING WALRUS

All measurements must be made with a ¼-inch flexible steel tape to the nearest one-eighth of an inch. Enter fractional figures in <u>eighths</u>, without reduction. Tusks <u>must</u> be removed from mounted specimens for measuring. Official measurements cannot be taken for at least sixty days after the animal was killed.

A. Greatest Spread is measured between perpendiculars at a right angle to the center line of the skull.

B. Tip to Tip Spread is measured between tips of tusks.

C. Entire Length of Loose Tusk is measured over outer curve from base to a point in line with tip.

D-1. Circumference of Base is measured at a right angle to axis of tusk. Do not follow edge of contact between tusk and skull.

D-2-3-4. Divide measurement C of LONGER tusk by four. Starting at base, mark <u>both</u> tusks at these quarters (even though other tusk is shorter) and measure circumferences at these marks.

* * * * * * * * * * * *

FAIR CHASE STATEMENT FOR ALL HUNTER-TAKEN TROPHIES

To make use of the following methods shall be deemed as UNFAIR CHASE and unsportmanlike, and any trophy obtained by use of such means is disqualified from entry for Awards.
  I. Spotting or herding game from the air, followed by landing in its vicinity for pursuit;
  II. Herding or pursuing game with motor-powered vehicles;
  III. Use of electronic communications for attracting, locating or observing game, or guiding the hunter to such game;
  IV. Hunting game confined by artificial barriers, including escape-proof fencing; or hunting game transplanted solely for the purpose of commercial shooting.

I certify that the trophy scored on this chart was not taken in UNFAIR CHASE as defined above by the Boone and Crockett Club. I further certify that it was taken in full compliance with local game laws of the state, province, or territory.
Date_____ Signature of Hunter_____
(Have signature notarized by a Notary Public)

Copyright © 1981 by Boone and Crockett Club
(Reproduction strictly forbidden without express, written consent)

OFFICIAL SCORING SYSTEM FOR NORTH AMERICAN BIG GAME TROPHIES

Records of North American Big Game

BOONE AND CROCKETT CLUB

241 South Fraley Blvd.
Dumfries, Virginia 22026

Minimum Score:
 Roosevelt 290
 American 375

WAPITI   Kind of Wapiti American

DETAIL OF POINT MEASUREMENT

		Abnormal Points	
		Right	Left

			Total to E			
SEE OTHER SIDE FOR INSTRUCTIONS			Column 1	Column 2	Column 3	Column 4
A. Number of Points on Each Antler	R. 6	L. 6	Spread Credit	Right Antler	Left Antler	Difference
B. Tip to Tip Spread			38 6/8			
C. Greatest Spread			46 6/8			
D. Inside Spread of Main Beams 41 5/8 Credit may equal but not exceed length of longer antler			41 5/8			
IF Spread exceeds longer antler, enter difference.						
E. Total of Lengths of all Abnormal Points						
F. Length of Main Beam				51 1/8	54 2/8	3 1/8
G-1. Length of First Point				16 3/8	17 4/8	1 1/8
G-2. Length of Second Point				16 2/8	17 7/8	1 5/8
G-3. Length of Third Point				17 6/8	18 5/8	7/8
G-4. Length of Fourth (Royal) Point				21	23 3/8	2 3/8
G-5. Length of Fifth Point				15 7/8	16 2/8	3/8
G-6. Length of Sixth Point, if present						
G-7. Length of Seventh Point, if present						
H-1. Circumference at Smallest Place Between First and Second Points				10 7/8	10 5/8	2/8
H-2. Circumference at Smallest Place Between Second and Third Points				7 5/8	7 6/8	1/8
H-3. Circumference at Smallest Place Between Third and Fourth Points				8 3/8	7 7/8	4/8
H-4. Circumference at Smallest Place Between Fourth and Fifth Points				7 6/8	7 3/8	3/8
TOTALS			41 5/8	173	181 4/8	10 6/8

ADD	Column 1	41 5/8	Exact locality where killed Mescalero Reservation, NM
	Column 2	173	Date killed 21 Sep 85 By whom killed Gregory C. Saunders
	Column 3	181 4/8	Present owner Gregory C. Saunders
Total		396 1/8	Address
SUBTRACT Column 4		10 6/8	Guide's Name and Address
FINAL SCORE		385 3/8	Remarks: (Mention any abnormalities or unique qualities)

I certify that I have measured the above trophy on __13 May_____ 19 86
at (address) __Nevada State Museum_____ City __Las Vegas__ State __NV__
and that these measurements and data are, to the best of my knowledge and belief, made in accordance with the instructions given.
Witness: __Horace Gore_____ Signature: __Frank E. Bertoia_____
OFFICIAL MEASURER

INSTRUCTIONS FOR MEASURING WAPITI

All measurements must be made with a ¼-inch flexible steel tape to the nearest one-eighth of an inch. Wherever it is necessary to change direction of measurement, mark a control point and swing tape at this point. Enter fractional figures in eighths, without reduction. Official measurements cannot be taken for at least sixty days after the animal was killed.

A. Number of Points on Each Antler. To be counted a point, a projection must be at least one inch long and its length must exceed the width of its base. All points are measured from tip of point to nearest edge of beam as illustrated. Beam tip is counted as a point but not measured as a point.

B. Tip to Tip Spread is measured between tips of main beams.

C. Greatest Spread is measured between perpendiculars at a right angle to the center line of the skull at widest part whether across main beams or points.

D. Inside Spread of Main Beams is measured at a right angle to the center line of the skull at widest point between main beams. Enter this measurement again in Spread Credit column if it is less than or equal to the length of longer antler; if longer, enter longer antler length for Spread Credit.

E. Total of Lengths of all Abnormal Points. Abnormal points are those nontypical in location (such as points originating from a point or from bottom or sides of main beam) or pattern (extra points, not generally paired). Measure in usual manner and enter in appropriate blanks.

F. Length of Main Beam is measured from lowest outside edge of burr over outer curve to the most distant point of what is, or appears to be, the main beam. The point of beginning is that point on the burr where the center line along the outer curve of the beam intersects the burr, then following generally the line of the illustration.

G-1-2-3-4-5-6-7. Length of Normal Points. Normal points project from the top or front of the main beam in the general pattern illustrated. They are measured from nearest edge of main beam over outer curve to tip. Lay the tape along the outer curve of the beam so that the top edge of the tape coincides with the top edge of the beam on both sides of the point to determine the baseline for point measurement. Record point length in appropriate blanks.

H-1-2-3-4. Circumferences are taken as detailed for each measurement.
* * * * * * * * * * *

FAIR CHASE STATEMENT FOR ALL HUNTER-TAKEN TROPHIES

To make use of the following methods shall be deemed as UNFAIR CHASE and unsportsmanlike, and any trophy obtained by use of such means is disqualified from entry for Awards.

   I. Spotting or herding game from the air, followed by landing in its vicinity for pursuit;
  II. Herding or pursuing game with motor-powered vehicles;
 III. Use of electronic communications for attracting, locating or observing game, or guiding the hunter to such game;
  IV. Hunting game confined by artificial barriers, including escape-proof fencing; or hunting game transplanted solely for the purpose of commercial shooting.
****

I certify that the trophy scored on this chart was not taken in UNFAIR CHASE as defined above by the Boone and Crockett Club. I further certify that it was taken in full compliance with local game laws of the state, province, or territory.

Date_____Signature of Hunter_____
(Have signature notarized by a Notary Public)

Copyright © 1981 by Boone and Crockett Club
(Reproduction strictly forbidden without express, written consent)

OFFICIAL SCORING SYSTEM FOR NORTH AMERICAN BIG GAME TROPHIES

Records of North American Big Game

BOONE AND CROCKETT CLUB

241 South Fraley Blvd.
Dumfries, Virginia 22026

Minimum Score:
mule 195
Columbia 130
Sitka 108

TYPICAL
MULE AND BLACKTAIL DEER

Kind of Deer Sitka blacktail

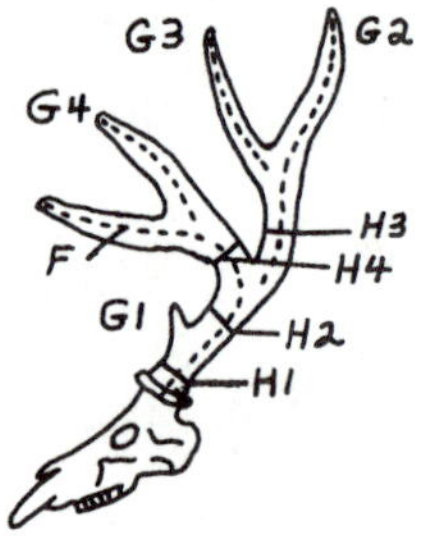

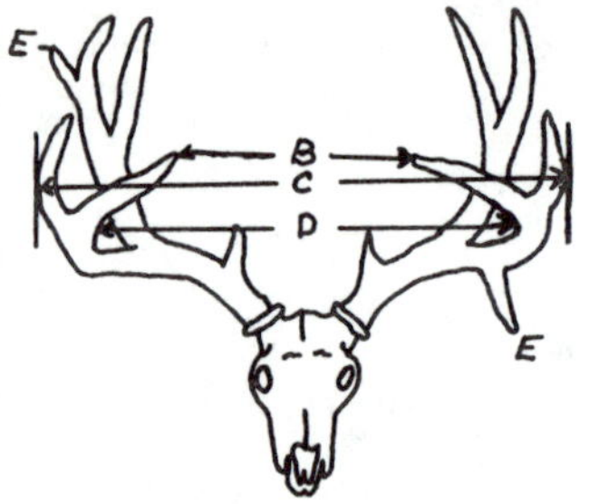

DETAIL OF POINT MEASUREMENT

Abnormal Points	
Right	Left
Total to E	

SEE OTHER SIDE FOR INSTRUCTIONS

				Column 1	Column 2	Column 3	Column 4
A.	Number of points on Each Antler	R. 4	L. 4	Spread Credit	Right Antler	Left Antler	Difference
B.	Tip to Tip Spread			8 3/8			
C.	Greatest Spread			19 7/8			
D.	Inside Spread of Main Beams	17 6/8	Credit may equal but not exceed length of longer antler	17 6/8			
	IF Spread exceeds longer antler, enter difference						
E.	Total of Lengths of Abnormal Points						
F.	Length of Main Beam				21 4/8	20 3/8	1 1/8
G-1.	Length of First Point, if present						
G-2.	Length of Second Point				10 2/8	8 6/8	1 4/8
G-3.	Length of Third Point, if present				3 4/8	6 5/8	3 1/8
G-4.	Length of Fourth Point, if present				6 7/8	6 4/8	3/8
H-1.	Circumference at Smallest Place Between Burr and First Point				3 6/8	3 6/8	
H-2.	Circumference at Smallest Place Between First and Second Points				3 5/8	3 4/8	1/8
H-3.	Circumference at Smallest Place Between Main Beam and Third Point				2 7/8	3	1/8
H-4.	Circumference at Smallest Place Between Second and Fourth Points				4 2/8	3 5/8	5/8
	TOTALS			17 6/8	56 5/8	56 1/8	7

ADD	Column 1	17 6/8	Exact locality where killed Uganik Bay, Alaska
	Column 2	56 5/8	Date killed 14 Nov. 83 By whom killed Donna D. Braendel
	Column 3	56 1/8	Present owner Donna D. Braendel
TOTAL		130 4/8	Address
SUBTRACT Column 4		7	Guide's Name and Address
FINAL SCORE		123 4/8	Remarks: (Mention any abnormalities or unique qualities)

I certify that I have measured the above trophy on ___14 May___ 19 _86_
at (address) ___Nevada State Museum___ City ___Las Vegas___ State ___NV___
and that these measurements and data are, to the best of my knowledge and belief, made in accordance with the instructions given.
Witness: ___Glenn St. Charles___   Signature: ___Philip L. Wright___
OFFICIAL MEASURER

INSTRUCTIONS FOR MEASURING MULE AND BLACKTAIL DEER

All measurements must be made with a ¼-inch flexible steel tape to the nearest one-eighth of an inch. Wherever it is necessary to change direction of measurement, mark a control point and swing tape at this point. Enter fractional figures in eighths, without reduction. Official measurements cannot be taken for at least sixty days after the animal was killed.

A. Number of Points on Each Antler. To be counted a point, a projection must be at least one inch long and its length must exceed the width of its base. All points are measured from tip of point to nearest edge of beam as illustrated. Beam tip is counted as a point but not measured as a point.

B. Tip to Tip Spread is measured between tips of main beams.

C. Greatest Spread is measured between perpendiculars at a right angle to the center line of the skull at widest part whether across main beams or points.

D. Inside Spread of Main Beams is measured at a right angle to the center line of the skull at widest point between main beams. Enter this measurement again in Spread Credit column if it is less than or equal to the length of longer antler; if longer, enter longer antler length for Spread Credit.

E. Total Lengths of all Abnormal Points. Abnormal points are those nontypical in location such as points originating from a point (exception: G-3 originates from G-2 in perfectly normal fashion) or from sides or bottom of main beam or any points beyond the normal pattern of five (including beam tip) per antler. Measure each abnormal point in usual manner and enter in appropriate blanks.

F. Length of Main Beam is measured from lowest outside edge of burr over outer curve to the tip of the main beam. The point of beginning is that point on the burr where the center line along the outer curve of the beam intersects the burr, then following generally the line of the illustration.

G-1-2-3-4. Length of Normal Points. Normal points are the brow and the upper and lower forks as shown in the illustration. They are measured from nearest edge of beam over outer curve to tip. Lay the tape along the outer curve of the beam so that the top edge of the tape coincides with the top edge of the beam on both sides of the point to determine baseline for point measurement. Record point lengths in appropriate blanks.

H-1-2-3-4. Circumferences are taken as detailed for each measurement. If brow point is missing, take H-1 and H-2 at smallest place between burr and G-2. If G-3 is missing, take H-3 halfway between the base and tip of second point. If G-4 is missing, take H-4 halfway between the second point and tip of main beam.

* * * * * * * * * * *

FAIR CHASE STATEMENT FOR ALL HUNTER-TAKEN TROPHIES

To make use of the following methods shall be deemed as UNFAIR CHASE and unsportsmanlike, and any trophy obtained by use of such means is disqualified from entry for Awards.

   I. Spotting or herding game from the air, followed by landing in its vicinity for pursuit;
  II. Herding or pursuing game with motor-powered vehicles;
 III. Use of electronic communications for attracting, locating or observing game, or guiding the hunter to such game;
  IV. Hunting game confined by artificial barriers, including escape-proof fencing; or hunting game transplanted solely for the purpose of commercial shooting.

****
I certify that the trophy scored on this chart was not taken in UNFAIR CHASE as defined above by the Boone and Crockett Club. I further certify that it was taken in full compliance with local game laws of the state, province, or territory.

Date_____ Signature of Hunter_____
(Have signature notarized by a Notary Public)

Copyright © 1981 by Boone and Crockett Club
(Reproduction strictly forbidden without express, written consent)

OFFICIAL SCORING SYSTEM FOR NORTH AMERICAN BIG GAME TROPHIES

Records of North American Big Game
BOONE AND CROCKETT CLUB
241 South Fraley Blvd.
Dumfries, Virginia 22026

Minimum Score: 240

NON-TYPICAL MULE DEER

Abnormal Points	
Right	Left
1 4/8	7 7/8
11 3/8	2 6/8
4 2/8	6 6/8
	6 4/8
	4 2/8
	3 2/8
	3 7/8
Total to E	52 3/8

SEE OTHER SIDE FOR INSTRUCTIONS

			Column 1	Column 2	Column 3	Column 4
A.	Number of Points on Each Antler	R. 8 L. 12	Spread Credit	Right Antler	Left Antler	Difference
B.	Tip to Tip Spread		20 3/8			
C.	Greatest Spread		40 6/8			
D.	Inside Spread of Main Beams 26 6/8	Credit may equal but not exceed length of longer antler	26 6/8			
	IF Spread exceeds longer antler, enter difference					
E.	Total of Lengths of Abnormal Points		52 3/8			
F.	Length of Main Beams			27 7/8	29 2/8	1 3/8
G-1.	Length of First Point, if present			1 6/8	2 5/8	7/8
G-2.	Length of Second Point			18 5/8	19 5/8	1
G-3.	Length of Third Point, if present			11	11 4/8	4/8
G-4.	Length of Fourth Point, if present			15 6/8	15 6/8	
H-1.	Circumference at Smallest Place Between Burr and First Point			6 1/8	6	1/8
H-2.	Circumference at Smallest Place Between First and Second Points			5 6/8	5 6/8	
H-3.	Circumference at Smallest Place Between Main Beam and Third Point			6 2/8	6 1/8	1/8
H-4.	Circumference at Smallest Place Between Second and Fourth Points			4 7/8	4 4/8	3/8
	TOTALS		52 3/8	26 6/8	98	101 1/8	4 3/8

ADD
Column 1   26 6/8
Column 2   98
Column 3   101 1/8
TOTAL   225 7/8
SUBTRACT Column 4   4 3/8
Result   221 4/8
Add Line E Total   52 3/8
FINAL SCORE   273 7/8

Exact locality where killed: Kane Co., Utah
Date killed: Oct. 50 By whom killed: Waldon Ballard
Present Owner: Alice Ballard
Address:
Guide's Name and Address:
Remarks: (Mention any abnormalities or unique qualities)

I certify that I have measured the above trophy on 20 April 19 85
at (address) 369 East 100 South   City St. George   State Utah
and that these measurements and data are, to the best of my knowledge and belief, made in accordance with the instructions given.

Witness: _____   Signature: Clair L. Huff
OFFICIAL MEASURER

INSTRUCTIONS FOR MEASURING NON-TYPICAL MULE DEER

All measurements must be made with a ¼-inch flexible steel tape to the nearest one-eighth of an inch. Wherever it is necessary to change direction of measurement, mark a control point and swing tape at this point. Enter fractional figures in eighths, without reduction. Official measurements cannot be taken for at least sixty days after the animal was killed.

A. Number of Points on Each Antler. To be counted a point, a projection must be at least one inch long and its length must exceed the width of its base. All points are measured from tip of point to nearest edge of beam as illustrated. Beam tip is counted as a point but not measured as a point.

B. Tip to Tip Spread is measured between tips of main beams.

C. Greatest Spread is measured between perpendiculars at a right angle to the center line of the skull at widest part whether across main beams or points.

D. Inside Spread of Main Beams is measured at a right angle to the center line of the skull at widest point between main beams. Enter this measurement again in Spread Credit column if it is less than or equal to the length of longer antler; if longer, enter longer antler length for Spread Credit.

E. Total of Lengths of all Abnormal Points. Abnormal points are those nontypical in location or points beyond the normal pattern of five (including beam tip) per antler. Mark the points that are normal, as defined below. All other points are considered abnormal and are entered in appropriate blanks, after measurement in usual manner.

F. Length of Main Beam is measured from lowest outside edge of burr over outer curve to the tip of the main beam. The point of beginning is that point on the burr where the center line along the outer curve of the beam intersects the burr, then following generally the line of the illustration.

G-1-2-3-4. Length of Normal Points. Normal points are the brow and the upper and lower forks, as shown in the illustration. They are measured from nearest edge of beam over outer curve to tip. Lay the tape along the outer curve of the beam so that the top edge of the tape coincides with the top edge of the beam on both sides of the point to determine baseline for point measurement. Record point lengths in appropriate blanks.

H-1-2-3-4. Circumferences are taken as detailed for each measurement. If brow point is missing, take H-1 and H-2 at smallest place between burr and G-2. If G-3 is missing, take H-3 halfway between the base and tip of second point. If G-4 is missing, take H-4 halfway between the second point and tip of main beam.

* * * * * * * * * * *

FAIR CHASE STATEMENT FOR ALL HUNTER-TAKEN TROPHIES

To make use of the following methods shall be deemed as UNFAIR CHASE and unsportsmanlike and any trophy obtained by use of such means is disqualified from entry for Awards.

I. Spotting or herding game from the air, followed by landing in its vicinity for pursuit;
II. Herding or pursuing game with motor-powered vehicles;
III. Use of electronic communications for attracting, locating or observing game, or guiding the hunter to such game;
IV. Hunting game confined by artificial barriers, including escape-proof fencing; or hunting game transplanted solely for the purpose of commercial shooting.

****

I certify that the trophy scored on this chart was not taken in UNFAIR CHASE as defined above by the Boone and Crockett Club. I further certify that it was taken in full compliance with local game laws of the state, province, or territory.

Date_____ Signature of Hunter_____
(Have signature notarized by a Notary Public)

Copyright © 1981 by Boone and Crockett Club
(Reproduction strictly forbidden without express, written consent)

OFFICIAL SCORING SYSTEM FOR NORTH AMERICAN BIG GAME TROPHIES

Records of North American Big Game

BOONE AND CROCKETT CLUB

241 South Fraley Blvd.
Dumfries, Virginia 22026

Minimum Score:
whitetail 170
Coues' 110

TYPICAL
WHITETAIL AND COUES' DEER

Kind of Deer **whitetail**

DETAIL OF POINT MEASUREMENT

Abnormal Points	
Right	Left
	2 2/8
Total to E	2 2/8

SEE OTHER SIDE FOR INSTRUCTIONS

			Column 1	Column 2	Column 3	Column 4
A.	Number of Points on Each Antler	R. 6 L. 7	Spread Credit	Right Antler	Left Antler	Difference
B.	Tip to Tip Spread	18 1/8				
C.	Greatest Spread	26 5/8				
D.	Inside Spread of Main Beams	24 — Credit may equal but not exceed length of longer antler	24			
	IF Spread exceeds longer antler, enter difference.					
E.	Total of Lengths of all Abnormal Points					2 2/8
F.	Length of Main Beam			26 3/8	27 1/8	6/8
G-1.	Length of First Point, if present			6 6/8	6 6/8	
G-2.	Length of Second Point			11 3/8	9 3/8	2
G-3.	Length of Third Point			12	10 6/8	1 2/8
G-4.	Length of Fourth Point, if present			10 4/8	10	4/8
G-5.	Length of Fifth Point, if present			4 4/8	7 3/8	2 7/8
G-6.	Length of Sixth Point, if present					
G-7.	Length of Seventh Point, if present					
H-1.	Circumference at Smallest Place Between Burr and First Point			5	4 7/8	1/8
H-2.	Circumference at Smallest Place Between First and Second Points			5 2/8	5	2/8
H-3.	Circumference at Smallest Place Between Second and Third Points			7 3/8	5 7/8	1 4/8
H-4.	Circumference at Smallest Place between Third and Fourth Points (see back if G-4 is missing)			5 6/8	6	2/8
	TOTALS		24	94 7/8	93 1/8	11 6/8

ADD	Column 1	24	Exact locality where killed **Whitkow, Sask.**
	Column 2	94 7/8	Date killed **18 Nov 83** By whom killed **Peter J. Swistun**
	Column 3	93 1/8	Present owner **Peter J. Swistun**
	Total	212	Address
SUBTRACT Column 4		11 6/8	Guide's Name and Address
FINAL SCORE		200 2/8	Remarks: (Mention any abnormalities or unique qualities)

I certify that I have measured the above trophy on __14 May_____ 19 86
at (address) __Nevada State Museum_____ City __Las Vegas_____ State __NV__
and that these measurements and data are, to the best of my knowledge and belief, made in accordance with the instructions given.

Witness: __Walter H. White_____ Signature: __C. Randall Byers_____
OFFICIAL MEASURER

INSTRUCTIONS FOR MEASURING WHITETAIL AND COUES' DEER

All measurements must be made with a ¼-inch flexible steel tape to the nearest one-eighth of an inch. Wherever it is necessary to change direction of measurement, mark a control point and swing tape at this point. Enter fractional figures in eighths, without reduction. Official measurements cannot be taken for at least sixty days after the animal was killed.

A. Number of Points on Each Antler. To be counted a point, a projection must be at least one inch long and its length must exceed the width of its base. All points are measured from tip of point to nearest edge of beam as illustrated. Beam tip is counted as a point but not measured as a point.

B. Tip to Tip Spread is measured between tips of main beams.

C. Greatest Spread is measured between perpendiculars at a right angle to the center line of the skull at widest part whether across main beams or points.

D. Inside Spread of Main Beams is measured at a right angle to the center line of the skull at widest point between main beams. Enter this measurement again in Spread Credit column if it is less than or equal to the length of longer antler; if longer, enter longer antler length for Spread Credit.

E. Total of lengths of all Abnormal Points. Abnormal points are those nontypical in location (points originating from points or from sides or bottom of main beam) or extra points beyond the normal pattern of up to eight normal points, including beam tip, per antler. Measure in usual manner and enter in appropriate blanks.

F. Length of Main Beam is measured from lowest outside edge of burr over outer curve to the most distant point of what is, or appears to be, the main beam. The point of beginning is that point on the burr where the center line along the outer curve of the beam intersects the burr, then following generally the line of the illustration.

G-1-2-3-4-5-6-7. Length of Normal Points. Normal points project from the top of the main beam. They are measured from nearest edge of main beam over outer curve to tip. Lay the tape along the outer curve of the beam so that the top edge of the tape coincides with the top edge of the beam on both sides of the point to determine baseline for point measurements. Record point lengths in appropriate blanks.

H-1-2-3-4. Circumferences are taken as detailed for each measurement. If brow point is missing, take H-1 and H-2 at smallest place between burr and G-2. If G-4 is missing, take H-4 halfway between G-3 and tip of main beam.

* * * * * * * * * * * *

FAIR CHASE STATEMENT FOR ALL HUNTER-TAKEN TROPHIES

To make use of the following methods shall be deemed as UNFAIR CHASE and unsportsmanlike, and any trophy obtained by use of such means is disqualified from entry for Awards.

  I. Spotting or herding game from the air, followed by landing in its vicinity for pursuit;
 II. Herding or pursuing game with motor-powered vehicles;
III. Use of electronic communications for attracting, locating or observing game, or guiding the hunter to such game;
 IV. Hunting game confined by artificial barriers, including escape-proof fencing; or hunting game transplanted solely for the purpose of commercial shooting.

****
I certify that the trophy scored on this chart was not taken in UNFAIR CHASE as defined above by the Boone and Crockett Club. I further certify that it was taken in full compliance with local game laws of the state, province, or territory.

Date_____Signature of Hunter_____
(Have signature notarized by a Notary Public)

Copyright © 1981 by Boone and Crockett Club
(Reproduction strictly forbidden without express, written consent)

OFFICIAL SCORING SYSTEM FOR NORTH AMERICAN BIG GAME TROPHIES

Records of North American Big Game

BOONE AND CROCKETT CLUB

241 South Fraley Blvd.
Dumfries, Virginia 22026

Minimum Score:
whitetail 195
Coues' 120

NON-TYPICAL
WHITETAIL AND COUES' DEER

Kind of Deer __whitetail__

Abnormal Points	
Right	Left
2 7/8 9 1/8	2 7/8 13 5/8
4 3/8 2 3/8	4 4/8 6 1/8
4 6/8 2 5/8	12 7/8 3 1/8
5 4/8 5 6/8	3 3/8 1 1/8
9 1/8 6 6/8	7 1
7 3/8 3 3/8	4 4/8 1 6/8
2 6/8 13 6/8	8 3/8 7
5 4/8 2 3/8	4 5/8
8	2
3 1/8	7 6/8
1 5/8	1
Total to E 100 4/8	**92 3/8**

SEE OTHER SIDE FOR INSTRUCTIONS		Column 1	Column 2	Column 3	Column 4
A. Number of Points on Each Antler R. 23 L. 22		Spread Credit	Right Antler	Left Antler	Difference
B. Tip to Tip Spread		21 2/8			
C. Greatest Spread		33			
D. Inside Spread of Main Beams 24 3/8 Credit may equal but not exceed length of longer antler		24 3/8			
IF Spread exceeds longer antler, enter difference.					
E. Total of Lengths of Abnormal Points					
F. Length of Main Beam			25 5/8	24 4/8	1 1/8
G-1. Length of First Point, if present			9 4/8	8 6/8	6/8
G-2. Length of Second Point			11 3/8	3	8 3/8
G-3. Length of Third Point			1 7/8	3 2/8	1 3/8
G-4. Length of Fourth Point, if present					
G-5. Length of Fifth Point, if present					
G-6. Length of Sixth Point, if present					
G-7. Length of Seventh Point, if present					
H-1. Circumference at Smallest Place Between Burr and First Point			6 2/8	5 6/8	4/8
H-2. Circumference at Smallest Place Between First and Second Points			5	4 6/8	2/8
H-3. Circumference at Smallest Place Between Second and Third Points			7 5/8	5 1/8	2 4/8
H-4. Circumference at Smallest Place Between Third and Fourth Points			2 4/8	1 6/8	6/8
TOTALS		192 7/8	24 3/8	69 6/8	56 7/8	15 5/8

ADD	Column 1	24 3/8	Exact locality where killed Portage Co., Ohio
	Column 2	69 6/8	Date killed early 40s By whom killed Picked Up
	Column 3	56 7/8	Present owner Dick Idol
	Total	151	Address
SUBTRACT	Column 4	15 5/8	
	Result	135 3/8	Guide's Name and Address
Add line E Total		192 7/8	Remarks: (Mention any abnormalities or unique qualities)
FINAL SCORE		328 2/8	

I certify that I have measured the above trophy on ___14 May_____ 19_86__
at (address) __Nevada State Museum_____ City __Las Vegas____ State _NV_
and that these measurements and data are, to the best of my knowledge and belief, made in accordance with the instructions given.

Witness: __Frank E. Bertoia_____ Signature: ___Horace Gore_____
OFFICIAL MEASURER

INSTRUCTIONS FOR MEASURING NON-TYPICAL WHITETAIL AND COUES' DEER

All measurements must be made with a ¼-inch flexible steel tape to the nearest one-eighth of an inch. Wherever it is necessary to change direction of measurement, mark a control point and swing tape at this point. Enter fractional figures in eighths, without reduction. Official measurements cannot be taken for at least sixty days after the animal was killed.

A. Number of Points on Each Antler. To be counted a point, a projection must be at least one inch long and its length must exceed the width of its base. All points are measured from tip of point to nearest edge of beam as illustrated. Beam tip is counted as a point but not measured as a point.

B. Tip to Tip Spread is measured between tips of main beams.

C. Greatest Spread is measured between perpendiculars at a right angle to the center line of the skull at widest part whether across main beams or points.

D. Inside Spread of Main Beams is measured at a right angle to the center line of the skull at widest point between main beams. Enter this measurement again in Spread Credit column if it is less than or equal to the length of longer antler; if longer, enter longer antler length for Spread Credit.

E. Total of Lengths of all Abnormal Points. Abnormal points are those nontypical in location (points originating from points or from sides or bottom of main beam) or extra points beyond the normal pattern of up to eight normal points, including beam tip, per antler. Measure in usual manner and enter in appropriate blanks.

F. Length of Main Beam is measured from lowest outside edge of burr over outer curve to the most distant point of what is, or appears to be, the main beam. The point of beginning is that point on the burr where the center line along the outer curve of the beam intersects the burr, then following generally the line of the illustration.

G-1-2-3-4-5-6-7. Length of Normal Points. Normal points project from the top of the main beam. They are measured from nearest edge of main beam over outer curve to tip. Lay the tape along the outer curve of the beam so that the top edge of the tape coincides with the beam on both sides of the point to determine baseline for point measurement. Record point lengths in appropriate blanks.

H-1-2-3-4. Circumferences are taken as detailed for each measurement. If brow point is missing, take H-1 and H-2 at smallest place between burr and G-2. If G-4 is missing, take H-4 halfway between G-3 and tip of main beam.

* * * * * * * * * * *

FAIR CHASE STATEMENT FOR ALL HUNTER-TAKEN TROPHIES

To make use of the following methods shall be deemed as UNFAIR CHASE and unsportsmanlike, and any trophy obtained by use of such means is disqualified from entry for Awards.

I. Spotting or herding game from the air, followed by landing in its vicinity for pursuit;
II. Herding or pursuing game with motor-powered vehicles;
III. Use of electronic communications for attracting, locating or observing game, or guiding the hunter to such game;
IV. Hunting game confined by artificial barriers, including escape-proof fencing; or hunting game transplanted solely for the purpose of commercial shooting.

****

I certify that the trophy scored on this chart was not taken in UNFAIR CHASE as defined above by the Boone and Crockett Club. I further certify that it was taken in full compliance with local game laws of the state, province, or territory.

Date_____Signature of Hunter_____
(Have signature notarized by a Notary Public)

Copyright © 1981 by Boone and Crockett Club
(Reproduction strictly forbidden without express, written consent)

OFFICIAL SCORING SYSTEM FOR NORTH AMERICAN BIG GAME TROPHIES

Records of North American Big Game

BOONE AND CROCKETT CLUB

241 South Fraley Blvd.
Dumfries, Virginia 22026

Minimum Score:
  Alaska-Yukon 224
  Canada 195
  Wyoming 155

MOOSE   Kind of Moose Canada

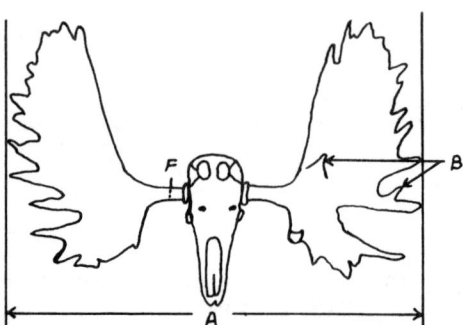
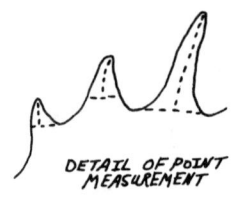

DETAIL OF POINT MEASUREMENT

SEE OTHER SIDE FOR INSTRUCTIONS	Column 1	Column 2	Column 3	Column 4
		Right Antler	Left Antler	Difference
A. Greatest Spread	58 2/8			
B. Number of Abnormal Points on Both Antlers	×	×	×	
C. Number of Normal Points	×	16	16	
D. Width of Palm	×	15	15 4/8	4/8
E. Length of Palm including Brow Palm	×	42 6/8	40 4/8	2 2/8
F. Circumference of Beam at Smallest Place	×	8 7/8	8 6/8	1/8
TOTALS	58 2/8	82 5/8	80 6/8	2 7/8

ADD	Column 1	58 2/8	Exact locality where killed Kennicott Lake, B.C.
	Column 2	82 5/8	Date killed 9 Sep 84 By whom killed Mike Popoff
	Column 3	80 6/8	Present owner Mike Popoff
	Total	221 5/8	Address
SUBTRACT Column 4		2 7/8	Guide's Name and Address
FINAL SCORE		218 6/8	Remarks: (Mention any abnormalities or unique qualities)

I certify that I have measured the above trophy on 13 May 19 86
at (address) Nevada State Museum   City Las Vegas   State NV
and that these measurements and data are, to the best of my knowledge and belief, made in accordance with the instructions given.

Witness: John G. Stelfox   Signature: Mike Wickersham
                                               Official Measurer

INSTRUCTIONS FOR MEASURING MOOSE

All measurements must be made with a ¼-inch flexible steel tape to the nearest one-eighth of an inch. Wherever it is necessary to change direction of measurement, mark a control point and swing tape at this point. Enter fractional figures in eighths, without reduction. Official measurements cannot be taken for at least sixty days after the animal was killed.

A. Greatest Spread is measured between perpendiculars in a straight line at a right angle to the center line of the skull.

B. Number of Abnormal Points on Both Antlers - Abnormal points are those originating from normal points or from the upper or lower palm surface, or from the inner edge of palm (see illustration). Abnormal points must be at least one inch long, with length exceeding width at one inch or more of length.

C. Number of Normal Points - Normal points originate from the outer edge of palm. To be counted a point, a projection must be at least one inch long, with the length exceeding width at one inch or more of length.

D. Width of Palm is taken in contact with the under surface of palm, at a right angle to the length of palm measurement line. The line of measurement should begin and end at the midpoint of the palm edge, which gives credit for the desirable character of palm thickness.

E. Length of Palm including Brow Palm is taken in contact with the surface along the under side of the palm, <u>parallel</u> to the inner edge, from dips between points at the top to dips between points (if present) at the bottom. If a bay is present, measure across the open bay if the proper line of measurement <u>parallel to inner edge</u>, follows this path. The line of measurement should begin and end at the midpoint of the palm edge, which gives credit for the desirable character of palm thickness.

F. Circumference of Beam at Smallest Place is taken as illustrated.

* * * * * * * * * * *

FAIR CHASE STATEMENT FOR ALL HUNTER-TAKEN TROPHIES

To make use of the following methods shall be deemed as UNFAIR CHASE and unsportsmanlike, and any trophy obtained by use of such means is disqualified from entry for Awards.

I. Spotting or herding game from the air, followed by landing in its vicinity for pursuit;
II. Herding or pursuing game with motor-powered vehicles;
III. Use of electronic communications for attracting, locating or observing game, or guiding the hunter to such game;
IV. Hunting game confined by artificial barriers, including escape-proof fencing; or hunting game transplanted solely for the purpose of commercial shooting.

I certify that the trophy scored on this chart was not taken in UNFAIR CHASE as defined above by the Boone and Crockett Club. I further certify that it was taken in full compliance with local game laws of the state, province, or territory.
Date_____Signature of Hunter_____
(Have signature notarized by a Notary Public)

Copyright © 1981 by Boone and Crockett Club
(Reproduction strictly forbidden without express, written consent)

OFFICIAL SCORING SYSTEM FOR NORTH AMERICAN BIG GAME TROPHIES

Records of North American Big Game

BOONE AND CROCKETT CLUB

241 South Fraley Blvd.
Dumfries, Virginia 22026

CARIBOU   Kind of Caribou Central Canada barren ground

Minimum Score:
- barren ground 400
- mountain 390
- Quebec-Labrador 375
- woodland 295
- Central Canada barren ground 345

DETAIL OF POINT MEASUREMENT

SEE OTHER SIDE FOR INSTRUCTIONS		Column 1 Spread Credit	Column 2 Right Antler	Column 3 Left Antler	Column 4 Difference
A. Tip to Tip Spread	28 7/8				
B. Greatest Spread	40 7/8				
C. Inside Spread of Main Beams 38 7/8 Credit may equal but not exceed length of longer antler		38 7/8			
IF Spread exceeds longer antler, enter difference.					
D. Number of Points on Each Antler excluding brows			12	13	1
Number of Points on Each Brow			5	10	
E. Length of Main Beam			52 2/8	51 1/8	1 1/8
F-1. Length of Brow Palm or First Point			21 2/8	18 2/8	
F-2. Length of Bez or Second Point			24 3/8	23	1 3/8
F-3. Length of Rear Point, if present			4 6/8	2 7/8	1 7/8
F-4. Length of Second Longest Top Point			13 3/8	14 2/8	7/8
F-5. Length of Longest Top Point			19 1/8	19 6/8	5/8
G-1. Width of Brow Palm			8 6/8	15 5/8	
G-2. Width of Top Palm			4 1/8	5	7/8
H-1. Circumference at Smallest Place Between Brow and Bez Points			4 6/8	4 6/8	
H-2. Circumference at Smallest Place Between Bez and Rear Point, if present			4 4/8	4 6/8	2/8
H-3. Circumference at Smallest Place Before First Top Point			4 4/8	4 4/8	
H-4. Circumference at Smallest Place Between Two Longest Top Palm Points			7	6 1/8	7/8
TOTALS		38 7/8	185 2/8	192 1/8	8 4/8

ADD	Column 1	38 7/8	Exact locality where killed Rendez-vous Lake, N.W.T.
	Column 2	185 2/8	Date killed 20 Oct 82 By whom killed Picked Up
	Column 3	192 1/8	Present owner Tom W. Barry
TOTAL		416 2/8	Address
SUBTRACT Column 4		8 4/8	Guide's Name and Address
FINAL SCORE		408 6/8	Remarks: (Mention any abnormalities or unique qualities)

I certify that I have measured the above trophy on ___13 May___ 19_86_
at (address) _Nevada State Museum_   City _Las Vegas_   State _NV_
and that these measurements and data are, to the best of my knowledge and belief, made in accordance with the instructions given.
Witness: ___Philip L. Wright___   Signature: ___George Tsukamoto___
                                                    OFFICIAL MEASURER

INSTRUCTIONS FOR MEASURING CARIBOU

All measurements must be made with a ¼-inch flexible steel tape to the nearest one-eighth of an inch. Wherever it is necessary to change direction of measurement, mark a control point and swing tape at this point. Enter fractional figures in eighths, without reduction. Official measurements cannot be taken for at least sixty days after the animal was killed.

A. Tip to Tip Spread is measured between tips of main beams.

B. Greatest Spread is measured between perpendiculars at a right angle to the center line of the skull at widest part, whether across main beams or points.

C. Inside Spread of Main Beams is measured at a right angle to the center line of the skull at widest point between main beams. Enter this measurement again in Spread Credit colum if it is less than or equal to the length of longer antler; if longer, enter longer antler length for Spread Credit.

D. Number of points on each antler. To be counted a point, a projection must be at least one-half inch long, with length exceeding width at the point of measurement. Beam tip is counted as a point but not measured as a point. There are no "abnormal" points in caribou.

E. Length of Main Beam is measured from lowest outside edge of burr over outer curve to the most distant point of what is, or appears to be, the main beam. The point of beginning is that point on the burr where the center line along the outer curve of the beam intersects the burr.

F-1-2-3. Length of Points are measured from nearest edge of beam on the shortest line over outer curve to tip. Lay the tape along the outer curve of the beam so that the top edge of the tape coincides with the top edge of the beam on both sides of the points to determine baseline for point measurement. Record point lengths in appropriate blanks.

F-4-5. Length of points are measured from the tip of the point to the top of the beam, then at a right angle to the lower edge of beam. The Second Longest Top Point cannot be a point branch of the Longest Top Point.

G-1. Width of Brow is measured in a straight line from top edge to lower edge, as illustrated, with measurement line at a right angle to main axis of brow.

G-2. Width of Top Palm is measured from midpoint of lower rear edge of main beam to midpoint of a dip between points, at widest part of palm. The line of measurement begins and ends at mid-points of palm edges, which gives credit for palm thickness.

H-1-2-3-4. Circumferences are taken as described for measurements. If rear point is missing, take H-2 and H-3 measurements at smallest place between bez and first top point.

* * * * * * * * * * *

FAIR CHASE STATEMENT FOR ALL HUNTER-TAKEN TROPHIES

To make use of the following methods shall be deemed as UNFAIR CHASE and unsportsmanlike, and any trophy obtained by use of such means is disqualified from entry for Awards.

I. Spotting or herding game from the air, followed by landing in its vicinity for pursuit;
II. Herding or pursuing game with motor-powered vehicles;
III. Use of electronic communications for attracting, locating or observing game, or guiding the hunter to such game;
IV. Hunting game confined by artificial barriers, including escape-proof fencing; or hunting game transplanted solely for the purpose of commercial shooting.

****

I certify that the trophy scored on this chart was not taken in UNFAIR CHASE as defined above by the Boone and Crockett Club. I further certify that it was taken in full compliance with local game laws of the state, province, or territory.

Date_____Signature of Hunter_____
(Have signature notarized by a Notary Public)

Copyright © 1981 by Boone and Crockett Club
(Reproduction strictly forbidden without express, written consent)

OFFICIAL SCORING SYSTEM FOR NORTH AMERICAN BIG GAME TROPHIES

Records of North American Big Game

BOONE AND CROCKETT CLUB

241 South Fraley Blvd.
Dumfries, Virginia 22026

Minimum Score: 82   PRONGHORN

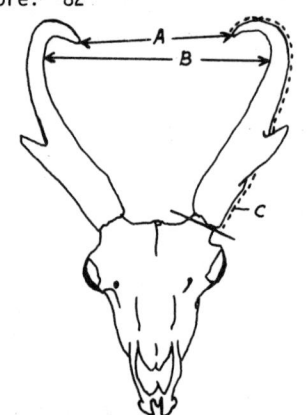 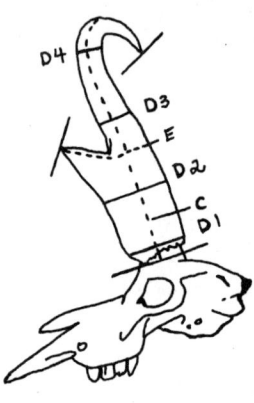

SEE OTHER SIDE FOR INSTRUCTIONS		Column 1	Column 2	Column 3
A. Tip to Tip Spread	8 1/8	Right Horn	Left Horn	Difference
B. Inside Spread of Main Beams	12 5/8			
IF inside Spread exceeds longer horn, enter difference.				
C. Length of Horn		17 6/8	17 4/8	2/8
D-1. Circumference of Base		6 7/8	7	1/8
D-2. Circumference at First Quarter		6 7/8	7 2/8	3/8
D-3. Circumference at Second Quarter		4 3/8	4 4/8	1/8
D-4. Circumference at Third Quarter		3 1/8	3 2/8	1/8
E. Length of Prong		8	8 2/8	2/8
TOTALS		47	47 6/8	1 2/8

ADD	Column 1	47	Exact locality where killed Coconino Co., Arizona
	Column 2	47 6/8	Date killed 20 Sep. 85 By whom killed Michael J. O'Haco, Jr.
	Total	94 6/8	Present owner Michael J. O'Haco, Jr.
SUBTRACT Column 3		1 2/8	Address
FINAL SCORE		93 4/8	Guide's Name and Address
			Remarks: (Mention any abnormalities or unique qualities)

I certify that I have measured the above trophy on 13 May 19 86
at (address) Nevada State Museum   City Las Vegas   State NV
and that these measurements and data are, to the best of my knowledge and belief, made in accordance with the instructions given.

Witness: George Tsukamoto   Signature: Walter H. White
                                        Official Measurer

INSTRUCTIONS FOR MEASURING PRONGHORN

All measurements must be made with a ¼-inch flexible steel tape to the nearest one-eighth of an inch. Wherever it is necessary to change direction of measurement, make a control point and swing tape at this point. Enter fractional figures in eighths, without reduction. Official measurements cannot be taken for at least sixty days after the animal was killed.

A. Tip to Tip Spread is measured between tips of horns.

B. Inside Spread of Main Beams is measured at a right angle to the center line of the skull, at widest point between main beams.

C. Length of horn is measured on the outside curve on the general line illustrated. The line taken will vary with different heads, depending on the direction of their curvature. Measure along the center of the outer curve from tip of horn to a point in line with the lowest edge of the base, using a straight edge to establish the line end.

D-1. Measure around base of horn at a right angle to long axis. Tape must be in contact with the lowest circumference of the horn in which there are no serrations.

D-2-3-4. Divide measurement of longer horn by four. Starting at base, mark both horns at these quarters (even though other horn is shorter) and measure circumferences at these marks. If the prong interferes with D-2, move the measurement down to just below the swelling of the prong. If the prong interferes with D-3, move the measurement up to just above the swelling of the prong.

E. Length of Prong- Measure from the tip of the prong along the upper edge of the outer curve to the horn; then continue around the horn to a point at the rear of the horn where a straight edge across the back of both horns touches the horn, with the latter part being at a right angle to the long axis of horn.

* * * * * * * * * * * *

FAIR CHASE STATEMENT FOR ALL HUNTER-TAKEN TROPHIES

To make use of the following methods shall be deemed as UNFAIR CHASE and unsportsmanlike, and any trophy obtained by use of such means is disqualified from entry for Awards.

I. Spotting or herding game from the air, followed by landing in its vicinity for pursuit;
II. Herding or pursuing game with motor-powered vehicles;
III. Use of electronic communications for attracting, locating or observing game, or guiding the hunter to such game;
IV. Hunting game confined by artificial barriers, including escape-proof fencing; or hunting game transplanted solely for the purpose of commercial shooting.

I certify that the trophy scored on this chart was not taken in UNFAIR CHASE as defined above by the Boone and Crockett Club. I further certify that it was taken in full compliance with local game laws of the state, province, or territory.

Date_____ Signature of Hunter_____

(Have signature notarized by a Notary Public)

Copyright © 1981 by Boone and Crockett Club
(Reproduction strictly forbidden without express, written consent)

OFFICIAL SCORING SYSTEM FOR NORTH AMERICAN BIG GAME TROPHIES

Records of North American Big Game
BOONE AND CROCKETT CLUB
241 South Fraley Blvd. Dumfries, Virginia 22026

Minimum Score: 115   BISON   Sex __male__

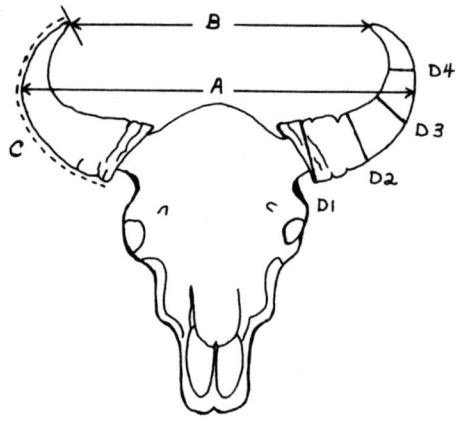

SEE OTHER SIDE FOR INSTRUCTIONS		Column 1	Column 2	Column 3
A. Greatest Spread	33 2/8	Right Horn	Left Horn	
B. Tip to Tip Spread	27 6/8			Difference
C. Length of Horn		18 6/8	18 4/8	2/8
D-1. Circumference of Base		14	14	
D-2. Circumference at First Quarter		12 3/8	12 6/8	3/8
D-3. Circumference at Second Quarter		10 5/8	11	3/8
D-4. Circumference at Third Quarter		6 4/8	7 6/8	1 2/8
TOTALS		62 2/8	64	2 2/8

ADD	Column 1	62 2/8	Exact locality where killed Coconino Co., Arizona
	Column 2	64	Date killed 19 Oct. 84 By whom killed Philip A. Sturgill
	Total	126 2/8	Present owner Philip A. Sturgill
SUBTRACT Column 3		2 2/8	Address
			Guide's Name and Address
FINAL SCORE		124	Remarks: (Mention any abnormalities or unique qualities)

I certify that I have measured the above trophy on 12 May 19 86
at (address) Nevada State Museum   City Las Vegas   State NV
and that these measurements and data are, to the best of my knowledge and belief, made in accordance with the instructions given.

Witness: Horace Gore   Signature: Frank Cook
                                         Official Measurer

INSTRUCTIONS FOR MEASURING BISON

All measurements must be made with a ¼-inch flexible steel tape to the nearest one-eighth of an inch. Wherever it is necessary to change direction of measurement, mark a control point and swing tape at this point. Enter fractional figures in eighths, without reduction. Official measurements cannot be taken for at least sixty days after the animal was killed.

A. Greatest Spread is measured between perpendiculars at a right angle to the center line of the skull.

B. Tip to Tip Spread is measured between tips of horns.

C. Length of Horn is measured from lowest point on under side over outer curve to a point in line with tip. Use a straight edge, perpendicular to horn axis, to end the measurement, if necessary.

D-1. Circumference of Base is measured at a right angle to axis of horn. Do not follow the irregular edge of horn; the line of measurement must be entirely on horn material, not the jagged edge often noted.

D-2-3-4. Divide measurement C of longer horn by four. Starting at base, mark both horns at these quarters (even though the other horn is shorter) and measure circumferences at these marks, with measurements taken at right angles to horn axis.

* * * * * * * * * * * * *

FAIR CHASE STATEMENT FOR ALL HUNTER-TAKEN TROPHIES

To make use of the following methods shall be deemed as UNFAIR CHASE and unsportmanlike, and any trophy obtained by use of such means is disqualified from entry for Awards.
  I. Spotting or herding game from the air, followed by landing in its vicinity for pursuit;
  II. Herding or pursuing game with motor-powered vehicles;
  III. Use of electronic communications for attracting, locating or observing game, or guiding the hunter to such game;
  IV. Hunting game confined by artificial barriers, including escape-proof fencing; or hunting game transplanted solely for the purpose of commercial shooting.

I certify that the trophy scored on this chart was not taken in UNFAIR CHASE as defined above by the Boone and Crockett Club. I further certify that it was taken in full compliance with local game laws of the state, province, or territory.
Date_____ Signature of Hunter_____
(Have signature notarized by a Notary Public)

Copyright © 1981 by Boone and Crockett Club
(Reproduction strictly forbidden without express, written consent)

OFFICIAL SCORING SYSTEM FOR NORTH AMERICAN BIG GAME TROPHIES

Records of North American Big Game
BOONE AND CROCKETT CLUB
241 South Fraley Blvd.
Dumfries, Virginia 22026

Minimum Score: 50   ROCKY MOUNTAIN GOAT   Sex __male__

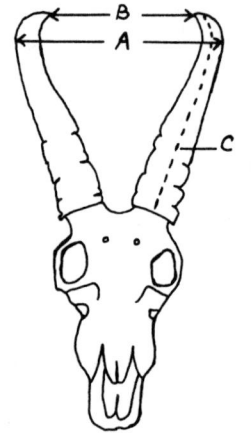 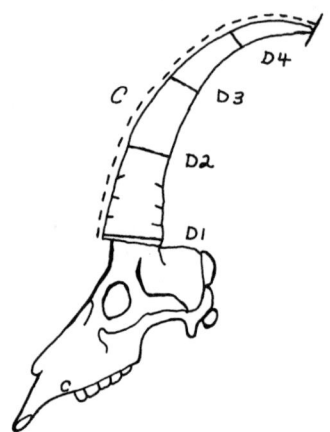

SEE OTHER SIDE FOR INSTRUCTIONS		Column 1	Column 2	Column 3
A. Greatest Spread	7 1/8	Right Horn	Left Horn	Difference
B. Tip to Tip Spread	6 4/8			
C. Length of Horn		10 4/8	10 4/8	
D-1. Circumference of Base		5 5/8	5 5/8	
D-2. Circumference at First Quarter		4 7/8	5	1/8
D-3. Circumference at Second Quarter		3 3/8	3 2/8	1/8
D-4. Circumference at Third Quarter		2 1/8	2 1/8	
TOTALS		26 4/8	26 4/8	2/8

ADD	Column 1	26 4/8	Exact locality where killed Reflection Lake, Alaska
	Column 2	26 4/8	Date killed 2 Sept 85 By whom killed Timothy F. McGinn
	Total	53	Present owner Timothy F. McGinn
SUBTRACT Column 3		2/8	Address
			Guide's Name and Address
FINAL SCORE		52 6/8	Remarks: (Mention any abnormalities or unique qualities)

I certify that I have measured the above trophy on 13 May 1986
at (address) Nevada State Museum   City Las Vegas   State NV
and that these measurements and data are, to the best of my knowledge and belief, made in accordance with the instructions given.

Witness: __Thomas A. Cavin__   Signature: __Charles E. Wilson, Jr.__
                                                  Official Measurer

INSTRUCTIONS FOR MEASURING ROCKY MOUNTAIN GOAT

All measurements must be made with a ¼-inch flexible steel tape to the nearest one-eighth of an inch. Wherever it is necessary to change direction of measurement, mark a control point and swing tape at this point. Enter fractional figures in eighths, without reductions. Measurements are most accurately taken before mounting of the trophy. Official measurements cannot be taken for at least sixty days after the animal was killed.

A. Greatest Spread is measured between perpendiculars at a right angle to the center line of the skull.

B. Tip to Tip Spread is measured between tips of horns.

C. Length of Horn is measured from lowest point in front over outer curve to a point in line with tip.

D-1. Circumference of Base is measured at a right angle to axis of horn. DO NOT follow irregular edge of horn.

D-2-3-4. Divide measurement C of longer horn by four. Starting at base, mark both horns at these quarters (even though other horn is shorter) and measure circumferences at these marks.

* * * * * * * * * * * *

FAIR CHASE STATEMENT FOR ALL HUNTER-TAKEN TROPHIES

To make use of the following methods shall be deemed as UNFAIR CHASE and unsportmanlike, and any trophy obtained by use of such means is disqualified from entry for Awards.
    I. Spotting or herding game from the air, followed by landing in its vicinity for pursuit;
    II. Herding or pursuing game with motor-powered vehicles;
    III. Use of electronic communications for attracting, locating or observing game, or guiding the hunter to such game;
    IV. Hunting game confined by artificial barriers, including escape-proof fencing; or hunting game transplanted solely for the purpose of commercial shooting.

I certify that the trophy scored on this chart was not taken in UNFAIR CHASE as defined above by the Boone and Crockett Club. I further certify that it was taken in full compliance with local game laws of the state, province, or territory.
Date_____Signature of Hunter_____
(Have signature notarized by a Notary Public)

Copyright © 1981 by Boone and Crockett Club
(Reproduction strictly forbidden without express, written consent)

OFFICIAL SCORING SYSTEM FOR NORTH AMERICAN BIG GAME TROPHIES

Records of North American Big Game
BOONE AND CROCKETT CLUB
241 South Fraley Blvd.
Dumfries, Virginia 22026

Minimum Score: 90 MUSKOX Sex male

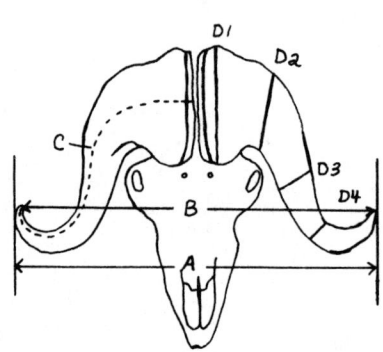 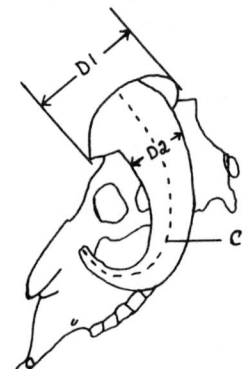

SEE OTHER SIDE FOR INSTRUCTIONS		Column 1	Column 2	Column 3
A. Greatest Spread	25 6/8	Right Horn	Left Horn	Difference
B. Tip to Tip Spread	21 5/8			
C. Length of Horn		26	26	
D-1. Width of Boss		9 6/8	9 6/8	
D-2. Width at First Quarter		5 6/8	6 1/8	3/8
D-3. Circumference at Second Quarter		9 1/8	9 3/8	2/8
D-4. Circumference at Third Quarter		4 5/8	5	3/8
TOTALS		55 2/8	56 2/8	1

ADD	Column 1	55 2/8	Exact locality where killed Banks Island, N.W.T
	Column 2	56 2/8	Date killed 28 Mar 85 By whom killed David V. Collis
	Total	111 4/8	Present owner David V. Collis
SUBTRACT Column 3		1	Address
FINAL SCORE		110 4/8	Guide's Name and Address
			Remarks: (Mention any abnormalities or unique qualities)

I certify that I have measured the above trophy on 13 May 19 86
at (address) Nevada State Museum   City Las Vegas   State NV
and that these measurements and data are, to the best of my knowledge and belief, made in accordance with the instructions given.

Witness: Murff F. Bledsoe   Signature: Philip L. Wright
                                         Official Measurer

INSTRUCTIONS FOR MEASURING MUSKOX

All measurements must be made with a ¼-inch flexible steel tape and adjustable calipers to the nearest one-eighth of an inch. Whenever it is necessary to change direction of measurement, mark a control point and swing tape at this point. Enter fractional figures in <u>eighths</u>, without reduction. Official measurements cannot be taken for at least sixty days after the animal was killed.

A. Greatest Spread is measured between perpendiculars at a right angle to the center line of the skull.

B. Tip to Tip Spread is measured between tips of horns by using large calipers, which are then read against a yardstick.

C. Length of Horn is measured along center of upper horn surface, staying within curve of horn as illustrated, to a point in line with tip. Attempt to free the connective tissue between the horns at the center of the boss to determine the lowest point of horn material on each side, near the top center of the skull. Hook the tape under the lowest point of the horn and measure the length of horn, with the measurement line maintained in the center of the upper surface of horn following the converging lines to the horn tip.

D-1. Width of Boss is measured with calipers at greatest width of base, with measurement line forming a right angle with horn axis. It is often helpful to measure D-1 before C, marking the midpoint of the boss as the correct path of C.

D-2-3-4. Divide measurement C of longer horn by four. Starting at base, mark <u>both</u> horns at these quarters (even though other horn is shorter). Then, using calipers, measure width of boss at D-2, making sure the measurement is at a right angle to horn axis and in line with the D-2 mark. Circumferences are then measured at D-3 and D-4, with measurements being taken at right angles to horn axis.

* * * * * * * * * * * *

FAIR CHASE STATEMENT FOR ALL HUNTER-TAKEN TROPHIES

To make use of the following methods shall be deemed as UNFAIR CHASE and unsportsmanlike, and any trophy obtained by use of such means is disqualified from entry for Awards.
  I. Spotting or herding game from the air, followed by landing in its vicinity for pursuit;
  II. Herding or pursuing game with motor-powered vehicles;
  III. Use of electronic communications for attracting, locating or observing game, or guiding the hunter to such game;
  IV. Hunting game confined by artificial barriers, including escape-proof fencing; or hunting game transplanted solely for the purpose of commercial shooting.

I certify that the trophy scored on this chart was not taken in UNFAIR CHASE as defined above by the Boone and Crockett Club. I further certify that it was taken in full compliance with local game laws of the state, province, or territory.
Date_____ Signature of Hunter_____
(Have signature notarized by a Notary Public)

Copyright © 1981 by Boone and Crockett Club
(Reproduction strictly forbidden without express, written consent)

OFFICIAL SCORING SYSTEM FOR NORTH AMERICAN BIG GAME TROPHIES

Records of North American Big Game
BOONE AND CROCKETT CLUB
241 South Fraley Blvd.
Dumfries, Virginia 22026

Minimum Score:
  bighorn 180
  desert 168
  Stone 170
  white or Dall 170

SHEEP   Kind of Sheep __bighorn__

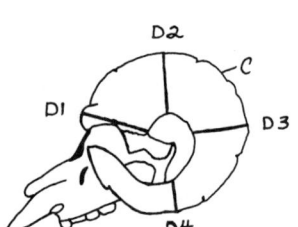
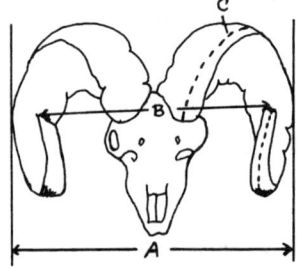

MEASURE TO A POINT IN LINE WITH HORN TIP

SEE OTHER SIDE FOR INSTRUCTIONS		Column 1 Right Horn	Column 2 Left Horn	Column 3 Difference
A. Greatest Spread (Is often Tip to Tip Spread)	24			
B. Tip to Tip Spread	24			
C. Length of Horn		41 3/8	40 4/8	
D-1. Circumference of Base		16	15 7/8	1/8
D-2. Circumference at First Quarter		15 5/8	15 4/8	1/8
D-3. Circumference at Second Quarter		14 2/8	14	2/8
D-4. Circumference at Third Quarter		10 1/8	9 5/8	4/8
TOTALS		97 3/8	95 4/8	1

ADD	Column 1	97 3/8	Exact locality where killed Granite Co., Montana
	Column 2	95 4/8	Date killed 15 Sep 84 By whom killed Steven L. Gingras
	TOTAL	192 7/8	Present owner Steven L. Gingras
SUBTRACT Column 3		1	Address
			Guide's Name and Address
FINAL SCORE		191 7/8	Remarks: (Mention any abnormalities or unique qualities)

I certify that I have measured the above trophy on 14 May 19 86
at (address) Nevada State Museum   City Las Vegas   State NV
and that these measurements and data are, to the best of my knowledge and belief, made in accordance with the instructions given.

Witness: __John G. Stelfox__   Signature: __C. Randall Byers__
                                                         Official Measurer

INSTRUCTIONS FOR MEASURING SHEEP

All measurements must be made with a ¼-inch flexible steel tape to the nearest one-eighth of an inch. Wherever it is necessary to change direction of measurement, mark a control point and swing tape at this point. Enter fractional figures in eighths, without reduction. Official measurements cannot be taken for at least sixty days after the animal was killed.

A. Greatest Spread is measured between perpendiculars at a right angle to the center line of the skull.

B. Tip to Tip Spread is measured between tips of horns.

C. Length of Horn is measured from the lowest point in front on outer curve to a point in line with tip. Do not press tape into depressions. The low point of the outer curve of the horn is considered to be the low point of the frontal portion of the horn, situated above and slightly medial to the eye socket (not the outside edge). Use a straight edge, perpendicular to horn axis, to end measurement on "broomed" horns.

D-1. Circumference of Base is measured at a right angle to axis of horn. Do not follow irregular edge of horn; the line of measurement must be entirely on horn material, not the jagged edge often noted.

D-2-3-4. Divide measurement C of longer horn by four. Starting at base, mark both horns at these quarters (even though the other horn is shorter) and measure circumferences at these marks, with measurements taken at right angles to horn axis.

* * * * * * * * * * * *

FAIR CHASE STATEMENT FOR ALL HUNTER-TAKEN TROPHIES

To make use of the following methods shall be deemed as UNFAIR CHASE and unsportsmanlike, and any trophy obtained by use of such means is disqualified from entry for Awards.
  I. Spotting or herding game from the air, followed by landing in its vicinity for pursuit;
  II. Herding or pursuing game with motor-powered vehicles;
  III. Use of electronic communications for attracting, locating or observing game, or guiding the hunter to such game;
  IV. Hunting game confined by artificial barriers, including escape-proof fencing; or hunting game transplanted solely for the purpose of commercial shooting.

I certify that the trophy scored on this chart was not taken in UNFAIR CHASE as defined above by the Boone and Crockett Club. I further certify that it was taken in full compliance with local game laws of the state, province, or territory.
Date_____ Signature of Hunter_____
(Have signature notarized by a Notary Public)

Copyright © 1981 by Boone and Crockett Club
(Reproduction strictly forbidden without express, written consent)

This book was:

Compiled with able assistance of:
    Lise Boorse Capobianco
    Michael V. Capobianco
    Michael J. Brown
    Carol D. Eads
    Jean B. Fry

Book design and layout by: Wm. H. Nesbitt

Typeset by: Capital Type
    Marlow Heights, Maryland

Printed and bound by: Haddon Craftsmen, Inc.
    Scranton, Pennsylvania